In the Shadow of the Bush

In the Shadow of the Bush

IN THE SHADOW OF THE BUSH

Ekoi Girl in Fatting-House Costume

IN THE SHADOW OF THE BUSH

By P. AMAURY TALBOT
OF THE NIGERIAN POLITICAL SERVICE

WITH ILLUSTRATIONS AND A MAP

NEW YORK: GEORGE H. DORAN COMPANY
LONDON: WILLIAM HEINEMANN
MCMXII

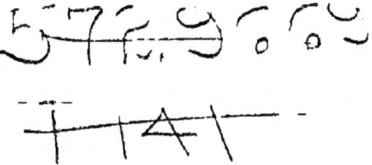

Printed in England.

To
THE DEAR AND HONOURED MEMORY
OF
LADY GALTON
THIS BOOK, BEGUN UNDER HER
KIND ENCOURAGEMENT,
IS GRATEFULLY AND AFFECTIONATELY
DEDICATED

through accident or adventure of our own, and it is for this reason that some personal incidents have been included.

I wish to take this opportunity of thanking the chief officials of my own Colony for their more than kind encouragement, and the authorities of the Natural History Museum for their unsparing kindness and generous help. Of the assistance given by my wife and her sister, I should like to say more, but am debarred by the very conditions under which their help was given.

CONTENTS

CHAP		PAGE
I.	On the Way to Oban	1
II	Religion	13
III	Religion (continued)	23
IV	Egbo	37
V.	Jujus	49
VI	Jujus (continued)	65
VII	Metamorphosis	80
VIII.	Oban to Niaji	89
IX.	Woman—Position, Etc	94
X	Woman—Position, Etc. (continued)	105
XI.	Birth Customs	120
XII.	Birth Customs (continued)	130
XIII.	Beyond Niaji	139
XIV.	The South Cameroons	151
XV.	Along the Border	160
XVI.	Ordeal	165
XVII.	Divination	174
XVIII.	Ojje or Witchcraft	190
XIX	Oberekkai to Etara	203
XX	Ekoi of the Cross River	216
XXI.	Funeral Ceremonies	221
XXII.	Ghosts	230
XXIII	Beyond Netim	242
XXIV.	Uyanga and Ekuri	255
XXV	Conditions of Life in Peace and War	262
XXVI.	Conditions of Life in Peace and War (continued)	278
XXVII.	Art	287
XXVIII	Records	304
XXIX.	Government, Etc.	310
XXX.	Treatment of " Members "	325
XXXI.	Folk-lore	335
	L'Envoie	Facing 404

CONTENTS

APPENDICES

APPENDIX		PAGE
A.	Tabus	407
B	Clubs	410
C	Anthropometry	414
D.	Orthography	415
E	Grammar	417
F	Vocabularies	424
G.	Nsibidi Signs	447
H	Botany	462
I.	Zoology	465
J	Mineralogy	474
K	Meteorology	476
L.	Geographical Survey	478

LIST OF ILLUSTRATIONS

Ekoi Girl in " Fatting-House " Costume (Coloured)	*Frontispiece*
	TO FACE PAGE
Kwa River .	2
Esuk Atimbo, Beach on Calabar River	4
Kwa River .	4
Oban-Obutong Road .	6
Farm Path with Offerings, near Ekong	8
Juju Circle at Oban	10
Egbo House and Juju Trees	10
The Lake of the Dead, near Nsan	24
Cotton Tree at Nsan .	30
Club Image, Ewaw	38
" Image " of Nkanda Grade of Egbo with Emblem " Ekabe Nkanda "	42
Hunting Juju " Image," Ekuri Ibokk, Oban	44
Juju Nimm Asam .	50
Juju Emomm	50
Juju " Images " with Attendants	54
Masks used in Religious Dances	58
Juju Heads—worn at Dances—and Fetish	58
Head Priest Akunane before Juju Ofiri at Ekong	66
Distributing Consecrated Offerings, Eja Festival, Oban	74
A Ceremony at Eja Festival, Oban	74
Partaking of Sacrifice to Eja at Obung	76
Dance at the Eja Festival, Oban	76
Chief Agbashan of Oban (a Were-Elephant)	82
Awaw Ita, the " Snake Woman " of Oban, with her Husband	84
Source of the River of Good Fortune	90
The River of Bad Fortune	92
Maia, the Priestess of Nimm	94
Nimm Neophytes .	98

LIST OF ILLUSTRATIONS

	TO FACE PAGE
THE HEAD PRIESTESS OF NIMM	102
PITS IN THE ROCK BY THE RIVERSIDE IN WHICH CAM-WOOD DYE IS MADE	108
TYPE OF LIANE IN THE EKOI BUSH	108
GIRL ATTENDANT ON JUJU "IMAGE"	110
EKOI INTERIOR, WITH WOMAN SEWING	114
AKWA YAFE FALLS	114
DANCE IN HONOUR OF THE BIRTH OF TWINS	120
JUJU LEFT IN DESERTED TOWN	124
MOTHER WITH TWINS MENTIONED ON P 120	124
A WOMAN FROM THE INTERIOR	126
JUJU "IMAGE" WITH ATTENDANTS	126
LEADERS OF THE CHILDREN'S AGARA CLUB, NCHOFAN	132
EKOI WOMAN	132
AFTER A HUNT, NDEBBIJI	142
EKOI HUNTER	150
OJOKK	150
NATIVE SUSPENSION BRIDGE IN THE SOUTH CAMEROONS	152
DR MANSFELD IN A HUT ON THE SHORE OF LAKE IJAGHAM	154
IJAGHAM (LAKE OF THE DEAD), SOUTH CAMEROONS	154
THE ORIGINAL HOME OF AKPAMBE AT OKURI	158
PASS NEAR MBINDA	158
RIVER AKWA YAFE	160
ENTRANCE TO UNDERGROUND CAVES NEAR AKWA YAFE RIVER	162
ODODOP	164
SEXAGONAL STONE DEDICATED TO NIMM, ABBIATI	172
ETAI NGBE, MKPOTT	172
ETAI NGBE, WITH TWISTED RODS, EGBO HOUSE, OKUNI	172
FALLS AT THE SOURCE OF THE IKPAN RIVER	190
RIVER SCENE, EKOILAND	192
JUJU AKPAMBE	198
PLAY AT OBAN, NSIKPE CLUB	198
CENTRAL FALLS, KWA RIVER	204
KWA RIVER	206
REST HOUSE, NSAN	212
EGBO HOUSE, NETIM	212
NEW COLA	214
NAPOLEONA ALEXANDRI	214
NEW ANACARDIACEÆ	214
DANCE GIVEN BY CHILDREN'S "AGARA" CLUB, NCHOFAN	216

LIST OF ILLUSTRATIONS

	TO FACE PAGE
The Great Drum of the Boy Scouts	216
Chief of Okuni, Upper Cross River	218
Type of Northern Ekoi Woman	218
Sacred Drum at Awaw Offong	220
"Image" of the Igumi Club	222
A Girl with "Ghost Marks" on her Arm	224
"Image" of Ojjen	224
A House in Oban where the Body of a Late Head Chief lay in State under the Protection of the Union Jack	226
Household Juju	226
Upper Falls on Kwa River	234
Nimm Stone, Calabar River	242
Ikum, Head Chief of Ojo Nkonmba	244
Source of the Calabar River	246
Interior of Egbo House, Ojo Akangba, showing Type of Native Fresco	248
Ojo Types	248
Crossing a River	250
An Oban Elephant	250
Type of Ekuri	254
Type of Uyanga	254
Juju Post at Ekuri Owai with Mummified Head in Fork	256
An Elephant Road	258
Dancers with Juju Masks at Ekuri Eying	260
Mourning Emblems at House of Dead Chief	260
Juju Obassi Osaw	266
Sacred Tree always brought to a New Town from the Parent Tree in the Old Town	266
Type of Ekoi Roof	270
Weaving Bags	270
Ekoi Calf	276
Leaf Men	276
Momodo Mandara, my Bornuese Skinner	276
Woman saved from being offered as a Sacrifice to Juju Mfuor	276
A Stilt Dance	284
Stilt Dance, "Lame Boy" in Foreground	284
Type of Ekoi	316
Ekoi Type	316
Type of "Member" from Slave Towns	316

LIST OF ILLUSTRATIONS

	TO FACE PAGE
Type of Ekoi	316
Types of Ekoi Coiffure	318
Types of Ekoi Coiffure	318
Types of Ekoi Coiffure	320
Types of Ekoi Coiffure, Female and Male	320
Types of Ekoi Coiffure, Small Children	322
Types of Ekoi Coiffure	322
People from the Interior waiting to welcome us	324
Lowest Falls, Kwa River	324
Village on Cross River	336
Cascade	346
Climbing Palms	346
Tree surrounded with Lattice Work Creeper which eventually kills it	356
Type of Vegetation	356
Native Tree-bridge	366
Cola Lepidota	374
Macrolobium lamprophyllum Harms	400
Group of pale Duck's-egg blue Fungi	400

INSETS

Decoration of Wall in Egbo House, Ekuri Owai	256
Map of the Oban District, Southern Nigeria	*at end of volume*

CHAPTER I

ON THE WAY TO OBAN

THE Ekoi people are divided into two unequal parts by the boundary which separates the Cameroons from Southern Nigeria. Their land is most easily reached by way of the River Kwa, which empties itself into the Cross River, a few miles from the latter's mouth. For some distance before its junction the Kwa is too broad to permit of a good photograph, and it is not till nearing the beach from which runs the main Calabar-Oban road, that one can be obtained.

The banks are fringed first with mangrove and screw pine, then, further on, by palm trees. When that part is reached which the Ekoi proudly term "our own water," the river narrows and becomes more beautiful. At its edge grow giant arums, green on the outer sheath, but cream splashed with purple within Behind these spring trees of every variety of shape and tint, from mimosas, with their delicate mauve or cream balls and feathery foliage, to the huge trumpet-shaped flowers of the Gardenia physophylla, the heavily-scented, purple-splashed blooms of the Kalbreyeri, or the great Berlinia, the white flowers of which shine with a pearl-like lustre from amid its dim, dark leaves.

Here and there, at a bend, one comes across beaches of clear white sand, glistening with mica, where crocodiles lie sunning On the single occasion when I went down the river, after having expended all my ammunition during a long "bush tour," the Fate which presides over such matters arranged an interesting tableau. On the branch of a great tree, which hung directly over the water, lay a creature such as I have never seen before or since. In shape it was like a medium-sized crocodile, but with a flat snout like that of a pig, and with six to eight black rings round its tail. As if aware of its perfect security, it lay quite still until we were almost level, and then slid out of sight.

Sometimes a monitor slips from a fallen tree-trunk as one draws near, or a great snake ruffles the surface as it swims across with a bird, just caught, in its mouth. Huge butterflies of gorgeous colouring flutter hither and thither, and now and then a flash of turquoise hangs for a moment over the water as a kingfisher swoops down, to rise again with a tiny fish.

These fishes, called Tatabonko by Efik and Ekoi, hold an important place in song and folk-lore. A little Efik ode to them begins—

"Enyenne nmonn asanga nben Tatabonko"
"Ye are the lords of the water. Ye walk near the banks. O tiny Tatabonko"

Every few minutes a grey heron rises, and over a small island, near the place where a Sierra Leonean has made a rice farm, circle flocks of mole-grey birds with breasts of vivid rose.

Now and again a space is passed, where the coarse grass has been cropped short by that strange creature the manatee. Save an elephant, this is the most valuable prize which can fall to the lot of the Ekoi hunter. Egbo Societies, those powerful secret associations which, before the coming of the white man, ruled the land, are known to give as much as £10 to £15 for a large one This is not only because its flesh is thought a delicacy, but because they believe that it confers magical properties on those who eat.

Magic is the key-note on which the lives of the Ekoi are attuned. The river itself is magical, and bold indeed would be that man or woman who should break an oath sworn on its name For somewhere in its depths dwells Nimm—the terrible—who is always ready, at the call of her women worshippers, to send up her servants, the beasts that flock down to drink and bathe in her stream, to destroy the farms of those who have offended. Nimm is, above all, the object of the women's devotion. She manifests herself sometimes as a huge snake, sometimes as a crocodile. Her priestesses have more power than those of any other cult, and the society which bears her name is strong enough to hold its own against the dreaded "Egbo Club"

Kwa River.

itself. It is during the rainy season that she is most to be feared. In 1909, at the height of the rains, one of my best paddlers was coming up with a consignment of goods from Calabar. Several of his friends were in the canoe, and they were all talking and laughing. Suddenly, as his hand neared the water at the down stroke, the head of a crocodile appeared above the surface. The cruel jaws closed on the man's wrist, and in a flash he was dragged under. "Nimm,"—whispered the terrified survivors, as they paddled on, "Who knows? Perhaps he had angered his wife, and she prayed to Nimm to avenge her."

As one passes up the river, further and further from Calabar and all it represents, one leaves behind not only one's own race, but one's own century as well, and glides backward through the ages, up the stream of time, to the childhood of the world—to a land full of mystery and terror, of magic plants, of rivers of good and ill fortune, of trees and rocks, ever lowering to engulf unwary wayfarers, where the terror of witchcraft stalks abroad, and where, against this dread, the most devoted love or faithful service counts as naught.

After awhile the banks grow steeper, and one enters a deep gorge which the water has worn for itself in the course of centuries. Down this rolls the thunder of the falls, and seems to shut out all sounds from the world one has left, just as the bush, creeping down around one, curtains off familiar sights. This gorge forms the boundary between the sedimentary deposits below and the crystalline rocks of the hilly country, of which the greater part of the Oban district is formed. The line of demarcation lies along this parallel of latitude to the Calabar River on the one side and the Akwa Yafe on the other.

Beyond Obutong beach, navigation is impossible, for the great curve of the first falls reaches from side to side in one white horseshoe. Above this again comes a stretch of foaming water, and then in rapid succession the higher falls, which are very beautiful for their size.

After landing on the little beach, a climb of about two hundred steps, steep as the staircase of many an old house at home, leads to a three-roomed Rest-house. On the first morning of my wife's arrival here, she was dressing with her sister Bimba in the latter's room, when suddenly a cry rang out, so evidently caused by terror, that it brought me hurrying to their door. My wife was sitting at the end of a bamboo bench, which runs along the wall, trying to tear off the long marching boot which she had pulled on, without taking the precaution of first shaking it upside down to make sure that neither snake, lizard, nor millipede was hidden within. For the moment the foot was stuck fast; beneath it something writhed and squirmed. One jerk and the boot was in my hand. I ran with it to the open house door, followed by "boys" and carriers, who crowded round with anxious, frightened faces, each armed with stick or matchet to kill the reptile as it fell. A violent shake, and the cause of the commotion slid into view—a small oval tablet of Roger and Gallet's soap! Roar after roar of laughter burst from the delighted carriers at the sight, and for the rest of the day we heard frequent bursts of merriment, or saw one of them suddenly double up with mirth as the recollection overcame him.

The fear of snakes is no idle one, for they literally swarm in the District. On another occasion when we were staying in the same Rest-house, my wife and her sister had both gone to bed, while I was still working in the central room. This time it was Bimba who called, and, on running in, we found her huddled up under a rug. A long snake had let itself down from the roof on to her mosquito net, the frail strings of which threatened to give way under its weight, and collapse, reptile and all, on to the little, shrinking figure beneath.

When the unwelcome visitor had been disposed of, it struck me that it would be well to make a thorough search of the roof. As a result, seven cobras from 4 to 6 feet long were accounted for. The roof was low, and I shot at close quarters, so that each snake fell down in several sections through the close criss-cross of palm stems which form the under roof. Each part seemed endued with a life of its own, so that before the little adventure was over the floors of the three rooms were literally covered with a carpet of writhing snakes. Later the District Commissioner, who came up to relieve me, asked if we had noticed some fair-sized holes in the floor. On having an affirmative answer, he told us that once during his stay there

Esuk Atimbo. Beach on Calabar River.

Kwa River.

he found a puff adder sleeping beneath one of the benches Subsequent investigations proved the holes to be entrances to the abodes of quite a family of these beautifully marked, sluggish reptiles.

This Rest-house lies close to the road which runs straight from Obutong to Oban Roads like this, only naturally broader and better in older Districts, are cut through the heart of dense "bush." They now cross the country in every direction, instead of the winding native tracks, often hardly distinguishable from those of bush animals, which were the only means of communication over a great part of Southern Nigeria up to 1902.

One hears from certain sources at home of the hardships entailed on the natives by the making of these roads. In an unimportant, thinly populated District like Oban, not only the making but the upkeep entails a considerable amount of labour on the scanty population. No one, however, is quicker than the natives themselves to see the advantages to be gained from such improved means of communication, whether as regards personal safety or trading facilities Whatever the people of the District have been called on to do in this direction has invariably met with a cheerful and willing response. On several occasions towns have offered, of their own free will, to do more than had been asked of them, and in some cases they have even made a new piece of road on their own initiative, as a surprise for my next visit to their part of the country It would perhaps be unnatural were they not willing to comply with the one demand made on them by Government in return for all that it gives, and even for this they are well paid.

Natives quickly realise the importance of the change. Not long ago a well-known black lawyer was discussing the matter with a native clergyman in my presence on board an Elder Dempster liner. His voice was so strident as to be heard from end to end of the deck. "You should go to Sapele," he said, "there you walk for 200 miles, safe as here. This Governor * makes good roads. We call him 'the road maker' I am black man myself, but I tell you for true. It is only white men who can make the way safe."

* Sir Walter Egerton

Not far from Obutong stands a compound which goes by the name of " Nwan's," but is now fast dropping to decay Round it plantains and bread-fruit trees are heavy with their unplucked burdens while behind them tower cocoanut palms, laden with great green globes. Calabash vines trail in all directions over the deserted dwellings, but those who planted them fear to come back and gather the fruits of their labour, for no "Juju" seems strong enough to keep the unquiet ghost in his grave. In the words of his family, " Nwan came back too much and made us fear " So they migrated to Esuk Aram, and left the deserted homestead and the little wayside grave.

The road from Obutong to Oban is of sand and gravel, firm enough for a bicycle, but on it the unshod feet of the carriers make no sound It leads under a continuous archway of boughs, so thick that the sunlight only filters through to dapple the roadway or sparkle on the many streams which cross it. All along one sees the spoor of bush animals which use the road as well as their two-footed brothers Antelope, buffalo, wild pig, leopard, and elephant all leave their traces—the latter too often in broken bridges, which, alas! were not constructed with a view to such heavy traffic. Here, as everywhere in the District, the streams are crystal clear, and ripple over pebbly beds or between boulders of quartz or dark gneiss—the former of these stones is thought to be male by the Ekoi, the latter female White, star-shaped lilies raise their heads above the water. These are often nearly 6 inches across, and usually four or five of them grow on a stem. They have a faint, sweet scent, and are in bloom for the greater part of the year. Occasionally the road passes through a village with its ' Egbo " house and " Juju " tree, or a little side path or farm track branches off from the main route, with offerings to gods or ancestors hung out on poles.

Near several of the towns are frail little huts made of posts driven into the ground, and supporting a palm-leaf roof Round these are scattered various pieces of property, such as plates, dishes, &c, all broken, and cloths which were once bright-coloured, but have grown faded by sun and rain. These are little funeral shrines, built over the graves of persons of distinction. The things scattered round are broken, so that their

Oban-Obutong Road.

ON THE WAY TO OBAN

astral forms may be set free, to be borne by the shade of their owner into the spirit world.

At each end of the village of Ekong, as in most Ekoi towns, dried palm leaves about 30 feet long are raised on high. These are stripped bare, save for a tuft at the top, and from them dangle small wooden objects, much the shape of a Moslem praying board. They form a charm to keep leopards from the town, as do also the sections of palm trunk which are found half buried across the pathway, flanked at either end with a small earthen pot containing "medicine."

After a 15-mile march Oban itself is reached. At the entrance, as in all Ekoi towns, ghost offerings are to be found, hung on either side of the way, or buried in the path. These are meant to propitiate the spirits, and keep them from entering the town.

The Ekoi have a wonderful folk-lore, and are never at a loss for story or legend, to explain their customs or beliefs. Many — of which the following is, perhaps, the best-known example — deal with the institution of ghost sacrifices at the entrance to the towns.

Charm against Leopards. Ekong.

Why Ghost Offerings are made before Towns.

Once a tortoise had two children, which were born on the same day. When only two days old they began to fight together, and so equal were they that neither could overcome the other. Three days later they went to cut bush, and make a farm for their father. While doing this they heard a far-off drumming. They followed the sound, and it led them to the ghost town.

The ghosts were beating their drum for a wrestling match. "Let us try if we cannot conquer these tortoises," said they.

The first tortoise stood forth, and overthrew twenty of the ghosts, one after the other, so that they fell down dead; for though ghosts have died once, they can die a second time, and so become more dead than before.

Now in this town dwelt a ghost named Ne-Achi-Esam (the Man with the twenty heads), who was a great wrestler. He was lying down in his house, sick with a very large boil, but when he heard the noise of the combat he ran out, and wished to take part in it He said to himself, " My boil will hold me back; what can I do?" He laid his hand upon the boil, and by magic transferred it to a post that stood near * So the post got the boil, and he himself grew well again. He went out and said, "Now I will see what I can do against Tortoise.' They closed, and he fought so well that Tortoise gave way before him. A great box had been brought out and placed near the drum. Ne-Achi-Esam drove Tortoise against this with such force that he broke in two, and fell to the ground dead. After this the second tortoise tried to avenge his brother, but met with a like fate.

Then the ghosts went and got magic "medicine," which they rubbed on all their companions who had been killed, so that they came to life again Next they cooked "chop" and ate it. Afterwards they all went back to bush to collect firewood with which to roast the two tortoises.

Now one of the ghosts had a beautiful daughter who was in the fatting-house.† She had pity on the tortoises, and when the other ghosts had gone, slipped out and went and got magic leaves These she crushed, and laid them on the mouths and eyes of the tortoises. After awhile the latter came to life again. She pointed out the road to them, and said, "Here is your way Go home now before the others come back." So they thanked her and went.

As the two hurried along, they heard the sound of the ghosts returning with the firewood, so they hid themselves in the bush till the way should be clear. When one of the ghosts reached the place, he stood for a long time, and said, " I think the two tortoises have escaped, and are hiding here."

* Compare the method of Paracelsus
† A room set apart in most compounds for the seclusion of girls, while being fattened before marriage

Then the ghosts called to the black ants, and sent them to search for the tortoises; also they called water from the river, and bade it flow round and seek them. In their terror the tortoises cried for help to Obassi Osaw.* So neither the ants nor the water could find them. At last all gave up the search and went home.

When the way was clear once more, the tortoises crept out and hurried onward. After awhile they saw a bunch of ripe plantains. Of these they took seven, and went on again till they came to a place where the road branched into two. There they laid down the seven ripe plantains and went onward.

When the ghosts got back to their town, and found that their prey had escaped, they said, "Let us follow." They ran very swiftly till they came to the place where the plantains lay.

The first ghost saw them, and began to count—1, 2, 3, 4, 5, 6 he counted, but could not add 7. The second ghost pushed him aside. "Go away," he said, "you know no addition." He also counted up to six, but could get no further. Then all the ghosts tried, but none of them could add the seventh number.

Meantime Obassi Osaw had seen the danger of the tortoises, and determined to help them. He counselled them to use every effort to reach their town, and there prepare to receive their pursuers. "There is one thing you can do," he said, "to keep the ghosts from entering your town. Kill goats and cows, get palm oil and palm wine and lay them before the entrance. When they see these sacrifices they will eat, and go back satisfied to their own place."

This the tortoises did, and when the ghosts came before the town they found a rich offering. All of them ate and were well content, save Ne-Achi-Esam alone, who said, "Let us enter the town"; but the others answered, "No, we may not enter."

Since then, when ghosts come to your house, seeking something, you inquire by the charm † what sacrifice they are asking, and having found out, you take it to the beginning of the road, and offer it there.

This is the reason why whenever you near a town you see sacrifices set out for the ghosts, so that they should no longer enter within.

* The Sky God
† See Method of Divination, p. 174

At Oban there are two circles of unhewn stones, each arranged round a "Juju" tree. Here mystic rites are performed when the moon is at the full, and on the rising of the new moon. The latter ceremony takes place near the compound of Chief Itaokui, not far from the "Egbo" house, and it is here that one of the most important of the women's "Jujus" is held. At the new moon the women and girls gather together. The head women sit round on the stones of the circle, and distribute "medicine" made of meat and plantains, mixed with Juju herbs and leaves. Even the very young girls partake of this. When all has been consumed they start a dance, which is only used on this occasion.

The object of the ceremony is to insure fruitfulness when the time comes for marriage, and it is firmly believed that any neglect of it would be punished by barrenness. Should a woman specially long for a child, she brings a goat to be sacrificed; then stands within the circle, and prays that a babe may be born to her. Her forehead is smeared with the blood of the sacrifice, and it is thought certain that her prayer will be granted within the year.

Neither men nor boys are allowed to approach during these rites, though women are not prevented from looking on when the men gather to carry out theirs before the Juju "Nchibbi." This ceremony is performed at the smaller circle, when the moon is at the full. The scene on bright moonlight nights is uncanny to a degree, and it is hard for any European, who has come suddenly on such a sight, to believe that he is still in the twentieth century, and has not rather stumbled on some witches' sabbat of the middle ages.

Near the greater circle of stones stands the miniature house of the Juju "Ta Amat," where the "small-pox medicine" and that used to ward off any epidemic is kept. When the people fear the approach of an infectious disease, the head chief enters the little hut and makes "medicine," compounded of magic herbs. This the people drink, and it is given to all strangers, especially to those who may have come from an infected area. In this way it is hoped that disease may be warded off, while as a further safeguard inoculation is practised. This is done by injecting into the arm the milky

Juju Circle at Oban.

Egbo House and Juju Trees.

juice of the leaves of a certain tree planted near for the purpose

Oban was chosen as the seat of government for the District, because it lies high and is easily reached from all parts of the Ekoi country. Half a mile from the town stands the station on a hill, the top of which had to be sliced off to make a level space large enough for the necessary buildings. This cleared land forms the most extensive open space in the District, and the view from the house is beautiful enough to make up for the plainness of the structure itself. In front, beyond the River Ataiyo, rises the rounded hill of Oban, clothed to the summit by masses of flowering trees, some of which are always in bloom. Behind this the sun sinks in a perfect wonder of colour, and perhaps the sunsets and sunrises, beautiful everywhere, are the most gorgeous sights of all this gorgeous land On all sides the " bush " sweeps down and shuts in the little clearing, while to the rear, beyond this green belt, tower the blue peaks of the Cameroons.

From the top of Oban hill a good view is to be had To the north lie clusters of peaks, of every shape and form, 3,000 to 4,000 feet high, wooded to the summit and forming the watershed of the country between the Cross River and the sea. To the south flow those streams which unite to form the Calabar, the Kwa, and the Akwa Yafe Rivers ; while to the north flow many of the main tributaries of the Cross River.

The rocks of the District are mostly metamorphic, and the hill, on which the station is built, is a good example of the geological formation of this part of the country. It is mainly composed of gneiss; but there is a large vein of manganese, and huge masses of quartz and felspar, with pegmatite dykes running through all. Traces of ilmenite, columbite, magnetite, tin and monazite are also to be found.

There is always a slight breeze here, and even to the most careless glance the difference in healthfulness between those children who live on the hill, in the new well-ventilated houses built for the station people, and their contemporaries in Oban itself, is very marked. The Ekoi are devoted parents, but it will take years of patient teaching before they grasp the importance of fresh air and the simplest sanitary measures for the health of their little ones. They are most particular in the matter of personal cleanliness so far as bathing and the washing of garments are concerned, but the old habit of crowding together for safety, in case of attack from a hostile tribe, still influences them to build their compounds of small, ill-ventilated rooms. They seem utterly indifferent to the existence of evil smells, and to this cause the high death-rate among the children is chiefly due. So high is it, indeed, as to be hardly more than covered by the birth-rate.

One day, sixty-two married women were chosen at haphazard in Oban town. To these it was found that 270 children had been born, of whom 163 had died. This gives an average of 4.3 children to each, of whom only 1·7 now survive. Of these sixty-two women, one had borne fifteen children, and seven others ten or over, while only four were childless.

Oban gives its name to the district, and from this fact and its position is regarded by all Ekoi under British rule, and even by many on the other side of the border, as the central point of their race.

Perhaps therefore, before going further, it would be well to pause here a little, and attempt some account of the influences which have shaped the character of the people.

CHAPTER II

RELIGION

THE religion of the Ekoi is altogether a fascinating study. Its principal features are the Cult of Ancestors and of Nature Forces These dominate the lives of the people to such an extent, and have such countless ramifications, that it becomes impossible to arrange definitely under headings, or say where one begins and the other ends. Ancestor worship, Nature Jujus, Secret Societies, the principal events of life, and the commonest actions of the day, all blend inextricably in a complicated ritual.

Of actual Deities there are only two, Obassi Osaw,* the Sky God, and the Earth God Obassi Nsi, but of the less powerful Genii of trees, lakes, rocks and rivers, there are countless hordes. The whole bush is peopled with these supernatural beings, its dim twilight thick with terrible, half-human shapes, akin to the were-wolves of our own Northern lands. Here, more truly even than in old Greece, the terror of Pan reigns supreme.

The shadow of the bush lies heavy over all; but beneath the thousand superstitions which have grown up, fungus-like, in its dark places, are still to be found traces of an older, purer form of worship—a relic possibly of that forgotten time when the Ekoi were a people living in open lands, swept by free air and bounded by wide horizons.

On every hand, indeed, indications are to be found, beneath modern corruptions and disfigurements, of a form of worship, which carries us back to the oldest known Minoan civilisation, and links the belief of the present-day Ekoi with that of the ancient Phœnician, the Egyptian, the Roman, and the Greek.

In some ways, indeed, the Ekoi form may be termed the most ancient of all, for whereas in the oldest representation

* Compare Osa, the supreme Deity of the Binis, and the Yoruba generic term for " Juju "

of Minoan bird and tree worship which have come to light, the tree is shown almost entirely conventionalised into pillar shape, and later as a mere pedestal for the bird, among the Ekoi it still keeps its original form, that of the actual, living tree.

The smallest town has its "Juju" tree. There are many varieties of these, but each stands alone, usually in an open space before the Egbo house. They are generally bound round with tie-tie, or surrounded by a little fence festooned with linked rings of the same. On the branches of these trees hang countless nests of one kind or another of the weaver bird. Even the smallest child knows that these are sacred, for on them depends the prosperity of the town. Should they be injured or driven away the women would become barren and the cattle cease to bear. The birds know that they are safe and flit fearlessly hither and thither, keeping up such a loud twittering and crying that it is almost impossible to hear oneself speak in their neighbourhood.

Surely in this we have the oldest picturing of the wedding of earth and sky; Sky Father and Earth Mother—for of all created things the bird is most akin to air and sky, while the tree, with its roots in the dark ground, reaching even, as in many Northern sagas, to the nether world, is the best and oldest personification of Mother Earth.

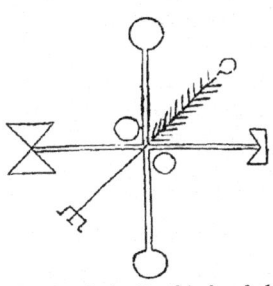

Ekoi Symbols Double-headed Axe, Knobbed Sceptre and Feather

Another possible picturing of this mystic marriage was found painted on the inner wall of the Egbo house at Mbeban. What first struck me was an apparent representation of the Cretan double-headed axe, lying horizontally across a knobbed sceptre. Over these again, diagonally, lies an Egbo feather. Without any hint from me these signs were explained in a way which tallied exactly with my own interpretation.

The cult of the double-axe is known to have prevailed in Egypt during certain dynasties. Vague memories came back to me of an axe and knobbed sceptre, used together as symbols of a deity. Attempts to verify this impression led me to read a paper on "The Cretan Axe Cult outside Crete,"* in which the following passages occur:—

"Longpérier also published an Assyrian cylinder in white agate, which had been brought from Constantinople by a certain M. Cayol. This shows a priestly personage presenting a fish to a deity, who is symbolized by an axe and a knobbed sceptre erected on a high backed throne. . . ."

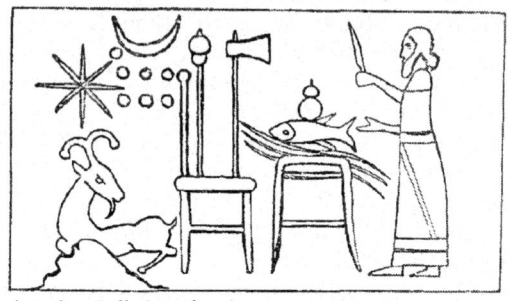

Assyrian Cylinder, showing Axe and Knobbed Sceptre as Symbols of a Deity.

"It will be remembered that the painted sarcophagus from Hagia Triada, in Crete, represents a pair of double-axes embedded in two supports of unique design. Professor von Duhn kindly informs me that these supports are apparently pillars or posts covered with leaves, most probably with cypress leaves. If so, they were obviously ritual substitutes for cypress trees. On either axe is perched a bird. . . ."

After going the round of the Mediterranean the author proceeds to gather up results.

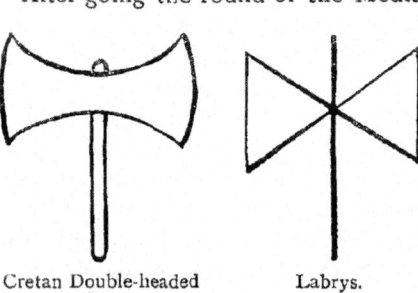

Cretan Double-headed Axe.   Labrys.

"It seems to me, then, that throughout the Ægean and Adriatic area (not to mention localities still further afield) we have to do with a cult of immemorial antiquity—the joint worship of a sky-father and an earth-mother. The former descends from above when the lightning flashes down, and, in old aniconic days, leaves his weapon as a tangible token of himself. The latter

* By A. B. Cook. Transactions of the third International Congress for the History of Religions, Vol. II., pp. 184, 189, 193.

ascends from below when vegetation springs up, and, at the same early epoch, gives visible proof of her presence in the sacred tree. Where, as was the case with the sarcophagus from Hagia Triada, we see the axe embedded in the tree trunk, there we must recognize the union of the sky-father with the earth-mother—a union essential to the fertility of crops, and beasts, and men. The axe embedded in a tree is the prototype of the axe embedded in a wooden column or a stalactite pillar. Ultimately a double-axe of the usual type is found serving as a symbol of the united deities, the axe head being the male, the axe handle the female, element in their union."

In the Ekoi representation, the cleft base of the axe may well be a highly conventionalized remnant of pillar or tree, while the feather, now that of the peacock sacred to Egbo societies, probably in earlier days was merely a bird symbol. The two circles may well be meant for eggs, and therefore as indications of fertility.

In the course of the ages, strangely enough, Mother Earth has become Father Earth in Ekoi legend. The two principal Deities, as has been mentioned, are now Obassi Osaw, the Sky God, and the Earth God Obassi Nsi. Still enough legends and fragments of ritual have been collected to show that the older idea has not yet quite died out. This may be seen from the following conversation with Ndum of Nsan, one of the most interesting of the Ekoi. He is as yet practically untouched by "White" influence, knows no word of English, and is a mine of folk-lore.

"Who is Obassi Nsi?" he was asked.

"He is Obassi who is kind to us," he answered.

"Where does he live?"

"Under the earth. There is a world beneath the earth whose king is Obassi Nsi."

"Which do you think the more powerful—Obassi Nsi or Obassi Osaw?"

"Both are powerful, but Osaw is cruel and Nsi kind and good."

"Why then do you pray to Obassi Osaw?"

"Obassi Nsi told us to do so, that Osaw might spare our lives, for the latter always seeks to kill us."

"How do you know that Osaw is fierce and cruel?"

"Because he tries to kill us with thunder and in many other ways. Also, he is not so loving and near to us as Obassi Nsi, for he cannot receive our offerings. We sometimes throw things up into the air for him, but they always fall back again to the earth. Obassi Nsi draws them down, that shows he is more powerful."

"How do you know that Obassi Nsi is good?"

"He never shows us terrifying things as Osaw does, such as thunder or lightning, nor the sun which blazes so hot as to frighten us sometimes, and the rain which falls so heavily at others as to make us think there will be no more sunshine. Nsi ripens our yams, cocos, plantains, &c, which we plant in the ground. When we are dead we are buried in the ground, and go to the world under the earth, to our Father Obassi Nsi."

"What do you think happens to you when you are buried?"

"When a man's body decays, a new form comes out of it, in every way like the man himself when he was above ground. This new shape goes down to its Lord, Obassi Nsi, carrying with it all that was spent on its funeral in the world above."

"You said that Obassi Nsi told you to make offerings to Obassi Osaw. Why then does he draw them down to himself, as you say he does?"

"He draws them back because he is greater than Osaw. Besides, he wants the latter to come to him, that they may divide the offerings between them. They are, of course, friends."

"Does Obassi Nsi ever want to kill you?"

"No, he would like us to live always; but when Osaw kills us, Nsi takes us to his country under the earth."

"You said that you were told to make offerings to Osaw, in order that he might spare your lives. How then can Nsi, who does not want you to die, partake of these?"

(Hesitation and shy laughter.)

"I told you that they are friends. They talk together and eat together. I think that Obassi Nsi is really our mother and Osaw our father. For whenever we make offerings we are taught to say Nta Obassi (Lord Obassi) and Ma Obassi (Lady Obassi). Now I think that the lord is Osaw, and the lady Nsi. Surely Nsi must be a woman, and our mother, for it is well known to all people that a woman has the tenderest heart."

After this Ndum could be drawn into no more answers, but only laughed softly in his shy way at attempts to get further information; and soon bade "good night" and went back to his compound.

Another story in which a feminine Deity also figures was told by Itambɔ Isom of Niaji.

How the Poor Boy came to the Land of Obassi Osaw.

Two great friends once lived in the same town. One was poor and the other very rich, and each of them had an only son.

Now, on a day, the poor man died, and, not long after, his rich friend also fell ill. The latter therefore called to the two boys and said .

"I do not think that I can live much longer on earth. I have gathered together everything necessary for the funeral ceremonies of my dead friend When I die I should like you two boys to dwell together." Next he told them to go to the farm and fetch yams. When these were brought he said :

"Cut them into pieces and boil them Mix them with palm oil, and let me try if I can eat once more."

When all was ready the boys brought the dish before him. Some of the food he put in his own mouth and threw some on the ground, calling at the same time on the name of his late friend. Soon after the offering had been made, he himself died.

The two children did not know that their protector was dead They thought only that he was very ill, so they left him, and went out weeping.

On their return they saw the body lying there, and the yams left almost untouched. These they ate, then licked up the palm oil, washed the calabash, and hung it up again in its place.

Now neither of the fathers had either brother or sister, so one of the principal men in the town took the boys to his house and cared for them. They grew up very quickly, and one day left their foster-father, and went back to the rich man's old compound.

Not long after, their late guardian saw them roaming and said :

"Why will you not live with me as you used to do ? Come, let us go back to my house. You are not yet old enough to live alone."

They answered, "We will not live in any house but our own."

RELIGION

So the man was angered and said, "From to-day I give up with you Never come to me any more."

The boys replied, "We are in charge of our fathers' property. We have neither brother nor sister to share it with us. We are strong and healthy and can take care of ourselves until we are fully grown."

When they were alone, the son of the rich man said to the poor man's son, "Come, we must perform the ceremonies for the deaths of our fathers. Let us give both plays at the same time."

The poor man's son said, "I do not agree. My father died first. Let us go step by step." So they began the rites for the death of the poor man. They killed two cows and two goats, and when all the first customs were finished, they began those for the rich boy's father For him they killed twelve cows and twelve out of their remaining fifteen goats. From what was left the poor boy took one goat and the rich boy two, each for his own.

Next day they bought a chicken. In course of time it grew to be a hen, and hatched out ten eggs, of which they each took five. Both tended the chicks, but a hawk came and carried off all those which belonged to the poor man's son. Also a leopard came and ate up his one goat.

Then Mkpaw-Ekett (Poor) went to Nsuma-Mbi (Rich) and said, "Hawk has taken away all my chickens and leopard has eaten my goat. My father is dead ; I have no relations to care for me ; I cannot endure such continued ill-fortune, and wish therefore to hang myself up and die." The rich boy comforted him for that time, but next day, very early in the morning, Mkpaw asked :

"Have you any eggs to give me that I may go and make sacrifice?"

Nsuma gave what his friend wanted, and then went to work on his farm.

As the sun rose, the poor boy stood with the eggs in his hand. He looked up at the sun, and held them so that they pointed towards it "Male God! Female God!" he cried, "Will you open the gate for me?" Then the eggs slipped from his hand, and out of each flew a small chick. These surrounded the boy, and flew with him up to the sky, to the kingdom of Obassi Osaw.

The first thing which Mkpaw saw on reaching this land was

a woman full of sores over all her body. She said to him, "Why do you come here, Earth-child?" He answered:

"I have come by reason of the loss of my property."

The woman said, "If you will wash my sores I will tell you something." He did as she asked, and she continued:

"Listen well. In this country there are two kinds of flies—Nkonn (Bee) and Mfut (Red-fly).* When you come to the house where Obassi sits in judgment you will see many chiefs. Watch Mfut, and when he settles on one of them, make the sign of supplication before him, for that one will be Obassi himself."

The boy did as he was bidden, and, when Mfut alighted on the shoulder of one of the chiefs, approached and bent down before him, with the fingers of both hands touching the ground.

Obassi said, "I know why you have come. It is about the loss of your property. Sit down awhile. The ghost people will soon come by, on their way to market, and I will show you your poor father and his rich friend."

First Nsuma's mother went by, next the two fathers, and after a little while Mkpaw saw his own mother, with her old cloth round her loins.

When all had passed by, Obassi said to the boy, "Here is a small box. Take it home with you. Whenever you want anything, ask this box and it will give it to you, but take care that it is never left open, and, above all, let no woman touch it."

When the boy reached earth again, he showed the box to his friend. The latter asked:

"Where have you been all this time?"

Mkpaw answered, "I have been with Obassi Osaw, who gave me this box."

As he said this, he went to it and asked for a fine cloth to give to his friend. When this fluttered out from under the lid, Mkpaw said·

"Here is a present for you, that you may know that I have come from the home of my parents." On this both were very glad and began to dance.

Now the rich boy had just married a wife. On hearing the sound of dancing and singing she ran in, and, before they could stop her, had laid hold of the box that she might see what it was.

So both sons died.

* *Chrysops silacea*, Austen.

RELIGION

This is the reason why, when we buy a strong Juju, the priest tells us to take great care of it and not allow our wives to touch it.

The rule is not for all Jujus, but for the principal ones. For instance, women must never touch Bigui or Mfam, or the Juju would certainly catch them.

As another indication of the original femininity of Obassi Nsi, it will be noticed that in the story quoted on p. 98, when Obassi Osaw and Obassi Nsi each built a town, the latter was the founder and protector of that set apart for women.

The two Deities enter into countless folk-lore stories, from which many details as to their nature and attributes may be gleaned.

In the central atrium of almost every compound is set a little group, consisting usually of a growing tree, carved post and sacrificial stone, sacred to one or other of the Deities. By far the greater number of these are dedicated to Obassi Nsi, as is shown by the coco yams planted, or laid in a small heap, close by. Those of Obassi Osaw can easily be distinguished by the clump of epiphytic ferns growing upon the tree trunk.

Emblems of Obassi Nsi.

Before beginning the work of the day, each man or woman who still clings to the old custom, takes a calabash of water and goes into the central court to wash. With eyes lifted to the newly-risen sun they pray:

"Eyo ofu, eyo egu, 'me eyange eyange."

"Sun of morning, sun of evening, let me (be) free from danger (to-day)."

This is done because the sun is supposed to be deputed by Obassi to receive all prayers offered on earth, and carry them before him.

Next, water is taken in the right hand and held on high, while the name of Obassi Osaw is invoked. Then a little is taken in the left hand and poured out on the ground to entreat the protection of Obassi Nsi.

In all ceremonies, whether connected with Juju or ancestor worship, the names of the two Deities must first be invoked.

When the new moon is seen in the sky, every man, woman and child comes out and offers a prayer in the following words:

" 'Mi mfe, 'Mi mfe ka osaw,   nkaiyen   njum ebi "
" Moon new, Moon new in sky, let me not see thing bad "

Or

" 'Mi kpe, afanikŏng   akajoi   na 'me."
" Moon this, trouble let not come to me "

CHAPTER III

Religion (*continued*)

Not far from Nsan, a town of some importance to the west, the road passes near to a small lake. This is supposed to be haunted by the ghosts of dead and gone Ekoi, and is looked upon as the dwelling place of a great Nature Juju, on which the prosperity of the surrounding country depends.* A rumour of this lake had reached my ears, but on first asking for its whereabouts, the question was met by expressions of the blandest and blankest ignorance as to the existence of any such thing When the line of march was altered in order to search, the carriers begged to be excused from accompanying us, and so were left behind.

A struggle through dense bush, in what seemed the most probable direction, brought us suddenly into a broad belt of fern Through this we waded knee deep, and finally emerged on a smooth stretch of grass, which was obviously a lake bed during the rains. Across this we could see the edge of the water, which shrinks in the dry season till scarcely bigger than a large pond. The surface was still; not a ripple stirred the grassy fringe. Near by grew bushes about 10 feet high, covered with what looked, at a distance, like tufts of creamy flowers, but proved on a nearer view to be the nests of that curious and little-known creature the tree-nesting frog †

One or two of our people had followed to the edge of the water. Among these was Eyiddimfonni (Hater-of-the-rich), the Priest of Eja, a cult for the protection of farms and cattle, in which certain forms of thunder worship are also mixed. Eyiddimfonni volunteered the information that he and his

---

* A far more beautiful example of a Lake of the Dead is to be found in the old home of the Ekoi, over the German Border For description see Chapter XIV.
† *Hylombatus rufus*

companions were very brave men to venture there, as the place was haunted by devils, into whose power fell all those who dared to set foot beyond the belt of fern.

Later, we learned that nothing must be allowed to trouble the water, even so much as at its utmost edge, otherwise the guardians of the lake would be enraged and bring disaster, in some dire form, such as famine or pestilence, on the whole countryside. The place is a sanctuary for all wild things, for no hunter would dare to penetrate the belt of fern in search of wounded bird or beast which had fled thither.

In walking round we came upon no less than five crocodiles' holes, and the tracks on the soft mud showed the owners to be "at home" in each case. These crocodiles are regarded as manifestations of the guardian spirits of the place, and therefore as specially sacred. Hither by night come the ghosts of long-dead Ekoi, to drift in sad companies, hopeless and wailing, over the surface of the water. Even in the bright sunlight the place has an uncanny look, and one can easily imagine that at midnight, when the white mists shimmer ghost-like in the light of the moon, people with the terror and mystery of the "bush" in their blood would rather sit chatting round the fire or dance by torchlight in the open spaces of the towns, than seek out this uncanny spot, on the chance of holding communion with the spirits of their long dead kin.

As we stood at the edge, gazing out over the water, its quiet was suddenly broken by a broad ripple, and little fish were seen to spring agitatedly above the surface. A great python was crossing, and this, we learned, shared with the crocodiles the guardianship of the Sacred Lake.

Everywhere in Ekoi mythology, the cult of the snake is found to be closely connected with that of the crocodile. In many of the Egbo houses a representation of the former is to be seen modelled in high relief on the wall at the farther end, while the crocodile is usually found carved on the principal pillar. Those families who are members of the Cult of Nimm,* never drive a snake from their houses, but take powdered chalk and strew before the visitor, very softly, so as not to frighten it in any way. Should a snake enter a house not protected by

* See p 94

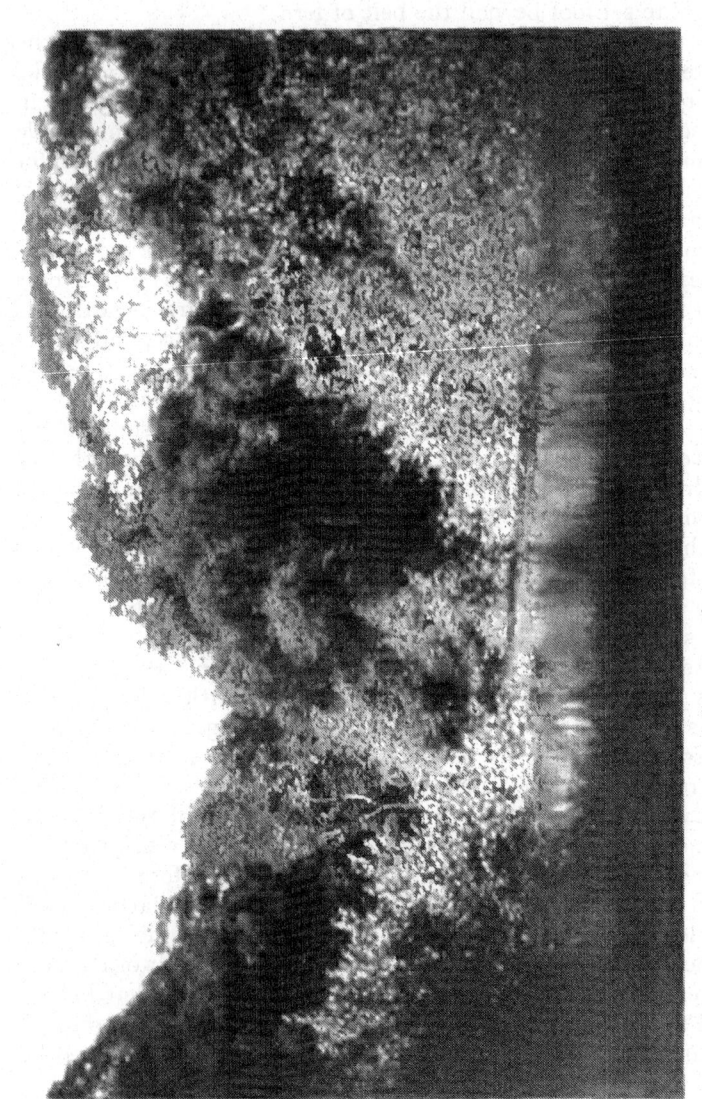

The Lake of the Dead, near N'san.

RELIGION

Nimm, the owner must consult the "Diviner" in order to find out if it is sent by ghosts or "Juju."

Possibly the cult of snake and crocodile has come down from very ancient times. It is well known that both were honoured in Egypt as tutelar gods, and if the Ekoi have trekked, as seems likely, from the east of Africa, it is probable that the original reason for deifying snake and cat, *i.e.*, that these creatures were the principal scourges of the plague-carrying rat, lies at the back of the powerful snake cult, while traces of cat worship are still to be found.* Rats are a great pest all over the land, and every possible means is taken to keep them down, though with little result.

In Egypt the snake was not only the guardian of house and tomb, but a snake goddess presided over the harvest festival, held in the month of Pharmuthi or April. Doubtless among other attributes she was regarded as the protectress of the garnered grain, and her cult grew from the practice of introducing non-poisonous snakes into granaries, in order to protect their contents from predatory rodents. Nimm also is looked upon as the guardian of farms and crops, and her great festival falls at the time of the gathering of the new yams.

Since writing the above, an article by Dr. W. Sambon, F.Z.S., has come to my notice. It appeared in the *Times* of February 4, 1911, and part of it bears so closely upon the subject in hand, that I venture to quote it.

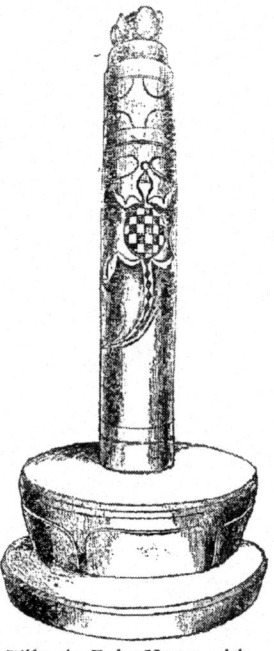

Pillar in Egbo House with carved figure of Nimm in crocodile form.

"A very interesting measure adopted by the ancient Romans to fight the plague was the introduction of rat-eating snakes. In the year 291 B.C. Rome was devastated by the plague. The Sibylline books were consulted, and it was decided to dispatch

* See p. 151.

ten ambassadors to Epidauros to confer with the Æsculapian priests. Valerius Maximus tells us how the tribune Quintus Ogulnius, chief of the embassy, returned with the snake sacred to the god of healing, and how a temple to Æsculapius was subsequently erected on the Tiberine island A beautiful medallion of Antoninus commemorates this event. A galley is represented passing beneath a bridge, and from its prow a snake moves towards the figure of the Tiber-god, who stretches out his right hand in sign of welcome. This legend, I have no doubt, refers to the introduction of rat-snakes in Rome for the purpose of destroying rats and thus stamping out the plague. In fact, Pliny clearly states that ' the Æsculapian serpent was imported in Rome from Epidauros, it was kept in the public edifices, and also in private houses' and we know from Ælian and other authors that the Egyptians kept domestic snakes in their houses and looked upon them as tutelar gods. Indeed, from the remotest antiquity throughout the East, snakes were kept in houses for the purpose of destroying rats and preventing rat-conveyed diseases. Certainly, non-venomous rat-snakes are a far better protection against plague than cats or dogs, because they are not likely to harbour fleas. For years I have thought that the guardian snakes painted on the walls of Roman houses might be a vestige of the long-forgotten introduction of rat-snakes to save Rome from the plague Only a few days ago, in looking through Dyer's book on Pompeii, published in 1871, I came across the figure of a painting found in a baker's shop of the Via Consularis. In this fresco are represented the two guardian serpents moving, as usual, towards an altar placed between them, on which is placed the incense-yielding pine cone sacred to Æsculapius, but above each snake is a bird darting after a fly. The tail considerably shorter than the wing, the peculiar marking, and the very action in which they are represented of hawking flies on the wing, show that these birds are the common spotted flycatcher. The association of the snake with the flycatcher, a bird even at the present day kept in the houses of Southern Italy for the purpose of destroying flies, proves beyond doubt that also the tutelar reptile is here depicted as an emblem of a house-pest destroying animal. The information just given explains, I believe, in a satisfactory manner why Æsculapius was represented leaning on a snake-entwined staff"

Early in 1909, an official, who was passing through the District, mentioned that in the course of his tour he had visited a tribe where the snake cult seemed very strong.

One of the carriers happened to kill a small python. He bore it back to camp, cut it into several "lengths," and laid one or two of these on a dish preparatory to cooking. News of what he had done reached the chiefs of the town and they came in a body, followed by an excited crowd, to ask that the man should be punished for his sacrilege. They also demanded the matchet with which the snake was killed, the dish on which it had lain, and a considerable fine to appease its "manes," lest it should return to trouble them.

A superstition connected with this cult came to light in July, 1911.

On our return to headquarters after a "bush" tour the warder mentioned in his report that a python, some 22 feet long, had been killed close to the prison. He had ordered this to be skinned, and had himself witnessed the extraction of the "bad parts," which he had intended to bury in a deep hole in a place known only to himself, so that they could not be used by witchcraft for the hurt of anyone. Before these could be buried, one of the chief clerks had demanded that they should be given up to him. At first the warder refused, but afterwards, reflecting that, while the Commissioner was away from the station, this clerk was his representative, he gave up the parts in question, on the distinct understanding that they were to be kept for my return. Needless to say they disappeared

Subsequent inquiries brought out the information that the most dreaded portion of these "bad parts" is the gall. This, used in a certain way, is capable of producing the most dire results. Of all animals, snake and leopard are most feared for the magical properties of their gall. This will be seen from the following legend told by Ojong of Oban.

How Slaves killed the Free-born.

Once all the hunters collected together for a great hunt in the bush near their town. Among other animals killed was a leopard, which they brought back and skinned. The meat was given to the slaves, for free-born Ekoi do not eat the flesh of leopards, but before dividing it, the gall was carefully taken out and kept, for it is used for a certain purpose.

One of the slaves thought to himself, " I will ask my master why the gall is always taken away before the flesh is shared." He did so, and the master explained that the gall was a strong " medicine," and would cause death if mixed with food or drink.

When the slave had learnt this, he called together all his fellow-slaves and explained to them how galls could be used as poison. Then they plotted among themselves, and said, " Let us kill the free-born and ourselves be free."

Now, one of the girl-slaves loved her mistress, and could not bear that any harm should come to her, so she said, " To-morrow touch no food and drink no water in the house ; only come into the bush with me, and I will bring you all that you need."

The woman, however, took no heed of what her slave had said, but drank what was offered her by other servants, and soon after died. She left a tiny girl-babe, and when the slaves prepared to leave the town and called to the faithful maid to go with them the latter said, " I cannot come ; I will not leave my mistress's child." When they urged her, she took up the babe, and carried it with her.

After they had gone a little way her sweetheart came and said, " What is this that you do ? All the other free-born are now dead. Give me the child that I may kill it also."

The girl saw that her charge could never be safe among the slaves, so she turned and ran back whence she had come. When she reached the house of her late mistress she laid the child down within, and shut the door. Then she went back again to rejoin her companions.

While the babe lay alone she began to cry, and, at the sound, one of the big calabashes, which hung against the wall of the room, called to her and said, " Do not weep any more." After that Calabash slid down off the wall and said to a basket and matchet which were lying near :

" Go to the farm of the child's mother and bring plantains."

Both went and did as they were ordered, and when the fruit was brought home, Calabash called to a pot and said :

"Go down to the river and fetch water." This also was done So Calabash cooked for the babe and tended her many years till she grew into a very beautiful maiden.

One day the son of Obassi Nsi went hunting in the bush. After awhile he came to a ruined village, in which only one house was still standing unharmed, and from this smoke was rising He went up to it and there saw a beautiful girl who had evidently just come out of the fatting-house. The room was empty save for herself and a great quantity of calabashes. So beautiful was she that he wished to have her for his sweetheart. She was willing, so he stayed with her for some time and then went back home.

Another day he went to visit her again and asked, "Do you live here alone, or is anyone with you?" This she would not answer. After a while he began to ask her to go with him to his father's town, but in the end had to go alone, because she was afraid to leave Calabash

After the young man had gone, Calabash said to her fosterling, "Next time your sweetheart comes, go home with him." The girl answered, "Why should I go, and leave you alone?"

That night, the son of Obassi said to his parents, "While I was hunting I found a town in the bush, and in it one very beautiful girl dwelling alone. I married her, but she will not leave her home and come with me " His father answered, "To-morrow I will send my people with you to bring her hither."

Next day, the Prince set out with a great train, and when Calabash saw them coming, she said to her fosterling, "Let us go now with your husband; only remember one thing. Pot and I stand to you in place of your mother. Allow no one to borrow us from you."

The son of Obassi gave orders to his people to gather together all his wife's property, and carry it to his father's town. When they reached their new home Obassi said, "This is the first time my son has taken a wife We will make a great feast for the wedding." One day, while they were making the marriage play, rain began to fall very heavily. The girl went to her door and looked around. Near by she saw the female slave who had taken care of her when she was small She recognised her, and called "Come into the house."

The woman came, and sat down by the fireside. She turned round and saw Calabash. At once she knew her and took her in her arms, crying as she held her. The girl said "Do you not know me too? I am the child of your former mistress."

The slave went out, and sought Obassi Nsi. "I am the foster-mother of your son's wife," said she. After me Calabash came and took care of her. The slaves killed all the free-born in the town with leopard gall. Among them the girl's mother perished also."

When Obassi heard this he called forth the Nsibidi * images, and bade them go through all the town and put to death all the slaves who had killed the free-born.

This was done. Then Obassi called the townsfolk before him and said, "From henceforth the free men must keep the gall themselves. It must never again be given in charge of the slaves."

That is the reason why we keep the custom even to this day. For after the kill, when it is time to divide up leopard or snake, no slave may go near till the principal men in the town have taken away the gall.

By the side of the main road, at the point most near to the Sacred Lake, stands a huge cotton tree, hung round with strips of cloth and other votive offerings. This is the special Juju tree for the town of Nsan. In this spot, therefore, the Genii of both wood and water may be worshipped in convenient proximity.

Everywhere in the bush grow giant trees, each with some special magic property, but perhaps the cotton trees are not only highest of all, but most dreaded. It is difficult to get good photographs of such, owing to the thickness of the surrounding bush, which would take too long to clear for a sufficient distance. The one shown in the illustration is a comparatively poor specimen which happened to stand at the edge of an open space.

Should man or woman among Efik or Ekoi wish to avenge themselves on an enemy, a sure way of bringing this about is to seek out one of these great trees in a lonely part of the bush.

---

* Officials of the Nsibidi Club, covered from crown to heel in long robes only pierced with eye-holes, acted as executioners in ancient times (see p 306)

Cotton Tree at Nsan. The Man Standing at the Foot was over Six Feet in Height.

If the petitioner be rich and of the Efik race, a white bull should be offered in sacrifice, together with a dish of rice flour and a flagon of palm oil. For the poorer Ekoi a white cock, or even lesser offering, may suffice.

The name of the enemy is called aloud The Genius of the tree hears, and from thenceforward lies in wait to wreak vengeance Should a child be born to anyone so cursed, the tree takes possession of it. Such a child will see strange black shapes from its birth, and be haunted by the demons of the bush. In time the tree will seize on and imprison the child, unless some powerful Juju man can be found to make strong " medicine," and so deliver it. There are two well-known ways of administering this "medicine." It should either be poured upon a lump of brass, from which anklets are made for the child to wear, or the face must be cut and the medicine rubbed in. Either of these methods will prevent the Genius of the tree from obtaining possession of its victim, though it may trouble him by means of dreams and visions till about the age of eight years.

For those too poor to provide a bull, or any costly sacrifice, there remains another and more dreaded way of enlisting the services of the Genius of the tree A man may buy vengeance, wealth, or power, by offering up himself. For a certain time he will enjoy the fruits of his sacrifice, but at length the call comes, and he must go, to exist, imprisoned Ariel-like within, as long as the tree endures.

On December 5, 1908, a case came up in Court against a man who killed his brother by forcing him to undergo the ordeal of eating Esere bean, in order to clear himself from the charge of trying to imprison their sister within a tree.

On another occasion an accident brought out the fact that tree affinities are well known among the Ekoi.

One Sunday evening cries were heard coming from the quarters occupied by the staff at Oban. Soon after, the Corporal was seen running towards the District House, with torn tunic and distracted air.

It seemed that one of the warders, Oji by name, had suddenly become delirious, and tried to run away into the bush. It was after the hour when station officials were supposed to be in quarters, and the Corporal tried to stop him, on which Oji was reported to have flown at him. Five policemen had, in the meantime, hastened to the scene of action, and in their hands he man was left struggling while the Corporal ran up to headquarters for instructions.

On my arrival Oji ceased to struggle, and begged to be allowed to go away at once, because his tree was calling.

In reply to questions as to what this might mean, he said:

"I come, as D. C.* knows, from the country of the Ibos. There the Oji trees grow and flourish, some in the water, and some on dry land. To all who, like me, bear the name of the tree, there comes a call at certain times of the year. When we hear our trees calling, wherever we may be, we must set out at once, by night or day, and run till we come to the place where they grow. We cannot stay for anything until we reach them.

"To-night I was very tired, and lay down on my bed. In my sleep my tree began to call 'Oji, Oji!' I woke, and still heard it call. So I started up to run out into the night. It always calls about the time of the new yams, sometimes earlier, sometimes later When they tried to stop me it called louder and louder. So I fought them to get away and go to my tree. That is all."

The torn tunics and battered limbs of the policemen seemed to attest that it was quite enough too!

The latter, mostly Yorubas, listened with an air of disdain to the "bushman's" foolish tale. Several of the Ekoi, on the other hand, who had come up to learn the cause of the disturbance, eagerly asserted that such things happened in their country also, and that, once heard, every man must follow the call

There are many stories about tree voices, and the ceremonies necessary for invoking the aid of the Genius of the tree. Perhaps the following is the best known of these.

Why Sacrifices are made to Cotton-trees.

Once a man was born with but one foot and one hand. When he grew up and married, the people of his town drove

---

* The contracted form of District Commissioner always used by natives.

him out from among them. So the couple went sadly away, and built themselves a little house in the bush. Here they dwelt for many years, hoping that Obassi would send them a son; but their hopes remained unfulfilled. One day they went together to the banks of the River of Good Fortune,* which flowed not far from their hut, and there prayed to Obassi to send them a child.

When they had prayed for a long time, the man asked his wife to help him back to their house. Some weeks later she told him that she thought their prayers were to be granted, and from this time he prayed more and more fervently.

One day a son was born to them. He came into the world bearing a Juju knife in one hand, and a small calabash full of Juju in the other.

When the father saw such an extraordinary child he trembled, and would have run away; but the babe said, "Do not be afraid, I am sent by Obassi to your help, because you have only one leg and one arm."

His mother brought him the usual offering of rain water, or plantain juice if no rain water is to be had, which is always given to new-born children. This the babe refused, and said in a strong voice, "Give me no water. Bring me chop to eat"†

Seven days after its birth the child could walk alone. People said, "How is it possible for a week-old child to do such things?"

The boy answered, "It is because I am sent from Obassi. My small brother will be coming soon."

One day he got his Juju knife, and held it out in his hand. The blade bent downwards of itself. He straightened it, and held it out again in a different direction. A second time it bent. A third time he did as before, but this time the knife kept straight, and pointed into the bush. The boy followed the way which the knife showed. After a time he came home and said to his mother, "Give me one single plantain."

She did as he asked, and he took the fruit and went out. He plucked leaves in the bush, mixed them with the plantain,

---

* See p 90.
† Compare the birth of Gargantua

and made " medicine," some of which he ate. Afterwards he returned and showed the rest to his mother, saying :

"This is the original food which Obassi ordained for me. I am a man of ability."

Next day at dawn, he took his knife as before, and held it out. It did not bend, so he followed where it pointed, and entered the bush. His way led him to the foot of a cotton tree. The tree called and he answered. It said to him " Where are you going ? " He answered, " I go where I choose, for the ' bush ' is the town of my parents."

The cotton tree said " Not so. This place belongs to me. Make ready, therefore, a sacrifice of young palm leaves, palm oil, palm wine, meat, and twisted creeper. Before you offer it to me call on the name of your true father, Obassi."

The boy did as he was bidden, and then went into the bush. Soon he heard the sound of a drum. At this he returned, and said to his foster-father, " I think there must be a town in the bush, for I heard a drum being played."

Next day the boy set forth again, and once more heard the sound of the drum, beaten as if for a wrestling match. He followed the sound, and came at length to a ghost town. In his hand he bore the calabash of "Juju," which made him invisible. So he passed unseen through the town till he came to the Egbo house, near which the Lame Boy* dwelt. There he saw ghosts wrestling together A matchet lay on the ground, and he noticed that if one ghost succeeded in thrusting another against this the latter died

After a while the new-comer wished to join in the wrestling, so he laid aside his calabash of Juju, and became visible to the ghosts. He started to wrestle. For a time he was successful and overcame several of his opponents, but at length one of them forced him backward on to the Juju matchet. The boy died, and the wrestling continued until only one ghost was left alive. Afterwards this ghost made Juju medicine for the others, and they became as before. Only the boy was left lying dead.

* The Lame Boy is the Ekoi Prometheus (see p 285), and the good fairy of their stories He is one of the principal characters in boys' plays and dances.

RELIGION

All the ghosts then went to bush to get firewood, in order to roast their visitor, that they might have a great feast, but before leaving, they called the fowls, and set them as a guard upon the body. To one of the cocks they said:

"Watch well, and, if you see the Lame Boy go near the dead body, crow loudly so that we may hear."

After they had all gone the Lame Boy said to himself, "I am sorry for the boy."

He went and got corn, and threw it on the ground before the fowls. They all ran to eat this, and forgot their charge.

Now, when the ghost made the Juju medicine to revive his dead companions, he had made more than was necessary, and what was left, he threw into the inner compartment of the Egbo house. While the fowls were busy pecking up the corn, the Lame Boy went thither, and got what remained of the magic medicine. He put this on the dead boy's eyes, and the latter stood up. When the Lame Boy saw that the stranger was alive once more, he said:

"Take your calabash of Juju, and go home quickly."

The lad set out, but had not got very far before the fowls had pecked up the last grains of corn which the Lame Boy had thrown down for them. They therefore went back to keep watch over the corpse, but found it gone. So the cocks crowed, to call back the ghosts. These came hurrying in with their firewood, but found that the visitor had been brought back to life, and had fled from them.

Then the ghosts said among themselves, "Let us pursue him; perhaps he may yet be overtaken."

When the boy reached the cotton tree, he related all that had befallen him in the ghost town. Cotton Tree said, "When you reach home, cook fufu * and fresh plantains, and offer them up before the house of your father."

The boy had just time to do this before the ghosts came. They found the place spread with offerings; so they ate these and returned home. After that he took a chicken and some palm oil, and went and placed them before Cotton Tree. The latter accepted them and said:

* Yam, etc., beaten up into a paste

"Now I will tell you about the ghost sacrifices. When the dead come to a town to catch a man, they will leave him unharmed, and go back, if they find plentiful offerings before the entrance to the town." The tree also said, " From to-day, should anything bad happen to you, or should you fall sick, and wish to find out the cause of your misfortune, come to me, and I will tell you. Come to me also should anyone harm you, and I will be ready to help."

This is the reason why native people go alone into the bush, if they are offended with anyone, and why they make sacrifice to the cotton tree, if they fall sick or wish to be avenged on an enemy.

CHAPTER IV

Egbo

THE whole country is honeycombed with secret societies, among which the Egbo Club is the most powerful. Before the coming of the " white man " this institution ruled the land, and even now it has more influence in many ways than Government itself, and has caused endless difficulty to administrators.

The Ekoi claim to have originated the whole idea of such clubs, which have existed among them for centuries, and are mentioned in some of their very old folk-lore tales. Later on, the Ododop and other tribes near Iffianga, Akwa and Efut in the South Cameroons, started a similar society, which gradually became more powerful than the original Ekoi one, and therefore more costly to join. The Efiks of Calabar were not slow to perceive the advantage of such institutions, and so founded the Ekkpe Club, which, with the growing importance of their town, through the coming of white men, soon became the wealthiest of all Egbo Societies.

As the Efiks held the monopoly of the Calabar trade they and their club obtained great influence over the Ekoi, who found it advisable to adopt many Efik customs and laws. This was especially the case with the Ekoi who live to the South of Oban, and therefore nearest to Calabar. Those to the North still keep their old Egbo practically unchanged, except the inhabitants of Ndebbiji, who have adopted that of the Ododop people, which is almost the same as the Efik one.

Calabar was practically the only place whence the Ekoi could obtain guns and gunpowder. To reach it, they had to pass through Efik territory. The roads were picketed by the latter people, and it was impossible to reach the factories save by their good will. Even if some men from the interior managed to reach a white official and attempted to lay their grievances before him, the Efik interpreter took care that the true state of things should not be translated. If a case was tried in the Calabar Courts the only chance which a "bush man" had of winning it was to enlist the help of some powerful Efik, and often the only way of doing this was to promise to become his "member." The arts by which Efik traders entrapped first one man and then the whole family, as slaves, were often cruel in the extreme. The only holds possessed by the Ekoi over their persecutors were that the Efiks feared their Jujus and wanted the dried meat killed and preserved by Ekoi hunters. The establishment of a Native Court at Oban did not much improve matters. Indeed, in some ways, it made them worse, as the clerk who ruled it was always an Efik and arranged that judgment should be given in favour of his own people.

It is natural that the most powerful society should be called by the name of the most dreaded denizen of the bush, for "Egbo" is supposed to express to the Efik "Ekkpe" and the Ekoi "Ngbe," i.e., Leopard.*

Possibly among the Ekoi, where totemism is still an article of belief, though most of them will deny the existence of any such idea, the Leopard Society originally consisted only of those who belonged to this totem. On account of the superior craft and power of the animal it would naturally draw to itself the largest following. Later, as totemism began to lose force, first one, then another prominent individual who was not properly speaking a "Leopard soul" might be allowed to join, until it gradually became open to all.

There are many indications which seem to place beyond doubt the fact that some form of totemism still enters into the ritual of the Egbo Society. For instance, at some of the bigger

* Compare the Leopard Society of Sierra Leone, which terrorised vast regions, especially among the Mendis. In 1903, while engaged in delimitating the Anglo-Liberian frontier, one of the carriers, who was a member of this Society and considered himself somewhat indebted to me, gave a considerable amount of information about it. Members can often be recognised at sight, as many of them have the sharply protruding forehead, caused by pressure applied in infancy by the mothers. When the Society wishes to kill a man certain members are chosen for the deed. These are armed with a set of iron instruments, fastened inside both hands, and track their victim, until they come upon him in a lonely part of the "bush." They watch their opportunity, suddenly spring upon him from behind, and seize him by the throat. Should the body ever be discovered, the marks so exactly resemble those made by leopard claws that the death is put down to these beasts.

"plays," while the principal performers or "images" as they are called, run up and down, now to the right, now to the left, the lesser personages form a circle, and keep time to a monotonous chant. In one case they sang·

"Okum ngbe ommobik ejennum ngimm, akiko ye ajakk nga ka ejenn nyamm"

The Egbo cannot walk straight, he is driven hither and thither by the movement of the beast.

On another occasion a prominent member of the "Egbo," who had the reputation of knowing more "Nsibidi"—a primitive secret writing much used in this part of the world—than any man now alive, was asked to give me a little help in the study of this script. He refused point blank, though a good remuneration had been offered for his services. He added as an "aside" to another member of the society, with no idea that his words could be understood by the "white man," "If I taught D C Nsibidi, he would know all the Egbo signs, and the secrets of the animals." He refused to give any further information, and soon after went away.

The importance of the society is obvious even to the most careless visitor to any land where it has gained a foothold, for the Club house is the principal building in every town. Even the smallest village has its Egbo shed, and when a town decides to migrate the first thing done, so soon as the fresh site is cleared, before even new farms are "cut," or the land divided up, is to fix the position of the Club house. A small shed, called Ekpa Ntan (the house without walls) is erected to mark the spot where the Egbo house is to stand.*

The many-sided character of Egbo may be judged from the immense powers which it has arrogated to itself in almost every direction. Under native rule it usurped practically all functions of government, made trade almost impossible for non-members, and exercised a deep influence on the religious and mystic side of the nation.

The ritual is certainly very ancient, and in it many Juju cults are mixed. The name of Obassi is invoked before every sacrifice, and an oblation of food and drink laid in front of the

* See story, p 350

Etai Ngbe (Leopard stone), the cut stone usually found before the second pillar of the Club house.*

It is difficult to discover more than the merest fragments of the secrets of Egbo, as any known informant would meet with a speedy death. Still from what has been gathered—mostly, as in the case already quoted, from snatches of song sung at different plays—there seems to be a close resemblance between these secrets and the Eleusinian and ancient Egyptian mysteries. Certainly a considerable amount of hypnotism, clairvoyance and spiritualism is taught, and only too many proofs have been given, that some of the powers of Nature are known and utilised by initiates, in a way forgotten or unknown to their white rulers

For instance, some of the esoteric members seem to have the power of calling up shadow forms of absent persons. Once an exhibition of this nature given in the central court of the compound of one of the head chiefs of Oban, was described to me.

It was midnight, and a bright moon was shining. Within the open space in the centre of the compound a fire was burning. On this from time to time " medicine " was thrown, which caused clouds of smoke to rise. These died down, save for isolated " puffs," which after a time assumed definite shape.

The spectators sat on the ground in a half-circle behind the fire, and facing a low mud wall, beyond which, against the background of the moonlit sky, dark silhouettes began to pass, each clearly recognisable as that of some person known to be absent at the time. There was no sign of any artificial means of producing these shapes, which continued to pass for about a quarter of an hour, at the end of which time they grew faint and at length faded.

The Chiefs claimed to have the power of calling up the shadow shapes of white men, but no case in which this had actually been done was cited.

There are seven grades which the aspirant must pass before he can be admitted to the deeper teaching or the revelation of any save the lesser mysteries. All may be entered by young boys, should their fathers be rich enough to pay the necessary

---

* See Chapter XXV

fees, but the secrets are not unfolded till middle age has been reached.

1. EKPIRI NGBE. Small Egbo.

2. EBU NKO (an old word, the meaning of which is not known). At a dance given by this grade, members must always wear their best clothes. Aspirants to each of these are marked with white chalk on both arms.

3. MBAWKAW (old Ekoi word adopted by Efiks). Aspirants to this are marked on the forehead with Ekui (cam-wood dye). These three grades are called collectively Abonn Ogbe, *i.e.*, children of the Egbos. They are neither important nor expensive to enter.

4. NDIBU (old word, meaning unknown, equivalent to Efik Nyampke). This is the second division, and one to which it is accounted a great honour to belong. It is often called " The Mother of the Grades." Its president holds the second place in the whole society. If it was found necessary to expel a member who had reached this grade, death followed as a matter of course, lest any of its secrets should be revealed by the outcast.

When a man joins Ndibu the head chiefs and officials stay in the Egbo house, while the young men dance and play round the town. The best friend of the aspirant brings forward a calabash containing a leg of meat, and two bottles of palm wine. The postulant then enters the Club house, and sits down before the Chief, who puts powder on his head, and recites all the names of the Egbo The new member next rises and invokes the names in his turn, while after each the chiefs call out " Owe," *i.e.*, our own. He then goes out and dances with the young men. The play is carried on for about eight days, during which time palm wine and meat are supplied to all.

At the present day at Oban, entrance to this grade costs about £30, which must be paid before full membership is allowed.

5. OKU AKAMA (the priest consents). This is not very expensive to enter, nor considered of much account, but it must be passed before further grades can be reached. The postulant is marked with yellow dye (Ogokk) on the abdomen and the back of his shoulders.

The old Ekoi grade was called Asian, but when Oban adopted the Calabar Egbo, the Efiks insisted on this being suppressed.

6. ETURI (metal or brass rod), Efik Okpokgo In the old days during a play, all fires had to be extinguished and no noise of any kind was permitted in the town. Formerly very few men succeeded in reaching this grade, but now it is usually passed on the same day as

7. NKANDA, the highest and final grade. Oban took this from the Efiks, who again insisted on the destruction of the old Ekoi equivalent " Isong," and of another old grade " Mutanda," of slightly lesser importance.

Nkanda is more expensive than any other grade, and most men only enter late in life. When a man has succeeded in joining this high grade, he is rubbed on head and chest with yellow powder (Ogokk). Five rings are made on front and back. Two yellow, one round each breast, a white one in the centre some few inches below, and, beneath this again, two more yellow ones, forming a square with those on the breasts

On the back the rings are arranged in the same way, but the central one is yellow and the four outer ones white. The arms are ornamented with alternate stripes of white and yellow, and till the last rite is finished, the man goes bare save for a long loin cloth which reaches from waist to feet.

The chief of Nkanda is the president of the Egbo Lodge, and by far the most powerful man of the town. His office is sometimes hereditary, and only free-born chiefs can aspire to it. In olden days a slave could not join Egbo, lest he should reveal its secrets to a new master. He could, however, be present at most of the ceremonies if his owner was a member of Egbo, and permitted

One of the chief insignia of the Nkanda grade is called the Ekabe (Efik Ekarra) Nkanda. This is a kind of hoop, covered with bright-coloured cloth. The attendant whose duty is to carry this, performs many curious evolutions with it. He is obliged to hold back the Okum (or " image") by its means if the latter, in a state of excitement, seems about to show himself to a non-member, particularly a woman, at a time when this is not permitted. Should the Okum succeed in evading the vigilance

"Image" of Nkanda Grade of Egbo with Emblem "Ekabe Nkanda."

EGBO

of the Ekabe bearer, a cow is killed, and a feast provided for the members at the expense of the defaulting official.

Another symbol, used by Nkanda and Ebu Nko alike, is the Effrigi (see drawing), a sort of wooden fan on which Nsibidi signs are inscribed.

The head priest of the whole Egbo Society is called Iyamba, the old Ekoi equivalent for which was Musungu.

Other officials are Murua, who carries the rattle during "plays," and Isua,* the master of ceremonies for the Abonn Ogbe. The head of each grade is called Ntui (chief) and acts as treasurer.

Those who belong to the four higher grades, and have paid the fees in full, may join in another ceremony called Mariba, or Etem-I-Ngbe (the bush leopard). This is performed in the depths of the forest and with the greatest secrecy. It is during the "Mariba" that the successive mysteries are unveiled. The ceremony may also be performed at the funeral "customs" of very great chiefs.

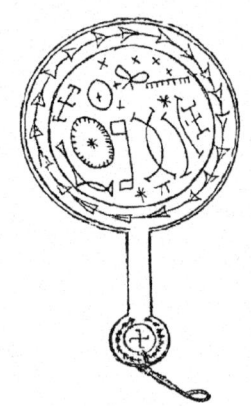

Effrigi Fan
(Notice svastika on handle.)

The danger run by non-members on such occasions, before the coming of white rule, may perhaps be better understood by a case which happened not long before my arrival to start the District.

During the "Mariba" the sacred images, &c., are carried to a part of the "bush" where a little hut of green boughs has been built to receive them. Sentries are posted to keep all intruders from coming within a mile of this spot. On this occasion, however, two young girls, sisters, happened to have missed the patrol, and trespassed unwittingly within the sacred precincts, probably in search of nuts or bush fruits, which abound everywhere They were caught by the sentries, brought

---

* This is also the name given to a particular dance never performed save on the death of one of the Chief Members, such as the Iyamba, or when fulfilling the latter's "customs"

before the "Egbo," condemned to death, and hanged almost immediately. Their brother, who was a member of the highest grade of the society, was allowed, as a great favour, to be present at their death and afterwards to carry home the bodies to his family. Of redress, in such a case, there could be neither hope nor thought.

Sometimes rich and influential women are permitted to become honorary members of all grades, but they are never allowed to be full members, nor to know any of the mysteries.

Each grade has its particular dances and tunes, and each its own Okum Ngbe or Egbo "image," which is never supposed to come out and show itself unless under direct inspiration to do so.

The so-called "image" is a figure robed from crown to heel in a long garment, of the colour proper to the grade, and pierced with eyeholes. It usually bears on its head a wooden framework covered with skin and shaped like a human head, often with two faces, one male and the other female. This represents the omniscience of the Deity looking both ways, into the future and back to the past, as also the bi-sexual character shown in the oldest conceptions of Obassi Osaw and Obassi Nsi, Sky Father and Earth Mother.

The Okum runs up and down accompanied by two attendants clothed in gorgeous, close-fitting, knitted garments, usually of red, yellow, and white. One of these carries a rod or whip, the symbol of the power of the society, which, under native law, had the right to flog to death any non-members who had seriously offended against its rules. The other bears the symbolic green boughs, which play so great a part in the lives of the Ekoi. At almost every important occurrence, from birth onward, green leaves of the kind proper to the event are used, and at the last are gently drawn over the face of a dying man, that his spirit may pass peacefully and without pain from this world to the next. Curiously enough the scientific name of the tree used on this last occasion is Croton *amabilis*, though the small, dark leaves and inconspicuous flowers hardly suggest such an appellation.

There is great rivalry between the different towns as to which can produce the most gorgeous robes for "images"

Hunting Juju "Image," Ekuri Ibokk, Oban.

and members. The financial state of a place can be told by a glance at one of the " plays," as the local resources are strained to the utmost in the hope of outdoing neighbouring towns. The chiefs of Oban volunteered the information that the play was so much finer on the second New Year after my arrival than formerly, because the opening of a Government Station had brought them an increase of wealth.

The most interesting figure in last New Year's dance, however, wore nothing either rich or attractive. This was the Ekuri Ibokk (Efik "axe-medicine") It is a very old Ekoi Juju, but was renamed a few years ago when the axe was placed between its jaws in addition to the other insignia.

The image was robed in a long gown of dark blue cloth, daubed with mud from the river-bed. This, to the Ekoi, as formerly to performers in the Greek Mysteries and to Flamen Dialis, is in itself a great " Juju." Over the robes of the image dark-spotted Juju leaves were fastened here and there. On its head it bore a crocodile mask, carved in wood, perhaps a representation of Nimm herself. It was attended by two hunters armed with flint-lock guns, a third bore a fishing-net, and a fourth a curious earthen trumpet covered with leopard skin The "image" was supposed to be deaf to human voices, and to hear only those of the bush beasts, save when awakened by the call of the trumpet. Ekuri Ibokk is the great "hunting Juju" of the Ekoi, and had never before appeared to a European. It is the Juju that is supposed to have the power of "smelling out" all others, and the axe in its jaws is a sign of its special fierceness. Powerful as it is, however, it is not proof against the very human weakness of wishing to have its photograph taken, and appeared, on this inducement, among its less exclusive brothers.

At such " plays " all the principal characters carry wands or whips, the symbol of the power of the society, which, as has already been mentioned, had the right to flog to death non-members who ventured outside their houses during an Egbo performance, or seriously offended in any way. Minor offences were punished by fines, and from these the main revenues of the Club were derived.

One great advantage to be gained from membership in the old days was the facility offered for the recovery of debts.

A creditor brought his case before the Egbo Lodge in the debtor's town. The Council considered the matter, and if the claim was thought justified, the Club drum would be beaten through the streets, and the defaulter ordered to pay. He was also bound to provide a "dash" for the Egbo Society Should he be unable to comply with both demands, his goods were seized, and, other means failing, himself or some of his family reduced to the position of slaves, in order to make good all liabilities.

There are many stories to account for the coming of Egbo, but perhaps the following is the best known.

How the First Egbo Image Came.

One day Nki * went into the bush to gather palm kernels. He cut down a great cluster from which one fell. This rolled down a crab's hole, right through to the ghost town, where the son of one of the chiefs found and ate it.

Nki climbed down from the palm tree, and went in search of his kernel. He followed it till he came to the ghost town. There he saw the young chief and guessed what he had done. So he went before the head chief and said ·

" Will you give me back the palm kernel which your son has eaten ? "

The old chief answered :

" Here is a drum. Take it and beat upon it It will repay you for what you have lost."

Nki did as he was told. Hardly had he struck the drum when a calabash full of fruit appeared. The chief said, " Take the drum with you," so Nki took it and went on his way.

When he reached home he called to his wives and said :

" Weep no more. I bring you food in plenty."

He beat the drum, and the calabash appeared as before. He ate of the fruit, and gave some to all his family.

After this there was always much chop in his house, for he needed only to strike the drum to obtain a fresh supply. He grew rich, and hired people to work for him instead of working himself as formerly.

---

* New Dormouse (*Graphiurus C. Dorotheæ*), discovered by me in 1911

One day he hired the men of the town to go and cut farm for him. All of them went save Ngbe (Leopard) alone. Each day Nki cooked twelve great calabashes of chop for his workers.

When the farm was cleared he hired the women to plant it, and prepared food for them as he had done for the men. The wife of Ngbe took her portion home. Her husband seized it and ate it up, whereon she said:

"When the others went to cut farm for Nki, you refused to go with them. Why then do you eat my chop?"

One day Nki went to visit his farm. He put the magic drum into an inner room and locked the door. Then he gave the key to the Lame Boy and said, "If anyone should come and ask for this do not give it."

As soon as he was out of sight Ngbe came and demanded the key. The boy refused to give it up, but Leopard said, "I will kill you if you do not give it to me." So the boy gave it.

Ngbe opened the door, seized the drum and bounded with it into the bush. There he made a small clearing, set up the drum and began to beat it. So strongly did he strike, that almost at once several calabashes appeared full of sweet things. There was too much for one to eat alone, so Ngbe ate what he could and left the rest, then broke up the drum and threw away the pieces. Afterwards he went off to his house.

When Nki came home, he asked the Lame Boy for the key of the inner room, whereon the boy told him all that Ngbe had done.

Nki was sad over his loss. After a while he went out into the bush as before. Again he cut palm kernels, but, as none of them fell, he looked round for a crab hole, threw a kernel into it, and pushed it down with a long stick. He then followed it through the hole till he came again to the ghost town. Here he saw a chief and said:

"One of your sons has taken my palm kernel. Give it back to me."

On this the chief gave him Egyuk, the long kind of drum which we now find in Egbo houses. Nki took it and went on his way.

When he reached the bush where he had cut the kernels he

set down the drum and began to beat it. Out sprang the Egbo "image" and started to flog him with the whip which it held in its hand.

Nki went on beating the drum, and after a while the image went back into it. Then he took up the drum and went home

Next day Nki went out as if he were again going to farm. No sooner was he out of sight than Ngbe came as before and demanded the key from the Lame Boy. This time the latter gave it without difficulty, as his master had told him to do.

Ngbe opened the door of the inner room where the drum was, took it, and sprang into the bush as before. He started to play with all his might, and so furiously did he strike that seven Egbo "images" sprang out, each armed with a whip, and began to flog him.

Full of anger and fear, he broke the drum, and threw the pieces into the bush. The "images" could no longer go back to their home in the drum, so they ran into the town, and beat all who came in their way.

That is the reason why the "images" run up and down to this day, and beat those who cross their path. It is because Ngbe broke the first long drum which was brought from the ghost town, and in which they used to dwell.

The reason we call them "Egbo" is because Nki gave that name to the first "image" which came out of the magic drum.

Beside the Egbo Club there are almost innumerable societies,* secret and otherwise, some partially religious in character, some formed simply for amusement and entertainment, some for mutual protection, and various other purposes, such as to carry out special celebrations at the funeral customs of members. In many cases such institutions grew from an "age class" which formed a club for its members; this became popular and outsiders were allowed to join.

* For list of Oban Societies, see Appendix B

CHAPTER V

JUJUS

THE term "Njomm," which can only be translated by "Juju," is so elusive as to defy definition, but as far as may be gathered from the vague conception of the Ekoi, it includes all uncomprehended, mysterious forces of Nature. These vary in importance from elementals, so powerful as to hold almost the position of demi-gods, to the "Mana"—to use a Melanesian term—of herb, stone, or metal. In another sense the word also includes the means by which such forces may be controlled or influenced, secrets wrung from the deepest recesses of Nature by men wise above their fellows, or mercifully imparted to some favoured mortal by one or other of the Deities.

Jujus vary in importance in different towns according to local opinion, but everywhere a dominant one is to be found, and whatever other attributes may be claimed for this, that of protection against witchcraft always ranks first. Each of the lesser Jujus presides over its particular department, though in many cases attributes overlap. As an example of the various kinds usually to be found, those existing in 1907 at the little village of Ekong, on the Obutong-Oban road, may be cited.

1. OFIRI, thought at the time to be the most powerful of all Jujus for defending the town against witchcraft and theft. So great was its reputation for destroying wizards that people came from hundreds of miles in order to join the cult. Each member wears a metal torque or anklet, on which some of the "medicine" has been poured, and carries back more "medicine" to be placed in a shrine at his own home.

2. NIMM ASAM (Nimm of the Spears). This is strong against witchcraft, and also helps hunters, but is chiefly valued

S.B.

for its power of warning members against poison in food or drink, especially against that made from ground porcupine quills, which is called "the poison of Nimm Asam," and is the Ekoi equivalent for ground glass or ground palm stem. Certain members of this Juju are thought to have the power of producing the rainbow, and therefore causing the rain to cease for a time.*

3. EGPATIM, against witchcraft and theft. This is of the same "family" as Nimm Asam.

4 NKAJOKK, the province of which is to ward off sickness from the town.

5. EBUP to ensure success in hunting and fishing.

6. NGAPONG, for protection against beasts of prey, especially leopards

These six Jujus are common to the whole town, but most families have, in addition, others which have been handed down from father to son, and mother to daughter for countless generations

In Oban, the most powerful Jujus are the very old ones of Okpata, Ejame† and Eja—the first two against witchcraft and theft, and the latter to increase the crops, ward off wild animals from the herds, and give protection from thunder and lightning. The feast of Eja is the chief one of the year, and corresponds to the harvest festival,‡ as do those of Mfuor and Animm in some towns.

Among the lesser Jujus at Oban is that which takes the place of the Ekong Ngapong. It is called Ngbe Abum Obbaw (Leopard knocks his foot), and was brought from Mkpott about two years ago. Before its arrival leopards had been a scourge. Five cows were once killed by them within twenty-four hours, while even in the middle of the town compounds were entered and goats carried off.

One night, before the Station was built, when I was sleeping in the doorless Court House, I awoke to find a leopard snuffing round my mosquito net. It was after a long march, and I felt too tired to exert myself to repel the intruder save by a sleepy "tsch—," but was punished for this laziness by the loss of several of my best fowls, which it took in default of bigger prey.

* See p 72   ‡ See dances, p. 295.
† See p. 74.

Juju Enoowu

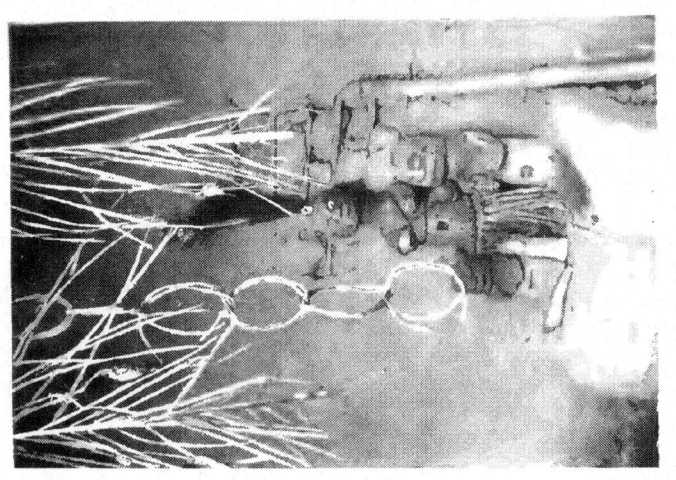

Juju Nnam Asam.

The same thing happened again at the station before the doors had been hung.

On returning to Oban after absence on leave, a remarkable change was found. Since the installation of the new Juju not a leopard showed itself within a mile of the houses, and not a sheep, goat or cow had been lost. The cattle, in fact, were wandering safely outside the town, eating my pineapples, and spoiling my rubber plantations.

The Juju is said to lose its efficacy if certain rites are not observed. Since its arrival palm kernels must be picked from the bunch before being brought into the town. Should this not be done, a leopard will come before dawn, and exact the penalty of cow or sheep. The same punishment is inflicted should any violent quarrel take place in the town, as also if a fire is lighted outside a compound's walls. The undoubted efficacy of the Juju may perhaps be explained in part by the purgation ceremony described on p. 220. It is possible that the strong-smelling pitch used to "renew the power" of the Juju may offend the nostrils of the keen-scented beasts of prey and cause them to avoid the town.

The four Jujus with the widest distribution are Mfam, Ofiri, Mfuor and Akpambe. All alike protect against witchcraft and theft. The first is the oldest, and was in the possession of the Ekoi when they arrived in this part of the world. It is held in some places to be so powerful, that it has had to be removed. For instance, in 1909 the people of Nsan came to beg that it might be taken away from their town, as many of the inhabitants were dying because of it. Even if a man thoughtlessly ate a single plantain when passing through a farm, without first obtaining the permission of the owner, Mfam was said to kill him for theft. Wherever this Juju is dominant, the entrails of any animal killed in hunting must be brought before its priest.

To revoke the tabu on entrails for the general public, an animal must be killed and brought into the town. Each man then takes his matchet and scrapes his tongue, refusing to be bound by the "Ntubi" (tabu). After this the entrails are divided and eaten.

Early in 1909 the cult of Akpambe invaded the District and

rapidly gained such a reputation that lodges were established in almost every town. The cult was started about a year earlier by a man named Obassi Abong, who was taught the necessary rites by his mother, a celebrated Juju woman of Okuri in the Cameroons, where its first shrine still exists (see photograph, p. 158). Many older cults were overthrown at the coming of Akpambe, but the shrine of Eburuk Pabi stands untouched. People even aver that the new Juju cannot enter a place unless Eburuk Pabi is there first; for the latter alone confers the power of "seeing" Akpambe. Certainly the "Okum" at each "play" bows before the shrine of Eburuk Pabi. It is somewhat significant that this last-named is looked upon as a female Juju. Some aver that Eburuk Pabi is an old name for Obassi, in which case it may perhaps be taken as a further indication of the original femininity of Obassi Nsi. The sign of Eburuk Pabi is an earthen pot—always a female symbol.

Shrine of Eburuk Pabi at Ndingane, with old Juju post overthrown at the coming of Akpambe.

Votaries of Akpambe, Ekuri Ibokk and Mfuor wear amulets of blue cloth containing "medicine," the chief function of which is to ward off witchcraft.

The "images" of all three Jujus wear robes of dark blue native cloth, bordered with a fringe of palm-fibre and decked with the silvery shells of a bivalve. From a certain resemblance in shape these are supposed to represent the human ear, and symbolise the all-hearing power of the spirit, like those pottery and enamel representations of the organ found in Egyptian temples. In each case the "image" bears a roughly-carved crocodile's head upon its own, thus seeming to link itself with the cult of the great nature goddess " Nimm "

When a man wishes to sacrifice, he must first call on Eyo (the sun) to carry his petition before Obassi. Should the ceremony take place in the morning the title Eyo Ofu (sun of the morning) must be used, but if after noon that of Eyo Egu (sun of the evening).

The ceremonies proper to the various Jujus are long, complicated, and contain many fragments of old ritual of which the meaning has long since been forgotten. An account of some of these may be not without interest.

At Oban on February 2, 1908, a sacrifice was offered by a woman named Ogai Etab for recovery of health When the townsfolk had assembled the suppliant advanced holding a calabash of food, covered with a white cloth

The priest received the offering, then took the cloth and held it up before the Juju, saying, " Here is cloth brought by Ogai Etab. By the charm you told her that the sickness had fallen upon her because she had not offered sacrifice for a very long time."

Next, dried meat was taken from the calabash, and offered with the same words, together with an earthen jar containing palm wine. After this the priest called for water and filled his mouth ; then laid two Juju leaves on the back of his left hand. He blew the water out upon them and called aloud, " Behold, here is food come from Ogai Etab. Answer whether or not you will eat of it, Obassi-o-o! Obassi-o-o!"

The names of all dead members of the cult were called, for ghosts have great power over the Juju which they served in life This is particularly the case with the " Founder," *i.e.*, the priest who first started the cult in a new town and is supposed to remain its guardian after death. Before any further step is taken the Diviner (Mboni) assures the people that the ghost of the Founder is present.

When the long list of dead was ended, the priest struck his right hand against the back of his left, on which the two leaves were lying. These fluttered down ; one fell face upward, and the other downward. This showed that the sacrifice was accepted.

Next the priest poured water into the earthenware pot, where the Juju is supposed to live, and said:

" Here is fresh water. Make our bodies cool and fresh as water, that fever may keep far from us ! " He then dropped in a little powdered white chalk saying, " Here is chalk. Give us good fortune." Next he added some palm wine and palm oil, saying " Make our blood rich and pure as oil and palm wine "

The meat was then cut into small pieces and divided among the worshippers, and dried corn, mixed with palm wine, was shared among them, after it had been held before the Juju.

When all had been eaten, the priest again laid two leaves upon his hand and said :

"Now we have eaten and drunken. May we go home satisfied ? "

He struck the leaves as before. If they had not fallen rightly, the woman, on whose behalf the ceremony had been held, must have gone to the Diviner to find out why her petition had not been granted. The latter would then practise the charm, and give some reason, for example, " The offering was not enough." In such a case more food must be gathered and the whole ceremony repeated.

On the occasion described above, the woman was very ill, and unfit to collect all that would usually have been thought necessary, but the priest allowed the ceremony to take place, on the understanding that the rest of the sacrifice should be offered later.

Another Juju for the recovery of health is called Ntuanto, *i.e*, the Soul or Outbreathing. This ceremony was witnessed one day at Nsan. As we went along the street, a low tomtoming, mixed with the sharper strokes of the Okankan (a musical instrument like two flat bells joined together), was heard from the compound of one of the minor chiefs named Atop Atun. We entered and found the whole family gathered in the central court round the Juju Ntuanto. Exactly facing it sat the head of the house, with a small table before him. On this lay five little fetishes, each robed in fresh green leaves bound on with fine tie-tie. Two were somewhat larger than the others, one male and the other female. These possibly represented the

Juju "Images" with Attendants.

special fetishes of the father and mother, while the lesser ones were those of the children. Before the Juju an iron spear (Osam), notched at the point like a gigantic fish hook, stood upright in the ground.

To the rear, at the right-hand corner, a tortoise was impaled head upwards, and front toward the spectators. In the foreground, on the right of the head of the family, knelt one of the "members," holding the black cock, destined to be sacrificed.

As we watched, Atop took up an egg which lay beside him, and broke it with great care, on the topmost barb of the spear. He then gently crushed the shell round the puncture, and pressed it against the spear in five different places, so that some of the yolk and specks of egg-shell adhered to the metal. The little dolls were then anointed in the same way, and what remained of the shell was crushed in the hand, and laid at the foot of the Juju.

A deputation of chiefs was waiting at the Rest-house, so it was impossible to stay till the end of the ceremony, the object of which was to restore health to Atop himself, who was sick.

On asking for the name of the Juju, I was told that it was called "Monni Njomm," *i.e.*, Little Juju, but when I shook my head and said I already knew that it was one of the lesser Jujus, and wished to learn its real name, my informant looked confused, though rather amused, and answered that it was called Ntuanto, *i.e.*, the Soul or Outbreathing.

Cocks and tortoises are sacrificed not only on an occasion such as that just described, but to nearly all the greater Jujus, together with the blood of animals killed in the bush During many ceremonies, pipes made from crabs' claws are blown. The legendary causes for these customs are to be found in the following stories.

WHY COCK AND TORTOISE ARE SACRIFICED TO THE JUJU

Cock and Tortoise dwelt together in a town where there was a great famine. No fruits ripened in the farms, and the yams and dried corn from last year's harvest were all eaten. So the townsfolk knew not how to stay their hunger.

Tortoise said to himself, "If I stay here, I starve," so he set out, determined not to turn back till he had found food.

After he had gone a long way, he came to a place where the ghosts had made their farm. They went hither and thither collecting plantains, yams, pumpkins, and other food. When they had got together a great store, they divided it among them, and returned homeward heavily laden.

No sooner had they gone than Tortoise crept out from his hiding place, cut a great bunch of plantains, and hurried back with it. When he got home he began to cook, and, while he was busy preparing the food, in came Cock. The latter saw what his friend was doing, and asked whence the plantains came.

Tortoise answered that he had seen them growing on a deserted farm. Cock asked if he might accompany him thither next day, but Tortoise refused.

On the morrow he set out again for the ghost farm, and came back at night with more plantains. Cock was awaiting him, and said, "It is not good that you treat me so."

Tortoise replied, "The reason I will not let you come with me is that you cannot hold your tongue."

Cock asked, "What have I spoken about?" Tortoise only answered, "Be satisfied. I will give you a share of my food, but cannot allow you to accompany me."

At dawn therefore he set out alone once more. This time, when he saw the ghosts preparing to go back to their town, he thought "I should like to know where they come from." So he followed behind them all the way.

Just before the entrance to the town, Tortoise hid himself in the bush, in a place whence he could see everything, but where no one could see him. He thought to himself "I have never seen so fine a town before. Perhaps later I may enter and find out how the ghosts live."

While he lay there hidden, some of the ghosts came by from the river. One of them said "I smell the odour of fresh meat. What is it that can smell so?" The other ghosts said, "Let us look around."

They began to search up and down. When they came to the place where Tortoise lay, he hid himself beneath his shell. The ghosts saw him but said, "This is only a stone." After they had grown weary of searching they returned to their town. Then Tortoise went back to the farm, and cut more plantains, which he took home as before.

Cock questioned him again, "Where did you get these plantains?" Tortoise said. "I will not tell. I went through great danger to get them. That is why I will not allow you to come with me. You are a babbler, and, should you come, you would surely make a noise; then someone would hear and come and kill us."

Cock said, "Of two friends it is not good that one should sit hungry in the town, while the other goes abroad and feeds in plenty."

Tortoise answered, "All you say is useless. You make too much noise to come with me."

Cock said "Good," and spoke no more.

Shortly afterwards Tortoise went away. No sooner had he left the house than Cock flew within. He found the bag which Tortoise usually carried, took out his knife, made a small hole, then scooped up some ashes from the hearth and put them at the bottom of the bag. He said to himself "No matter how secretly you go to-morrow, I will know where you get all this food."

Next morning when Tortoise set out, the ashes fell along the road. Cock followed, and both arrived at the ghost farm.

After the ghosts had taken their food and gone away, Tortoise went to cut plantains as before. When he turned round to go back he saw Cock. He was afraid and said, "Why did you come? Now we must hurry back. I fear that the owners of the farm may catch us." Cock said, "Even if I make a noise I do not think they will do me any harm."

Tortoise replied, "If you make a noise, not you alone, but both of us will die." In great fear he hurried home, and for four days did not leave his town.

At the end of that time all the stolen plantains were finished, so he was forced to set out in search of more.

He said, "I will go back to the farm." He went in front Cock walked behind. When they reached the farm they saw the ghosts gathering their fruits.

Tortoise said to Cock, "Do not go near to the ghosts or they will catch you. Stay hidden until they have gone."

Cock kept still for a little time, but after a while he saw a great heap of coco-yams, and ran to get some. One of the ghosts saw him and cried, " What is this ? " Cock ran away. He was frightened and began to make a small noise.

Tortoise had already started to run, and, when Cock caught him up, said·

" Did I not tell you to keep well hidden, and, above all, to make no noise ? " Both hurried home, and fasted that day rather than return to the ghost town.

Next morning, however, driven by hunger, Tortoise resolved to go once more. When he got to the place, he looked round and saw Cock coming. Tortoise said:

" You give a great deal of trouble "

On this occasion none of the ghosts were present. The two friends began eagerly to gather as much food as they could carry away. They took enough for four days. Cock grew so excited that he started to crow once more. Tortoise said, " It is too much. I am weary of all the worry you cause me. I am going to the town to-day. If they catch me I shall at least be rid of you."

Cock said, " You at first told me the ghosts would do us harm. Why then do you go to their town ? However, if you go, I will come along with you."

Now when Tortoise had lain hidden near the ghost town, he had seen the Lame Boy sitting outside one of the houses. To this place, therefore, he went, and entered into the small room belonging to the Lame Boy.

The latter said, " We have never seen a man like you in our town before. You must hide yourself and let no one see you. They bring food for me here, and I will give you some of it."

Cock entered also. Tortoise said to him, " Above all things I beg you not to make a noise."

For two days they stayed there safely, but on the third, Cock saw a small boy strewing corn before the house. He began to crow

Tortoise ran to him and held him fast. " Why do you cry out ? " he asked. Cock said, " I saw corn, therefore I had to crow." He wanted to run outside and peck it up, but Tortoise held him by the waist and said:

"You will bring death on us both. We must get back to our town."

The Cock struggled and crowed. All the town heard his crowing. The townsfolk ran and filled the house. They caught Cock, who said

"It was Tortoise who brought me. I never came here before."

Then the ghosts asked, "Whence do you come? We have never seen anyone like you."

Cock shook with fear, and could only answer "Tortoise brought me."

Then the ghosts said, "What shall we do with him, because he has dared to enter our town?" and Cock answered.

"I came down from the sky. If you ask what is the best thing you can do for yourselves I must tell you. Get white cloth and hang it round my neck. Then tie me up on a high palm tree, and pray to Obassi Osaw Say "Here is the Cock. We have not killed him for nothing, but because he came, uninvited and without permission, into our town. Therefore he must die.'"

This the ghosts did, and from thence came the custom that a cock should be sacrificed to many Jujus. In the beginning of things. before Cock went to the ghost town, men did not take him to sacrifice before the Juju.

When all was finished with Cock, the ghosts turned to Tortoise and said:

"What then shall be done with you?" and Tortoise answered "I also must be sacrificed to the Juju. Take a long stick, sharpen it at one end, and drive it through me under my shell so that the pointed end holds me upright in the ground. Thus it is ordained that I also should suffer because I came uninvited to the town of the ghost people."

This too was done, and we see Tortoise impaled to this day before many Jujus.

WHY TORTOISE IS ALWAYS SACRIFICED TO THE JUJU.

Once when Obassi Osaw lived on earth, Tortoise was very sad, because all the women of his town were friends with the men, and took presents from them, but gave none to hi

He thought within himself, "What can I do to get presents?"

Now one day, as he went hunting, he met a slave who belonged to Obassi Osaw. As he passed her he noticed that she looked very ill. When he came back from hunting she lay dead by the roadside. He stood looking at her, then said to himself:

"To-day I see a way of getting presents." So, when it was dark, he took up the body and carried it into his house.

In the morning he went out and said to the townfolk:

"I have a daughter who is very beautiful. She has been in the Fatting-house for a long time, but will come out to-day. Will you come and play?"

The people came. They beat drums and sang songs. Tortoise went inside and ornamented himself as is done in honour of a girl who is coming out of the Fatting-house. Then he began to dance.

The people cried, "Let the maiden come out that we may see her", but Tortoise said "Wait."

Meantime someone went to Obassi Osaw, and told him about the matter.

Obassi sent to Tortoise and said, "Do you not know that all the most beautiful brides must be brought to me? You also must not forget to offer your daughter." With this message he sent the sweetheart and marriage presents.

These Tortoise accepted, and Obassi bade him fix a day to bring the new wife.

This was done, but Tortoise asked that during the wedding day no man should be allowed to go from his town to that of Obassi, nor from Obassi's town to his. Also he said, "Leave the small door open that we may enter, but keep all your people within the house that no man may see us come When my daughter is prepared to receive you, I will call."

At dawn he carried the dead body of the slave over his shoulder till he came to the room which Obassi had prepared Here he saw a bed covered with rich cloths and many fine pillows He arranged the dead body among them, then went and said to Obassi.

"Before you enter I have something to say. My daughter

will sometimes act like a dumb woman, and not answer when one speaks. To-day she is very tired. You must let her rest till I have gone."

Obassi ordered that chop should be prepared for Tortoise, but the latter said:

"It is too hot. I cannot stay till it cools. Tell your people to bring me some large leaves, that I may wrap them round it and carry it away."

Before leaving, he said:

"This is the only daughter I have. She lies quietly in your bed. Take care of her, for now you cannot blame me if any bad thing happens. Should she die, I claim her back from you."

To this Obassi agreed.

When Tortoise had left, Obassi entered the bride-room and called, "Dearest, dearest." As no answer came, he thought "I have heard of this silent habit." So he went away and returned with rich food and drink, and said "Will you open your mouth?" Still she lay without moving.

Then Obassi touched her head and said:

"Will you wake up?" but the hair came away.

He took her hand in his, and the hand broke off.

The people heard the sound of weeping, and ran in. They saw the dead body and said to their lord

"Do not weep. Let us carry out the dead woman and examine her." Then they cried, "This is your female slave who was sick a few days ago. Do you not know her?"

Tortoise was called. He came shouting, "I had told Obassi about my daughter. It is he who has killed her."

At daybreak Obassi called a meeting of the townspeople and said to Tortoise, "Why did you do such a thing as to bring the dead body of my slave and say that it was your daughter?" Further he said to all the townsfolk, "I cannot punish Tortoise, because of the compact he made with me before I saw the dead body, but from to-day all sacrifices shall be made with Tortoise."

That is the reason why native people always offer Tortoise to the Juju

WHY CRAB'S CLAW IS USED IN MANY JUJUS.

One year there was no fruit in the land, and all the people were hungry. Mbaw (Dormouse, *Graphiurus Hueti*) went into the bush to cut tie-tie. He came to a river, and walked along the bank. After a while he saw a calabash floating on the water. He called "Calabash, come here." It came at his bidding, but within, instead of food, he found a foul thing. So hungry was he that he tried to eat, but could not, so he covered it up once more and sent it away. Next he saw a log of wood floating down. Some plantains were lying on it. He called to the wood to come to him. It came. He ate some of the fruit, kept the rest, and sent the log away. When he got home he gave some of the plantains to his friend Nki (Dormouse, *Graphiurus C. Dorotheæ*).

The latter said, "Where did you get such sweet fruit? I should like to go with you to-morrow and find some for myself." Mbaw said "No."

Very early in the morning Nki woke up, filled a leaf with ashes from the hearth, then crept into Mbaw's house, made a small hole in his bag, and put in the leaf full of ashes. Then he went back to his own home.

At daybreak Nki went again, and called his friend, but the people said that Mbaw had already gone out to hunt.

Nki sought about till he found the marks of ashes. He followed the trail till he met his friend down by the river. Another calabash had just came floating by. In it was the same as in the first. Mbaw asked Nki if he would taste it, but he said :

"No, I will not eat rubbish," and threw it back in the water. Hardly was it out of sight before a second appeared full of plantains.

Nki called the calabash, and as it drew near the bank sprang upon it. It floated away with him down the river. The whole day long they floated, and at evening time came to the ghost town.

Nki hid in the bush and watched, for he was a curious man. The very first ghost he saw was his sister who had died a year before. He called to her, and she took him to her house and hid him there. Then she began to prepare the evening meal. A friend came in to help her make the fu-fu.

While they were doing this, the friend said, "There is a smell of fresh flesh here," for ghosts can always smell out any live thing. The sister sent her away, and then called Nki to come out. She gave him coco yams, but he said, "That is not enough." So she replied :

"I have no more. If you must have some, go to the head chief of all the ghosts. Bend down before him, and touch the ground with your hands. Perhaps he may give you food."

Before Nki could reach the chief, all the ghosts came crowding in. They brought a little thing like a trumpet, made from a crab's claw. They cried, "If a live person is here, let him die." Then they blew on the small instrument, and Nki died.

When the evening meal was ended, the ghosts played on the crab's claw once more. They had forgotten about Nki, but at the sound of the magic notes he came to life again. They hung up the trumpet on the wall of the house, and went away, while Nki hid till morning.

At dawn he saw children going to the spring to fetch water. He took the magic claw and followed them. Near a small stream he saw a crab This he caught and broke off a claw, which he hung up in place of the ghost trumpet, for he was very cunning.

When he was ready to escape he blew on the magic pipe, and sleep caught all the ghosts, so that they could not follow. All day long he walked, and towards nightfall neared his home Then he blew again on the crab's claw, and the ghosts woke up and found him gone.

They got another pipe to call him back. They played it long. Nki heard, and shook the claw instead of answering, for ghosts can hear if you shake a crab's claw.

They blew again, and again, and always he answered with his hand. Then he ran to Etuk (Bay Duiker) and said, "Will you please hold this for me ?" but Etuk refused.

Nki ran a little further, and came across He-goat. To him he said the same thing. He-goat took the claw Then Nki went back to his house.

When the ghosts blew again, the crab's claw answered from the hand of He-goat. The latter was frightened and shook his hand to be rid of the strange thing that made a noise by itself. The claw held tight, and he could not free himself. The ghosts followed wherever he went, for they heard the sound of the claw.

Then He-goat dug a hole and buried himself, but left one foot above ground. When the ghosts reached the place, one of them knocked against the foot. Then they set to work and dug him up, and asked how he came to have their trumpet. When they heard, some of them said, "Let us kill him," but others said, "No, only take away crab's claw." This they did, and then threw foul things upon his body, so that goats remain evil-smelling to this day.

It is because ghosts can hear when you play upon such claws, that crab is used in many Jujus.

Emblems of Juju Mfuor, Egbo House, Aking.

CHAPTER VI

Jujus (*continued*)

SEVERAL times it has come to my knowledge that Jujus have been used against me in Court, in the hopes of securing a favourable decision, or of causing temporary dumbness and even sudden death, should an adverse judgment be contemplated Probably something of the kind goes on every time a Court is held throughout the country, but knowledge of the fact seldom reaches the judge's ears.

On one occasion a man named Nsa Obassi brought a complaint against some members of the Egbo Club who had beaten him for being found outside his house during an Egbo performance. In the course of his evidence, he stated:

"It was Inyan Ita and Oberi Oye who beat me most cruelly" The latter said, "You cannot bring an action for this, as almost all the town is concerned in the matter. Besides, even should you try to bring trouble upon us on account of it, you cannot succeed, for I have a strong Juju which I should take into Court against you. When I stamp with my foot on the ground, the Judge will become dumb, and so will be unable to pronounce judgment for you."

It is useless to attempt to revoke any Juju without the proper offerings and full rites. In a case which came before the Native Court in 1907, Oyonmba, the head priest of Nfam at Ntebbashott, said in his evidence that the Juju had not been properly revoked, as it had been done without full ritual and empty handed.

As an example of the revocation of a Juju, that of Ofiri, witnessed at Ekong in December, 1907, may be quoted.*

Akunane, the head priest of the cult, stated:

"One of my sons named Atananingba quarrelled with his

---

* For revoking Juju Mfam, see p 139

wife, and swore by Ofiri that he would eat no coco-yams which came from her farm. Afterwards they became friends again, and he repented of the oath he had sworn. First he went to the Diviner (Mboni), who found out by the charm that he must take coco-yams before Ofiri, and offer up a sacrifice consisting of plantains, dried meat, a mat, a cock, palm oil and red and yellow powder. My son got together all these things and brought them to me.

Very early in the morning I washed my face and hands, and brought out the three Juju images (small wooden fetishes) and the horns containing " medicine," and set them on the altar.

First I took water and an egg. This latter I pointed towards the Juju, and called on Obassi Nsi and Obassi Osaw.

"Obassi, everything was made by you. You made earth and heaven. Without you nothing was made. Everything comes from you. You it is who give Ofiri power to protect the town."

Then I called on the names of all the dead who used to belong to the Juju, and laid the meat and plantains on the ground for them to eat.

After that I poured out water beside the altar, saying, " Here is water. I wash your face and hands; then I will bring you food, Ofiri"

Next I called on the name of Ofiri. I took two leaves, held them out on my left hand, and showed them before him and asked:

" Have you waked up or not ?"

The leaves fluttered down, the one fell on its face and the other upward, which showed that Ofiri was awake. Had they fallen otherwise, I must have waited a while and then showed the leaves again.

Next I took a piece of plantain and some meat, chewed them and put them inside the pot. I lifted the cock on high and said, "Here is food from my son. He swore not to eat coco-yams from his wife's farm. He has come to make confession to-day that his oath was against your custom. He asks to be set free, so that he may eat coco-yams as before. Forgive my son, O Lord, for the oath he swore was against himself alone. No one has been harmed through his fault." Then I poured palm wine within the pot, saying, " Here is palm wine. Drink as you eat, my Lord."

After that I chewed red and yellow powder in my mouth, and spat it out on the pot, over the fetishes and on all the worshippers, saying :

"Here is powder for you, red and yellow as our custom is, that we may get red blood in our bodies like the red powder, and that Ofiri may protect the whole land."

Then I showed the leaves again to see whether or not the offering was accepted, and asked:

" Do you receive the offering of my son ? " The leaves fell as before, so I knew that all was well.

After this I held up the mat, saying, " Here is the mat. Let no one sleep long upon it " (*i.e.*, fall ill).

Lastly I poured out the rest of the palm wine, crying, " Let all our goods remain safely in our houses "

As has been said, the pot represents the female, and the three fetishes, the male attribute of the Juju. When eggs are offered, one of them is usually broken and the forehead of the petitioner marked with the yolk just above the junction of the eyebrows, over the pineal gland, according to Descartes the seat of the mind. This is done with the avowed purpose of giving clear vision. Afterwards the egg is crushed small and deposited on the creepers round the Juju post.

It will be noticed that there is a very strong resemblance between the ritual described above, and the daily service of the chief Egyptian temples, save that here actual food is offered to the Deity in lieu of incense

It is somewhat curious that a lamb, regarded in most parts of the earth as an acceptable offering, should here be forbidden for sacrificial purposes. The mythical reason for this tabu is given in the following story.

Why Lambs should not be Sacrificed

There was once a lamb whom Leopard-child wished to eat. The latter therefore said : " Let us be friends , we will play together, and always trust one another." Lamb answered, " Agreed. As a first proof of friendship let us change our skins." To this Leopard-child consented in his turn No sooner had Lamb donned the gay new coat of black and yellow than a boar came out of the bush. Lamb felled him with one stroke. Little Ise (*Cephalophus melanorrheus*—Blue duikerbok) ran out a few minutes later, and a like fate overtook him. Some time after a young bush cow came tramping forth. Lamb sprang at his throat, and he too died.

After that Leopard child came up and said, "Give me back my skin now, and we will feed on all that you have slain with my teeth and my claws." Lamb said "Very well" He sprang upon Leopard-child and killed the latter also.

When Leopard heard how her son had died she was very angry, but went to Sheep and said, "Let us be friends." Sheep answered, "I am willing." One of the little lambs, however, said, "Leopard only wants to be revenged on you because your eldest son has killed her's If you do not hide me carefully she will certainly cause my death."

One day when Sheep was going to farm, the Lamb said again, "Please hide me under the floor mat. I am sure that Leopard will come as soon as you have gone" So Sheep hid her little son very cunningly.

Just at this time Obassi Nsi wanted a new "boy," so he sent to Sheep and asked that one of her small sons might be sent to live with him as his servant. To this Sheep consented.

When Leopard heard that Lamb was living with Obassi, she went to his house and brought a great "dash" She spoke cunning words, and made a bargain that the lamb might be given her to kill. Obassi agreed for a great price. He said:

"Go and hide yourself in the bush near my farm, and I will send Lamb to gather vegetables; then he will fall into your power"

Now Lamb knew, by the knowledge which was within him, how they had agreed together, so when he was sent to fetch yams from the farm, he went very cautiously and knew by the scent where Leopard was hiding. He went round by the other side, took the yams quickly, and ran back home. When Obassi saw him return in safety, he wondered how this had been done.

Some time after, Leopard went and said, "Will you send Lamb on a message? Then I may catch him on the road."

To this Obassi agreed, but Lamb said, "You engaged me as a personal attendant, not as a messenger." So Obassi replied "Very well. I will send someone else." He therefore chose out some men and bade them go by river to a great city where they were to buy a big box, bring it back, and leave it on the beach near his town. This they did, and, while those who had charge of the canoe were busy, Leopard went and hid herself in the box.

On the way to the river a canoe-man met Lamb and said, "Be careful when you get to the landing place, for Leopard is hiding in the box."

Lamb said "I thank you; she is one of my enemies." So he turned back, and got a padlock and key, then went slowly on his way to the landing place. The box stood open. He crept round behind, jumped on the lid, pressed it down, and then leant over and locked it. After that he pushed the box into the water and kept it there till Leopard was drowned. Then he drew it up, and carried it, with the dead leopard, before Obassi

The latter looked at the body and saw that it was quite dead. He said "Leopard made a fool of herself and spoilt her own life." Therefore he ordered his people to bury the body.

One day Lamb went to his master's room, and found there many rich clothes. The most splendid of these he made into a bundle and carried away with him. Then he took his gun and went out to the bush. He walked for some time till he came to a great cotton tree. Here he unfolded the clothes, and hung them all round the tree. When he had done this he went home and said to his master:

"I have found the place from which, in the old days, people used to get all their fine clothes. Yesterday I went into the bush and found a cotton tree from which gay robes were hanging"

Obassi said, "I should like to see this thing. Can you lead me thither?" and Lamb answered:

"If you are willing, you and I will go there together, but you must tell no one whither we are going, for it is a great Juju. Also we must take an axe with us."

When they got to the place, Lamb said, "Let us cut down the cotton tree, so that we may find out how it can produce such things as these." To himself he thought, "Obassi tried to betray me to Leopard, so I myself will try to kill him to-day!" He took the axe and said further.

"I will cut the tree, for I am your servant; but I beg you to be careful, so that none of these rich robes touch the ground."

Lamb struck at the tree with such strength that after a time it was ready to fall. Obassi put out his hand to hold up the garments, but at that moment the great trunk came crashing down and buried him in its fall. On this Lamb ran back to the town weeping, and said "My master is lost; I do not know where he may be."

The people all went out to search. They found the dead body and brought it home, but Lamb went to his mother's house and told her all that had happened to him since he went to serve Obassi Nsi. Also he said, "Earth is no longer safe for us. Let us flee to the sky." He went outside and made a Juju, then he looked upward and prayed, and lo! a great rope began to come down from the sky.

When it reached to the ground, he said to his mother "Will you go first? I myself will come later." He stood and watched while the rope drew her gently up, and then went back to his place in the house of his master.

About a week later, while the townspeople were playing for the death of Obassi, Lamb went outside and stood before them. He looked up into the sky and called "My mother, my mother, send the rope down to me now." She heard the voice of her son and threw down the rope. He laid his hand upon it and then said

"I will confess about the death of my master. It was I who deceived and killed him in the bush, because he would have given me over to Leopard." Then he quickly climbed up the rope and disappeared in the sky.

That is why we do not sacrifice a young sheep. After such behaviour he would not be an acceptable offering.

According to Ekoi belief Obassi Osaw and Obassi Nsi made all things between them. First they dwelt together, but after a while agreed to have different lands. Obassi Osaw fixed his dwelling place in the sky, while Obassi Nsi came down to earth and lived there.

After this separation Nsi grew in power. " for when a child is born it falls to the earth, and when a man dies he returns to the earth, whence all things have sprung. Nsi is the governor of all crops which the earth ripens. The sky is bad, for sometimes it sends too much rain, sometimes not enough."

Often people who are Efumi* of crocodiles make rain for themselves, especially in midsummer, when the water grows too hot and low for their comfort.

When a farm has been cut and prepared for sowing, the owner cannot plant yams until some rain has fallen, so he goes to the priest of the great rain Juju and asks him to make the rain fall. Members of the cult of Ekuri Ibokk have special power in this direction. At the time of the new moon, they go forth into the bush and gather magic leaves. These they bring home and dry carefully in bundles When rain is wanted they cut them open, and either pour water upon them out of a calabash, or lay them to soak in a bowl of water. Then it will surely rain.

Chief Ita Sakese of Oban was said to be able to produce rain by drinking water mixed with magic potions, or stop the downpour by refraining from taking water for two or three days at a time. During this period he was not debarred from palm wine.

Early in 1909, a man near Obutong was shown a famous rain Juju, and told that it was so powerful that rain would fall, even at the height of the dry season, if certain rites were performed before it. He was a sceptical soul, for no sooner had he heard than, in a spirit of bravado, he seized the Juju and performed the rites. Unfortunately the rest of the season was wet enough to strengthen belief even among the most doubting. In the words of the Ekoi—"Njokk I mbuta eya nji '—" an elephant of rain fell this year. ' The man paid for his scepticism, probably at the hands of the owners of the ruined farms, for he disappeared, and no trace of him has ever been found.

* The Ekoi word Efumi denotes a person who has the power of sending his spirit into the form of some animal

It is only another paradox, such as is constantly cropping up among the Ekoi, that importance should still be attached to rites for rain-making, in a country where about 200 inches fall in the year; for such customs are seldom found, save where the rainfall is precarious. The ceremonies practised to this end are probably another survival from the time when the Ekoi dwelt in parklands, but, as is to be expected under the present conditions, rain-stopping by magic arts has now assumed greater importance than the older ceremonial for its production.

Once on visiting Effion Iyawe's, a settlement not far from Ekkonnanakku, I noticed two bundles of thin roots wrapped round by leaves hanging over a fire. The chief assured me that no rain could fall so long as the flame was kept burning

A few hours later, on our way back, the rain came down in torrents. Two or three days afterwards we met the weather-prophet and asked why his Juju was not working. He began eagerly to explain that the mishap must not be put down to the Juju, but solely to the fact that he himself had been called away from home on urgent business, and the man deputed to tend the fire had neglected his duty and allowed it to die out.

Another way of stopping a heavy downpour is to produce a rainbow. Certain Juju men claim to be able to do this without special difficulty. Ntui Itabon of Oban, for instance, is credited with the power. He has but to take powdered cam-wood, mix it with certain magic medicines in his palm, and then throw the red paste up towards the sky. This he did one day at three o'clock in the afternoon, and an hour later a splendid rainbow spanned the heavens.

Many members of the cult of Nimm Asam are supposed to have this power, but in varying degrees. Those of little importance can only produce a rainbow, the results of which will last for a few hours, but those more deeply versed in the mysteries can guarantee fair weather for several days.

The bow itself is supposed to arch over the earth, one end resting in one river, and the other in another, a long way off.

Most winds are sent by Obassi Osaw, but those which

cause the greatest damage to farms usually come from the great wind Juju " Mfepp "

Members of this cult only use their power to work ill on others. They never acknowledge that they belong to the Juju, but use it against hostile towns, debtors who will not pay what they owe, or any one against whom they have a grudge. They prove their power to aspirants by sending a sudden wind to blow down some forest giant, usually a cotton tree, which they have previously pointed out as an object on which to show their might.

Opinions differ as to the causes which produce Thunder (Nsann) and Lightning (Nyanga Ainya). Some think that the former is a giant, who marches across the sky, others a great sheep which runs up and down in the house of Obassi Osaw. Some people again believe that Lightning is the servant of Thunder, others that they are enemies. Many Ekoi will put out all lamps during a storm, lest Thunder should notice their gleam and send his bolt to crush them. " When Thunder sees Lightning," they say, " he is very angry, and growls ' r-r-rong,' ' r-r-rong,' to drive it away."

" Nsann " is the name of a great Juju cult, members of which claim the power to produce storms and direct the lightning. As the initiates of the Mfepp Juju can show their might by overthrowing great cotton trees, so those of Nsann demonstrate theirs by pointing out some tree, usually a cocoanut palm, and then causing it to be struck by lightning, for which these palms are thought to have a peculiar attraction. The Father Rector of the Catholic Mission at Calabar said that he considered them as great a protection as any conductor, for houses near which they grew. In a storm he had often watched the peculiar movement of the leaves, all of which swept upward to a point, and only returned to their normal position when the storm was dying down.

Lightning is said to be attracted to rocks and peaks because of the fire within them; " For many stones contain fire, which a hunter can bring forth by striking them with his matchet."

When Lightning flashes from out a clear sky, the people

whisper "A man will die to-day," for they think that all members of Nsann are powerful poisoners, and that the flash is a sign that a new victim had been singled out for death The only Juju great enough to save a man from the power of Nsann is Eja, the festival of which is the chief one of the year, and is celebrated at the time of the new yams. This cult, as already mentioned, is supposed not only to produce plentiful harvests, but also to protect human beings, farms and cattle from damage by lightning and thunderbolt

No one who has attended the festival could fail to be struck by the resemblance between the present-day Ekoi ritual and those descriptions which have come down to us of the old Adonis-Attis-Osiris worship. The ecstatic frenzy of the dancers, the trances into which some of them fall, and the jealousy with which all strangers are excluded, show that this ceremony holds a very special significance.

One day, while speaking to the chief of an important town about the local "Eja," he remarked that it had been brought from the interior many years before, and was a most powerful Juju. To ensure its continued efficacy, however, sacrifices must be offered every two years. It struck me that this had not been done since my arrival in the District, and I asked the reason for the neglect. The old man grew confused, and stammered that it had not been possible to confirm the Juju for three years because they had been unable to procure the most necessary ingredient for the "medicine." When questioned as to what was missing, and whether it would not be possible to help them in the matter, he grew more and more confused, and at length answered that it was nothing that could be procured by a white man. None but a native could get it, and that only under certain circumstances. He further added that he dared disclose no more, or the Juju might kill him.

From later inquiries it turned out that the ceremony had been performed with the utmost regularity before the coming of the "white man," and the fact that there had been difficulty in providing the necessary ingredients ever since his arrival seemed highly suspicious. Nothing more could be learned at the time ; but some weeks later, a man came up to the house where we were staying, with the news that there would be a plentiful supply of fresh meat next day. All the hunters had gone out, he added, to provide game for the feast to be held in honour of the "confirmation of Eja."

This was interesting news, but I said, as casually as possible, "I thought that they did not possess the ingredients for confirming the Juju!" The man answered quite unsuspiciously, "Formerly they did not, but now they have got all that is necessary."

Everyone knows that the easiest way to extract information from natives is to assume more knowledge than one really possesses. In this case the man took for granted that I knew all about it, for in answer to the question, "Do they kill, or only mutilate their victim?" he answered, "They could not cut away so large a part without causing death." After this admission it was comparatively easy, under promise of not revealing the name of my informant, to get many further details.

As I had grown to suspect, the ingredient, which had been so difficult to procure, since the coming of the "white man," was the same organ as that flung to the symbolic tree in the Osiris ritual described by Dr. Frazer. Among the Ekoi, however, a woman is usually chosen as the victim. This is natural when one remembers that up to quite recent times with them, woman, not man, was the head of the house.

Somewhere in the bush a poor woman had been done to death, that her mutilated body might bring prosperity to the Ekoi farms. It is useless, according to their belief, to employ the necessary part of any corpse which had met its death by accident, or from natural causes. The victim must be slain purposely, or the rite is of no avail. None of the townspeople had disappeared on this occasion, so that the murdered woman must have been some poor soul brought down from the interior or one kept prisoner in a lonely bush farm, till it was thought that the time had come for her to be sacrificed without the knowledge of the "white man."

So jealously was the secret guarded, that the most anxious inquiries failed to find actual proof of the murder, or bring to justice those responsible. A mass of evidence, however, came to light, as to the frequency of such sacrifices in former days.

On one occasion, during our visit to the Cameroons, after a long march through the beautiful pass of Okuri, we arrived at the village of Mbinda, and settled down in the Egbo house. The day had been a good one from the point of view of the Botany collection, and we were all in the highest of spirits. Suddenly one of my companions, who was sitting opposite, stopped in the midst of a sentence, her eyes fixed in a stare of horror on something above my head.

An upward glance showed three gruesome objects dangling from the roof. They would not bear minute description save in a strictly anthropological work, but as will be seen from the accompanying little sketch, each of the bowls which composed the body was set on a pair of widely opened human jaws which formed a foot or stand.

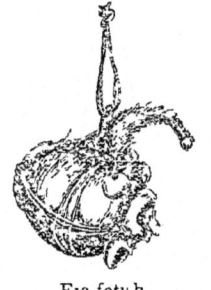

Eja fetish

One glance was enough to show that these were Eja symbols. Later we learned that the fetish consists of two parts. The bowl, always the feminine sign, is called Ekum Oke, while the curved male symbol represents Eja himself. It has not been possible to learn anything concerning the origin of the names. We were only told vaguely that "Eja" always consists of the two personalities mentioned above. "Eja, he is man, and the stronger of the two. Ekum Oke is a woman, less strong than Eja; nevertheless without her he can do nothing."

At every great Eja festival the following song is sung. It is perhaps worth noticing that Ekum Oke is first invoked —

THE SONG OF EJA AND EKUM OKE.
"Ekum Oke, 'me njawe na 'we
Ekum Oke, I am staying with you.
O 'me njawe na 'we
O, I am staying with you
Num Eja, 'me njawe na 'we
Man Eja, I am staying with you
O 'me njawe na 'we
O, I am staying with you

```
O kare mana              njum ka          obbaw chang
O give  now  (there is)  thing in (your)  hands   no
O kare ntung eya, O kare mana.
O give throat your, O give  now"
```

The meaning of the last two lines, which is somewhat obscure, seems to be as follows :—

Should a poor man have nothing of sufficient value to offer to the Juju, his full brother or full sister must be sacrificed. The term "throat" includes all the children of the same father and mother

At Obung, roots rubbed with charcoal enter into the composition of the Eja "medicine." When an Obung man goes to another town to attend a "play" at which many people are expected to be present, he rubs some of the medicine on his forehead, and some on the soles of his feet, as a protection against any witch or wizard who may be among the crowd.

One of the chief ceremonies at the festival is the bringing in of the first fruits. Each family sends a representative bearing a basket of yams, the greater number of which are eaten during the feast, but part is reserved to be offered up at the entrance to the town

Till the Eja festival comes round, neither fu-fu nor fresh yams may be eaten. Men may begin to partake of these on the first and second days, but women may not touch any till the third. On the first day neither food nor drink may be taken by either sex, till the sun has reached his zenith.

At the actual offerings of yams, the following song is sung :—

```
"Achibong,           aba yi aiyu o-or we.
(Name of original
 priest of Juju),    come eat yams o-or-we
Nta Asu,  aba yi aiyu o-or-we
Lord Asu, come eat yams o-or-we."
```

On one occasion at which I was present, an old slave had been placed in a crouching position within a little fence by the Juju. He probably represented the human sacrifice formerly offered up at this time.

Now that Government has at least succeeded in making such offerings extremely dangerous, the people have looked anxiously round for substitutes, which as far as possible might replace those now forbidden. The little vase-shaped ant hills, or "bush-men," as they are called, are therefore often used. These abound everywhere, and are so strongly built as to be easily movable. They are often found at the entrance to towns, farms or compounds,* bound round with a piece of cloth. To quote the Ekoi, " dress him up fine—say, ' take him and spare me ' "

The chief of one town, when questioned as to the uses of these offerings, answered in an aggrieved tone .

"We give 'bush-men' to the Juju, because our father, the D. C , no longer allows us to offer real ones."

As a substitute for human sacrifice, however, the Drill Ape (*Papio leucophæus*)—so rare in most places that the skulls forwarded by me to the British Museum are said by the authorities to be the first ever received by them—holds first place from its near resemblance to man. It exists in vast quantities, but is by no means an easy prey, owing to its strength and fierceness.

The Ekoi firmly believe that Drill Apes, and indeed all anthropoids, are degenerate men. The story of their degradation is told in the following tale :—

Why Ape People no longer Live in Towns.

By Ntui Nenshaw of Mfamosing.

Once long ago a man named Nshum (Drill Ape) lived in a town. The other men were building houses, but Nshum only ran round, ate their chop, and would do nothing to help. One of the chiefs called to the idler and said, "Why do you not work like all the rest ? " To this Nshum did not answer.

A few weeks later all the townsfolk went to cut farm, but Nshum refused to go with them and remained idle in the town

Again the chief called and said, " Why do you not go and cut farm like the others ? "

On this Nshum was angry, so he said, " I will live by myself, I will not stay in your town any more." With that he left them, and went into the bush.

* See Nsibidi Sign 43, Appendix G

The head chief ordered the people to take their nets, and go out to catch him. They tried to do this, but he went too far and so escaped them.

At that time men did not like to kill Nshum, because he was a man like themselves, though a very bad one, but in course of years all the lazy people gathered together in the bush, and not only drove away the good people who went near them, but tried to do them harm.

One day a hunter went into the bush. He saw some creature moving in the branches of a great tree and shot it. It was Nshum.

Then the hunter caught up the body and dragged it home to his town. He took it before the charm and said to the Diviner:

"I have brought this creature who was once a man, but has now become a bush-beast. You may practise on him on account of his laziness."

The Diviner practised the charm and said·

"He is no longer a human being, but only a wild animal now. You may kill him and eat his flesh."

This is the reason why it is no longer unlawful to eat Nshum. Before the charm was practised, no one ate him. His name is still that of a person, and if a man is lazy we sometimes call him "Nshum."

CHAPTER VII

Metamorphosis

The head-dresses representing bird or beast, worn by the "images" of the Egbo and other clubs, seem originally to have been connected with the common belief in Metamorphosis. It is quite usual to hear one of the Ekoi say of another, "he (or she) possesses" such and such an animal, meaning that the person alluded to has the power to assume the shape of that particular creature. To primitive people like the Ekoi, such cases seem on the same plane as those recorded from other continents, where the souls of mystics or sick people, are supposed temporarily to quit their bodies. It is an article of belief that, by means of constant practice and hereditary secrets, a man can leave his human form and take on that of some wild creature. They say that every man has two souls, one which always animates the human shape, and a bush soul, which at times is capable of being sent forth to enter the form of the animal "possessed." When a man wishes to send out his bush soul, he drinks a magic potion, the secret of which has been handed down in his family from time immemorial and some of which is always kept ready for use in an ancient earthen pot set apart for the purpose.

After drinking the potion the bush soul is supposed to leave its human form, and float invisibly through the town till it reaches the forest, where it begins to swell, and, safe in the shadows of the trees, takes on the shape of its were-body. The commonest animals "possessed' in this manner are elephant, leopard, buffalo, wild boar and crocodile.

Different potions are naturally necessary for the assumption of each shape.

All the totem animals were once the eponyms of the families which possess them. A man cannot belong to a totem to which neither his father nor mother belonged.

One of the advantages of being able to take on animal form is that the farms of enemies may be devoured during the night-time. That is why men with buffalo, elephant or wild boar "bush souls" are usually found in the neighbourhood of places where there are large, well-kept farms.

At Oban, where, owing to the unenterprising nature of the inhabitants, the farms are neither extensive nor particularly fruitful, there are very few farm-devouring creatures, and the favourite were-beasts are leopards and crocodiles. Townsfolk declare that in crossing rivers, especially the Calabar and the Awa, which separates the British Ekoi from their kinsfolk in the Cameroons, men bearing loads have been attacked by a crocodile and terrified into dropping their possessions in the hurry to escape. Occasionally goods have been returned by a friend, who explained that it was only a trick played by him as a joke while in crocodile form, but usually were-crocodiles have a particularly bad reputation, as they are supposed to overturn canoes in order to seize both goods and men.

Early in 1911, a deputation from Netim, one of the largest towns in the District, brought a chief and his son to the Commissioner at Oban. These were accused of having, in crocodile form, killed two women while the latter were crossing the Calabar river. Some men stated that they had watched the women enter the water, and, about mid-stream, saw them dragged under by crocodiles. The chief and his son, who had long been suspected of such crimes, were at once seized, and a meeting held in the town. The dominant Juju was brought out, and the accused were asked to clear themselves by swearing their innocence upon it. This they refused to do, and were therefore brought up before the D. C., who was administering the District at the time. He, very naturally, said that it was not in his power to do anything in such a case, as more proof was necessary. The people returned to the town and held another meeting at which the accused were asked to swear their innocence on the "Broom Juju." This is held in considerable veneration, because it enters into every little corner in cleaning out the compound, so no part of the house is supposed to be safe from it. The son confessed that both he and his father were guilty, that they had killed and eaten seven other men and women, but that in this case, as in all others, it was his father who had taken the lead. He asserted, however, that one of the women was not dead, but that after reviving her by magic arts, they had drawn her up out of the water, and then, in their human forms, taken her to Uyanga, where she had been sold as a slave. The body of the other had been placed in the fork of a tree just beneath the surface, where it was kept to devour at leisure.

The people swore that they went to the place indicated, and found the body exactly as had been said. They then sent to Uyanga and found the other woman. She at once pointed to the chief and his son, and said that it was they who, as crocodiles, had dragged her down to a house which they had beneath the water. There she lost consciousness, and only recovered when they restored her, and forced her to follow them into slavery.

After being confronted with the woman, the chief also confessed the truth of the accusation, and within ten days both he and his son were dead—killed, as the townsfolk said, by the Broom Juju, but more probably by poison administered by avenging neighbours.

Should women strew fish poison in the water above the dwelling place of a were-crocodile, the Efumi of the crocodile dies within seven days.

Soon after my first arrival at Oban, information was brought that something of an unusual nature was happening. On investigation, it appeared that a certain chief had fallen under the suspicion of having, in the guise of a were-leopard, killed several cows and goats. Preparations were on foot for ridding the town of him in a summary manner, when the arrival of the "white man" put an end to the proceedings of the extempore tribunal.

Chief Agbashan, a splendid hunter, is believed to have the power of transforming himself into an elephant, an accomplishment that would certainly be of great use to him when out after these creatures. During the last few months before my arrival, he had killed thirty-five elephants with his own hand.

A man of considerable intelligence, educated in England, the brother of a member of the Legislative Council for one of the West African Colonies, offered to take oath that he had seen Agbashan not only in his elephant form, but while actually undergoing the metamorphosis.

Those who have elephant affinities know at once should any beast, which happens to be killed, be "possessed" by a man's soul. In the latter case they would not eat of it. Were-elephants are said to be seldom seen in the day-time, but there is a curious superstition with regard to were-leopards. At noon of day or night, such creatures are supposed to rise on their hind legs and walk upright. Occasionally when the people of a bush farm have left the compound and gone to work, one of these uncanny beings will creep up to the deserted dwelling and reconnoitre. If all seems safe he will enter, with the object of carrying off one of the domestic animals. In such a case it is thought that he walks upright, holding his tail with the left hand, and hiding his face behind a bunch of green boughs held in the right. Sick folk, left behind while the rest of the family went to work, have repeatedly testified to having watched through door or wall chink while their terrible visitor approached lamb or kid, in the manner described, then suddenly pounced upon its prey and bore it off to devour in the bush.

An old woman of Oban, Awaw Ita by name, was suspected of a still more sinister familiar. Her husband, by whom she is standing in the photograph, had a sore on his ankle. Somehow or other the idea got about that this could not heal because a snake came out of her mouth every night to lick the wound while they slept. Curiously enough, as in similar cases in our own country during the Middle Ages, she herself firmly believed in the truth of the story, and owned to it when she thought that such a confession might cost her her life.

The following is the account of her trial by the Egbo Society, given in her own words.—

"Last month I was in my house, when the Juju Image entered the compound at night-time, with many companions. He called me 'Awaw Ita, Awaw Ita.' I answered, and he said, 'Come out.' I followed him. He led me into Ntui Iterem's compound, where all the Jujus are kept. Many people were gathered together. They said to me, 'You possess a snake?' I answered, 'Yes,' because I have it for true. In my country, Okorroba, which is a long way from here, both snakes and hippopotami are possessed by women. I left my snake in the bush of my land, when I was brought from my home. When I sleep and dream I sometimes see my snake, but not very often. In the day-time I have not seen it since I was brought here as a slave many seasons ago."

Fortunately for all parties the wound was soon healed, by means no more romantic or mysterious than the application of a little clean water and some ointment.

Cases of this kind are always coming on before the Native Court of the District. These Courts are mines of information as to customs and beliefs, and the intelligence obtained from them can be relied on; for, should one party to a suit volunteer a false statement, it would be quickly rectified by the other. Three chiefs, unconnected with either side and from different towns, are always chosen to sit as an advisory committee, and give information as to native custom and law, which is followed except when in opposition to British justice.

Another interesting case came to our notice lately. In 1909, while marching toward Ekkonnanakku, the new town built by a branch of the Ododop tribe, which came to settle in the District about five years ago, I noticed the skull of a great bush-cow. It stood at the base of the Juju tree in the centre of the settlement, where the Head Chief, Awaw Anjanna, dwelt about twelve miles from his town, and was so unusually fine a specimen that I asked the chief if he were willing to sell it. He answered that he would rather not, as he liked to see it there, and could not easily get another so large. He spoke naturally, even carelessly, and I attached no importance to the matter.

Between the settlement and the town, all along the way, lie huge boulders, water-worn and rounded like those on the seashore. On our first visit, Awaw Anjanna took us along a hunters' track, about a mile from his dwelling, which led to the foot of a colossal boulder. Here he stooped down, and, bending aside the bushes, showed us a hole through which we proceeded to crawl After going for a few yards in this cramped position, we emerged into a hunter's cave—apparently formed by a great piece of rock which had split off from the main block, swung over by its own weight, and been held up by two small pinnacles which stood in its way. These now form rough pillars to which the fallen boulder acts as roof. Once in the cave it was found roomy enough to hold a hundred people, and quite light, for the side between the pillars is open.

In revisiting Awaw Anjanna's two years later, we found it deserted. The chief, we thought, had at last yielded to the entreaties of his people, and gone to live among them.

Just before reaching the old dwelling place, one of our attendants, a man half Yoruba, half Bini, asked my wife, who was a little ahead, to come back a few paces. She found him gazing with peculiar intentness at some tracks in the soft sand. "Makee look, lady," he said, " These be bush-cow tracks They come and they go. Every day there be fresh one for Awaw Anjanna's farm."

His tone was intensely sad, but my wife thought this probably due to a fear that rations might be hard to get, as at so many places, owing to the ravages of the bush beasts.

All along the road, we looked for the figure of the chief, who, in immaculate white linen coat and dark blue loin cloth, had been in the habit of coming out a long way to greet us There was no sign of him, and though, on our arrival at Ekkonnanakku, the head men of the town were assembled to meet us, we still sought in vain for his familiar figure. My first question was as to his whereabouts. There was a moment's silence, and then one of the men answered ·

"He died long since."

No other information was volunteered. Our condolences were received in silence, and the people obviously did not wish to be questioned on the subject.

Soon after the townsfolk had gone, the same man who had pointed out the tracks came in, and after looking anxiously round to make sure of not being overheard, startled us by announcing.

"When D. C. Talbot go for his own country, the new D. C. kill Awaw Anjanna for Oban"

There was obviously something wrong here, as, on the face of it, such a thing was impossible. After a while the whole story came out.

It seems that the chiefs of the Ododop tribe are supposed to be mysteriously linked with buffaloes. When one of them dies, his soul enters into one of the last-named beasts. At night, too, the bush soul goes out into the form of his affinity. Hence the skull beneath the Juju tree.

All Ododop people are supposed to have some totem or other, mostly wild boar or antelope, though some, like the chiefs, are buffalo souls.

Now Awaw Anjanna had been, according to custom, to attend Court at Oban, for he was a particularly intelligent man and took a great interest in learning everything possible about the administration of justice. He returned home in excellent health, and two days afterwards was sitting talking with several of his people, when he suddenly struck his hand against his body and cried out:

"They kill me for (*i.e.* at) Oban."

It was four o'clock in the afternoon. At that hour a buffalo was seen to come down to drink at a stream which runs through the station garden. The Commissioner shot the beast, and it turned round and ran off badly wounded. It was followed, but got away for the time. In the excitement of the chase, two men were shot by mistake, one in the arm and the other in the body; fortunately, however, both recovered. Two days later the buffalo was found dead in the bush, and an hour or so before this discovery Awaw Anjanna died at his little settlement over ten miles away. Just before his death he sent a message to Ekkonnanakku to warn all people who belonged to the buffalo totem to keep away from Oban, as it was too dangerous there.

Now his brother rules in his stead. The old dwelling place stands lonely and deserted, with carefully padlocked doors; but the farms seem still to be tended, that the soul of the dead chief, roaming up and down in buffalo form, may see that the space he reclaimed from the bush is kept in good order

Whatever may have been the case in earlier times, there is now no restriction as to marriage between the various totem peoples For instance, a wild boar man may marry an antelope woman, or *vice versa*, and the children of such a marriage seem given the choice of totem. A bush-cow man will never shoot a beast of his own affinity, though he may kill antelope or wild boar, but, after having done this, should he think that his kill is not an ordinary animal, but one "possessed" by any of the townspeople, he must go through certain ceremonies over the body of the beast, and then hurry back at topmost speed to take a particular "medicine" to the man whose totem it was. Otherwise the Efumi must die.

It was unfortunately impossible to extract information as to the nature of this medicine, but some few indications seemed to show that it was a part of the animal itself

There are differences of opinion as to the moment of death Some assert that the man's coincides with that of the animal, others that the possessor lives, though with decreasing strength, so long as the body of his affinity remains entire. Should a man unknowingly eat a beast of the family to which he is mysteriously linked he would fall sick. On this he must consult his Juju as to the cause of the illness, and would recover, after making the required sacrifice. Should he eat knowingly, however, he would surely die.

Amid these weird beliefs, one curious fact stands out. While nearly all other tribes in the District have been driven to despair by the depredations of boar, bush cow and other wild beasts, the Ododop farms remain untouched. Tracks are everywhere to be seen, but never a plantain is trodden down, nor yam uprooted. Here, strangely enough, the bush beasts seem to leave the farms alone, and feed only on wild herbage.

The same man who had offered to take oath as to having seen Chief Agbashan when changing into his elephant form, wrote out and sent the following account of a ceremony at which he claimed to have been present. I give it in his own words, for what it is worth:—

"In the month of June, 1908, I was wakened from a peaceful

slumber in the middle of the night by a noise which seemed unearthly. I got up shivering with fear, and found that the light which I always kept burning till the small hours of the morning had unaccountably been extinguished. I fondled (fumbled?) under my pillow in search of matches and a candle which were usually kept there in case of emergency, and when I had secured these, I ventured outside.

"There I saw shadowy persons of both sexes and all ages sitting on stools and benches, and talking in undertones. Among the crowd was my landlord. In front of him stood two native wooden bowls, about 24 inches wide and 12 deep, filled with what the natives call " Ekpo Juju " and also some bottles charged (sic) with herbal decoctions. On one of the bowls lay a brush made of palm branches, with which, when he saw me watching, he sprinkled some of the contents in my direction. I then irresistibly fell headlong, and entirely lost locomotion. The candle was snatched from my grasp, and the compound plunged into utter darkness.

"After a few minutes I crawled along on my elbows till I reached a certain point where an empty stool was standing. On this I sat down.

"The rain began to fall in drenching torrents and lightning flashed vividly, which enabled me to discern the features of the members of this company, all of whom are capable of assuming the forms of ferocious animals, and in olden days used to feast on human flesh.

" Suddenly a flash of lightning revealed my whereabouts; my landlord again threw some of the decoction over me, and I became insensible. For hours I lay in the drenching rain, and when I began to recover consciousness thought that my end had come. After a while I heard the voices of some people talking to the head of the house, and saying that I had been kind to them. On this he wrenched open my jaws and forced a 'pillet' down my throat. I lay as still as the dead, though shaking with fright lest he should really put an end to me. After this he began some incantation in the vernacular. Then all present assumed the shape of ducks, and began greedily to drink at the pools of rain, save the paramount chief himself, who took on the form of a large elephant."

CHAPTER VIII

Oban to Niaji

To the north-east of Oban live those Ekoi of purest blood They show hardly a trace of having mixed with Efifs or any other people, and are of a more enterprising character than the rest of their race.

The way leads along a forest path, 8 to 10 feet wide, clear of trees, fern-fringed and carpeted ankle-deep with a thousand little flowers, amid which small Acanthaceæ raise their pure white or deep purple heads, recalling with curious vividness the violets of Worcestershire spinneys Amid this wealth of flowers winds the foot-wide track, bare and smooth, which is all that natives use.

The first river to be crossed is the Ojuk. On its banks, by the ford, a powerful Juju was formerly buried So many people died after crossing, that the "Okum" Ekuri Ibokk, described on p 45, was taken down to smell out the magic. He indicated a spot between the gnarled roots of a tree, and, after digging for a considerable depth at this point, a pot containing Juju medicine was discovered and removed. The path was then declared safe once more—but we did not find it so.

One evening we reached the river bank a little before sunset. I was ahead with my gun, next came Bimba, and then my wife, followed by our botanical collector. Suddenly I heard a warning cry, and looking back saw my wife pointing to a small cobra which had crossed the path between herself and her sister. Bimba at once passed me, so as to be out of the way, and our positions then formed a triangle, with the snake, between my wife and myself, for its apex. I shot, and thought that the reptile had been blown to pieces, as it disappeared. Next moment our collector sprang into the air with a yell of terror. The cobra had been "lofted" by the shot at a seemingly impossible angle, had hit my wife across the mouth with its tail, and then fallen just beyond her feet, in close proximity to the bare brown toes of our black companion. Almost at the same spot, an Oban man had been bitten in the heel by one of this species a few days before, and had died within the hour.

Beyond the river, the first town to be reached is Aking, a small place nestling at the base of the beautiful purple hills of the same name. Here on one occasion the children gave a particularly charming series of games, singing all the while in the pretty lilting way usual among them. Nothing could be more graceful than the waving arms and swaying limbs of the little brown forms as they bent and moved, always in perfect time to their song.

After leaving this town the next stopping place is Ako, where a specimen of that rare and wonderful creature the Goliath beetle was secured. Up to this point the road from Oban, though hilly, is one of the most level in the District, but from now onward it grows steep and rocky.

At the next town, Ntebbashott, the walls of the houses were covered with rude black-and-white frescoes, which stood out boldly from their dull yellow background. Inquiries as to the meaning of the paintings elicited the explanation, somewhat reproachfully given, that they were representations of the District Commissioner as he rode through on horseback some time before. This is the furthest point in the District to which it is possible to ride, and my horse was the first ever seen in this part of the country. The Ekoi have no proper name for

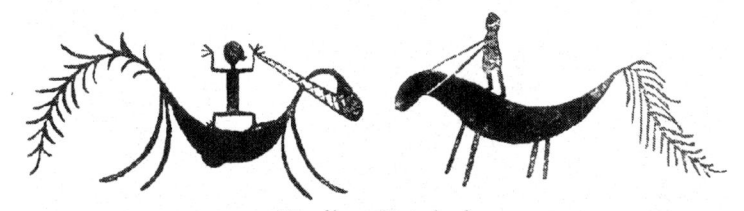

Myself on Horseback.

the animal, but always call it "the white man's cow." A feeling of vanity in this testimony to the grace of my seat prompts me

Source of the River of Good Fortune.

to venture on reproducing two of the more striking positions depicted.

After leaving Ntebbashott the way leads down a steep, rocky slope into a charming little dell, through the centre of which flows a stream of clearest water. The carriers always set down their loads and run forward to drink of this; then after plucking leaves from the banks, form into an irregular procession, and proceed to a heap of leaves which lies a few yards off Here they rub those they have gathered across their foreheads, saying :

"'Me nfonn ofa!
(May) I have luck!'"

and then drop them on the heap.

The reason for this little ceremony is that the stream is called the river of Good Fortune, and anyone who conforms to the rite above described is supposed to have good luck throughout the current year. It is specially practised by traders who go up to the German Cameroons.

Another heap of leaves, with which a similar ceremony is connected, for the prevention of evil fortune, is to be found on the bank of the Calabar River (see p. 242).

Lesser mounds may occasionally be seen on the roadside. If these be pushed aside, they will usually be found to cover a dead chameleon. According to the law of the old men, should one of these creatures be killed on the road, it must not be thrown into the bush, but left by the wayside. Each passer-by then takes a few leaves, spits upon them, and drops them on the dead animal, saying, " Look! Here is your mat."

"Enn! mkpa eya
Behold! mat your."

The reason is that when a chameleon has been killed, his spirit is supposed to go before Obassi Nsi, and pray for revenge on the race of those who have caused his death.

The rite is intended to placate the "manes" of the dead creature, and avert punishment.

When a poisonous snake is killed, this also is left lying across the road, so that all who pass by may step over its body. It is thought that by so doing danger from snake-bite will be averted till a new moon shines in the sky.

Niaji, the first town to be reached beyond the river of Good Fortune, lies at the base of Osaw Ifogi (High hill with holes *i e*, caves) This is a conical peak, over 3,000 feet high, covered with flowering trees. On a single visit six varieties new to science were discovered.

In 1909 the summit had been cleared for theodolite observations save for one tree, which stood amid its fallen brethren a lonely sentinel, visible for miles around. The top of the hill was too narrow to allow of the tents being pitched there with any degree of safety, so camp was made on the slope, about 50 yards below.

I began to take angles, but storm clouds gathered, and the sky became overcast At four o'clock, Itamfum, our second "boy," who naturally took his time from the sun, brought the lamps, under the impression that it was 6 p.m. A strong wind arose, branches began to crash in every direction, and a few minutes later the storm burst upon us in all its fury.

We took refuge in one of the tents. For awhile the wind tore at the frail structure, as though to carry it away Then suddenly we were enveloped in a blaze of light. At the same moment came a deafening crash, and we were thrown to the ground by a force there was no resisting.

When consciousness returned it was to find both my companions senseless, and apparently dead, beside me. I dragged them outside into the downpour, where pandemonium reigned. Carriers and "boys" were screaming at the highest pitch of terror, tearing helplessly hither and thither, too frightened to think what to do, while cook, cook-mate, the Interpreter, and one of my "boys" still lay in a helpless heap where they had been flung downhill by the force of the stroke.

When my wife recovered consciousness, she explained that when she first felt the blow which struck her down, it flashed through her mind, "This is death." There was no time for fear, only a feeling of interest that the experience, which must come at some time, and in some guise, to us all, was there so swiftly. Afterwards she knew nothing until, she declares, a voice, very thin and far away, as if over a distant telephone, came to her ears. "Are you killed?" it piped. "Are you killed?" and then, "Oh, you're *both* dead!" She

The River of Bad Fortune.

thought for the moment that I was raising a death wail—a circumstance which she insists quite cheered her by its picturesqueness. She soon, however, realised that she was still alive, and sat up, and a few minutes later Bimba too revived.

The next hour or so was the most unpleasant of our lives. We all suffered intense pain, and it was a long time before I could stand upright, while my wife bore for weeks the marks of scarlet zigzags, and Bimba's left arm became white and crinkled almost like tissue-paper.

Niaji Peak is the centre of a huge amphitheatre of hills. As we sat in our soddened deck chairs amid a solid downpour, the storm receded from us, to rumble round and return again and again, breaking overhead in deafening crashes, and flashes which seemed to render transparent closed eyelids and sheltering hands.

The actual blow which had felled us had come so suddenly that there was no time for fear. Sitting there, counting, from the time between flash and crash, whether the storm were receding or returning, with the expectation that next time it broke above us it must surely finish its work of destruction, would, I think, have tried the strongest nerves. The peaks are needle-pointed, there is much ironstone, and the storms here are among the worst in the world. Later we heard that one of the carriers, employed by a surveying party while delimitating the Nigerian Cameroons Boundary, had been struck and killed on a hill not many miles off.

When the storm had at length rumbled away in the direction of Calabar, we walked along the topmost ridge of the peak. Far as the eye could reach chaos reigned. No sign of human habitation was in sight, and pacing from end to end of the long narrow summit gave one the curious sensation of being on shipboard, the sole survivors of a world overwhelmed in some mighty convulsion of Nature.

All around lay white mists, billowing and breaking like the crests of angry waves, which stretched, sweep upon sweep, to the great dark hills beyond. Above lowered a sky of sombre grey, broken here and there by splashes of stormy orange, while in the distance, over Calabar, the mutter of the dying storm might still be heard.

CHAPTER IX

Woman—Position, Etc.

Just outside Niaji is to be found the only attempt at a portrait statue known in the Oban District, though others existed till lately on the further side of the Boundary.

The figure is a representation of Maia, priestess of Nimm. It is modelled, rudely enough, in mud on a framework of sticks, and is placed above the grave of the woman it commemorates. Over it a little hut has been built, and round this are hung most of the things once used by the dead woman. These are all broken according to custom.

As has already been stated on p 2, Nimm is the special object of devotion to Ekoi women, and her cult, founded, according to tradition, by a Divine woman who came down to earth for the purpose, seems to provide satisfactory expression for the religious feelings of her human sisters. Every eighth day is sacred to her, and is called " the women's day "

"Ofu ane akai.
Day of persons female "

On this women have even more power than usual, and no work must be done. Should any transgress the law and go to work upon their farm, Nimm would be angered and send up her servants, the beasts, to destroy it.

Those freshly initiated into the mysteries of Nimm are rubbed over with red cam-wood dye. Afterwards they have the right to wear special ornaments round neck and arms and carry the " feathers of Nimm " in the right hand and in their coiffure, while in the left they bear a Juju knife.

Each " Nimm woman " has a little shrine built in the corner of her room. On this stands a pot, usually an ancient earthenware one, containing " medicine," peculiar to the cult,

Maia, the Priestess of Nimm.

together with some queerly shaped pieces of carved wood, corn cobs, a Juju knife, and the feathers of the white "Ebekk." Sometimes in addition they have pieces of the "Ngaw" creeper, supposed to be used by were-crocodiles to draw men down to their death.

Across the door of the room hangs a split palm leaf, so arranged that all the "spikes" hang downward, while among them corn cobs and Juju leaves are usually tied.

Nimm women are supposed to have the power of foretelling the future. They strew white chalk over the floor of

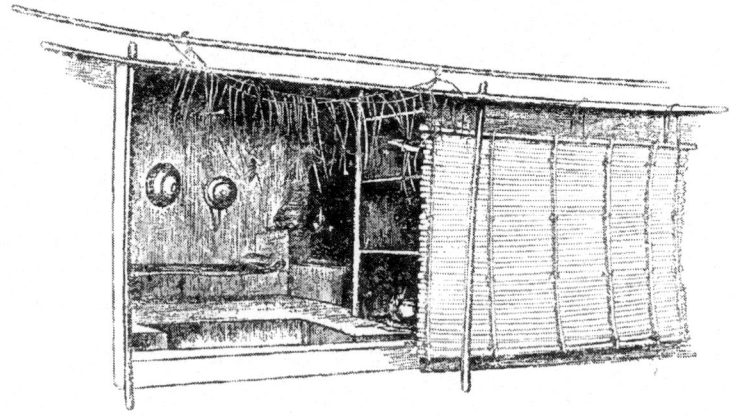

Nimm Woman's Room, with Corner Shrine.

their room immediately before the shrine. On this space a little pile of white feathers is laid. A light is then applied, and when nothing remains but ashes the priestess sits gazing intently into their midst till the desired answer can be given.

All Nimm women have not equal powers of divination, but those who have won a reputation for their oracles are treated with great respect.

When one of the priestesses gives a dance, the townspeople are supposed to bring offerings of roasted corn cobs, palm oil, and pieces of dried Nsun (Ogilby's duiker) flesh. In the old days a Nimm woman never appeared outside her compound without a Juju knife in her left hand and the symbolic white Ebekk feather in the right. These are now only obligatory on occasions of ceremony.

All stones rounded by water action into oval form are sacred to Nimm. Those too heavy to be moved are left standing *in situ* and used as a kind of rustic altar, while the smaller ones, of about the size of eggs, are carefully collected and placed in compounds and farms. Sometimes such stones are inserted in a

Mboandem Woman's Room, with Shrine, Cupboard, and Shelves beneath Niche Bed.

little hole made for the purpose in the mud base of the principal pillar in the Egbo house. The object of all is to promote fertility. They are looked upon as the "Eggs of Nimm," whether in crocodile or serpent shape.

No man is permitted to share in the mysteries of Nimm, and not even the fear of death would induce a male Ekoi to intrude at the celebration of her rites. A woman is, however, occasionally chosen as the head of powerful Jujus, to which both sexes may belong. Such an one was brought from Nsan to Ndingane by an Aking man. It is specially strong as a protection against witchcraft and the breaking of oaths sworn in its name.

The cult of Nimm seems to bear a strong resemblance to that of the "Mboandem Frauen," described by Dr. Mansfeld ("Urwald Dokumente," p. 70). It has not, however, been possible to discover any of this designation on the British side of the Frontier.

At Niaji, in one of the compounds, the Juju Enyere is to be seen. This consists of a growing "Egakk" tree, to which an earthen pot is attached by a coil of thick bronze wire, which continues down the stem. The pot is closed by a flat earthenware lid, and decorated with a fringe of split palm leaves and two Nimm feathers.

The head man of a family is the priest of its Lares, but should he die and leave no male relative to take his place, all other Jujus are banished from the compound and "Enyere" raised in their stead. This is the only Juju permitted to a family which consists solely of women.

Juju Enyere.

The Ekoi are a polygamous people, but till several years after my arrival, the chief wife, not the husband, was regarded as head of the house. This is still true to a great extent, but there are indications that native customs in this, as with children, property, &c., are beginning to be influenced by those of white men; especially in places near European centres, such as Calabar. At Niaji, and the more northern towns, the change has hardly had time to make itself felt, and old customs still obtain. Each wife has complete control over her children, and the latter almost invariably go with her if she leaves her husband.

S.B.   H

So strictly are woman's rights guarded by native law that even now it is not at all unusual for a wife to summon her husband before Court on the heinous charge of having made use, without permission, of some of her property, perhaps a pot or pan.

The following stories give some idea of the position of the sexes :—

Why Men must serve Women.

Long ago, Obassi Osaw and Obassi Nsi determined to build two towns; the former one for men, and the latter one for women. Each was to be separate from the other. When both were inhabited, the people of the two towns began to interchange visits. Sometimes men visited the women's town, sometimes women went to the men's. In course of time disputes arose as to the ownership of the intervening bush, and the men began to fight their neighbours.

Obassi Nsi and Obassi Osaw said to one another, "What can we do to prevent this? Let us hold a meeting."

When they had considered the question, they decided that it would be better for men and women to live together in one town. The women refused, and said, "Men began to kill us. Why should we go to live in their town? If the men want to dwell with us, let them come and live in ours."

To this the men agreed, and that is the reason why, when we marry a woman, we must serve her so long as she lives with us.

The next story goes even further.

How Men came on Earth.

At the beginning of things the world was peopled by women only.

One day, Obassi Nsi happened to kill a woman by accident.

On hearing this the rest gathered together, and prayed him, if he meant to slay them, to bring destruction on all together, rather than kill them slowly one by one.

Obassi Nsi was sorry for the grief that he had caused. So he offered to give them anything they should choose out of all

Nimm Neophytes.

his possessions, to make up to them for their fellow-woman whom he had slain

They begged him to mention what he had to offer, and said that they would all cry 'Yes" when he named the thing which they wished.

Obassi began, and mentioned, one by one, all his fruits, fowls, and beasts, but at the name of each they shouted "No."

At length the list was nearly ended. Only one thing remained to offer. "Will you then take man?" said Obassi at last.

"Yes," they roared in a great shout, and catching hold of one another, began dancing for joy, at the thought of the gift which Obassi was sending.

They took man, therefore, as compensation for the fellow-woman whom they had lost. Thus men became the servants of women, and have to work for them to this day. For, though a woman comes under the influence of her husband on marriage, yet she is his proprietor, and has a right to ask any service, and expect him to do whatever she chooses

---

It is not unusual in these stories for a man to lose his life, rather than fail to gratify some whim of his wife's, as, for instance, in the following :—

The Man who understood Animals' Speech.

Once, long ago, a man went into the bush to hunt. He saw an antelope, and tried to kill it, but could not do so. The beast got away, and ran down a great hole in the earth. The hunter followed and found himself in a ghost town.

When he arrived, the antelope's mistress was questioning it as to why it had returned so hurriedly. It replied that a hunter had tried to kill it in the world above. While speaking, it turned round and saw the very man, standing aghast. It pointed him out to the ghost-woman, and said:

"That is the man."

Now the hunter heard the sound of voices, but could not understand what was said.

The ghost-woman called her ghost friends, and told them what the stranger had done. So they tied him to a post, where he stayed all through the night.

Next morning the grown-up folk went into the bush to gather firewood with which to roast the prisoner, that they might make a great feast. No one was left in the town but the captive and the small children.

The man noticed that the little ones were sad-looking and dirty, and that their hair was long, matted and verminous. So he called them to come and sit round him.

Before the ghosts left the town, they had loosed his bonds a little, and put "medicine" in his ears, that he might understand their speech. He now began, in turn, from the first child to the last, to cut off the hair from their heads and wash them all properly with water.

When the ghost people came back, they found their ugly children made neat and very clean. They embraced the hunter, and thanked him heartily for what he had done. Those who had elder children with matted and dirty heads, brought them to him, that he might tend them as he had done the others. So well did he work, that the ghosts said he should not be killed, but, on the contrary, should be free to go home When his work was done, they gave him for reward the power to understand the language of all beasts; but warned him that he must not reveal this to any living being, or he himself would die at once.

The hunter thanked them and returned home. His townsmen were glad to see him again, and he told them where he had been, and how he got back, but kept the secret of the language of the beasts

One day his wife's mother heard of his return and went to visit him. She sat on the verandah of the house, and ate corn which her daughter brought her. As she bit the grains from the cob, a few of them fell down, and a hen who was near saw this, and began to call her chickens.

"Agbaw Okpok, Agbaw Okpok," she cried—for that is the way a hen calls her brood—" If you want to pick up the fallen grains, do not go near the woman's right hand, but go as close as you please to her left eye, because she is blind on that side, and cannot see you."

On hearing this the man burst into a loud laugh, for, indeed, his mother-in-law had lost her left eye. His wife thought that he was laughing at her mother, and grew vexed with him. The husband explained that he was not laughing at what she thought, but only because he had just remembered a story which had once amused him. His wife asked to be told what it was, and would not be satisfied till he granted her request. When he found out how much she wished to know, he told her what the hen had said, and how he came to understand her speech. He then fell dead on the spot, as the ghosts had warned him would happen if he told the secret.

This man was the only living being who ever understood the talk of animals. He told his wife what the hen had said simply to please her, and in full knowledge that his death would follow.

Why Children Belong to the Mother.

There was once a beast called Ejimm,* who had two Ejimm sons, by name Obegud and Igwe. They lived in the bush, near the dwelling of a poor couple who had twelve children.

One day the parents left their little ones at home and went to farm. While they were away, the children sang and played happily together, but the wicked beast Ejimm heard their voices. She told her son Obegud to go to their house and say that he had something for sale. This the beast did, and the children asked him to show his wares.

As soon as he had succeeded so far in his errand, he went back singing :—

> "Obegud Obegud ayaya-ay
> Bia koko ayaya-ay
> Ajima anwa nwa ayaya-ay."

(The narrator repeated this song very carefully, but had no idea as to its meaning. It has apparently come down from very ancient times.)

When Ejimm knew from the sound of her son's voice that all

---

* 'Ejimm" is the name of the iron instrument used by the Ekoi to spear lumps of meat from out a boiling pot. The monster in this story was probably so named on account of the long sharp jaws with which she seized her victims.

was well, she rushed to the hut, and stood in the doorway—a fearful sight! Then she thrust out her long mouth, seized a child, and carried it off to her den in the bush.

On their return from farm work, the parents missed one of their children, and heard from the others that a monster with a very long mouth had killed him and borne him away

Long they wept for their lost child, and when the time came to go to farm next day, the father bade his wife go alone while he waited at home to kill Ejimm.

At first the woman would not go, but after a while her husband persuaded her, so she left him.

At noon the beast sent out her other son Igwe, with instructions to say what his brother Obegud had said before He did so, and again the children bade him bring out his wares, whereon he ran homeward, singing as he went:

> " Igwe Igwe Igwe Iya
> Bia koko Iya
> Ajim anwa nwa Iya "

On hearing this Ejimm again set forth in search of prey, and came to the threshold as before. The man was well armed, but at the horrible sight of the beast his courage failed him. He ran for his life through the back doorway, leaving his children helpless before the greedy monster.

Again Ejimm seized a child and carried it off, rejoicing greatly over the prey she had found.

When the mother came back and heard that a second child had been taken, her grief knew no bounds. She turned fiercely on her husband, and asked why he had not saved his child. To excuse his cowardice, he told her that he had been very ill, and had had to leave the little ones for a while, during which time the monster had come

The children, however, all cried, " No, mother. Our father fled in terror at the sight of the beast, and left us to face the danger alone."

Filled with fury at this, the woman bade her husband begone. He did not need to be told twice, but went out and hid himself in the bush near by.

The mother determined to risk her life to save her little ones.

She armed herself with a very sharp matchet, and waited for the beast, who came again as before, and thrust in her head to seize a child.

Then the woman stood forth bravely, and killed her enemy, whereon the children raised a cry of triumph The father heard, and came from his hiding place, in the hope that all danger was now over. The two sons Obegud and Igwe, however, had heard the noise of the struggle, and now sallied forth to the aid of their mother. When the man saw them he fled once more, but the woman held her ground bravely, and killed these two beasts also.

When all was indeed over, out came the timid husband from his hiding place, and asked for a sharp knife, that he might divide the kill between himself and his wife. All the best of the flesh he kept for his share, and gave the heads only to the woman who had slain the beasts.

To this division she refused to agree, and called upon Obassi to decide between her husband and herself. Obassi heard her cry, and sent a messenger to fetch the couple before him.

When they appeared, the wife stood forth, made obeisance and said:

"After promising to fight Ejimm and defend our children, my husband ran away, and left them for the beast to kill. I am the person who stood bravely fighting, and slew, not her alone, but her two sons. Yet my husband would give me the heads only, of all my kill. So I come to claim my right before our Lord."

Obassi then asked the husband what he had to say in his defence; but the man could only confirm what his wife had said.

Thereupon Obassi gave order that, as the woman had such a brave heart to defend her children, from thenceforward no man should claim any property which his wife had risked her life to get.

Further Obassi gave judgment, that, should the woman choose to take the remaining ten children away from her husband, she should be allowed to do so; for she had suffered much for their sakes. Obassi also said that a woman was sure to risk her life for her children, though there were but few men who would do so.

It is in obedience to the above decision that when a woman leaves her husband, she may be asked to give up all gifts received from him, but not her children, nor any other thing for which she may have risked her life.

CHAPTER X

WOMAN—POSITION, ETC. (*continued*)

BY native custom a man who wishes to marry an Ekoi maiden must serve her people for some considerable time, usually from two to three years. His work mostly consists in helping to clear bush for the next season's farms, but other services may be required of him

During this time he is expected to make presents to the relations of his future wife, the value of which varies according to his means. A very usual list of gifts offered to father and mother, or guardians, is the following:—

1 demijohn of palm oil.
1 head of plantains.
1 piece of dried meat.
2 bottles of rum.
2, or more, heads of tobacco.

Maidenhood in a bride is not considered of the first importance, though parents usually watch over their daughters with great care, and in some cases girls are not allowed to go out alone.

Even should young girls be allowed considerable freedom before marriage, they may be regarded as fairly faithful once the ceremony has been performed. This is partly due to fear of the Jujus invoked by the husband, and partly because considerable damages may be claimed from the co-respondent, and also from the woman, should the husband consider the affair serious enough to demand a divorce.

The wedding ceremony is not regarded as possessing any religious character, and there is no trace of ritual symbolising former marriage to a deity.

The actual marriage, according to native law, consists in the acceptance, by the bride from the groom, of at least one wedding gift, on the distinct understanding that it is received *as such*. Acceptance must be followed by public proclamation of the marriage before chiefs and people, after the bell has been rung round the town for the purpose. The actual words used in most towns are "Oho Oho Owe," but in some places "Ora Ho, Ora Ho," is called instead   The expressions are practically identical, and mean "Our own." After these words, the names of the couple are usually added

The proclamation is mostly a precautionary measure on the part of the husband. Ekoi women are unfortunately all too fond of inducing suitors to give them as wedding gifts offerings which they afterwards declare they only regarded in the light of "sweetheart" presents, and therefore not binding them to marriage.

The following is a list of the dowry demanded by one Aret Offiong of Oban. It finishes, as will be seen, by a frank declaration, transcribed and translated by a friend whose store of English was somewhat limited.—

5 silk handkerchiefs, 5s.
1 piece of cloth, 5s.
1 bead necklace, 5s.
1 tin plate, 6d.
1 spoon, 3d.
1 piece of cloth, 2s. 6d.
1 looking glass, 6d.
1 razor, 6d.
1 comb, 6d.
1 pair scissors, 6d.
1 piece of black cloth, 1s 3d
1 piece of white cloth, 1s. 3d.
5 balls of string, 1s. 3d.
1 earthenware plate, 1s.
1 knife, 3d.

"I told him that if he will not me all this things I will not married him—
                    I am ARET OFFIONG."

Before their wedding, all free-born Ekoi girls, of well-to-do parents, spend a time in the 'fatting-house.' During this period they may not wash their faces and are not supposed to go out or do any work. If the parents are too poor to keep their daughter in idleness, and provide her with sufficient food to fatten her during this period, she is looked down upon by her companions before marriage, and also by the members of her husband's family when she joins them.

Should an Ekoi mother not approve of the man of her daughter's choice, she can sometimes induce her to give him up by the threat of not providing her with a good "fatting-house," i.e., not letting her have as much, or as rich, food during the time of her seclusion, as if she had chosen a suitor whom the mother favoured.

A case of this kind came before the native Court on March 3rd, 1909, when Mane Okon claimed damages for breach of promise to marry from Itakui Mbing Atan. The latter stated:

"I promised to marry him, but said I did not want to take his present yet, as, if I accepted it, my mother, who did not approve of him as a husband for me, would not give me a good 'fatting-house' like the others. After two months spent in the 'fatting-house' I looked at him again, and said to myself 'He does not seem to be a clever man. I do not think he would make a good husband.' I therefore chose another, and pointed him out to my father as the one I would have."

The period spent in the fatting-house varies, according to the wealth of the parents, from a few weeks up to two years. It is very usual for a girl confined in this way to amuse herself by

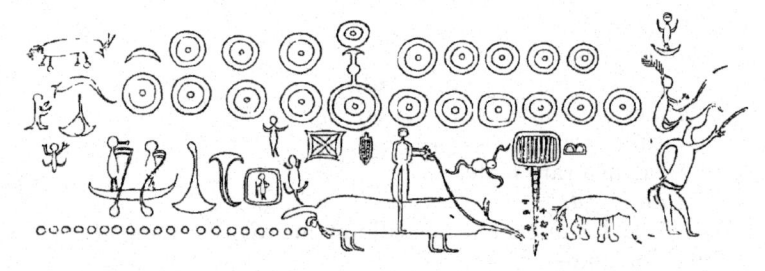

painting on the walls of her room a series of circles to represent the number of "moons" she has spent in seclusion.

The accompanying drawing, copied from a wall at Nkami, shows that the artist had spent twenty months in this manner.

The little row of circles at the left-hand corner represents the first tally kept. This was later elaborated in the manner shown above.

Usually before leaving the fatting-house, the girl undergoes clitoridectomy, but this operation is sometimes performed in infancy, and sometimes not till after the birth of the first babe.

When a girl leaves the fatting-house, it is an occasion of much rejoicing. A great feast is made and dances are given. The girl herself is smeared from the waist downward with a red dye made from the cam-wood tree. Fatting-house ornaments, consisting of tassels and chains made of dried palm-leaf fibre also dyed red, are hung round her neck, while a cross-piece of the same is usually passed beneath the breasts. Her girdle of beads, cowries and palm, is also rubbed over with the same dye. Her face is painted in various patterns and colours, and her hair dressed in a very elaborate way and decorated with combs, and large " pompoms " of white feathers, while over all nods a plume of the dark green and creamish feathers of the Nkundak (Greater Plantain-eater)

Unless my memory misleads me, some such custom also obtains among the Bavili of the French Congo, where a girl is secluded for a time in the " Paint House," so called because, after being carefully fed and tended there in enforced seclusion, she is painted red before being led to the dwelling of her future husband.

At a wedding, beside the gifts presented to the bride and her people, offerings must also be sent to the chiefs of the town. A feast is made for the " Nkan " or " age classes " of bride and groom. By this expression those townspeople born within two or three years of one another are meant. The men of about the same age form a sort of club to themselves and the girls and women likewise.*

Immediately after marriage, if the husband be wise, he will try to induce his wife to swear with him before the Juju Njomm Ekatt (the Foot Juju), which is supposed to keep wives faithful to their husbands.

The method of procedure is as follows :—The newly-wedded pair take mud from the river-bed. This in itself, as has already

* See p 283

Pits in the Rock by the River side in which Cam-wood Dye is made.

Type of Liane in the Ekoi Bush.

been mentioned, is supposed to possess magic properties. Hen's eggs and a quantity of Mfu leaves are collected, and the latter placed in a vessel of fresh water; the woman then holds an egg in each hand, while the man pours water over them. Next she lays the eggs on the ground and places two leaves beside them. The husband advances his left foot, and, while standing in this position, crushes up the leaves in the vessel of water. Into this the woman carefully stirs the mud brought for the purpose, and, after awhile, when it is well mixed, dips in her hand, and makes a mark with the liquid on her husband's forehead. He in turn does the same for her.

The object of this ceremony is to prevent women from having lovers after marriage. Should they do so after the rite above described, it is thought that Njomm Ekatt will "catch" them and give them a sickness, from which they can only recover after confessing to their husbands and inducing these to revoke the Juju.

Another way of ensuring fidelity in a wife is to swear with her before Njomm Aiyung (the Blood Juju).

Each of the contracting parties sucks a little blood from the wrist of the other as in the ancient marriage rite. Certain death is thought to follow any infraction of this oath. The blood of the husband which has entered the woman's body is said to rebel at the first sign of unfaithfulness, and course so furiously through her veins as to bring about speedy death.

A third way will be found described on p. 224.

On marriage the wife becomes a member of her husband's family, and goes to live in his compound. A man's first wife is always the head of the house. The younger wives obey her and consider her in everything. Therefore a wife likes her husband to marry plenty of other women. The chief complaint of cruelty brought by the wife of Njabong of Oban before the Native Court was that her husband refused to marry anyone but herself.

Should a wife's father die after marriage, it is usual for the husband to support his mother-in-law, but this is not obligatory. Each wife is given one side of the central "atrium," and two fireplaces are made for her, one for her own use and one for that of her children. When the number of wives exceeds the accommodation afforded by one compound, another is built, and so on till there is room enough for all. The husband has his own private room where he entertains his male friends.

As a rule the only objection offered by a man's wives to his visiting other women is that, if the latter receive his attentions, they ought to do their share of house and farm work for his family. This was brought out during a case which came up in Court on May 17th, 1907. A man named Akari Ntui claimed a certain Atim Okon as his wife. She disavowed the claim, and in her sworn evidence stated

"I was never a proper wife of plaintiff's, nor was I his proper 'friend.' Okon Asibong was my real 'friend.' but plaintiff used to visit me, till his wife warned me that if her husband came to my house again, she should reckon me as one of his wives. I then summoned the plaintiff, to prove that I was not married to him. This happened at Obutong about five years ago."

There are practically no marriage restrictions among this people. A man may marry a woman of the same name and tribe, or of another. It is not even forbidden by native law for half-brothers and sisters to marry, though cases of this kind are extremely rare. Such a one came before the Native Court on October 4th, 1909, between Ma Mfon Ita and Ntui Obassi.

In her sworn evidence the former stated, "When I was a small girl my father Itu gave me as a child-wife to Ntui Obassi. When I grew old enough for motherhood the latter gave me in marriage to Ita Nken. I was not willing. I was never willing to live as a wife with either of them. I am Ntui's half-sister"

She was declared free by native law as her consent had never been given.

There is nothing repugnant to Ekoi ideas in the marriage of uncle and niece, as is shown by another case heard before the same Court. In it Ared Asham of Mfamosing claimed that she was not the wife of her uncle Njokk Abang. The plaintiff stated on oath.

"My father told me that I was the wife of Njok Abang, but that when I grew up I need not have the marriage confirmed unless I chose. When my father died, defendant claimed all the property of the deceased because he was his brother. About six months ago, my uncle came back from Esuk Aje and seized me. He tried to tie me up so as to force me to become his wife, but I would not consent."

Ma Kokk (sworn) : " I am the mother of plaintiff. My husband gave my daughter to defendant as a wife, when she was a very small child; but defendant never gave any gift to my daughter since she became of marriageable age."

Njokk Abang (sworn) stated :

"At plaintiff's birth her father gave her to me. I used to take care of her. Now I claim her as my wife."

The claim was disallowed by native law, on the same grounds as the former one.

From the last case it will be seen that parents occasionally promise their daughters in marriage without the consent of the latter. Such an arrangement could never become binding, however, unless the girl herself agreed to it, when of marriageable age, and accepted the wedding gift.

Very small children are sometimes induced to take presents, and afterwards claimed as wives, on the ground that these gifts, accepted years before, bound them to marriage. Little Ekoi girls are therefore very cautious about accepting offerings from their boy companions. That they have need to be wary is shown by the following case, heard on January 3rd, 1908, in which Ma Obassi of Ayabam claimed the restitution of her daughter from Chief Nenkui. She declared on oath :

" I sent my daughter Baii to Mfamosing. She went out to play with the children. Etim, son of Nenkui, gave this ring to her saying, ' Here is a present.' Baii asked, ' Are you giving this in marriage ? ' Etim answered, ' No, I only give it as a dash.' When Baii had taken the ring, the relatives of the boy caught hold of her, and took her to their compound. There they kept her. She was about eight years old at the time.

" I went to Nenkui and begged him to give Baii back. He said ' No,' not unless I ransomed her by the payment of many pieces of cloth.

"Afterwards I went to Obutong. My daughter escaped and ran away to me there. Nenkui sent after her and had her seized and taken back. In doing this they broke down the door of my house and did damage."

If a man claims a girl as his sweetheart, and she wishes to show that his suit is hopeless, she calls for water and washes her hands before him.

This was done by Ikwo Okon, who stated on oath ·

"Once Ntui Akam sent a messenger to ask me to go to his house. I did so, thinking that something good would happen. He asked me, 'Why will you not accept my love? Are you afraid of your mother?' I said 'I am too young for marriage.' Next morning he brought palm oil to my mother. My big brother Usimebin took some of this, and my father took some also. A little while after, defendant asked me to go and eat food with him. I went, and after we had eaten he rose up and said, 'Now you are my " friend," and we will continue like this till we become permanent husband and wife.' At once I washed my hands and went away, telling him not to come to my mother's house, and saying that I would never be his friend.'"

When more than one man loves the same girl, magic rites are practised by the suitors in order to secure her affection, or to keep another from winning her Two well-known ways of bringing this about came up in Court on February 3rd, 1908. Obiri Awaw (sworn) stated:

"Two years ago my sister Ekpo Awaw gave Usin to me as a 'friend.' Obassi Ndo tried to take the girl away from me. So I took my company * 'Ekpe Kusua,' and crossed two sticks before her door, that defendant should not visit there any more

"Some time after I saw Usin sitting by Obassi on his verandah. I told her to go away, and he ran up to me, and said very angrily, 'I know that you want to kill me.' I raised my hands on high and said: 'God knows my father knew nothing of poison, nor do I.'"

"One morning I went to salute the mother of the girl, and saw defendant tying up her food with a piece of native rope This was a Juju to prevent the food from nourishing her if she carried on friendship with anyone but himself."

Should a wife refuse to live with her husband, without having

* Age class

freed herself by any of the usual rites, the Juju Eburuk Pabi, if invoked by the husband, may bring death upon her unless revoked in time.

On March 3rd, 1909, Ekoli charged her husband before the Native Court with trying to bring about her death in this manner. She stated:

"One and a half months ago I quarrelled with my husband Itui Ita. While he was away my child died. On his return he asked me where it was. I said, 'It is dead.' He said, 'Whenever you have a child it dies.' I answered, 'It is not I who kill them, but Obassi.' One night he called me to go to his room. I refused to go with him and said, 'It is no use. Whenever I have a child it dies.'

"He took his Juju named Eburuk Pabi, held a matchet in his right hand and the Juju in his left, and called 'Eburuk Pabi! Eburuk Pabi! If Ekoli will not come to me, may you catch her! If she comes, may you not catch her.' Soon afterwards the fever took me, and I sent and told Effion Archibong."

The latter stated on oath:

"When the woman was ill, I sent for accused, and told him to gather meat for the sacrifice that he might revoke the Juju. He did not deny that he had sworn Juju against her, nor make any objection to gathering the meat for the sacrifice, so the charm was revoked and the woman grew well."

Divorce is extremely easy under native law. The most common rite for freeing a wife is to rub white chalk on both her hands. If a woman wishes to free herself without the consent of her husband, she usually rakes out the fire and pours water on the embers till they die out. She then cuts her hair and covers herself with white paint. After this, even if both parties wished it, she could never return to her husband. Such a case occurred on December 3rd, 1908, when Awaw Otu stated on oath:

"Machott was my wife. One day she pulled out the kitchen fire on to the floor, and poured water on it till it died out. Then she cut her hair and covered herself with white. This is against our rule; so now she cannot come back to me as my wife."

By old law also, it appeared that a woman could divorce

herself by giving a slave or "member" to her husband instead of herself. This will be seen from the following case, which incidentally throws a curious sidelight on the relations of husband and wife.—

On December 4th, 1908, Awo Otu stated: "One day I was lying down by the fireplace in my compound. My other wife asked me to come and dine. Then my wife Machott caught me and beat me, and prevented me from going to my food. She then abused me. I replied, ' Look at you with a mouth as wide as a bag!' Then she said, ' Here is my member Ndo Tammi. You can have her instead of me. I give her to you."

In cases of divorce public sympathy is usually on the side of the wife, as will be seen from the following story:—

Why Wives sometimes Leave their Husbands.

Once an animal named Mbaw, and his wife Ma Ndikange, were eating young coco-yams. He said to her, " I will go and set a trap." So he went to the bush for the purpose. Next morning an Etuk (duiker) was found within. He gave it to his wife and said, " Boil this, but for you it is tabu, as it is the first animal caught in the trap."

Next day and the next, he said the same, and ate all his kill. On the excuse that each was caught in a new trap, he gave none to Ndikange, though she had cooked it.

The third day he caught a pig. This he took home, and said to his wife, " Boil it well. I think you will eat of this pig." After the meat was cooked, however, he made the same excuse as before, and ate all himself.

Then the woman thought within herself, " What can I do? All this time I am eating only young coco-yams. Of the beasts my husband traps, he gives me none." She made a plan.

She got her basket and went out; then collected magic leaves, mixed them together and made " medicine." Next she went down to the river-side, and poured the medicine into the water. Soon the river dried up because of the magic medicine. So she walked along its bed, and caught four baskets full of fish, of a very good kind, called Noi-oshi. She then went home, cooked these and ate her fill of them, for they were sweet to the taste ; but what was over, she left standing upon the fireplace

At daybreak the husband said he felt very sick, so the woman left him to rest in the house, and went alone to farm. No sooner had she gone, than he sprang up and tasted the fat left in the pot from the fish his wife had caught. At once he said to himself, "Oh, what a sweet taste! This is what my wife ate yesterday."

Now the fish was inside a native pot, and before the woman left her house, she had put a Juju upon the fish to protect them.

So greedy was the husband, that he stuck his head right inside the pot, that so he might more quickly eat up the good fish.

When he had done, he would have pulled his head out again, but the Juju caught him and held him fast.

He knocked his head up and down, and tried to break the pot, but still the Juju held, and he could not free himself.

All of a sudden, he heard his step-son, the lame boy, salute Ndikange as she came back from farm. The lame boy was the son of the latter.

Mbaw did not want to face his wife in that state, so he ran out, his head still covered with the pot, and stuck it in the deep gutter before the house. He thought that all of him was hidden, but alas! his feet stuck out.

The woman said to her son, "Where is my husband?"

The boy answered, "He has eaten your fish. When he heard you returning he ran outside to hide. Here he is, with his head in the gutter and his feet sticking out."

The woman went and caught her husband by the feet She pulled him out and said to him :

"You killed three animals. All these you ate without giving me any. Look at your head covered with the pot! Obassi sees everything. That is his judgment on you. You have stolen my fish."

The husband went out with the pot on his head, and called together his " age class." When they were all gathered before the house, he said to them .

"I have stolen my wife's fish. When she went away, she

left it in the house with some Juju to protect it. Therefore the Juju keeps my head in the pot."

His companions took his part, and said that the matter went against the woman, and that she must take off the pot.

She said, "Why should I do so? If the pot be taken off his head, I will not be his wife again for ever."

Then she threw some medicine on to the pot, and it fell away. The man's neck and head swelled up. The woman ran from them all, and said, "I will be his wife no longer, but will marry another man."

The husband remained full of sorrow. Then he disguised himself and followed her. He went round by another way, and lay down in the road where she must pass by. When the woman came up to him, he said

"You have left your husband. Here am I. Come marry me."

She said to him, "You are too like my former husband. I will not marry you, but someone else." She then went on her way.

Again the husband disguised himself, and ran on. He caught her up, and accosted her as before. She said to him:

"Very well, I will marry you temporarily, to see how you will be. If you behave badly, like my first husband, I shall divorce myself again, and leave you."

This is the reason why women divorce themselves, and marry other men. Whenever they marry a husband, and find that he is good, they stop with him. Ndikange remained with this husband, and had six children by him. She often said to herself, "If I had stayed with my first husband, I should not have done so well as this."

During all this time the husband took such good care of her and her children that she became very rich.

The reason why people sometimes say "Women are too roaming" is because these women have not found good husbands. When they find a good husband they stop with him, and do not want to leave him to go to another.

Divorced wives may marry again, but a widow must not listen to the proposals of any man until the mourning for her late husband is over.

On July 17th, 1909, a case came up before Court, in which Asot Ankpe confessed, " During the mourning for my husband I accepted a certain man as a ' friend.' " According to native custom in such a case, a woman must be handed over to her children, and the latter will have no right to their late father's property.

During another trial on August 3rd, 1909. Ekpri Nwan Ndifon stated on oath :

" Okon Ene Okpo said to me, ' What about the widow of your late master ? ' I said, ' She is still mourning. You must not talk about sweethearting yet. After the mourning is over you can speak to her, but not now.'

" Later I said to him, ' Our custom is that when a widow is released from mourning for her husband, you can approach her as to a new marriage, but not now.' Another day I said further, " After the mourning is quite over, you may bring a gift of one bottle of palm wine to the widow, but even then you must not talk of sweethearting at once."

The respective duties of husband and wife are clearly laid down by native law, and will be found fully treated on pp. 269 *et seq.*

Custom also insists that no favouritism may be shown to one wife above another, save for the privileges enjoyed by the first wife. An elderly woman has no cause to complain of neglect on the score of her advancing years, for what she loses in youthful attraction is made up by the reverence accorded to age.

Custom regulates even the smallest matters. In spite of the growing liking for European finery, no Ekoi woman could be induced to wear a hat. For them such a thing is " tabu," and as a reason the following legend is given :—

Why Women Do Not Wear Hats.

Obassi Osaw had five wives. Among them was one named Ekwaw, whom he loved above all the rest. She did no work, but stayed at home all day, while the other wives were made to wait upon her.

One day Obassi brought a little slave, and said to his

favourite wife, "I bring this young girl, that she may attend on you, and do all you wish."

After some time Ekwaw said to her maid, "To-day you must go to market. Come back and tell me what you have seen there."

When the girl returned she told her mistress, "I saw seven young men, each handsomer than the other. Never before have I seen such as these. Shall I bring them to you next time?"

To this the woman eagerly assented.

Another day the maid was sent as before. Again she saw the seven young men, and said, "My mistress calls you." They asked, "Who is your mistress?" When she did not answer they refused to follow her. She went home and related this to Ekwaw.

The mistress said, "Next time you go, take a great jar of palm wine, and beg them to come to me."

This the maid did. The young men drank the wine, and agreed to follow her. She brought them secretly to the compound.

When they came into the presence of Ekwaw she made a great feast, and kept them in her own room. Then she sent a message to her husband, "I cannot cook chop for you to-day. I have no time."

Next day one of the slaves went to Obassi and said, "Yesterday I saw some men go into your wife's house." He was very angry, and ordered the slave to be killed for accusing his wife.

Another time one of the wives went to Obassi and said, "I wish to tell you something, but fear that you will have me put to death like the slave." He answered, "No, I will not kill you You may tell me what you wish." She said, "Come with me. If you listen you will hear people talking in Ekwaw's room."

Obassi went, and found that the statements were true. He came back to his own house and sent to call the guilty wife before him. When she came he said to her · "For six days you have cooked no chop for me, neither would you admit me to your room."

The woman answered, " I have not been well all this time;" but her husband sent a message to the townsfolk, and said:

"In seven days you may play the play called Nsibidi. I will find out what is happening in my house."

When the seven days were over chains were put upon the woman, and upon the little slave, and on the seven young men, and Obassi ordered Nsibidi to kill them all; but before they died he called Ekwaw before him.

In the time when they were loving together, they two had changed hats. Now, therefore, he gave her back her hat, and she returned his also.

After she was dead a law was proclaimed. "From to-day no man shall change hats with his wife."

Women always have bad consciences. After they have married they should not be unfaithful at all. Up to that time if you loved your wife you used to change hats with her, but since Ekwaw deceived her husband women must not wear hats any more.

CHAPTER XI

Birth Customs

Like most primitive peoples, the Ekoi have the haziest ideas as to the causes of their being. Those who have come under white influence during the last few years affect, it is true, amusement over the foolish stories of the " bush people "; but in the interior the old vague myths still hold their ground.

There are many interesting beliefs as to the advent and death of babes. One charming superstition forbids all quarrelling in a house where there are little children. The latter, so it is said, love sweet words, kind looks, and gentle voices, and if these are not to be found in the family into which they have reincarnated, they will close their eyes and forsake the earth, till a chance offers to return amid less quarrelsome surroundings.

As an instance of how near primitive thought sometimes reaches to the most cultured minds of our own time, perhaps it may not be without interest to mention the Ekoi equivalent for the Song of the Mothers who come forth to welcome the new-born in M. Maeterlinck's play, " The Blue Bird." Once on arriving at a little town among the hills, in the interior, after a long, hot march over hard country, we stopped for the night at the Egbo house, in the centre of the town, as one always does where no Rest-house has been built. From a compound near by came the sound of singing, accompanied by tomtoms and okankan. As Bimba had developed a bad headache on the march, and found the noise very trying, the inhabitants were requested to postpone their rejoicing, or carry it out in a less noisy manner. On hearing this a little deputation was sent by the head woman of the compound, to say that twin sons had just been born to her, and that if the family ceased singing and playing to show their joy, the new-born would think themselves unwelcome, and go back whence they came.

As will be seen from this, unlike in many parts of Southern

Nigeria, twin births are here a cause of great rejoicing. The accompanying photograph is of a dance given to celebrate such an event. The father and mother were rubbed over with native red dye, and the latter further decorated with white chalk spots. The babes were carried by the two oldest of the chief women of the town, who hold much the position of godmothers to the new-born, and are called "mother" by them in later life. Parents and "sponsors" wear round their necks ornaments made of young palm leaves. On this occasion they danced to the accompaniment of the following song:—

"Ofung okupba, ojokk okupba
Buffaloes come, elephants come.
                  Aya aya pong ki pong
Egunamfuk, ka osaw are aje, ka nsi are ayingi.
Corktree, in air are leaves, in ground are roots"

The refrain "Pong ki pong" is added to give onomatopoeically the tramp of the oncoming buffalo and elephant, and may perhaps be compared with "Iliad," XXIII., l. 116,

"πολλὰ δ'ἄναντα κάταντα πάραντά τε δόχμιά τ'ἦλθον",

and the "Æneid," VIII., l. 596,

"Quadrupedante putrem sonitu quatit ungula campum"

Two very old songs in honour of the birth of twins run as follows:—

I

(Sung by the Mother)

"Nchitt, Nchitt, eyama ngaw ka aya
Egg plant, Egg plant, mine is in (the) water (or river)
Mbonga chang, Mbonga chang.
Picker out none, picker out none.
Tuk awmenge awbonga, Aiyamba?
Can you know (how) to pick it out, Eldest born?
Tuk awmenge awbonga, Manyo?
Can you know (how) to pick it out, Second born?
Nchitt, Nchitt, eyama ngaw ka aya
Egg plant, Egg plant, mine is in (the) river"

It is perhaps over-fanciful to find in this little song an echo of two old mid-European beliefs as to the origin of new souls. One legend places the home of the unborn in the water kingdom—the mother of all—and one in the realm of the dead, thus completing the circle of life.

According to Ekoi superstition, all egg-shaped substances, such as oval stones, etc., exert a favourable influence on generation It is perhaps not without interest to note that many of their legends affirm that both egg-plant fruits and native tomatoes were gifts from the nether world.*

II.

(Sung by the Family to the Guests)

" Awfat   are,   ibin,   ikumi,   nji, aha.,
Twins   are (born), dancing, sit down, go, aha.
Aiyamba o e-e,   manyo   o-e-c, o-e-c.
First born o-e-e second born o-e-e, o-e e."

At the end of the celebration, before the guests go home, the family sing with charming frankness :—

"Ntemm, akuri   eye   nju.
Friend, go away into house."

To which the visitors respond :—

" ' Me nkuri eyama nju
I   go   my   house."

On the way home the latter sing .—

" Ikuri ka   oju,   oju.
Going to (our) houses (our) houses "

The third line from the end reminds one somewhat of the hint afforded by the dish placed on Polish tables as an intimation that a guest has outstayed his welcome.

Should a woman be childless for several years after marriage, it is thought that there must be some special reason for the non-appearance of the babe. The cause is usually attributed to the "ill-wish" of some witch in the town, often a jealous fellow-wife or relative, who, like the mother-in-law in "Willie's Lady," or the deserted mistress mentioned in the "Metamorphoses of Apuleius," has used magic arts to prevent the birth of the babe.

The greatest efforts are made to overcome all such evil magic, for barren women have but little influence among their

* See pp 236, 238

BIRTH CUSTOMS

fellows. Such an one will spend all she has in the purchase of "medicines" or offerings, and her husband usually helps her to the utmost of his power.

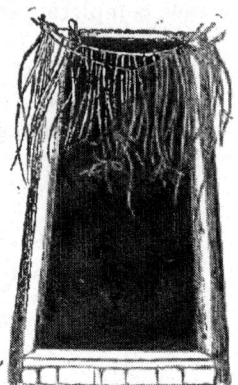

The principal Juju used to protect women about to become mothers, or those suffering from barrenness induced by witchcraft, is named "Isse Obassi Nsi." It consists of two different parts. First a double string of knotted palm-leaf strips hung up over the door of the woman's room, and secondly a little shrine within. On the latter a small lamp is to be found, unlighted by day, but burning all the night-time. Corn, meat (regarded in many parts of the world, and especially among North American Indians, as a fecundating substance), and oil are offered to the guardian spirit. Iron, too, must always be present in some form or other, for this the witches dread. Should a witch enter a room so protected she will surely die.

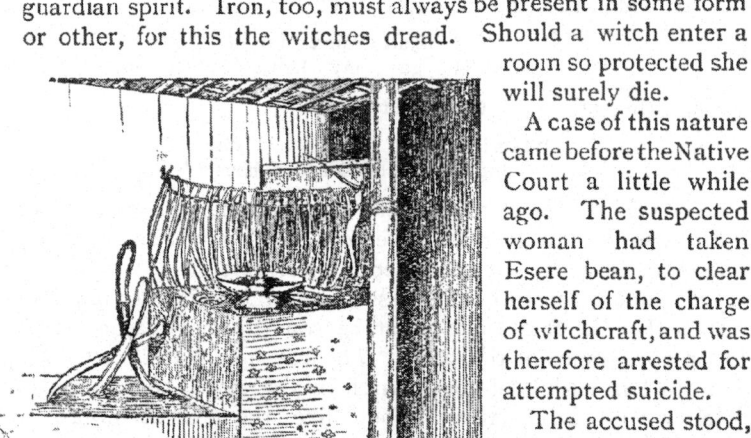

Juju Isse Obassi Nsi—Exterior.

A case of this nature came before the Native Court a little while ago. The suspected woman had taken Esere bean, to clear herself of the charge of witchcraft, and was therefore arrested for attempted suicide.

The accused stood, a picture of hopeless misery, with arms folded and eyes glancing hither and thither like those of a hunted animal, or with bent head, and face half hidden in her hands. When she was asked why she ate the Esere bean she said—in a voice

Juju Isse Obassi Nsi—Interior.

so sad as, in Gray's beautiful phrase, to touch "the very heart strings of compassion":—

"I had a child, a son named Itagbo, who wished to marry the daughter of Aya. First they were only sweethearts, but one day I saw that a grandchild was coming to me. I took the girl to my house and looked after her. When the babe came, I looked after both till they became strong. Then I sent to Aya to ask her to come, as I wished to circumcise him. She came, and all was done according to our custom, but some time after the boy died.

"Aya did not say that I had killed the babe, but her daughter went back for a time, and then a proper marriage was proclaimed between the latter and my son. Twice the girl conceived, but each time her child died. Then Aya said it was I who killed the children. She said that I was always passing invisibly through the house where her daughter was, both by day and by night, and so by my witchcraft brought about the death of the babes.

"I went to Aya and said, 'Do you say that I killed the children? In the old days I should have known what to do to show that I am not guilty; but now it is Talbot's time, and we may no longer undergo trial by ordeal.' So I did not eat Esere.

"Once more the girl conceived, but the fact was hidden from me. One day I went to the house where she was, and saw the Juju Isse Obassi Nsi before the door of her room, and the same Juju within it. I knew that the reason they put this there was because they thought that I was a witch, and that if I entered to do her harm the Juju would kill me.

"I laughed for a long time and was not afraid, for I knew what was in my heart, and how I wished for a grandchild. Then I went out and said publicly that the townspeople should ask Aya if she accused me of witchcraft.

"Again a piccan was born. This time it was a girl child. They concealed the fact from me, and the mother was sent away from the town so that I should not know. I called my son and said to him, 'Where is your wife?' He answered, 'I think that she has gone to Ndebbiji'—not suspecting that I knew anything about it.

"Not long after, the great Juju Akpambe arrived at Okuri. When Aya heard this she sent to her daughter and told her to go before Akpambe. This the girl did, and on her way thither my children wanted to go out and salute her, but I prevented them, and said, 'They hide her from me because they accuse me of having the evil eye with regard to her. Therefore I beg you to let her go by unnoticed.' She came and asked Itagbo to give her a bottle of rum to pour out before Akpambe. My son came to me and said, 'What shall I do?' I answered, 'I do not want you to do it for myself, but if you do not give it they may say that I prevented you from doing so because I am a witch.' So, at my prayer, he did as she asked him, and himself took her to Okuri, but the Juju would not give her any answer. After some time my son said:

"'I will return to Niaji, and afterwards come back for you.'

"No sooner had Itagbo gone, than the charm was practised, and afterwards an Okuri man told him that Akpambe had said it was I who killed the children.

"Not long after one of our chiefs died, and the Okuri people came to Niaji for the funeral play. They boasted about the power of Akpambe, but I said to them, 'Your Juju does not say anything at all. The mother of the girl had accused me of witchcraft before the Juju said that I was guilty. I do not believe that Akpambe can find out anything.' Then I took one piece of cloth and a bottle of rum, and said, 'I myself will go before Akpambe and question him face to face, that he may openly tell me anything he has to say.'

"Itambo Isum of Niaji said 'I will go with you.' So we set forth; but when we got half-way, we heard that the German D. C. was coming to Okuri, and that the people were packing up their things to cross over into English territory. So Itambo prevented me from going on.

"The Okuri people discussed the matter, and said if I were a witch there would be a sign in my house. So I watched and waited.

"Then my children began to suffer from pains and wounds, and I thought to myself 'Can this be what the Okuri people meant when they said that a sign would come?' I thought within myself 'I will not wait till my children die. I will go to

Aya, who has accused me of being a witch, and settle it once for all.' So I published the matter at Niaji town; but the people took no notice, though all of them heard.

"Next some sunbaked mud fell down from the roof of my house, and struck one of my children, so that it hurt her. I picked it up and went before the Okuri people, and said:

"'You have prophesied that there should be a sign in my house to prove whether I am a witch, as Aya says. Is this what you mean?'

"Then they answered me, 'If you are accused of witchcraft, why do you not clear yourself by eating Esere before all the people?'

"Up till then I had been afraid to eat the Esere bean, because white rule had come to our land; but when I heard the Okuri people say this, and Ekuri San, who was a member in the District Court, said nothing to stop them, I thought 'Perhaps the white man no longer forbids the trial by ordeal.' So I took the bean and ate it in the presence of Aya."

When a woman is childless for several years after marriage, it is thought that the babe has lain for all that time in the womb, waiting till the right moment should come for it to be born.

Such a case is told in the following story:—

Seven Years in the Womb.

Once, long ago, God made a man and a woman, and placed them in a little hut which he had built for the purpose.

In a few months the woman began to think that she ought to have a child. Nevertheless she remained childless for seven years.

One day when that time had passed by, the husband went off to hunt. He went very far from their hut, and was gone for many nights and days. When he came back he saw a boy sitting in the house.

Now while he was away his wife went into the bush to gather firewood. On the road she felt that her time had come. She laid her hands upon a tree and held it firmly. Then, instead of a tender babe, behold! there appeared a boy whose size was nearly equal to her own. At once the latter took her by the hand and led her home, for she was very faint, from bringing forth such a person.

When the husband came back and saw the boy, he asked the latter whence he had come. "I am your son, Tata,"* answered the child.

"How can that be?" asked the man.

"I am born of my mother, who is your true wife," answered the child, "but as I knew that you needed a helper, I would not come to you for seven years. I finished my time of helplessness in her womb and am now ready and able to help you both."

The man could hardly believe the boy's story, and was very much afraid. He thought he was going to die after seeing such a wonderful sight. "Perhaps," thought the father, "he is sent by the ghosts to fetch me."

So his thoughts wandered, although the wife also told him that the child was really his son.

For four days the boy stayed at home, and looked after his mother. On the fifth day he begged his father to give him a matchet, with which he could go to " bush."

In one hand he carried the matchet, and in the other he held a two-edged knife called Isawm The latter was a magic knife, and pointed out the direction of any place to which its owner wished to go. For instance, should he want to reach a town which lies to the south, the knife bent of itself if pointed towards the east, north or west, yet kept quite straight if held to the south.

The boy laid snares as he went along. He went on and on, making traps, till at last he thought the time had come for him to return. On the way back he found many birds caught in the snares he had set These he took home to his parents, and they thanked him heartily.

Next day again he went out to set more traps, and just as he was turning to come back as before, he heard a distant music played as if for a wrestling match.

Now the lad was very fond of wrestling, so he hurried back home and told his parents that he had heard the sound of

* Native name for father

wrestlers' music, and would start on the morrow to find whence it came. His parents advised him not to go, but he would not be put off, and started with Isawm in his hand.

When he reached that part of the bush where he had before heard the playing, he stopped and listened, but the woods were all silent. By the help of Isawm, however, he found the way, and went on and on, till about three o'clock in the afternoon he heard the music once more. The magic knife had led him straight to the place whence it came.

At the sound he flew forward, as if winged, and found himself at the foot of a very steep mountain, from the summit of which sounded, clear and sure, the long-sought, longed-for music.

The face of the mountain was so steep and slippery that no mortal foot could have climbed it unaided. The boy set to work, however, with Isawm and made two holes for his feet, then standing in these, he made two others higher up, and so continued till at length, in this way, he reached the top of the mountain. At the moment he reached it, he saw and was seen by the people who dwelt on the plateau above the precipice, up which he had climbed. At once he joined in the wrestling.

Now the best wrestlers among these people were seven in number, but the newcomer beat them all.

Obassi heard the din of the strife, and came at once to see what was the matter, for the town was his. He saw the boy, knew him for the one he had sent to help the poor couple, and signed to him to come near.

Now to-day was the seventh day since he had been born, but he was already grown to manhood. Obassi said, "You have overcome all the others; therefore I will adopt you as my own son."

The youth was so beautiful that, when Obassi's chief wife saw him, she at once fell in love with him. At first, the boy refused her love, but it was not long before he fell into temptation, and foolishly accepted her proposals. Obassi knew all, for nothing can be hidden from him. He asked the woman if she would own what she had done, but she denied it. He then asked his adopted son, who admitted his fault, and Obassi therefore at once forgave him.

After staying for a week the boy told Obassi that he would like to go and see his other parents, but would come back.

To this Obassi agreed, and gave him a rich present to take to his poor parents, and the boy started, well content.

When he had got half-way on the homeward road, he heard a sound in the bush at the side of the path. The branches were pushed back, and out stepped the woman whom he had left in the mountain town. She had heard the conversation between her lover and his adopted father, and had quickly followed.

The boy, who had by now learned the benefit of having a mate, was glad to take her to his home, and never returned to Obassi any more.

The latter knew that his wife had gone away with the lad, but was patient, thinking " Perhaps he will come back to ask forgiveness as he did before." When the boy did not return, however, after a long time, Obassi sent out his war-men to punish him.

Now, on adopting the boy, Obassi had shown him the Jujus of good and evil.* When the war-men appeared, therefore, this wicked youth put forth a strong magic, and bade them fight among themselves. So each man's hand was turned against his neighbour, and they fought together till all died, save a very few. These went back to their Lord, and told him how they had fared. When Obassi heard what the boy had done, he was very angry and shut the gates of mercy to mankind. Were it not for the fault of this couple, we might at any time have run to Obassi, and pleaded forgiveness for whatsoever evil we had done, and he would have pardoned us at once and spared our lives. Since the sin of this pair, however, the road to mercy is blocked for ever.

* Cf Genesis iii 5.

CHAPTER XII

Birth Customs—*continued*

From the moment a woman knows she is about to become a mother, she must take many precautions to ward off ill. For instance, she must be careful in passing along a road, or through the bush, never to go near the tree Njo Uru, the bark of which is used in fishing, otherwise the child will die.

Neither she nor her husband may eat elephant flesh, and she must also abstain from porcupine, water chevrotain and the leaves of gourd or pumpkin. It seems probable, from certain indications, that these plants were once regarded as totems. She must sacrifice to her houshold Juju—the most ordinary one of which is Osam (Spear). For this rite, a calabash, or native pot of lightly-baked earthenware, is filled with food, and the spear driven through it.

Just before the birth is expected, the head women of the town assemble, and administer soothing draughts to the mother. From the moment of their entry until after the washing of the babe, no man may approach the house, though the father and his male relatives may be present at the anointing with palm oil.

After the birth, the mother is secluded for one or two months, and, should the grandmother be still alive and in a position to bear the expense, she generally goes to the fatting-house for a period varying from four to six months, during which time the husband does not visit her. On returning to ordinary life, the young mother must sacrifice to her Juju, while the husband makes an offering to his.

When a babe is first carried outside the birth-room, the mother herself, or her mother, must bear it to the threshold between her two palms One of the female relatives, either grandmother, sister, or aunt, then throws water on to the roof so that it drips upon the child. Should this not be done it would get fever. A week later it is rubbed over with white chalk to bring good luck, and is then carried round to the houses of friends. On this occasion gifts are presented to the mother.

The first curl on the head of a babe is carefully cut by the grandmother, wrapped in a cloth and hidden in a box.

Should a woman be unable to suckle her babe, she may give it to her sister to nurse; but this practice is looked upon with general disfavour, and the mother must be doctored so as to tend her own child as soon as possible. After two or three months, plantains are crushed and given in addition. When the infant is thought old enough, the wrist is cut, and magic medicines rubbed within. That generally used to give strength is made from the index finger of the Nyokk (Chimpanzee, *Anthropopithecus troglodytes*), and for quickness and activity crushed Nsoii—the large, fierce black ants (*Paltothyreus tarsatus fabricius*)—are used.

A child is usually given its first name from the day, time, or place of its birth. For instance, should it be born on a native Sunday it would be called "Edet" if a boy, and "Ared" if a girl. If it came in the night-time it would be called "Okun," or "Akun" (night). If born at a farm, "Etim," or "Atim" (bush). The name is given immediately after birth. In many cases Efik names are chosen, as they are often shorter than their Ekoi equivalents.

Should the child continue healthy for a full year, the name first given becomes its permanent one, but, should it fall sick, the parents carry it before the "Mboni" (Diviner). The latter tells them to get ready a sacrifice, consisting of meat, plantains and coco-yams. On the appointed day the family assembles, and calls a meeting of the townspeople. The head of the house then slowly recites the names of the ancestors on both sides. As each is called, the Diviner answers "No," until at length one is mentioned to which he assents. This name is given to the babe, in the belief that the soul of this particular ancestor has reincarnated in him. The illness is thought to be sent as a sign that the spirit wishes the Diviner to be consulted, in order that the right name may be given.

The name of the father or father's brother is added as a surname, though not often used in everyday life.

After the ceremony above described, should a child sicken, the illness is usually ascribed to the influence of witchcraft, and all possible precautions are taken, and charms practised, to safeguard it from being "overlooked" by the evil eye. Should the child die through no fault of its parents, such as quarrelling, &c., but merely through the ill-wish of an enemy, it may return again and again to the same family. It is, therefore, not unusual, for parents who have lost several children, one after the other, to say of the first they have succeeded in rearing, "He has been born three times," or "seven," as the case may be. Subsequent children are usually given a protective name, such as Ajomm (Jujus), or Obassi (God), in much the same way as many Israelitish names were compounded, of Yahweh, Baal, Bel, or El. All children sent as a result of special prayer to the Juju are called Njomm or Ajomm. Before the birth of a babe, the mother generally makes a pilgrimage to the shrines of greatest repute in her part of the world.

In olden days, if man and wife were childless, or if an old woman was lonely and longed for a son or daughter, there were many ways, so legends assert, of securing babes. Fruits, flowers, vegetables, and even fungi, might, on the prayer of the childless, open, and provide them with son or daughter. Indeed, in many cases, prayer was unnecessary, the mere intensity of the wish was enough to bring about its fulfilment.

Perhaps, in the belief in flower and fruit births, some faint, far-off echo may be traced of those vague myths, the loveliest of which grew into the story of the birth of Adonis.

To quote the "Golden Bough" (p. 281), "His (Adonis') connection with vegetation comes out at once in the common story of his birth. He was said to have been born from a myrrh tree, the bark of which, bursting . . . allowed the lovely infant to come forth." And again (p. 298), "His origin is further attested by the story that he was born of a virgin, who conceived by putting in her bosom a ripe almond or pomegranate."

The tales next given are typical of the Ekoi version of such legends.

Leaders of the Children's Agara Club, Nch-fun.

Ekoi Woman.

THE FLOWER CHILD.

By Effa Mbop, Woman of Niaji.

There was once a woman who was very sad, because she had never had a child. She said to herself, "What can I do, so that a babe may come to me?" She went into the bush and sought around, then came back and planted what she had found. Each day she tended it well, and it sprouted, and always she said, "Other women have many children, but none come to me." One day she went to her plant, and lo! it bore great flowers, while at its root sat a beautiful boy. This she carried home, and kept hidden in her room. All day she talked to him and was very glad. The child said, "Let no one know whence I came."

One day someone said to her, "With whom are you always talking in your room?" She answered, "I talk to myself."

Later she had to go to farm with the other women, but, after they had started, one of them ran back to the compound, opened the door of the Childless-one's room, and saw who was within.

When they came back the two women had a quarrel, for the one accused the other of having stolen the babe she had found. While they quarrelled a third came up. "It is no proper child at all," said she, "but only the son of the flowers of the tree."

The Childless-one went into her room and took the little babe in her arms. "If you are born of a flower," said she, "you are just the same as my own to me."

The boy began to cry bitterly, and said: "I told you that no one must know you had found me. Now that all men know I am a flower-child, I must go back whence I came."

Next day, very early in the morning, the boy said, "Now, I go." He ran from the room and into the bush. The Childless-one followed, but though she searched, she could not find him. At length, when the day had grown very hot, she came to a place where a great plant bloomed full of the flowers beneath which she had first found the babe. There, at the foot of the plant, he lay dead.

Up till then, if a woman had no child, she could get one from a fruit or a flower, but since the boy ran away from this woman, no one can get a child from a plant any more. If this one had stayed with his foster-mother, it would still have been possible to get children in that way.

White people call the plant "bitter leaf," because its leaves have grown bitter from the tears of the woman, as she buried her little dead child at its root.

The Fruit Child

By Ikpuma of Ndebbiji

Two young men were great friends. The name of the one was Okun and the other Eret.

One day both went into the bush to hunt. On the way they saw an Mbum fruit which was quite ripe. This they gathered and carried with them.

When they came to the hunter's hut where they were to spend the night, they laid the fruit down on the bank of a stream which flowed close by. This was in the evening. Next day both went out to hunt, and, when they returned, a calabash of food stood ready, and all was prepared for the meal. Both wondered who could have cooked for them, but one said, "Anyhow, let us eat. We are hungry." So they ate, and the food was very good.

Next day again they went forth to hunt, and once more, on their return, the meal stood ready. They ate it and said, "To-morrow we will go forth, but will come back early and watch."

Okun reached the hut before his friend and hid in a hollow tree. After he had waited awhile, he saw the fruit open and a beautiful girl step forth. She began setting everything in order, and then cooked chop for the evening meal. Okun came from his hiding place and would have spoken to her, but when she saw him she tried to run away. He, however, said, "Do not leave us. We have something to say to you." He then called his friend, "Eret, Eret. Come, I have found out who it is who has worked for us."

They persuaded the girl to stay with them, but when many moons had gone by she said to Okun, "I must go back to my place." "Why should you go?" asked he. "Because I shall soon bear a child," she answered, "and I fear that someone will tell of me that I came out of the fruit Mbum." He comforted her, however, and she stayed.

One day, when her child was a few weeks old, she left it in the house, and went to work at the farm. While she was away the child cried. The husband's sister said to it, "Hush! You son of a fruit!"

Though the mother was afar off, the wind bore the sound to her, and she ran home crying, "All of you promised that none would ever say that I came out of a fruit."

She took the child in her arms, and ran to the great Mbum tree which was growing near. This opened, and she stepped within, and it closed over her and her child.

In those days if a woman had no child she could go into the bush, and ask Mbum to open and give her a babe, but since they said to this little one, "You are the young child of fruit," no one can get children in this way any more.

The Fungus Daughter.

By Bai Effiong, a Girl of Nsan

There once lived an old couple who had never had any child at all. One day the old man went out into the bush and searched and searched to find a child. He found nothing but a great Ebbuya ball, which the Ekoi people use to grate up fine, and then put into the soup to thicken it. This he took, and put into his bag, for he said to himself, "I have heard that when the lucky person finds a thing like this, he can carry it home, and it becomes a child to him." When he reached his hut, he heard a voice from the bag, which said, "Take me out of the bag, my father, for it is very hard for me to breathe here."

The old man put his hand into the bag, and, instead of the Ebbuya ball, drew forth a beautiful young girl. You may think how pleased he was to have found a child so easily! His wife also was delighted when she heard the good news, and did everything she could to make the new daughter happy. After a while the girl grew old enough to be sent to the fatting-house. The old couple arranged everything for her, and gave her a little slave to attend on her, while they themselves went to work at their farm.

When the foster-daughter spoke to this maid, however, and asked her to cook or do any other service, she answered " I do not recognise you at all as my mistress, for I well know that you are not the proper daughter of those whom you call your parents. You are nothing but an Ebbuya ball!"

On hearing this unkind speech, the foster-daughter went sadly back to the bush, and once more became a fungus.

When the old couple returned they found their fosterling missing. Now in the same house there lived a lame boy, who had overheard the whole matter, and told them all. Then the old people knew that their child had gone back whence she came, and would never come to them any more.

Again the old man set forth to look for Ebbuya balls, but, though he found many, none ever turned into a child again.

Had it not been that the little slave taunted the Ebbuya maiden with not being the proper daughter of the family, she might have remained with them, and from thenceforth it would have been the custom for man or woman to get a child this way, if he or she were lucky enough to find the right Ebbuya ball.

The Herb Daughters.

By Akon Ekpo, a Woman of Nsan.

There was once a woman who was very very old, and had never had a child. Round her hut grew many edible herbs which she had planted. Among them were Etigi, Etinyung Ikaw, and Etidut roots.

Day by day the woman left her home and went into the bush to search for nuts and wild fruit, and each day when she had gone, four beautiful girls crept forth from the herbs. They went into the house, cooked food on the hearth, ate, and then went back to their herbs once more.

One day a neighbour passed the hut, and, as she went by, heard voices within. She knew that the old woman had no children, and wondered who could be talking so gaily. So she went to the hut and looked within it. To her surprise she saw four beautiful girls, who started up and ran quickly to the herb bed, where they disappeared. She went away as if she had noticed nothing, but next day told her neighbour what she had seen. "Do not go to farm," she said, "but hide yourself somewhere, then come back stealthily, and you will surely see something which will please you."

The old woman did not need to be told twice, but did just as her neighbour had said. She pretended to go out as usual, but hid herself near the hut, and soon came back and peeped stealthily within. There she saw four beautiful girls, cooking and eating merrily in her house. Before they could run away, she stepped forward, and begged that they would stay with her and be her children. They promised to live with her so long as the herbs from which they had sprung were never given them to eat, Etinyung, Ikaw, Etidut, and Etigi. This the old woman promised, and most carefully kept her word, for she did not need to be told how sad it is for one of her age to be left alone.

As time went on, she noticed that her daughters grew bigger and more beautiful, especially Etinyung, who was the loveliest of all. So beautiful was she that a great prince named Ekpenyong Obassi fell in love with her as he saw her one day, near the hut.

At first the old woman refused to give her consent to the marriage, but Ekpenyong was not to be put off. He tried and tried to persuade her, and at last prevailed. The old woman, however, made him agree to the following conditions:—

Etinyung should not be troubled to do any work whatsoever, as the other wives did. Once in every four days she should be brought back to see her foster-mother, and last, but most important of all, none of the herb Etinyung should ever be mixed in her food. The secret of the girl's birth was confided to him; he was willing to do all that was asked, and went home to get together suitable marriage presents.

When the prince came again, he brought sixteen slaves laden with offerings, and all these were left as servants to the old woman.

Then Etinyung was given to him to be his wife, and the attendants spread skins and rich cloths all the way from the old woman's hut to the house of the bridal pair. With singing and dancing they went away together, and their feet never touched the ground the whole of the way. Ekpenyong grew so fond of this new wife, that he spent all his time with her. One of his other wives became vexed at this. Somehow or other the latter found out that Etinyung must not eat of the herb that bore her name, lest some great evil should befall her. The jealous wife therefore plucked some of it in secret, and mixed it with the food that was set before the bride. No sooner had Etinyung eaten this than she said to her husband·

"I must go home to my mother, even at this very moment."

How sad was the prince when he found that she had eaten of the forbidden herb! In vain he begged her to remain with him She told him that she was forced to leave him, and could no longer be his dear.

As she hurried towards her mother's hut she sang—

"Etigi eyene ka 'mi di inyawng-o
Okro sister come to me we must go-o
Etidut eyene ka 'mi di inyawng-o
Etidut sister come to me we must go-o
Ikaw eyene ka 'mi di inyawng-o
Ikaw sister come to me we must go-o"

As she sang thus, calling her sisters Etigi, Etidut, and Ikaw, who had in the meantime been married, they all rushed from their husbands' houses, back to the hut of their foster-mother. There they told what had happened to them, and once more became the herbs which they had been before.

Had not Ekpenyong's other wife been so cruel as to give Etinyung the forbidden herb to eat, it would have been possible for a woman of any nation, who had grown too old to get a child in the ordinary course, to be lucky enough to obtain one or more in the way of this old woman.

When the herb-daughters had left, the foster-mother had to be content with the servants given to her by her son-in-law, but Ekpenyong's grief at the loss of his sweet wife was more than can be told.

CHAPTER XIII

Beyond Niaji

AFTER leaving Niaji, the first village to be reached is Ikpai, which has a great reputation as one of the homes of " Mfam " Behind the Egbo house is a tiny shed, built over this Juju, and close by stands the Mfam tree, the scientific name of which is *Croton amabilis*. It is small-leaved, with insignificant, almost invisible flowers, and, so far as could be learned, possesses no medicinal properties. Its importance in the mystical herbal of the race is therefore hard to understand.

When a rich or influential man is sick, he sends for the priest of Mfam to bring him some of the boughs of the sacred tree, and, unless the Fates are spinning the last strands of life, the mere touch of the leaves is said to restore health.

To rich and poor alike, when at the point of death, the boughs are brought. The priest stands by the side of the dying man and draws them gently over his face that his spirit may pass painlessly to the realm of Obassi Nsi.

On August 19, 1907, I was present at the revocation of the Juju

Obu of Ikpai had sworn " Mfam " against anyone who should try to take from him a young girl named Nkoiyu, whom he wished to keep in his family.

When all the members of the Juju had gathered together before the shrine, naked to the waist, Itagbun, the head priest, opened the Juju shed and took from it six horns containing " medicine." These he laid on the ground, and, after drinking a little palm wine, sprinkled some over the horns.

Next he took up two of these, one in each hand, and calling on the names of Obassi Nsi, Obassi Osaw, and of the ghosts, prayed :

" Behold ! Obu has come to take off the Juju which he swore, when he asked that if anyone should take the girl from his house, Mfam might kill them. He has now come to pray the Juju to take off the curse that the whole business may stop."

While Itagbun spoke to the Juju, the people knelt or stood with their eyes reverently lowered. He then drank a little more palm wine and tried the leaves to see if the Juju agreed. The answer was favourable.

Obu himself next stepped forward and said, "Look! I come to take off the Juju from the girl. Let the Juju oath be cancelled. Let her go to her former mistress Idan Awaw. Let the Juju not interfere with the business again. I leave her now to Idan Awaw. Let the Juju not fall upon Idan!"

Itagbun continued, "O Juju, hear the thing that I say. Obu has come to tell you he has nothing more to do with Nkoiyu. Make nothing able to touch her to her hurt. Should anyone try to do harm to Nkoiyu or Idan, may you stop them!"

He then sat down, poured palm wine into a small calabash, drank some and threw the rest on the ground before the Juju. Then he rose and placed two leaves beneath it. Next he poured palm wine on the six horns and prayed:

"This is the palm wine that Obu gave. Accept it and let all be well for the persons who have come before you to-day."

After this he laid the two leaves on the back of his left hand and struck his right hand upon them, saying, "If you accept the palm wine and everything is finished, tell me now."

The leaves agreed, and the people shouted "Ohe!" (It is good!).

All the chiefs drank a little palm wine. Then the meat brought by Obu was cut into small pieces. Some were laid on each of the horns and the rest distributed.

Itagbun next stood before the Juju and said, "This is the beef which Obu has given you." He then took up a cloth and waved it over the horns, saying, "Look, O Juju, at the cloth Obu has given. Set Nkoiyu free from the curse which was sworn against her in your name."

A third time he took up the leaves and asked, "Everything is finished. Do you agree?" To this again the leaves gave a favourable answer.

Itagbun then called Nkoiyu. As she stepped forward she dropped the long cloth which she wore, and stood before the Juju, clothed only in a small loin cloth.

Itagbun said, "Come, hold forth your hands." She held them together, palm to palm, as if to receive a gift. Then he spat solemnly into them and said, "Everything is finished. Go in peace."

Last of all Idan was called, and the same rite gone through with her.

After this the priest replaced the horns in the little shed, and the people went back to their homes.

Itagbun, priest of Mfam, has amassed great wealth from the offerings of pilgrims who come from many miles round to invoke the Juju. His "treasure house" is elaborately decorated, as will be seen from the ornamentation of one of its seats. The most valued possessions of rich Ekoi consist in collections of glass, pottery and china.

Seat in Itagbun's Treasure House.

Among the latter, beautiful old specimens, amassed during the slave-trading days, are often to be found.

The Etai Ngbe, or Egbo stone, in the local club house has a particularly clear sharp edge.

At Ndebbiji, the next town of interest, another fine example of these stones is to be seen. It stands before the base of the Egbo pillar, on which there are some curious drawings.

The animal represents an antelope, the upright rods are meant for native money, and the figure in Egbo dress is holding out its hand in the traditional attitude to indicate the telling of news.

Hunting Customs.

The Ekoi are a race of hunters, but the northern towns, such as Niaji and Ndebbiji, are the most celebrated in the District for their skill in the chase. So long as gunpowder was available, they never failed to arrange a good drive on each visit, and some of their hunting customs are of great interest.

Usually, before the hunt, each man sacrifices to his own Juju. Should a leopard have been lately killed, Juju leaves are rubbed over its skull and prayers are offered to its spirit that it will go on the left hand, and drive the gentler game towards the hunters who keep to the right. It is also entreated to help in the killing of other leopards or any dangerous beast, should such be met with.

On one occasion we started at seven o'clock, with about sixty guns and a large number of beaters, and marched to a little glade about three miles off Here we separated to take up our several stations.

Usually nets about 6 feet high and, when joined, half a mile long, are stretched across the angle caused by the junction of two rivers. Here the principal guns are posted, while the rest, when they have reached a sufficient distance, form a huge semicircle, and, on a given signal, bear down towards the apex, driving all before them.

The wait is more exciting than might be imagined by those unaccustomed to this method, as there is an interesting uncertainty as to what game may first appear. On one occasion a leopard flashed past within a few feet of me and cleared the net before it could be dropped.

It is not often that an Ekoi hunter misses, even in the thick undergrowth and with primitive flint-locks. Among the animals killed in this hunt were seven fine antelopes, one of which, a harnessed antelope, was apportioned to the carriers.

A few minutes after the distribution had taken place the interpreter came up and said, Might he be allowed to mention that the carriers did not like the skin of the animal? When I suggested, with some astonishment, that they were not expected to eat the skin, he showed obvious embarrassment, and at length explained that none would dare to eat the flesh of a

After a Hunt, Ndebbiji.

spotted antelope unless the proper rites had been performed. Otherwise the Juju would catch them; they would die and the spots appear on their bodies. When one of the party pointed to a Bay duiker, and asked if its dark stripe would have a like fatal effect, they seemed much amused. Luckily some of the old chiefs of the town were capable of performing the necessary ceremonies, in which "Egakk" leaves played a great part. After these rites had been duly performed carriers and "boys" feasted merrily on the Juju antelope.

This tabu, like many others, probably had its origin in totemic causes.* Others were imposed for sanitary reasons, and many from the desire of the old men to obtain a share of what was killed by their juniors, as in the following story —

WHY A HUNTER MAY NOT EAT APES KILLED IN THE BUSH, BUT MUST FIRST BRING THEM BEFORE HIS FATHER OR THE HEAD OF HIS HOUSE.

Once, long ago, a man named Atai Ikot (Ikot the hunter) went out into the bush. He saw a great many Nyori nuts, so collected them into a heap. Then he made a fire, and sat down to break the nuts between two stones.

Some Oiyokk (chimpanzees) came down and watched. After a while, when the hunter had gathered together many kernels, he went off a little way. When he looked back, he saw that the monkeys had come down. They took the Nyori in their hands, and tried to crush them with stones as he had done, but only hurt their hands. The hunter laughed at them, and, when his friend Okun came to join him, Okun laughed also. They went to spend the night in a hunter's hut, and while there Ikot said:

"Let us go back to the place where the monkeys are, and pretend to fight together, then we will leave our cutlasses. Very likely they will take them and kill one another."

The two friends did this, and when they had gone away again, the Oiyokk came back and picked up the cutlasses. One chopped at his friend, and the latter cried.

"How is this? Blood is coming out from my skin." He

* For list of Tabus see Appendix A.

himself then took a cutlass, and struck at the beast who had wounded him. Both fell down dead, and the others continued fighting with the cutlasses till all were slain, save one, very old and wise, named Etim Aiyaiyokk. This last picked up the matchets, turned them over and over and said " What can these things be ? " Then he broke them both and went away.

Ikot and Okun gathered together all the bodies and laid them by the fire, but Etim Aiyaiyokk called together all the monkey people to come and look at their dead friends.

The hunters saw that the apes wanted to kill them, so they made a great fire, and began roasting nuts. They ate the kernels and threw away the shells, and then hid themselves to watch.

The Oiyokk also wished to roast nuts and eat them, but did not know how to do it properly, so burnt their fingers and threw away the nuts, kernels and all.

Okun said to his friend, " You see, they do not know how to eat such things ! but if they catch us with all the Oiyokk meat they will kill us, for they are too many for us. Let us run and fetch help." So they ran to their town and called all the people to come out and bring in the kill.

When the townsfolk learned what had happened, they said, " You have done well, because you bring all this meat to the town instead of eating it yourselves in the bush."

After this a law was made that whoever should kill an ape in the bush, must not eat of it, but must bring it before his father or the head of his house.

The next tale explains other hunting rules.

Why the Owner of a Gun gets all of his Kill save one Leg.

By Itamfum of Oban.

All the men in Elephant's town went out hunting. Crab fired the first shot, and killed an antelope, and at the second shot killed a bush cow. Elephant was angry, because he himself could shoot nothing, so he took Crab's gun away from him.

Crab went home, and got out all his nets. He hung them up

round the bush. When the next shot was fired a water chevrotain started up. It ran into the nets which Crab had spread and was caught On this Lord Elephant took the nets and burnt them. He also took the water chevrotain, for he said, "It is not right that Crab should kill so much when the others have caught nothing"

Crab took up the ashes of his nets, and made a strong Juju over them. Then he went round all the bush strewing the ashes. If any beast came where they lay he was caught by the magic and held fast, just as in a net. Elephant again took away all thus caught.

Then Crab was very angry. He went home and got out his water Juju. Next he went to every spring and every little stream in the bush, and put some of his Juju into each. Everywhere the water dried up Into the river by Elephant's town he poured the same Juju, and that also dried.

Crab went back, and entered the compound where all the women were cooking. He said, "I am a messenger from Lord Elephant. He bids each woman put much pepper in the food to-day, and also throw away all water. There must be none left in the town when my Lord comes home."

After a while Crab went again and said, "I have come to see that you have obeyed the order, lest Elephant should blame me." He inspected the houses and saw that not a drop of water remained, so he said, "I will tell Elephant that all has been done according to his command." After this he went away and hid in his own hole.

When Elephant came back from the hunt, he said to his wife, "I am thirsty Give me some water." She answered, "There is none." He said, "Why is this?" and she replied, "Crab said that you had ordered all the water to be thrown away"

Elephant was very angry, but all the people said. "We know Crab. He is a sensible man Eat your food, and when he comes back he will explain about the water"

All began to eat, but the pepper burnt their mouths, and made them more thirsty than before, so they cried out. Ise was sent to call Crab, but could not find him. Then Etuk was sent, but he was faint with thirst and lay down on the road.

Meantime three of the beasts had died for want of water, so they called Pig, and said to him, "Find Crab, or all of us must perish."

Pig went round in the bush, and dug up all the ground with his snout. At length he came to Crab's hole, and rooted him out. He said, "You are wanted by the Chief," but Crab answered, "I will not go I also am a chief."

On this Pig said, " Please respect my orders and let us go " Crab replied, " First get back my meat, and my gun "

Pig went to his house, took his own gun and some meat that he had, and brought them to Crab, who accepted the offering.

The latter said.

"You are my friend, and have behaved justly. For your sake I will give back the water."

So these two went before Elephant, and Crab said:

" Before I give back that which you desire, you must proclaim one thing throughout your town. That is, that whenever we go hunting, the townsfolk may have one leg of each beast killed, but the rest shall belong to the actual slayer, to be divided by him according to hunters' law."

All the people agreed to what Crab proposed, and confirmed it, for they said, " Many people have died of thirst already, and we must have water."

Crab then announced to Elephant, " Though you are bigger than I, yet the water is mine and I have control over it." He took his Juju and poured it into the streams, whereon the water flowed once more.

This is the reason why, when Ekoi men go hunting, one leg of all their kill is the right of the townsfolk, but the rest belongs to the hunter or the owner of the gun, to be divided by him among all those to whom a part of his kill is due, such as the head of his house, his parents, wife, etc.

As one follows a bush path, rough platforms of sticks may often be seen, fastened across the branches of some tree, the fruit of which bush-beasts love, or, should the trunk of the actual tree be unforked, little shelters may be found in convenient

BEYOND NIAJI—HUNTING CUSTOMS

nearness to such. On this frail perch the hunter crouches till his prey comes to feed on the heap of fallen fruits spread out below.

Sometimes too, in unfrequented parts, one stumbles on a deep pit dug by the wayside, and hidden by green boughs, to ensnare the feet of unwary buffalo.

It is probably to their highly developed musical sense that Ekoi hunters owe their marvellous faculty for imitating the cry of any beast for which they lie in wait. So perfect is the imitation that the animal nearly always follows the sound, to its destruction.

The ordinary West African form of trap is much in use for catching leopards, genet and wild cat, and there are many bird traps, mostly on the lever principle.

Although there are no Ekoi words to express the points of the compass, the sense of direction is very keen, as is usual with forest peoples. It is rare for men to be lost in the bush, no matter how far they may follow their prey. They are quick to read woodland-signs and are wonderful trackers —in this the hunting dogs are of great help. Certain rites are performed over the latter before they are given the freedom of the bush. as is mentioned in the following:—

Concerning Hunting Dogs.

One day the Ennying (francolin) was sitting on her eggs. She grew very hungry and went out to find some food. While she was away, Njaw (dog) ate her eggs. Then he went off, stole some feathers and covered himself with them, so that he should not be found. When inquiry was made about the egg-thief, Porcupine said, "It is Njaw who is guilty." The dog therefore thought, "From to-day Porcupine is my enemy." He ran after her, but she got to her home and hid within it. Njaw got nets and hung them round the hole. Then he waited, and after a while she tried to come out, and was caught.

That is the reason why, when a hunting dog goes into the bush, he always seeks out the place where Porcupine lives. They have been enemies for many years. Whenever he can, Njaw goes down the hole, kills Porcupine, and then comes back to his master, wagging his tail. The master follows the dog to the hole and gets the porcupine.

Often a man buys a young dog, and confirms him by Juju for hunting. Till the proper rites have been carried out, the dog is not of much use to his master. Afterwards, when he grows big, he can go out alone and hunt.

Some dogs go with their masters, but many go alone. When they have killed anything, they go back and wag their tails. Often the master sees blood on their mouths.

Before starting out after elephant, the hunter almost invariably sacrifices to the special fetish which is to be found in most villages. This act is supposed to be of the first importance, as it is universally asserted that none have been killed unless the sacrifice has been neglected. The rites are also efficacious in another way, for a man so protected, is in no danger of shooting a were-elephant in mistake for an ordinary animal. The beast always gives some sign, by which it can be known. Usually this is said to be done by lifting the right fore-foot, and at the same time bending down the head.

An unsuccessful hunter almost invariably attributes his failure to witchcraft. In order to break such evil spells, he takes an offering of dried meat and plantains to some place on the road outside the village. There he spreads out the sacrifice and pours a libation of spirit upon the ground, praying at the same time to Obassi and the ghosts, that they will set him free from the spells which hold him.

Supposing the ill-luck continues, the hunter next consults a Diviner, who, after questioning the charm, tells him that the witchcraft is very strong, and can only be broken by recourse to a powerful Juju. On such an occasion the prayer is always offered, "This hunter begs you to protect his gun and himself, that no ill-spells may have power upon them."

At the conclusion of the ceremony, when all the members of the Juju have feasted at the hunter's expense, the Diviner returns the gun to its owner with the words:

"Go into the bush, and may good fortune attend you.

BEYOND NIAJI—HUNTING CUSTOMS

Should you kill, bring back an offering to the Juju, and to its priest."

It is indicative of a certain side of the Ekoi character, that they deem it necessary to explain the right by which a hunter may kill the bush beasts. The reason for this is given in many tales, of which the following is perhaps best known:—

How all the Beasts came upon Earth.

By Ndum of Nsan.

Obassi Osaw and Obassi Nsi were, as we know, great friends.

Once upon a time the former told the latter, that he was going to fix a day to invite him, with all his people, to a great feast at his home in the sky.

Obassi Nsi answered that he should be very pleased, and, when the day came round, went, with a great following, to the feast given by Obassi Osaw.

Up to this time, all the beasts had lived in the sky, and we human beings only, then as now, lived on earth with Obassi Nsi.

The guests ate their fill, and were afterwards entertained with dances and games. When the time came to say "farewell," Obassi Nsi thanked his host, but said that he thought he himself could give a still more splendid feast, if his friend would come with his people to visit him on earth. The day was fixed, and all promised to attend, but Obassi Nsi warned them that they would not be able to eat in a year the half of what he would spread before them at this one day's feast.

Obassi Osaw said that this was well, and no sooner had his guests gone back to earth, than he sent round to announce to the sky people—for the heavens were then peopled by every kind of animal—that on the appointed day all the beasts must go with him to earth to visit his friend Obassi Nsi. No excuse would be accepted from any who should fail to come.

When the time for the feast came round, all the animals, from the smallest ant to the biggest elephant, followed their Lord Obassi Osaw earthward, to the land of his friend.

Now the day before, Obassi Nsi had gone round the whole

earth and bidden every tree and bush to bring forth abundance of fruit. This they did, and yielded to the utmost of their power, so that the whole land was beautiful with ripe fruits, which hung down temptingly from every stem and bough. Besides all this, Nsi ordered great calabashes of cooked food to be prepared, and many drinks got ready to receive his guests.

All the beasts came down from the sky and saw an infinite number of trees clad with fruits of the most enticing ripeness. They broke from their master, and spread themselves over the land, eagerly feeding. The monkeys were busy with bananas, the swine rooted for cassava, while the birds hardly knew what to choose of all the feast provided for them.

Obassi Osaw was asked by his friend why his people did not attend him, and answered, very sadly, that they were coming behind. He saw at a glance that he was surely exceeded by Obassi Nsi, just as the latter had said. However, he sat down at table and enjoyed all the good things. It began to grow dark, but still none of his people came back to him. Again Nsi asked him where his people could be, since they did not come to attend him. Osaw answered nothing, but, sadly and alone, went back to his home on high.

Afterwards he sent word to Nsi that he and his people might hunt the beasts and kill them, for they should no longer be sky people, but only food for the earth men, as they had disgraced him, their Lord, and refused to return to their own land.

This, then, is the only ground, by right of which we may kill the beasts and eat their flesh, and this is truly the way in which the animals came to this world. Some of them were free, from this time, to prey upon others, as leopards, bush cats, crocodiles, etc., but they have long since forgotten the way back to their old home in the sky, and must now stay here, whether they like it or not.

Ekoi Hunter.

Ojokk.

CHAPTER XIV

THE SOUTH CAMEROONS

AFTER Ndebbiji the road leads up positive precipices to the towns of Ojokk and Obepp. These were once great centres of the slave trade, but now lie, veritable palm gardens, sunny and peaceful, at the foot of their crescent-shaped mountain background.

About three miles further stands Nkami, the last British town, the inhabitants of which are among the simplest and most charming of their race. Here, as well as at Ekoneman in the German Cameroons, some traces of cat worship still remain. In the night-time, when a play of this nature is given, the people spring upon the roofs just as cats do. Especially famous in the cat dance is Ntui Esame of Ekoneman.

A few miles beyond Nkami flows the Awa River, which is roughly taken as the boundary between Southern Nigeria and the South Cameroons. At the moment of writing, the actual frontier-line has not been ratified by the Governments concerned.

Over this river the courteous German Commissioner, Dr. Mansfeld, had had a new suspension bridge built, and had told the chief of the nearest town to put up a Juju, so that no one should use it before the arrival of our party.

Nfunum is only just on the other side of the water, and here our complimentary escort, a coloured sergeant-major with a couple of privates, was awaiting us. In one of the houses was a small "treasure chamber," the wall design of which seemed worth copying (see p. 152).

Dr. Mansfeld had suggested meeting us at Lake Ijagham, the sacred lake of the Ekoi, which he had discovered about three years ago.

The way thither led through ruined villages or almost deserted towns. Here and there along the roadside, amid the luxuriant growth, a fallen Juju post or Egbo drum showed the site of some abandoned settlement. So rapidly does vegetation spring up to cover the rain-levelled walls that, save for indications such as these, one would pass, unnoticed, sites where thriving towns had stood only a few years before.

Just beyond the River Agegam, over which a second excellent native suspension bridge has been built, are a series of beautiful little cascades. Beyond these the road gradually rose, and for the last hour led along a narrow ridge with a deep gorge on

Treasure Chamber at Nfunum.

either side. The vegetation, for a considerable way, was much the same as that on the other side of the boundary, but this suddenly changed. Dense bush gave place to comparatively thin clumps of a palm new to science and as yet unnamed, which extends in a narrow irregular belt far into British territory. The former style of bush reasserted itself, however, before Lake Ijagham was reached.

Dr. Mansfeld met us on the road, and took us to the houses which he had had built for our accommodation, in full view of the beautiful lake.

It is indicative of the jealous way in which a primitive people like the Ekoi guards its secrets, that a Government station had existed for years within a few miles of this spot, yet no hint of the lake had reached German ears. It was only through

Native Suspension Bridge in the S. Cameroons.

noticing the recurrence of the word "Ijagham" in the phonograph records of folk songs which he was collecting, and the fact that no translation could be got from the people, that Dr. Mansfeld's suspicions were aroused. After a long time and by means of considerable bribes, one man was induced to explain that it meant a great water which existed in the neighbourhood. It was still a matter of difficulty to discover the actual situation, but in time this also was accomplished.

The word "Ijagham" bears a strong affinity to "Ejagham," the name by which the Ekoi call themselves; but so far it has been found impossible to induce them to give any explanation for the similarity. The word Ekoi itself is Efik, but it is the only name by which the people are generally known, and is therefore a more convenient designation for them.

Like the smaller Lake of the Dead, near Nsan,* Ijagham, or Toten See, as the Germans have named it, is supposed to be haunted by the ghosts of dead-and-gone Ekoi.

According to legend, the centre of the lake is of immense depth, and contains a whirlpool into which all are sucked who venture to bathe in its waters, or attempt to cross them in a canoe. No such evil fate, however, overtook the little Berthon boat in which we crossed. Perhaps the Genius of the lake was too chivalrous to harm the first white women to visit his shores.

As in the Nsan Lake of the Dead, a great snake dwells beneath the waters, and this at least is fact, not legend alone, for Dr. Mansfeld informed us that a skin was found not 100 yards from the huts he had built on the shore. It had only just been cast, and measured 18 feet. Wild ducks cling in coveys to the branches of dead trees which raise their bare limbs above the surface, while hawks and eagles circle continually in the clear air above.

The lake is in the shape of an oval cup, ringed round with high trees, which reach right down to the water's edge. There is no encircling belt of reed or fern, and noticeably little undergrowth. The bed is of clean white sand, which seems to

* See p 23

stretch from rim to rim Through the clear green water hundreds of fishes dart hither and thither, of different sizes, but only one variety. They are much like trout to the eye and taste, but need no salt for cooking. The natives say "They have salt in their bodies," and experience would seem to prove them right. Possibly the fact that the lake lies in the centre of a circle of thirteen salt springs may have something to do with this peculiarity, though the water of Ijagham itself is beautifully clear and sweet

Strangely enough, the temperature of the water at the bottom of the lake is, even on the hottest day, far higher than that of the surface. On September 24, at 8 a.m., 81° on the surface and 84° at a depth of 72 feet was obtained. No river enters and only one flows from it, which eventually empties itself into a tributary of the Cross River.

Before the sun sank, it caught the tops of the trees which ringed the far side, and turned their fresh green into a glory of russet and gold. As the glow faded, and we sat watching the shadows darkening round the quiet surface, a ring suddenly appeared near the centre of the lake but a little to the right This spread in our direction—a thin circle of mist—till it enclosed about one-eighth of the whole area. From that point it faded, spreading always outward, and growing fainter and fainter until quite swallowed up in the darkness. It had the appearance of steam rising from some giant cauldron.

After a while a splendid moon rose over Ijagham, turning its surface into a mirror of silver.

For much of the information contained in the foregoing account I am indebted to Dr Mansfeld, who also most kindly raised no objection to our visiting all that we wished to see of the Ekoi country under German rule.

We marched to Ekoneman by the way we had come, and thence over the 2,000-feet-high hills by Naretim to Mbabong.

For some reason or other the inhabitants of this place have earned, among their kinsfolk, much the same reputation as that of the Bœotians among the keener-witted Greeks around them. Endless stories, of the same character as the three following, have been invented at their expense :—

The Folly of the Mbabong.

By Ndum Agurimon of Nsan

I.

There was once a very handsome young man of Mbabong, who had an old mother. He was quite poor, but promised that when she died he would get a cow and kill it, that the people might eat, and honour her memory.

At the beginning of the year in which the death occurred, he made his farm close to the cave in which a buffalo lived. One day he went into the bush near by, to cut sticks, on which to train his yam vines. In the cave he saw the buffalo lying asleep, and went back quietly so as not to disturb it. He warned his wife not to make any noise when she went to the farm, lest she should frighten away the cow which Obassi had sent.

The wife was a good woman, so she carefully attended to this warning.

Not long after, the old mother died, and as soon as she had ceased to breathe, the son sent his wife to announce the death to the town.

When the people began gathering together for the mourning, the man took a rope and went toward his farm, saying that he was going to bring the cow for his mother's funeral feast. He tied the rope properly round his waist, made a slip knot in the other end, wide enough for the head of the cow to pass through, and laid the snare across the entrance of the cave. He then hid himself and set up a great shout. On hearing the noise, the buffalo dashed out. Over hill and dale she ran, through bush and river, dragging the poor Mbabong to a terrible death.

A wise man would have asked some strong men to go with him, to help hold the rope, or else would have made it fast to the trunk of a great tree. In either case he would have won the cow with hurrahs! On account of this folly, when we wish to express contempt of anyone, he or she is simply called "Mbabong."

II.

This second story is of another Mbabong man, who was also very ridiculously foolish

One day he stood watching a friend of his climb a palm tree by means of an " nded " loop. This is a rope used to climb trees with smooth straight trunks. First it is tied round the bole of the tree, but so loosely that though one side of the circle touches the trunk there is a space of about 3 feet between it and the other. The climber slips the loop over his head, and lets it fall to his waist. He then presses his feet against the tree, and his back against the rope Next he makes a short leap, raising the rope at the same time in both hands. A good " nded " climber will go up 2 feet at each leap.

The Mbabong man saw his friend climb the palm tree to the very top, and then give another long leap. At this the rope slipped, and the man fell dead on the ground below.

The second Mbabong could not think what had happened, and went to try for himself. As a good climber he went leaping up proudly, but gave the same unnecessary leap at the end, and also fell down dead.

Because of this it has become the proverb of the country—

" Mbabong agyut obi, echi ekin.
Mbabong climbs a palm, head half.
Akin mfong ngu, nkipp.
Dries cow - hide, flayed side downwards "

On our visit, my interpreter produced roars of laughter from his own countrymen, and embarrassment to the inhabitants of the town, by asking, with a would-be innocent air, to be shown the famous palm tree.

III.

A third Mbabong went hunting in the " bush." Almost as soon as he had left his town, he saw an antelope. He fired, and the beast fell dead, after running a little way. Although it lay motionless on the ground the man kept on firing at it, till a hunter from another town drew near, guided by the sound of the shots. The newcomer asked, "At what are you shooting?" On which Mbabong answered, "I shoot at the antelope which has fallen over there, and shall go on shooting till I have made it come over here to me."

The other man explained that this was impossible, as it was dead, but that, were it alive, it would run further away instead of coming near him. "If you ever happen to shoot another beast," said he, "I should advise you to run towards it, and not go on wasting shot in trying to force it to come near you."

Were they not foolish people in those days? We may hope that they have grown wiser now.

As the greater number of Mbabong, like many other Ekoi, have left their old homes in the Cameroons, and migrated to the Oban district, in order to avoid the poll-tax, imposed over the border, I venture to echo the pious aspiration of the narrator.

The people seemed simple and friendly, and, after a few sufferers had been given the various medicines which they came to beg, the inhabitants came out in crowds to ask for medicaments.

The town stands on the top of a hill, from which a splendid view can be obtained of the mountains to the south and south-west. From Babi, our next stopping place, the way, which is a mere hunter's track, led through the beautiful pass below Okuri Peak. In the course of this march, two hills, each over 2,000 feet high, were crossed. On the summit of the last was a small cleared space, called "Anwan Nsibidi,"—the place of cunning words. This name was given in the old slave-dealing days, when chiefs of the principal towns on each side met here to arrange a treaty, by which they mutually bound themselves not to raid one another's territory for the purpose of seizing captives to sell to the slave-dealers at Calabar.

At the next town, Mbinda, we bought the Eja fetish described on p. 76.

The town is surrounded by an amphitheatre of mountains, mist-wreathed and purple-tinted in the soft light of a late rain's sunset. Looking backward, the pass through which we had come could be clearly seen, a cleft in the surrounding wall.

We had been specially anxious to visit Okuri as, till recently, it had been a town of considerable importance and the home of many powerful Jujus. Thence it was, for instance, that Akpambe crossed the border to invade the Oban district. Dr. Mansfeld has described the elaborate decoration of the Egbo house, which was the largest in the whole countryside. Now only low mounds remain to show its original dimensions. Within these a smaller building is in process of construction, but of ornamentation there was no sign.

On the road, not far from Okuri, is a sad memento of the Ekoi struggle for independence. As we passed along we noticed a group of carriers who had laid down their loads, and were clustered in the shade of a great tree. They looked unusually sad, and down the cheeks of some great tears were rolling As we came up, one of them bent down and drew back the creepers from the base of the tree. Low on its trunk a round hole showed, made by the bullet which killed the chief of a neighbouring town. The latter was a near relative of some of our men, and, according to their story, had been shot because he first protested against his yams being taken without permission by the soldiers, and then tried to escape after being arrested. He was retaken, made to stand before the great tree, and shot by the officer in charge.

Night travelling is not popular among the Ekoi, but this road is specially shunned after sunset, through fear of the unquiet ghost which is thought to wander there.

We had already passed another sad memento of the struggle. Near to Ekoneman stands the tree from behind which Leutnant Queisz was shot in the breast in November, 1899. An echo of this tragedy was heard a few months ago, when the man who had fired the shot was caught and hanged. On the suppression of the rising he had fled, but, drawn by the yearning for home, had crept back later to his own town. For ten years he had dragged out a wretched existence, hidden in a hole in the ground, behind some boulders in the bush near by. His secret was faithfully kept till some accident revealed it to a native official, who, as in duty bound, reported it to the " white man." One would think that it would be almost a relief when the long agony of such an existence was over, and he paid with his own life for the life which he had taken.

The Original Home of Akpambe at Okuri.

Pass near Mbinda.

The period of the Ekoi struggle for independence was necessarily one of great suffering. How intense this must have been is shown by a fact related by Dr Mansfeld in his book " Urwald Dokumente," p. 21 :—

" Von mehreren Seiten," he says, " habe ich bestimmte Mitteilungen erhalten, dass die Mutter wahrend des Aufstandes fast alle Sauglinge getotet haben ; als Grund wurde mir angegeben dass die Sauglinge Stets den Soldaten Patrouillen durch ihr Geschrei, besonders bei Nacht, die Verstecke im Wald verrieten."

The Ekoi are such devoted parents that the idea of a mother killing the babe at her breast to ensure safety is almost inconceivable. Possibly the want of proper nourishment, combined with the necessity for constant trekking and hiding in the bush, entailed such hardships on the little ones, that the mothers killed them in pity for their sufferings, and in the firm belief that their spirits would return to earth as soon as all was peaceful once more.

Sad indeed is the description given by Dr. Mansfeld of the state of the country at the end of the war :—

" Trostlos war der Anblick, den das Land in Herbst 1904 machte : Uberall niedergebrannte Hutten ; die leeren Mauern dort, wo sie durch den Regen nicht eingesturzt waren, uberwuchert von allerlei Grasern, violetten und gelben Bluten und zahlreichen Schlingpflanzen. Die Wege fast unpassierbar, da sie ein Jahr lang nicht gereinigt waren. Die Farmen alle leer, keine Banane weit und breit zu kaufen ; kein Mensch, keine Ziege, kein Huhn zu erblicken ; geht man vom Lager aus auf Buschwegen auf die Suche nach Menschen, so trifft man auf einzelne bewohnte Stellen, die aus einem mit einem Mattendach uberdeckten, sonst aber ganz offenen Feuerherd bestehen, und aus dem in wilder Flucht Manner und Weiber mit ihren kleinen Kindern entlaufen."

CHAPTER XV

Along the Border

THE last of the German Ekoi are to be found at Ndebbiji Itaokui, an almost deserted village, tenanted by only two men.

Soon after re-entering British territory, as we were crossing a small river, a dark object was noticed swimming rapidly down stream. The carriers called out that it was a big fish, and begged me to shoot it. It was below the surface, but from the ripple I felt sure that it was no fish, but probably a monitor. A shot seemed likely to settle the question, and so it did, but in a way astonishing to all. The supposed fish sprang to the bank, and disappeared in a series of graceful bounds—a water chevrotain confessed.

This beautiful little antelope, so rare in most parts of the world that travellers are advised to forward skin and skull of every specimen procured to the Natural History Museum, is here so common that a drive is practically never arranged without securing at least two. It is strange that so small and graceful a creature should be, in some respects, intermediate between deer on the one hand, and camel and boar on the other.

I believe that we were the first Europeans fortunate enough to see a water chevrotain actually swimming beneath the surface, though Major Powell Cotton once saw one take to the water.

Along these roads, as everywhere in Ekoi land, stones about the size of the palm of the hand are to be seen, tightly wedged into the forks of small trees. Should a casual visitor chance to ask a native the reason for this, the latter will probably answer vaguely that someone has put them there to mark the place where he has hidden his kill, or where rubber vines are to be found, or maybe where he should return later to gather ripening fruits or nuts. When one has gained their confidence, however, through long dwelling amongst them, quite a different story is told.

When a man has occasion to go to a neighbouring town to

River Akwa Yafe.

visit a friend who is not expecting him, he picks up a medium-sized stone and presses it firmly into the fork of a tree on the right-hand side of the path. As he does so he says:

"Mbongi aiyipp (name of man sought is here inserted) akadji mfum,
Heart heavy   ,,   ,,   do not go anywhere,
ta nji mkpoi 'we.
till I go meet you."

The spirit of the stone then hastens on before, till it reaches the house of the man to be visited. Should the owner be within, it lies invisibly upon the threshold, thus blocking up the exit, and, all unknown to the inhabitant, keeping him a prisoner till the arrival of the man who has wrought the spell.

Sometimes, instead of stones, bare corn cobs may be seen, similarly held in the fork of a tree. For a long time when questioned as to the cause of this, the men answered with a shrug, "For no reason, Sar." At length one day someone, whose store of tobacco had run short, came up on the road, and, in the hope of thus earning a fresh supply, explained that the corn spirit gets very angry should even the bare core be left to rot on the ground. As this decays the body of the man who had discarded it would waste away also. In dread of such a fate the core is placed where, after rain has fallen, sun and air may dry it again, that it may be preserved for as long as possible. Subsequent inquiries proved the truth of this explanation.

The first town in British territory is Ako, which has already been described, but leaving this on the right, one can pass on to Okarara, where on our last visit the inhabitants were even more clamorous than most, on the subject of the bush-cow and elephant which were devouring their farms. On one occasion during our stay in the neighbourhood news was brought of the presence of a herd of six, which had grown so troublesome that the children feared to go down to fetch water or cut plantains.

A few minutes was enough to strike the trail, and after an hour or two's careful tracking the elephants were caught up in a little clearing, which was evidently one of their playgrounds.

A shot from a ·470 just at the tip of the ear laid one of them low. The other five crowded round, regardless of danger, and began stroking the dead beast with their trunks, uttering all the time a kind of mournful trumpeting.

The sight was too pitiful to permit of further destruction, but it was necessary to drive away the rest of the herd. A couple of shots fired just over their heads effected this, and soon afterwards the delighted townspeople arrived to take possession of the "beef."

The bush hereabouts is honeycombed by elephant roads, often far broader and more distinct than the little-used native paths. So clear are they at times that, on his way to visit us, Dr. Mansfeld followed one for several miles, under the impression that he was walking along the regular road. The whole stretch of land along the frontier indeed, by the rivers Awa and Akwa Yafe, forms a natural forest reserve, for it is all but uninhabited, and teems with animal life.

Near the falls of the Akwa Yafe, we were fortunate enough to happen on an interesting discovery.

Less than a mile from the bank, on the British shore, a bush path leads down a cup-like depression, at the bottom of which, in the wall-like side, looms a great cave. From the blackness within, countless bats shrill ceaselessly above the dull rush and boom of water, for just beyond the opening, two underground rivers join. Save for the heavy odour of swarms of bats, disturbed by our approach, the air was clear and pure, showing the presence of many openings. This system of vast underground halls and vaulted tunnels reaches for miles, in many cases with roofs smoothly curved as though hewn by the hand of man.

The caves are said to extend up to the first falls, but time did not permit of anything like thorough exploration. They are the property of the Ododop people, and much valued on account of the bats which inhabit them in vast numbers and are looked on as a delicacy.

The method of capture is as follows:—

At each known entrance stand men armed with long sticks, with which to strike down the escaping bats. The principal hunters then enter the caves, accompanied by lantern bearers, and carrying triangular nets fastened at the end of long poles.

Entrance to Underground Caves near Akwa Yafe River.

With these they sweep the roofs, enmeshing hundreds of the dusky denizens, and driving the rest toward the entrances.

When first disturbed, the din, caused by the screams of the startled bats, and the whirr of their thousand wings, was indescribable. Great clouds of them made for the exits, to fall, line after line, under the blows of the beaters outside. The sight of the strewn ground was hideous in the extreme, for half the wounded, writhing creatures bore young beneath the breast, and even in their death agony rolled over, in a last effort to protect them. Many too carried, in addition, young perched upon the back.

The Ododop, or, to use their own name, Korawp, are an interesting people. To quote Professor Keith's remarks, on measurements taken by me,* they represent "what Sir Harry Johnston has named the Forest-negro type. The stature is short, the arms long, the face, the head and the nose massive, but the head is proportionally long as in most of the Northern negro tribes." They appear particularly gentle in character, and the most careful enquiries failed to find any trace of cruel rites or customs.

On my second visit to their town, I was astonished to find that they had, on their own initiative, erected a little three-roomed Rest-house. This was the more good of them, as they were new arrivals from the Cameroons, and their own plantations were too young to supply palm leaves for the roof mats, every one of which therefore they had been forced to buy from the next town, Mfamosing.

Since the Rest-house had been built as a surprise for me, it was not possible to have any voice in the choice of site. A position right in the middle of the town had therefore been chosen, instead of, as in those fixed upon by me, at a sufficient distance to ensure quiet.

As ill-luck would have it, on our visit, my sister-in-law had developed malaria on the march, which caused a very bad headache.

Surrounded on all sides by bleating goats, screaming children, and the thousand and one noises of a crowded native town, it seemed useless to hope for the necessary quiet. A few minutes

* See Appendix C.

after I had explained the state of affairs to the Chief, however, a strange stillness seemed to settle over the town. The goats were led off to distant pens, but how silence could have been so successfully imposed on the usually noisy babies remains a mystery, while only the most sympathetic co-operation on the part of every inhabitant could have stilled the stir and bustle of everyday life

Just as we had started to go to the next town after our last visit to this tribe, the cords of my wife's hammock suddenly broke, and she was thrown out backwards, all the weight of her body falling on to her head, which struck the ground with such force as to stun her. At first I thought that her neck must be broken by the fall, but after a door had been unhinged and brought, she revived, and, strapped to this, was carried over the twelve-mile march to Mfamosing, in order to get at least that much nearer to a doctor, in case it should be necessary to summon one. A deputation of Korawp accompanied us the whole way, and spent the night away from home in order to make enquiries next morning. On learning that the injuries were not as grave as had been feared, the Head Chief made a charming little speech, expressing how great would have been the grief of his people had any grave mishap happened to their white visitor.

Ododop. The principal figure is a Buffalo Soul. The figure in the background is a Boar Soul.

CHAPTER XVI

Ordeal

Up to 1907, Mfamosing had been the scene of a veritable reign of terror under Chief Nenkui. The latter was a giant of a man, with a huge bull neck and the arms of a prize fighter—a good chief according to his lights, but so obsessed by the terror of witchcraft that every single person in the town was forced by him, at some time or other, to undergo trial by ordeal, in order to clear themselves from the suspicion of black magic. Many died from the tests imposed, others suffered horribly. He had killed two of his wives in this way, and forced his own children to take Esere. This is the most ordinary form of ordeal among the Ekoi. The bean itself is to be found in a wild state all over the District. The ordeal is practised by giving it ground up and mixed with water to the accused person, who must then drink the potion.

The superstition is that wizard or witch will die on drinking, but that no ill effect will be produced on innocent persons. As a matter of fact, should the bean have been boiled before the ordeal is tried, it will result only in intense pain, followed by vomiting. This, however, is a jealously guarded secret. Some natives assert that the danger varies in proportion to the quantity administered. Should either an under- or overdose be given it will only result in vomiting. The exact amount is known only to initiates.

The ordeal by boiling palm oil is far less dreaded. not only because its results were practically never fatal, but because the physical anguish entailed is acknowledged to be less intense than that produced by Esere.

When the surviving townsfolk of Mfamosing found that the "white man" was strong enough to protect them against Chief

Nenkui, they brought charge upon charge against him; and the following cases may be cited as typical :—

I.

Itagbo Arap of Mfamosing had reason to believe that his wife Ada was unfaithful to him. She acknowledged her fault in part, but he thought that she was still concealing something. He stated on oath:

"Nenkui said that the charm ought to be consulted in order to see if my wife had confessed all, so I told her to 'practise' with palm-oil We boiled the oil and brought coco-yam leaves, and laid them on the ground. Then we took the shell of a great snail (Achatina marginata), dipped it into the pot and poured boiling oil on the leaves. We knew that, if they should shrivel, it proved that the woman had lied. The leaves perished utterly, but the woman would not confess.

"Then she herself sent for some oil, and demanded that it should be tried in another way. A new pot was brought, and again we boiled the oil. When it was ready we told the palm-oil all about the affair, pointing to the woman. We put medicine in the pot. Fire caught it, the flames rose up, and we found that the palm-oil pronounced her guilty a second time. Still she would not confess properly.

"Then Nenkui shouted, 'Pour the oil on the hands of the woman'

"Ada stated: 'I was not willing that they should pour the boiling oil upon me, my heart trembled, and I grew weak with fear; but Nenkui shouted to me again and again to do it. So at length, in terror of him, I held out my hands. The oil burnt both my palms so fiercely that I could not endure the pain, and at last confessed all my fault.'"

II.

Bail Barine of Mfamosing stated on oath·

"My daughter Enok Eijuni was ill, and Chief Nenkui said that I had bewitched her. So I went to the Diviner and asked him to practise the charm. I sat down before the Juju and said, 'Ask if it is I, her mother, who is bewitching my child?' The charm answered that it was not I. On this I said to the Mboni, 'It is enough. You may take away the charm.'

"Nenkui said, 'Not so. I must know who is guilty.' So the Diviner was told to practise again. Nenkui asked if one of his own people had bewitched the girl, and the charm answered 'Yes.'

"Then the Chief said, 'All my people have undergone the ordeal except Obassi Nenkui, is it he?' The charm answered, 'It is he.'

"After this I went away, but a little later Nenkui came after me and said, 'I have been trying to find out about the accused, and he swears that he knows nothing of the matter.'"

Obassi Nenkui stated

"Chief Nenkui called me to have the charm practised. The Diviner said it was I who had bewitched the girl. On this the Chief told me to go to her mother, and ask for Esere. The woman said, 'It is not I who accuse you, but Nenkui.' I went back and told him this. He answered, 'If you are not guilty, why do you not go and eat Esere?'

"So I went into the bush and ate the bean. Afterwards I vomited. When I had grown well again I went home, for now no man could say that I was guilty."

"Afterwards," Bau continued, "I said to Nenkui, 'Since it is not Obassi who has bewitched my daughter, and since you accused me also, I myself will take Esere.'

"When day broke I did as I had said. Then I went to my daughter's room that I might die by her."

Enok Eijuni, the daughter, stated:

"Early in the morning I woke up and saw my mother lying by the fire in my room. She said, 'I have eaten Esere.' I sprang up to go to her, but just then a woman named Ndu Mojong came in, and asked what had happened. When she understood, she said to me, 'I will tend your mother. You yourself must not go near her, because you are about to bear a child, and it is not lawful that such an one should touch a woman who has eaten Esere.' Then she called other women to my mother's help, and they tended her till she grew well again."

III

Awo Mbu of Mfamosing stated on oath

"My son Okon Itagbo was sick at Mfamosing. I gathered together all that I had to sacrifice to the Juju, so that he might be made well again. One day Nenkui came to my room. He stood looking at me, and said:

"'You are a witch You are killing your son because you wish to give him as an offering to your witch company'

"I answered, 'I am no witch, but if I were I would beg my witch company to take me and spare my son.'

"Nenkui still said, 'I know that you are a witch. If you wish to prove that you are not bewitching your son you must eat Esere.' So I went to my town and did as he bade me, to show that it was not I who was harming my son."

IV.

Ngob Anyok of Mfamosing stated·

"I had two children, both of whom died. Chief Nenkui came to me, and said, 'Your mother was a witch. She took Esere and died You also are a witch, and have caused the death of your children.'

"I ate the Esere bean, so that, if I were a witch and had killed the children, I might die also, for I did not want to live if I had harmed my little ones This happened a long time ago, before Government came to Oban."

V.

Mojong Akpamit of Mfamosing stated on oath.

"Whenever a child was born to me it died Chief Nenkui came and said, 'Do you think that I do not know what you do? You are making a custom of bewitching your children. All those which you have had, you have killed already. Have a care that you do not destroy any more!' Five months later he came again and said, 'You have had another child, and that too has died. You have killed it like the others.' He called his daughter Njenamba, and said·

"'Do not go near this woman, else she will bewitch you also.'

"At daybreak therefore I took Esere and ate it in the bush My heart was clean, so it did me no harm."

VI.

Njenamba, daughter of Nenkui, stated on oath.

"My father accused me of witchcraft. One day while playing I touched his eye. He said, 'You are shutting my eye. You have shut one; now you can shut the other.' I said, 'What have I done to shut your eye?' He said, 'You have already shut one with your hand It pains me.' Therefore I went out and ate Esere Abassi Nenkui was present and heard."

Abassi Nenkui, sworn. "I heard Nenkui accuse Njenamba of witchcraft."

Njenamba stated further, "My father also swore Juju that if any man wanted to marry me the Juju should kill both me and my lover, unless the latter would pay 500 great logs of ebony, which was the dowry Nenkui himself gave before wedding my mother"

VII

The sister of Chief Nenkui, Makok of Mfamosing, stated on oath:

"I am the mother of Nse Nyo She had a little child, who died while her husband Okun Omin was in Calabar. When he came back and found that his boy was dead, he was very angry, and said that it was I who had bewitched the child He proclaimed before all the people, 'I will not believe that Makok has not killed my son, unless she will swear before a powerful Juju like Mfam or Ofiri.'

"They brought in the Oka Juju. I blew pepper-corns seven times towards the Oka. Then the owner of the Juju took the Oka knife and pointed it at my breast, crying 'Swear before the Juju that you will tell the truth in this affair.'

"I answered, 'I call upon you, Oka If it is I who have killed the child, or if I possess any animal, or other witchcraft within my body, may you catch me, O Oka!' Then gunpowder was laid on the big knife of Oka. The owner of the Juju held it beneath my breasts and put fire upon the powder. There was a great explosion, but I remained unhurt. Next, palm wine was brought and given me to drink. After I had drunk, the owner of the Juju said, 'If Oka catches her, I will not remove the curse unless one cow is given to me as payment.'"

Okun Omin stated, "I did not force her to swear the Juju. She herself wished to do so. She had sworn Juju against my wife that if the latter had a child it should be a girl, or if a boy it should die. Chief Nenkui told me this. She also used witchcraft, so that, when her daughter bore a babe, the milk might dry up within the breast.

"Next my wife grew sick, and I practised the charm for her. It answered that the ghosts had caught her. My babe was dead, and the townsfolk taunted me and said, 'Goats have kids and fowls chicks, but you are a childless man.' So I called a meeting and asked what I should do. Nenkui stood up and said.

"'About thirty children have died in my town. You must eat Esere to prove that it is not you who have killed them.'

"I went back home and said to Makok, 'Your brother, Chief Nenkui, has ordered me to eat Esere.' She answered, 'There is some in the basket.' So I put in my hand and took it out. My wife ground it for me, and put it into a calabash. I drank it, but it did not kill me, so I was pronounced guiltless."

* * * * *

These are but a few of the stories told by survivors. Of the far more terrible cases, in which countless victims died, no trustworthy information was forthcoming. As a result of the trial Nenkui was condemned to four years' imprisonment at Calabar.

His family consider him as dead. The part of his compound once sacred to his use is left unrepaired. Sun, wind and rain have faded the bright colourings of his mural paintings. Many of his carved pillars lie rotting on the ground, while others lean at a perilous angle. The roof has fallen in. Only the Juju tree still flourishes amid the ruins, like the promise of new life springing from the wreckage of the old.

ORDEAL

Another form of ordeal is by pepper inserted in the eyes. Should this produce no injury the accused is declared innocent.

Nenkui's Deserted Compound.

If inflammation sets in he is thought guilty. Very often the pain induces confession.

This ordeal was tried in the case of Ndifon of Ndebbiji, who was accused of having shot a fellow townsman in the bush.

After leaving Mfamosing, the road next leads through the old site of Abbiati, a town which was deserted nearly two years ago, because a half-witted woman in quarrelling with her husband threw salt upon the ground and cried, "So may God do with you all." In order to avoid this curse, the whole town fled into the bush, and has never gathered together again. So rapidly does the vegetation grow up and efface all signs of human habitation, that hardly a trace is now left to show that a town once stood here.

Before the site of the old Egbo house stands a hexagonal stone, about 6 feet above the ground, and, the natives assert, almost as much below it. The inhabitants of Abbiati, while searching for a site for their town, came upon this carved stone and took it as an indication that they should settle in that spot.

It was then raised up before their Egbo house, painted with black and white circles, called the stone of Nimm, and sacrifices were offered before it as the guardian of the town.

Many such stones lie buried in the bush, and when discovered are objects of great reverence to the Ekoi. Even those who have been educated in Government schools insist that all such stones are the work of Obassi alone, and that no man has carved them. Yet they are clearly cut, not split by fire, and show the presence of some old race to whom stone shaping was well known. No legend of such a race can be found, though this is, after all, natural, as the Ekoi themselves only arrived to take possession of the country a few hundred years ago.

Each Egbo house has one of these cut stones called "Etai Ngbe" or "Leopard Stone," erected before the second pillar, and we ourselves have come across countless examples in the bush. From some of these sharp angles have been cut out, seemingly for the insertion of corresponding ones protruding from other blocks, roughly in the manner of Inca masonry. Many stones show merely natural fractures, to be expected among the gneiss and granite of the District, but a careful examination shows that all could not be accounted for in this manner.

The subject has great fascination, and a closer study seems to point to the possibility of a Carthaginian origin. When the latter people circumnavigated Africa in their small coasting ships, it is improbable that they would have passed by the Calabar River, one of the best natural harbours on the coast, without putting in for shelter, refitting, or provisions. In such a case it is easy to surmise that some of the crew should have remained behind, either as a small colony or as captives or deserters.

Sexagonal Stone Dedicated to Nnim. Amovrr.

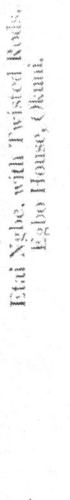

Etai Ngbe. Mkvort.

Etai Ngbe, with Twisted Rods. Egbo House, Okuni.

This might account for the strongly Phœnician types sometimes to be met, as also the presence of articles occasionally disinterred, which seem to show a Mediterranean origin. A small object, made from a mixture of copper and brass, looped as if for a pendant, and with delicate spiral ornamentation. was found by me near Aking When shown to one of the greatest authorities in Europe, it was at once pronounced by him to be the work of some early Mediterranean civilisation, though, on its place of discovery being disclosed, the trained eye of the connoisseur detected indications of a nearer and less interesting origin.

CHAPTER XVII

DIVINATION

This practice, which among the Ekoi is called "Ebu,"* or by the older title "Efa," but is more generally known to Europeans under its Efik name "Idiong," is in very general use. Almost all questions are referred to the Diviner (Mboni), and answered by him after consulting the charm, which consists of two pairs of strings, each composed of four "Osing" shells. These are laid side by side on either hand of the Diviner. Those on the right are supposed to be male and on the left female. Each pair must "confirm" the other, by falling in exactly the reverse manner. If the pairs do not agree, everything must be begun again, and should the question be at all important, it is often repeated several times.

A man who wishes to qualify as a Diviner (Mboni) must first learn how the charm (Ebu) makes its communications. He then goes to an old Diviner, and asks him to "confirm" the power. This is done by gathering leaves and bark from various Juju trees. The old man chews these and spits out small quantities into the shells. The aspirant then takes the latter, and places them high up in the roof-thatch, that they may listen to Obassi Osaw and talk with him. After a while they are taken down and carried outside the town, to a place where cross-roads meet, and there buried, to talk with the ghosts, and with Obassi Nsi. After a few days the strings are dug up again, and the man starts practice as a full-fledged "Mboni."

Osing shells are the dried covering of the seeds of the Osing tree, which in itself is sacred; but they cannot be used for purposes of divination until an elephant has taken the ripe fruit into his mouth and then ejected the seeds. These are

* Compare Ebo, the Bini name for minor deities.

DIVINATION

afterwards split open, and the half shells strung together as described.

Other objects, always spread out before the magician, are—First, the egg of a bush fowl. It is thought that this bird calls up the dawn each morning,* so the Diviner holds up its egg, pointing toward the sun, and prays "As the bush fowl cries for the light, so may light be shed on what we wish to know." Secondly, a quill and tail of a porcupine are held up, because in all legends Porcupine is the great diviner. White chalk is laid out to bring good luck, and a boar's tooth is used, like Neapolitan coral, to ward off evil influences from the questioner. After having been held out towards the latter, the shells are touched with it, one after another.

The small horns usually to be seen are those of Ise, the blue duikerbok, because it is looked upon as the ally of magicians, and is thought, like the dog, to have "four eyes," *i.e.*, to be able to see by night as well as day, and to recognise ghosts, witches, and all such uncanny beings, when they pass invisible to human eyes.

The shells composing the four strings are naturally capable of falling in almost innumerable combinations, and, as a consequence, an expert Mboni has an extensive system on which to work.

As an example of the vocabulary used—

One shell turned upward and all the rest downward means a young man.
Two shells   ,,   ,,   ,,   mean water.
Three ,,   ,,   ,,   ,,   ,, food.
Four   ,,   ,,   ,,   ,,   ,, sickness.

* See story, p. 384.

An instance of consulting the charm was observed at Ndingane in 1907, when a sick woman went to inquire the cause of her illness. After the preliminaries described above, the Mboni called to Ebu:

"Wake up"
A "We are awake"
Q "Why does the woman call you?"
A "Because she is sick"
Q "What is the matter with her?"
A "Something bad has caught her"
Q "What has caught her? Ghosts, Juju, or witchcraft?"
A "A noise has caught her."

(If ghosts quarrel near a person, some sickness "catches" the latter unless sacrifices be made.)

This answer was contradicted by the second hand; so the query had to be repeated. The next answer was a laugh of ridicule, and the questions had to be started again from the beginning.

Q "Is it witchcraft?"
A. "No."
Q "Is it Juju?"
A "No"
Q. "Is it ghosts?"
A "Yes."
Q. "Is it mother's ancestors or father's ancestors?"
A "Mother's family'
Q "Man?"
A "No"
Q. "Woman?"
A "Yes"

All the names of female ancestors on the mother's side were then called, till the charm signified which of them had caused the sickness.

Q. "What does the ghost want?"
A. "Libations."
Q "Anything else?"
A. "Yes Food sacrifices"

The inquirer then proceeded to make a round basket of palm leaves. In this she put some palm wine, together with a small quantity of rum. She then went before the town and put the basket down on the ground, as is usual for the ghosts. Sometimes, however, the offering is placed on poles, which is always done when the sacrifice is made to Obassi Osaw. She called on the ghosts and said: "Here is drink and food"; then poured out the libation on the ground, and said "Here is what you asked of me. Do not let me be sick any more."

After that she paid the usual fee to the diviner, 3d. in kind and 3d. in money, and then returned home.

The spirit of Osing, which inhabits all Osing trees, gives the power of divination to the shells "Akparhe Osing." In the beginning, the tree itself had the power of talking to human beings, but lost it in the way related below.—

Why Osing Tree can no longer Speak to Men save by the Charm.

In the beginning of all things, both Ojje (Witchcraft) and Osing (the Spirit of the Osing tree) used to live with Obassi Osaw, and accompany him wheresoever he went.

One day Obassi disguised himself like a man, and journeyed through the length and breadth of the earth, to see how people were faring In course of time he came, with his two companions, to the place where a peasant was cutting bush for his farm.

Obassi asked what he was doing, and how many people there were in that place. The man answered that there was only one other beside himself, that he was making a farm, and next year was going to clear a larger space, adjoining that on which he was now working.

Obassi bade "goodbye" to him, and went on to the second man, of whom he asked the same questions. This latter answered that there were two of them, and that, God willing, he hoped to continue his work next year.

Now Osing stood near and heard both replies. Afterwards he went back to the first man and told him how foolishly he had spoken, and how wise was the second man in saying "If God wills" before anything he intended to do; for the questioner was Obassi himself, who greatly disliked over-free and presumptuous speech.

The first man took the lesson to heart, and next time Obassi came in disguise to question him, he answered, modestly enough, that he hoped to extend his farm if God were willing.

Now Obassi saw at once that this change of speech was due to Osing, who had thus taught the man how to draw down a blessing upon his future projects.

If Osing had continued to tell such secrets, men would have learnt all those things which are able to bring trouble or danger upon them, and at last be freed even from death itself. So Obassi ordained that Osing should no longer be able to talk unrestrainedly. Yet he allowed him to communicate with men when the hard shells of his seeds had been made into a practising charm. Now the fruits of this tree are edible and something like mangoes. Diviners collect the seed shells, and through them Osing can still speak, and give answer as to whether accused persons are innocent or guilty, and on many other subjects. When the charm is proclaimed in this way it is given the name of "Efa," or "Idiong."

Thus Osing lost his right to be the companion of Obassi Osaw, and also the advantage of speaking freely with whomsoever he chose. Had he been left to do so as before, we should by now have learnt how to avoid the consequences of wrongdoing, sickness, trouble and even death.

Ojje, on the contrary, told no secrets, but kept them all hidden in his breast. Therefore, he was not driven away from the fellowship of Obassi Osaw, and can communicate as he chooses with his evil followers, both witch and wizard.

Another story gives the following explanation:—

WHY "OSING" MAY ONLY SPEAK THROUGH THE CHARM.

There was once a town in which all the inhabitants were rich save one, who had lost the goods which his father had left him. So poor was he that neither he nor his wife had anything to eat.

One day the people of the town were holding a feast for the dead. Now, when the poor man was young, his father had paid the necessary price for him to become a member of the Egbo Club. So he went to join the play like all the rest, but the people called out, "You are too poorly dressed; you cannot join in our celebration," and drove him away.

It was evening time, so he went to his house and slept, but at daybreak he went into the bush to hunt. All day long he followed the bush tracks, but found nothing, and at length, as twilight fell, returned hungry and sad to his town. As he neared it, he heard voices in the darkness. He walked very softly, and found that seven ghosts were talking together before a small hut. He went behind this, and watched the ghosts. Each of them held in his hand a calabash containing a black Juju, which they rubbed on their faces, saying, " May this make me invisible." Then each hung up his calabash on the wall of the little house, and went into the town.

When the seven were out of sight, the man crept into the house, and took down one of the calabashes. He poured some of the black Juju on to his hand, smeared his face, and said the same words which he had overheard from the ghosts. Then he took the calabash to his home, left it there, and went on to the place where they were playing for the dead. There he saw all the people feasting, and the ghosts feasting with them. The others did not know that the ghosts were there, but the poor man knew it, for he had used their Juju and therefore could see them.

One of the richest men in the town stood up and served out much food. He then poured out rum into a glass. One of the ghosts was about to drink the essence of the spirit, but the poor man stretched out his hand and said, "Stop, do not touch it"

The ghost stopped still, and for the rest of the feast the poor man prevented any of them from eating or drinking with the living. The ghosts said within themselves, " What can be the matter? Someone is preventing us from eating with the living as we used to do."

Before dawn broke, the ghosts had to go back to their own place. When they reached the small house, the Head-man said, "We have left our Jujus here. Let us take them away with us." Then all but one took down his calabash from the wall. The one whose Juju was missing cried out very loudly, and the poor man, who had followed them all the time, came forward and said, " It is I who took your Juju." The ghost said, " Go, and bring it to me." The man did so, and then the ghost continued, "Now go and get me another calabash."

This was done, and the ghost made the same Juju for him and said, "Take it home with you, but allow no one to touch it; for if anyone should do so, it will run away from you, and you will die. Listen carefully, and I will tell you what to do. Hang it up in a room in your house, and fasten the door. The first day when you enter you will find that it has given you fine clothes to wear, and after that it will give you all that you need till you become very rich."

The poor man gladly did as he was bidden, and next day opened the door. There within he found a great piece of very fine cloth. He cut off as much as he needed, and tied it round him.

When his wife came back from farm she said, "Where did you get that cloth? I have never seen any so fine." The husband answered, "It is a gift from the Egbo."

The wife thought "I should like to know whence such a beautiful thing came." She watched till the man went down to the spring to bathe, and no sooner was he out of sight than she opened the door of the room where the Juju was kept. When she saw it, she stretched out her hand, but no sooner did she lay so much as a finger upon it, than it sprang up, and floated out of the door, back to the ghosts. At the same time she felt a stinging pain, like that of a lash, curling round her body.

When the husband returned, he saw that his wife had a great cut across back and breast. He asked her "How did you get this mark?" She answered, "It is your Juju that flogged me."

Her husband said, "You have killed me, for the rule of that Juju is that no one may touch it, save the owner."

He went into his room, and sent for his brother. When the latter came, he said, "My wife has killed me, for she touched my Juju."

Then he made a coffin and lined it with the fine cloth which he had got from the magic calabash. When all was ready, he lay down within it and died.

His brother called a meeting of the townsfolk and said, "This woman caused the death of her husband, so I ask that she should die too."

The meeting called the woman before them and asked her, "Have you anything to say about the death of your husband?"

She answered, "Yes, for since he brought the Juju home, he never told me about the rule that none may touch it."

The brother said, "In spite of this, the woman must hang"; but Osing tree, which stood near the house, shouted out, "The woman shall not hang. If anyone die by accident, it cannot be helped."

Obassi Osaw heard all that passed. He came down and stood among the people. He held up his right hand, and said to the Osing tree, "Because you give judgment without being asked, from to-day you shall no longer be able to speak whenever you choose, but only through the shells of your seeds when they are used to practise the charm."

In animal stories, when any beast is in trouble he goes to Porcupine to find out the cause. Sometimes men also consult her, as has already been mentioned. This will be seen again from the following three tales:—

I.

Porcupine Witch.

By Itamfum of Oban

Once the women of a town arranged among themselves to choose a day on which they would all go to catch fish. This they do by throwing a great number of Adhatoda leaves into a place which they have prepared in the river. The juice of the leaves stupefies the fish as they pass through the water, so that they rise and float on the surface, where the women catch them.

On this occasion, though many leaves had been collected and thrown into the river, no fish rose.

After awhile, a great crocodile was seen eating up all the leaves, and so preventing them from harming the fish.

The women went back to their town. When they got there they went to Porcupine, and asked her to practise the charm to find out who it was who sent the crocodile.

Porcupine said, "It is the Head Chief of the town, who

lay there in that guise. All of you go to him and ask why you might not poison the fish."

They went, as the Diviner had ordered, and the Chief said, "It is true that it is I who possess this witchcraft. In the shape of a crocodile I protect the river. The reason why you could catch nothing is that you went without permission to fish in my stream. For the future women shall not go alone to poison the fish. Men and women can both go. Women, you are not strong enough to do this alone. Arrange it among yourselves."

The women explained the new order to the men. All went into the bush, gathered leaves, and brought them to the Head Chief. The latter said:

"You have not brought enough." So they went again, and gathered still more, till he said:

"That will do."

Then all set out gaily, both men and women. They spent three nights in the bush, gathering fish, till they had caught a great quantity, when they retured home.

Each gave one fish as a "Dash" to the Chief, but no one gave any to Porcupine, who was the priestess of the charm.

The latter therefore went to the Head Woman, and asked for her share of the catch.

They refused to give any, whereon she said, "Very well." She then announced to the townsfolk, "The charm shall be practised for none of you any more."

On this they were afraid, and answered, "When any woman conceives, she must practise the charm."

At the same moment one of them conceived. She went to Porcupine and asked her to practise the charm.

At first Porcupine refused, but all the townsfolk begged her most earnestly to take pity on the woman They brought yams and palm oil, and promised to go out and get plenty of fish. So Porcupine at last consented.

After the woman's child was born, and she had grown strong again, she went fishing by herself, and brought all that she caught to Porcupine.

The latter was very pleased, and announced, "I remove the law I made. All priests may practise the charm as usual."

DIVINATION

This is the reason why when a native woman conceives, she goes to the "Mboni" to practise the charm for her.

II.

How Obassi Drove Forth His Unloved Wife.

Before Obassi Osaw left the earth, he married many wives. Two of these he loved, but the others he did not care for. One day one of his favourite wives saw a woman weeping in the compound. "What is your trouble?" she asked, and the woman answered, "I weep because I am the wife of Obassi, yet I may never come near to my Lord."

The favourite wife had pity on her, and at night led her privately into their husband's chamber.

Some months later, Obassi chanced to pass by this woman, as she sat working, and saw what had befallen her. He thought she had been guilty of unfaithfulness, and therefore ordered her to be driven away from the town.

The woman fled into the bush, and there her child was born. For several years they dwelt together, till the boy grew tall and strong.

One day the people of Obassi set out to cut "bush" for new farms. While doing this, they saw a boy coming, and said to their master, "This youth is very like you." They roasted yams and offered them to the new arrival, but he said:

"I cannot eat the food of Obassi, neither can my mother, because he drove her away without cause."

Another day the woman also came to visit them, and, on seeing her, the second of the favourite wives approached her husband and said, "Here is the woman whom you turned out of your compound. Her son is named Effion Obassi."

Obassi caught his discarded wife, and handed her over to the people that they might put her to death, but Effion stood forth and said.

"I want to know why you wish to kill my mother."

The wife who had at first befriended her also said:

"Why should the woman be killed? What is the name of her son?" and they answered, "He is called Effion Obassi."

This wife went to her husband and said: "It is I who

have deceived you. I brought the woman to your room in my place in the night time, and her son is yours."

No sooner did Obassi hear this, than he ordered his people to build a house for his discarded wife, and allowed her to dwell there with the boy.

One day the sons of Obassi were sent to market to buy and sell. All of them made unprofitable bargains save Effion only, who did well. From that time he was entrusted with the disposal of all merchandise.

Once he was preparing to set out for market as usual, when his father called to him and said, "The time draws near when I must leave the earth If you should see a fresh leaf fall down before you on the road, or in the market place, you will know that I am dead."

Effion left home and, in time, reached the town where the market was held. While he bought and sold, a leaf fluttered down, and fell at his feet. At once he left his business and hastened home, but alas! his father was already dead.

After the funeral, Effion wanted to enter the place where the treasure was kept, but his half-brothers prevented him. On this he went to Porcupine, who was a witch, and ask her to practise the charm for him, to find out what he should do in order to gain some of the goods of his late father.

Porcupine said, "On your way back, you will meet a man who is covered with sores. Follow him and he will tell you what to do."

He met the man, who led him along a road which passed the foot of a hill. There he saw a bell hanging The man said, "Presently some people will come down from the top of the hill. They will ring the bell, and then take up the loads which are awaiting them. These they will carry back whence they came, and you must follow."

Effion did as he was advised, and followed till he had climbed a long way. Then he saw all the people enter a large house. He too went in, and saw someone lying by the hearth. Effion bent down and held out his hands towards him, touching the ground with his fingers. The man was Obassi. He arose and looked and knew the lad for his son, and bade him wait for one night.

At daybreak Obassi ordered all the people to go out hunting, but Effion he kept in the house. When they were alone he took the boy, and opened the door of his treasure house. As they entered, one of the boxes shouted, "Whom do you bring?" Obassi answered "My son."

On this the box opened of itself and all kinds of food poured out. The boy ate till he was satisfied, for he was very hungry.

Then Obassi got some "medicine" and rubbed on the boy's eyes. At this the room faded from sight, and, when Effion looked round him, he saw that he was standing on a grave, but in his arms he held the magic box.

He saw people coming towards him, and ran inside the bush to hide his treasure, for his father had said that he must tell no one of his secret, else he would be able to get nothing from it save with much trouble.

After he had gone a long way, he sat down and rested. No one was in sight, so he called to the box. It opened and within it he found yams, ready for planting. He called again, and from it stepped, one after the other, a long line of slaves. These set to work, built a town, laid out farms and planted them with everything that was necessary for food. After this, troops of sheep, goats and cattle appeared from the box.

When all was finished, Effion went back to the town where his mother dwelt. He brought her with him, together with his brothers and sisters. When they arrived he made a great feast for them, and "dashed" them very fine linen. They said that they never wished to go back, but would always dwell there with him.

After a time he made a great play for the death of his father. To this he invited all nations on earth, but, great as was the number of those who came, the box provided enough for all, both of meat and drink.

Like his father, the youth married many wives, but he also cared for only two of them. One day he brought a present to the wife he loved best of all, but she refused it. Soon after this he left home to go to a far town, but, before setting out, gave the key of his treasure house to his eldest son.

One day the mother of the boy took the key while he slept, and opened the store house. As she entered, the magic box shouted, "Who are you?" and she answered:

"I am the wife of Effion Obassi." Then the box opened and a piece of very fine cloth fluttered out, and hung upon her hand.

Now Effion was a long way off, but at that same moment he knew within himself what had happened between his wife and the box.

At once he hurried homeward, and entered the treasure house. He asked the box "What sacrifices must I offer to you so that you may be to me as before?"

The box answered, "Send to the bush, cut down a great tree, and fashion it like a canoe." This Effion did, and when all was ready, the box said:

"Carry me down to the river-side, and place me within the canoe."

This was also done, and Effion himself embarked. The box said "Sit down," and he sat down. Then it said "Pull at right hand, pull at left hand." He paddled for some hours, as far as from Ekoi land to Calabar.

When the people saw a man with a great box approaching their town, they made a sacrifice of white cloth and young palm leaves in token of peace, and offered it at the landing place

Then Box said to his master, "You may not leave this place any more. We must stop here for ever."

III.

THE MAGIC FISH.

BY IDEM MBAIFONGE OF AKO.

Three girls once went down to the river to gather snails One of them saw a small black fish named Mbonne, in the water. She caught it, and brought it back to the place where her companions were bathing. As she showed it to them, it fell from her hand and slipped under the edge of some great stones, which stood half in and half out of the water. The girl dived after the fish, but did not reappear.

When her two companions saw that she did not come back they went to the town, and told her parents.

Not long afterwards, a man, who was building a house, went into the bush to cut tie-tie, for binding the roof-ribs together. As he walked by the river-side, he saw some tie-tie lying on the stones. He pulled at it, and, as he did so, heard the girl's voice from the water beneath. At once he went home and told her parents, "I heard your daughter's voice beneath the stone." They followed him to the place, and offered a sacrifice. When this was ended, the girl came up, with the fish in her hand. The parents said, "Let us go home," but she answered, "You go; I will come in a little time."

When she reached her father's house, they gave her chop. She took it, and went down to the river to eat with the fish to whom she gave some of all she had.

At evening time again, the same thing happened, and dawn saw her once more by the stones with her morning's meal. She struck her hand on the fish as she fed him, and said, "Grow as big as my father's goats." Next day she came and did as before, but this time she said "Grow to the size of my father's cows," and again on the third day, "Do not cease growing till you become as big as the elephants."

One day some people watched her, and came to her parents and said, "Your daughter is accustomed to eat with the fish." So when she came home again her father said.

"To-day you will go to the market." The girl answered, "I will not go."

He replied, "It is my order, and in spite of everything you shall be sent."

She answered, "If it must be, it must; nevertheless some bad thing will happen—perhaps I may die."

This time she cooked chop herself, and went and ate it with the fish. She told him "To-day I go to market. Should anyone come and call you, do not answer. If they kill you, your blood will call and let me know."

That evening, after she had set out for the town whither she was sent, her small sister took chop alongside the river, sang to the fish, and called him, "Mbonne, Mbonne, come out to me." This she did, so that she might kill him. He would not answer, so she ate alone, and returned home

Next day she went again with several people, who surrounded the stone. She sang more sweetly than before, and this time the fish came out. No sooner did it appear above the stone, than one of the men killed it.

The blood flew up to a cotton tree which stood near, and thence a little stream ran till it reached the feet of the owner of the fish. So the girl knew that her fish was dead. She scooped up a little of the blood, and put it in a small calabash. Then she went on, as far as from here to Ndebbiji.

The people saw her coming with the calabash of blood in her hands, and asked:

"Has your father killed any elephant?" She said, "Whether or not, I have eaten nothing of his kill"

Next she went on so far as to Owam, where the people asked her the same question, to which she replied as before. At each town the same thing happened, and at length she arrived at her home.

As she returned her parents saluted her, but she said:

"I do not want any welcome."

She got some Juju leaves, and mixed them with the blood. Then she went down to the river, and with the mixture smeared a palm tree which grew near by. At daybreak she asked her father to go with her to the water. When she had reached the place, she begged him to climb up the palm tree and gather her some clusters of kernels. He did so, but no sooner had he climbed to the top, than she called to the palm tree "Grow up," and at once it grew so high, that her father fell down and died. She hid his body, and went back to the house.

Next she asked her mother to go with her to the river. When they got there, she made the same magic, and her mother died also.

She returned home, but there was no fire on the hearth, so she went to the house of some neighbours and begged that they would give her a lighted brand. They, however, drove her away and said, "It is you who have killed your father and your mother."

After this the girl went from door to door begging for fire, but all the townsfolk said the same thing, and at length drove her forth into the bush.

Then she grew afraid because of what she had done, and went to Porcupine, to beg her to practise the charm.

Porcupine said "Get yam and palm-oil and bring to me."

This the girl did, and Porcupine said further, "Now I will show you a magic medicine, which will bring your parents to life again."

The girl did all that Porcupine had told her. She made the medicine and rubbed it over the bodies of her father and mother, so that they were cured of the hurt of their fall, and stood up alive. Then all returned home together, and the neighbours brought brands and relit the fire on the hearth.

Some of the medicine with which she had cured her parents remained over. This she threw away on the rubbish heap.

Now hawk had watched all the time, when the girl went to consult Porcupine, and again when she made the medicine, and brought her parents to life. That is the reason why you often see a hawk circling round and round over a rubbish heap, because he wants to get the medicine which the girl threw away, so that, if his parents die, he also may be able to bring them to life again.

The last paragraph is really a separate story, entitled "Why hawks haunt rubbish heaps." The narrator, however, joined it to the last story in the way given above.

CHAPTER XVIII

OJJE OR WITCHCRAFT

It is perhaps during long "bush" tours that one comes nearest of all to understanding forest folk such as the Ekoi.

During the night, when the voices of the tired carriers have at last died down, and one lies awake, listening to the myriad sounds of Africa the sleepless, one is aware of a soft undercurrent, the murmur of countless streams, rippling over pebbly beds, the far-off splash of little cascades leaping from rock to rock, the gentle rustle of encircling leaves, or the sleepy chirp of the cricket and its even smaller brethren—"The manifold soft chimes, that fill the haunted" vastness of the African night. Against this restful undercurrent, sound, with startling distinctness, the harsh cries of night jars, the howl of a leopard, or the scream of a giant cicada, as yet unnamed, close to one's ear. This latter sound almost invariably makes the newcomer spring up to search around, so like is it to the cry of a child in pain.

The camp clearing is often as much as 100 feet by 50 feet, but the great branches still arch high above one, shutting off all but the merest glimpse of blue sky beyond.

In the whole land there are no open spaces, save those which have been cleared as sites for villages or farms. The heavenly bodies play but little part in the life of the race, for, as one of the men remarked, " Ekoi people do not trouble themselves about the stars, because the trees always hide them." Very few have distinctive names. Among these are:

Nkai Okott 'Mi.   The woman of the moon's love (Venus).
Nkai Nkokk Obassi.   The hen of Obassi (Aldebaran).
Aati Ikang Aiyu.   The yam rack (the girdle of Orion).
Nkokk Abonn.   The hen's chicks (Pleiades).

Besides these, none seem to have particular significance.

To those of us whose interests are to a large extent geographical and botanical, the study of the part played by the land itself in moulding the character of its people must appeal in a special degree, and it is the all-enfolding mysterious bush that, more than any other influence, has formed the Ekoi. To this they owe that leucocholy which lies deep down beneath the surface gaiety of their natures, and makes the dread of the unknown the dominant note of their lives.

The bush, with its soft green twilight, its dark shadows and quivering lights, is peopled by many terrors, but among these that of Ojje reigns supreme. Some people, indeed, believe that there are good Jujus which are stronger, but many think that none but Obassi himself can give protection against this dread, which walks by day or night, and may manifest itself in the least suspected ways. Mother, sister, or sweetheart may be witches in disguise. The bird which flies in at your open door in the sunshine, the bat which circles round your house at twilight, the small bush beasts which cross your path while hunting,—all may be familiars of witch or wizard, or even the latter themselves, disguised to do you hurt In this world of magic, shape-shifting is an everyday occurrence, and it seems scarce harder of belief that a man should be able to change into leopard or crocodile than that tiny flowers, no bigger than a pin-head, should become huge fruits, hanging from tree and liane, ready to fall on, and stun, the passer-by. To those who know the depths of virgin forests—with their strange solitudes, filled by the thousand unexplainable sounds, which together make up one vast silence—such beliefs seem not only natural but inevitable.

Witchcraft and all bad Jujus are thought to have been sent to earth by Obassi Osaw, while the good ones came from Obassi Nsi. Sometimes people pray to the latter to destroy Ojje, for it is well known that no witchcraft can stand against his might.

A case which came before the Native Court on January 5, 1909, shows how the smallest event is sometimes thought to have been caused by supernatural agency.

On being questioned as to why she took Esere bean, a woman, named Awaka, stated:

"One day when I sat alone in my house, a white bird flew

in. When my husband Atean returned I told him about it. He said:

"'Perhaps someone wants to destroy my Juju.'

"At evening time, he sent to call the man who practised the charm, and asked him to find out whether a ghost or living person had sent the bird.

"The Diviner decided that a living person had sent it to try to injure the Juju. At that time we were three women within the compound, but the men remained outside.

"First Iamba was called before the charm, and it was asked if she were guilty. It answered 'No.' Next the second woman was called, with the same result. Lastly the Diviner called my name, and I also was pronounced guiltless.

"After some time I asked, 'Have you got the person?' and Mboni answered 'Not yet.'

"From that day my husband gave me no part of the animals which he killed in the hunt. I was vexed and went into the bush and ate Esere, because my name had been called before the charm. I took the bean to prove that I was guiltless of witchcraft, and had nothing to do with the coming of the white bird."

Those possessed by Ojje have a power which warns them of the approach of others similarly possessed, as the magic knife in the girdle of the king's daughter rang on the coming of Weland.

Should witch or wizard wish to kill a man, they gather together at night time in front of the town, and dance, not upon the ground, but a few feet above. While dancing they often grow to giant size. No noise can be heard, and they are invisible to all who have not the "four eyes."

E. E. Offiong, one of the best-known chiefs of Calabar, claims to have the power of witnessing these witches' revels. He says that he has often seen them dancing in the moonlight, and that after looking on for a long time one night, he went next day to each of the men and women whom he had recognised, and forced them to confess that they were possessed by Ojje.

Perhaps the most terrible power held by witch or wizard is that of "sucking out the heart" of a man without his

River Scene, Ekoiland.

knowledge. They can sit on the roof of the house at night and suck out the heart while he sleeps, and, without the aid of some strong Juju, he will never know what is killing him. A man wasting away from consumption or Beri-beri, is usually thought to have been bewitched in this way.

When the witch knows that her victim's last hour draws near, she sends Ekpangpang in the night time to the town of the dying man. This is the bat (*Hypsignathus monstrosus*) which is always looked upon as the servant of witch or wizard, and its sinister reputation is well borne out by its hideous hippopotamus-shaped head and large unwinking yellow eyes. One afternoon we watched a couple flying, in blazing sunlight, from side to side of the Kwa river. Great was the joy of the paddlers when one fell to my gun, and was retrieved from the water in a butterfly net.

The name Ekpangpang is the same as that of the brass pan used in Ekoi-land for washing hands. When not needed for this purpose it is often held up, and the knuckles struck against the back to form a sort of gong. When put to this use it produces a sound from which its name is onomatopoeically derived. The same name has been given to the bat, because its dull monotonous cry "Pangpang" sounding out of the darkness is taken for the blows on the nails driven into the coffin, which it has been ordered to prepare for the burial of some victim. When such a sound is heard during the night, it is a matter of faith that at dawn there will be one dweller the less in the little town.

In old days, if a man was thought to be a wizard, he used to be taken into the bush to be "examined." There he was bound, and a hole cut in his body just above the liver. From this the officiating "Juju man" usually succeeded in withdrawing the suspected familiar, generally in the form of a bird, toad, or other small creature, but sometimes in that of a tiny man. If nothing was found, the victim was cleared of all suspicion, but alas! death always resulted from the treatment.

Even now the bodies of those who have fallen under the suspicion of witchcraft are examined in this way after death. Should the ceremony be omitted, and the familiar remain unkilled, it is thought that it will sally from the grave at night time, and bring disaster on the dead man's town. As a precaution the corrosive juice of a species of cactus is dropped into the eyes of the corpse, and the mouth is filled with the leaves of the Egakk tree,* so that the soul should be unable to sally forth through these apertures.

A case in which two familiars were exorcised by a witch-doctor from a live woman, Antikka by name, came before the Native Court on December 4, 1908.

The husband, Ojokk, stated on oath:

"It was during the dry season, while I was cutting farm. My little child came to call me, and said that her mother was dying. I ran home and found my wife very ill I gave her eggs and kernel oil. I got water, boiled it, and washed her. Then again I gave her eggs and kernel oil. I held her in my arms and called, and called, her name. She answered very slowly and feebly. Then I took pepper and ground it on a stone. I boiled yams and beat fu-fu. All these I gave her. She ate and grew better. Next I began to question her. 'What is the matter with you?' She said 'I have eaten Esere on account of the death of my child. Take me to Aiyu, the great witch-doctor who lives near Okuni.'

"I questioned the people. They said that the man was indeed strong to drive forth witchcraft and all bad things from the heart. So I took my wife before him. We spent twelve nights on the way, and found him at length at his farm plantation called Ibara Nshi. He went to the bush and gathered dark leaves. These he crushed in mud, mixed with water, and gave to Antikka to drink.

"After this, Aiyu gave me a matchet and told me to dig a small hole. He then bade my wife stand forth and look at the hole. First he asked her to confess what she had done, and she said

"'The children which I bore were twins. One of them died. It was I who killed it. One of my sisters was named Ogaba; her I killed also.'

"After she had finished confessing the evil she had done, she

---

* Both cactus and "Enyere" are called Egakk. The first is looked on as female and the latter male, and they are supposed to hold the position of husband and wife, as are also "male" and "female" ebony

began to vomit the medicine. First there came out of her mouth a bat, the small kind, and after that a frog. Then the priest said to me:

"'Take your wife home. Give her one Esere bean to drink. Should she die, come and take back all the goods you have paid to me, but if she does not die, you will know that I have done well in driving forth the witchcraft from out of her, and that the goods are therefore mine.'

"When I reached home, I explained everything to the townsfolk, and to my elder brother Mbe, who got the bean and ground it on a stone. My wife drank, and vomited as the priest said she would. When she was well again I went out hunting. No sooner was I gone than she ran away to Akot Ekpim, and complained to him that all the townsfolk had seen her shame, so she did not wish to live in my house any more."

Another case was brought to my notice in which a great Juju man had exorcised a witch's familiar, in the form of a black butterfly. This he drove forth from between her lips, after laying his own hand across her mouth.

As was the case in Europe from the fourteenth century onwards, there are thought to be far more witches than wizards, and, though both can transform themselves at will into the shape of any animal, they more often take the form of bat or owl than of other creatures. All witches have a special cry like that of a bird. This is believed, not by the Ekoi alone, but practically all over West Africa. The shell of the ground nut is their boat, and in this they can travel through air or by water.

There are some trees, for example, the Mbaghe, which, like our own rowan, has the power to keep witches at bay. The leaf of this, pressed against the nostrils, will save a man from death if he is suffering through witchcraft, and green boughs are also often burnt over a fire, so that the smoke may drive witches away. Should one of them be forced to drink water into which Esere has been scraped, she will confess all her misdeeds before dying.

In much the same way as with us, the owl is looked upon as a bird of ill omen, and a familiar of witch and wizard. The origin of this belief is explained in the following way:—

Why Owl is the Witches' Familiar.
By Ntui Mfum of Niaji.

Egut (Parrot), Nkundak (Greater Plantain-eater), and Ekku (Owl) were all great friends. One day they consulted together and said, "Let us pretend to die, that we may see whether our children mourn for us or not."

First they acted as if they were very sick, then all three lay down and pretended to die. When the children saw their mothers lying motionless, and seemingly dead, the daughter of Egut began to weep bitterly, as did Nkundak's daughter also. The son of Ekku, however, did not mourn at all, but went gaily away to the place where the dried meat was kept, and began to eat it up greedily. When Ekku heard what he was doing, she called to her friends, "It is time to wake up. My son has eaten up almost all the dried meat in the house." So they arose, and told their children the trick which had been played on them. Nkundak put her daughter into the fatting-house, as did Egut also. When the right number of moons had gone by, they both made ornaments for their daughters as a reward for the affection shown by them. Nkundak gave her child glistening feathers, and Egut brought red tail-feathers for hers. That is why these birds are so fine even at the present day.

Ekku, however, said to her son, "Because you had no love for me, and did not mourn my death like the others, from to-day, wherever your cry is heard, people will swear Juju against you."

This is the reason that whenever native people hear an owl hoot they say "A bad man is near." When such a cry is heard, they go at once to the Juju man, and ask him to make a "medicine" to protect them from witchcraft, for since the day on which Ekku cursed her son, he has been driven away from among the other birds, and has become the familiar of witch and wizard.

Crab claws form an important part of a witch's stock-in-trade. This crustacean is never eaten by the Ekoi, who, when questioned as to the reason, usually answer, "We never eat Crab because he is the grandfather of us all." The relationship does not, however, prevent him from being used in nearly all Juju sacrifices The reason for this is explained in the following story, another version of which has already been given (p. 144):

Why Crab's Claw is Sacrificed.

Once the Lord Njokk (Elephant) sent out to his people to tell them that they must come together on a certain day to hunt for him.

All the animals brought good guns, save Crab alone, whose weapon was so old that it appeared quite useless. The other beasts taunted him and asked, "How can you expect to kill anything for our Lord with such a miserable gun?" Nevertheless, when the hunt began they all missed everything at which they aimed, while Crab alone killed five great antelopes, one after the other.

Then the beasts were very angry and took away from him all his kill. They took the gun away also, and wrecked it utterly.

Crab said nothing, but left them in the bush, and went back to the town. He entered the compound where Elephant's wives were, and said to them :

"Your husband has sent me to tell you to get ready his chop. You are to put in it much pepper and plenty of native salt. When you have done this, you are to throw away every drop of water that is in the compound, and none is to be fetched until after his return, for he wishes that all should be brought him fresh from the spring."

Next, Crab went off to his home by the river-side, and drank up all the water, so that the stream ran dry.

When the huntsmen returned they began hungrily to eat up the food that had been prepared for them. Soon they grew very thirsty because of the pepper and salt. They went to the water-pot, but found nothing there. All had been thrown away by Elephant's wives.

At once they sent to the river to get water, but found that all had dried up.

Elephant called Ise, the little grey duiker, and bade him fetch water. On his way, Ise saw Crab run to his hole, and knew that it was he who had brought the trouble upon them. He therefore went back and told Lord Elephant.

Next the latter sent Etuk (Bay duiker); but Etuk always wants to sleep, so no sooner had he reached a good place in the road than he lay down and slept.

Day dawned and he did not come back, so Njokk sent out Pig, with orders to bring water at all costs. Pig began to root about, till he came to the place where Crab's hole was. Then he broke up the hole and crushed Crab. No sooner was the latter dead, than the water began to flow again. Pig filled a great jar and carried it back. Njokk drank and quenched his thirst.

Then the Chief called all his people together and gave orders that whoever makes a sacrifice to the Juju should put a piece of crab in it. This is the reason why natives always add a crab's claw when they sacrifice. Sometimes it is filled with Juju medicine and hung round the neck of the man who makes the offering. Also, when some "companies" carry their "image" round the town, a man goes by the side of the Okum blowing on a crab's claw, for the Juju can hear the sound.

Akpambe is now almost universally supposed to be the strongest Juju for smelling out witchcraft, but the Oban people still believe in the superior power of their own "Okum," Ekuri Ibokk. Not long ago an Oban woman died. She was buried with the usual rites, and, some time after, people began to fall sick and die. This was put down to witchcraft, practised by someone in the town, but, as Government does not allow suspected characters to be "tested" in the way already described, the inhabitants could only seek safety by going to outlying farms. Then the Juju "image" declared that every night he saw the ghost of the dead woman rise from her grave, and walk through the town spreading pestilence among its people.

The District Clerk was appealed to, and he, in company with the Station Carpenter, went down to the grave to investigate matters. There they found a small hole like the entrance to a rat's run,—which it probably was. They sprinkled pepper on a piece of paper, and laid it inside. On the morrow this had disappeared, so the people were sure that the ghost had come out by that way. All the town collected together and made a great bonfire. Then they dug up the body and burnt it, and after

Juju Akpambe.

Play at Oban, Nsikpe Club.

this there was no more sickness in Oban. Almost exactly the same thing happened at Aking, a little later.

Some hold the belief that witch or wizard passes on death from out the human form to take up its abode in that of an animal.

There are supposed to be seven different kinds of witchcraft, as will be seen from the following :—

The Seven Witchcrafts.

Once, long ago, seven different witchcrafts dwelt together in a little town. Four were wizards and three witches. They dwelt all alone because everyone feared them.

At that time people did not know about making offering against witchcraft. They only knew how to hang up charms to keep these evil creatures out of their houses. One day the seven witchcrafts gathered together and said, "We are all hungry, yet we cannot enter into men's houses to take food from them. Let us devise some way by which they may be forced to bring us offerings."

The first said, "I will choose out a man, and put a bad Juju in the path to his farm, so that he shall become cold and sick when he steps across it. In a few days he will die, and I will let the people know that if they do not set offerings for us on the farm paths, they also will perish in this way."

The others said "Good." Next morning all seven went out to the farm road and buried medicine in the ground.

Not long after, the owner of the farm came along. He crossed the spot where the magic was buried. Afterwards he began to feel cold.

As he went back home he crossed the place again, and saw the seven kinds of witchcraft standing there; the four wizards on the one side, and three witches on the other

They said to him, "Go home, and tell all your people. If no offerings are made against witchcraft in the path, all the town will die as they go to farm. You yourself will die, that all men may know what we tell you is true."

The man went home and gathered his friends around him.

He told them what had befallen him, and lay down and died. All the townsfolk feared very much, so they made offerings before their farms as the evil beings commanded.

After this, the second called all the seven together and said: "It is not enough. Let us go to the place in the road where the big rocks stand. There we will make a magic, and wait till a man comes by. When he comes we will fasten him in the rock." The others said, "It is well. We will put him within the rock, save one hand, which shall remain outside, that all who pass by may see and fear our power, and offer sacrifice."

Next morning, very early, they did as they had said. Then they waited, but no one came

About noon they heard a man coming. He came very gaily. Behind his ear he wore a red flower, Akpane Besin, as a sign that he had overcome the wrestlers in his town, and was now going to another to challenge all comers.

Him the wizards seized, and shut up within the rock; only one hand they left free, so that all passers-by might see it and take warning.

During the afternoon six of the townsfolk came by. They were taking their farm produce for sale to a village some way off. As they passed the rock one of them stopped and said:

"I see the hand of a man." The second said, "I do not see it." The third said, "I see it, and it is holding the red flower that 'Ne Ikomm (Strong Man) wore behind his ear." The fourth said, "It is surely the hand of a man. Some wizard must have killed him and put him within."

Since this, everyone knows that a man may be imprisoned in rocks and great stones.

All the other magicians killed a man in some way, each after his kind. So men learnt to make offerings, and hang up charms in many places, that wizards and witches might be powerless to harm them.

Some time ago in one of the larger towns, the people were dying so fast that it was thought witches must be killing them. To stop this, the Chief proclaimed that the inhabitants must come together on a certain day. When all were present he ordered that the Juju " Njomm Aiyung " (the Blood Juju) should be practised. A cut was made in the body of each, and a few drops of blood allowed to flow into a calabash half full of dry corn, which had been brought for the purpose. None were exempt, even the babies born that day gave one drop of blood, and, when all had been collected, each man, woman and child was made to partake of the corn. This was done so that witchcraft might no longer be practised against any of the townsfolk; for, after mingling blood and then partaking of it, should one of the parties attempt to harm another, Njomm Aiyung would catch them, and the evil they had tried to inflict would fall on themselves.

Much the same ceremony is used, though more rarely, to bind friends in a blood bond. In this case, after cuts have mutually been made, the blood is allowed to flow into a small clay basin, in which some strong Juju "medicine" has already been placed This is then drunk by the celebrants. Should one of them afterwards act in an unfriendly way towards the other, the Juju will catch him and he will die.

Sometimes the terror of witchcraft will scatter a whole town. Such was the case with Oberekkai (" Obet Ekkai," Crab mud), which stands on a little tributary of the Kwa river. This was, in old slave-dealing days, a large and prosperous town, and its Chief, Nataba, was the wealthiest man in the District. As more labour was needed to develop his great cocoa and other plantations, he sent to buy workpeople from the German Cameroons.

In course of time the emissaries returned with a band of some thirty captives, whose great limbs and strong appearance gave promise of excellent labour material.

The newcomers kept apart from the people of Oberekkai and refused to take any share in the social life of the town When "plays" were given, they hung together at the edge of the crowd, looking sombrely on, but more often gathered by stealth in the night time, at a farm hut belonging to one of them. After a while strange stories began to spread of midnight rites practised before unknown Jujus, brought by the newcomers from their own land. Then the townsfolk sickened. One after another they died, and the survivors whispered that the captives were wizards from the Cameroons, and were "eating out the hearts" of those who had enslaved them, so that soon neither man, woman nor child would remain of the free-born folk of Oberekkai. Terror took the people, many fled, and in a comparatively short time the inhabitants were reduced to a mere remnant. Nataba, and those of his family who still survived, determined on desperate measures. One after another the slaves disappeared. Their magic was powerless to protect them from the vengeance of the infuriated survivors, and Oberekkai remains, with its untended plantations, over which the bush is rapidly creeping, a shrunken survival of its former prosperity.

* * * * *

One of the real causes of the decrease in population became painfully evident during our stay, and proved to be nothing more mysterious or romantic than the insanitary conditions prevailing. When this was pointed out to Chief Nataba, he answered in a bewildered kind of way that native people did not notice bad smells like white men, but professed himself willing to obey orders about cleaning up the town, and ended by saying, "Almost I believe what White Man says, that this is the cause of the deaths of my people." A great improvement in the sanitary conditions has now been made.

CHAPTER XIX

Oberekkai to Etara

A few hours after leaving Oberekkai, Obutong was reached once more, and that evening, as we sat working in the Resthouse, after dinner, a timid tap came on the door. Outside we found the Interpreter and a tall, slim girl, clothed in the graceful native style, which is now fast disappearing. She wore a piece of cloth passed under the right arm and knotted over the left shoulder, beneath which her only garment was a ribbon-like strip round the waist, with ends falling down on the left side where the upper cloth swung slightly open. Round her slender ankles and wrists were strings of dark blue beads, and the whole length of her left arm, almost from shoulder to wrist, was ornamented with carefully made round scars, about the size of a wafer. These, she told us, it was the custom of her people to make on their arms, because after death the ghost could remove them one by one, and sell them to the spirits in exchange for food. This is a widespread belief among the Ekoi, though all scars to be seen on their arms must not be attributed to this superstition. Many of them are due to a simple desire for ornament, and others to the marks of native inoculation described on p. 10.

The girl had come down from a town about 60 miles off, to ask protection from her father, who was trying to force her into marriage against her will. When asked the reason for her unwillingness, she answered, modestly enough, that she was too young for wifehood, and did not wish to be wed until she had learnt to know herself better, and also understood more thoroughly the meaning of marriage.

On the following morning we set off for a climb along the river-side to the uppermost of the Kwa falls.

The world has countless falls more splendid than these, yet

the place has a quiet charm all its own. On both sides the high banks are covered with tall trees, which throw a cool green light on the dark, swift-flowing water. Scarcely a ray of sunlight filters through, and no flowers, save a few heavily-scented white landolphias, break the restful green of the gorge.

The rocks here are of foliated gneiss, mixed with a considerable amount of manganese The century-old lap and wash of the water has worn the stone into great dark folds, which in places enclose little stretches of golden sand and shining pebbles. The rocks in many parts of the District are highly garnetiferous, and gold dust and sapphires are reported from many streams, though, in our case, careful washings only resulted in the merest trace of " colour."

In the midst of the river, immediately above the falls, is a great " pot-hole," more than 7 feet across, and very deep

On the further shore the ground slopes down to a little bay, over which the trees arch from side to side, till it looks like a dim cool arbour. As we sat, watching the lace-like mist rise from the edge of the fall, a fawn and kid came down to drink at the brink. The golden brown of their coats stood out with startling distinctness against the twilight of the alcove, but, though so near, we sat motionless, and passed for the time unnoticed Suddenly the fawn looked across, and seemed to give a warning signal. Both stood for a while petrified with astonishment at the sight of the strange white creatures on the other side, but they seemed more curious than fearful, and after watching us for some time turned and trotted off in a leisurely manner.

It would have taken a harder heart than any there to mar the beauty of the picture, or break the silence of the place by the crack of a rifle; so fawn and kid got off safely for the time.

The way from the falls leads past several leopard lairs, over tree trunks covered with orchids and flowering creepers, down to Obutong beach. Here a dug-out canoe is stationed for the ferrying over of traders, to supplement the somewhat dangerous tie-tie bridge which spans the river immediately over one of the highest falls.

On the other side a scramble of several hundred feet led up

Central Falls, Kwa River.

to the top of the bank. It seemed to me that this climb was too steep and dangerous for traders, especially women traders, who come down in considerable numbers with heavy loads, *en route* for Calabar; so a broad flight of steps has now been made like the one on the other side of the river.

The way from Obutong to Mbarakpa is a bush road, but clear and broad, and bordered almost continuously by an endless variety of cauliflorous trees and bushes. These strangely flowering growths are so rare in most parts of the world that, as we learned from the authorities at Kew, they had remained almost unstudied, for no collection of importance had been made. Here, however, they occur in vast numbers, and almost countless varieties, several hundred of which have now been sent to England. The strangeness of their appearance is equalled in many cases by their loveliness; for, in the case of Napoleonas and many of the more showy species, one happens suddenly amid the deep green of the bush, on a great trunk, covered from root to branches with myriads of flowers. At first sight the trees look as if wreathed round by garlands, such as were offered at some festival in Arcady, or brought as gifts to the fairy folk by little old-world children, like those of Domremy in the time of Jeanne d'Arc.

Above the town of Mbarakpa stands the Rest-house, in a clearing at the top of a little hill. On their own initiative the inhabitants had made a broad road leading up to it, which was particularly charming of them, as the town is a small one, and the task of keeping even narrow roads in good order is by no means popular.

On one occasion, soon after our arrival, a boy came up with a bird which he had snared, and brought in as a present. This was placed in an extemporised cage on the verandah. During the night it seemed to flutter and beat its wings; then there was a noise as of something falling. I was about to go out to investigate, but the march had been a long one that day, and laziness counselled waiting to see if anything further would happen. I must have dropped off to sleep again, for suddenly the voice of " small boy " woke us all with a start.

" Sar, Sar," he yelled, " leopard catch one fowl, seize him and run for bush."

It did not take long to pick up my rifle and follow. The trail led to the edge of the clearing, but the light of the few hastily brought lanterns failed to show anything further. Next morning unmistakable signs were found that the beast had devoured his prey in the shadow of a bush, the outermost branches of which must have brushed my rifle Before seizing the chicken he had paid a visit to our verandah, and the noise we had heard had been caused by the fall of the cage, which he had knocked over in trying to get at the bird. The latter had escaped, flown through the ventilation space at the top of the mud wall, and taken refuge on Bimba's mosquito net, where it was found and liberated next day.

At Mbarakpa the children have a Club, in close imitation of the "Egbo Society" of their parents. They usually came up to give a "play" before the Rest-house during our visit, at the end of which we often threw handfuls of "tenths" among them, for the children dearly love a "scramble." These coins are, as their name denotes, of the value of one-tenth of a penny. It struck me that the little "Okum" or "image" was heavily handicapped by the cloth which concealed his face, so, as he passed by, I thoughtlessly pulled off the covering.

A cry went up from the children, all of whom stopped the scramble as if at a word of command. The little "Okum" covered his face with his hands, and the elders hastened up to rearrange the veils about him, volubly explaining that the face of the "image" must never be seen by his companions.

* * * * *

The whole country is honeycombed with waterways, which meander in every direction, through the green of the bush, like the veins in some giant leaf. Across many of the smaller streams stepping-stones are placed, while, over larger ones, tree trunks have been felled to serve as bridges.

On one tour, when nearing the river before Nsan, terrified screams were heard, and, on hurrying up, some women were found huddled together on the near bank, while, from a branch overhanging the far end of the rough bridge, a great snake dangled. The water was too deep for fording, and the reptile hung, darting its wicked head threateningly hither and thither,

Kwa River.

as if fully conscious of the terror it caused. A shot cleared the way, and gave me a fine skin some 14 feet in length.

The name Nsan (Thunder town) is a common one in Ekoi folk-lore. One of the dangers to which Obassi Osaw, Obassi Nsi, or indeed any unjust father, doomed his unloved son was a visit to a town of this name, usually in the underworld, on a mission planned for the youth's destruction. Such a tale will be found quoted in the Creation stories ("How the Two Brightest Stars came into the Sky"), but there are many others, among which the following are perhaps the best known.—

About Obassi Osaw and his Unloved Son.

Obassi Osaw married a woman, who bore him two sons, one named Oru and the other Agbo. The first work given to them was making native traps. Before they set about this, both went and asked their father to give them each a matchet. He gave one to Oru but refused Agbo. This last, therefore, went and complained to his mother, "Our father refuses to give me a matchet." His mother gave him an old one, which was the best she had.

Both sons went into the bush. Agbo caught many birds in his traps, while Oru caught none. Agbo "dashed" twenty of his birds to his brother, and they took all before their father. The father refused the birds of Agbo and drove him away, but accepted those from Oru. Agbo therefore took the birds to his mother and said, "My father refuses them." The mother took them and ate.

When the boys were old enough to use the gun, both went to their father to ask for one. As before, Obassi gave to Oru, but refused Agbo, and said, "I do not like you at all." Both asked for gunpowder, but this again was refused to the unloved son. The mother, however, supplied him with a very old gun and a little powder.

Both lads went into the bush. Agbo killed many antelopes, then called his brother who had slain none and said, "Let us divide them, half for me, half for you."

They then went into the town, and Agbo said. "Take the meat home, it is for yourself and your wife."

When Agbo got back to the compound, he took his kill to their father, who refused it and drove him away. Then he took it to his mother, who accepted and ate it.

At evening time Obassi sent to call Agbo. He pointed to a cotton tree and said, "To-morrow go and cut it down."

When Agbo saw the huge girth of the tree, how tall it was, and how strong, he wept, and went as usual to his mother, who bade him be comforted. When night had come, she went with a witch to the place, and together they sucked out the inside of the tree.* At dawn the boy went with his matchet, and after two or three blows the tree fell down.

Next Obassi pointed to a very high rock and said, "To-morrow go and break it into pieces."

Again the lad complained to his mother, and once more she went with her witch friend in the night time, and together they ate up all the inside of the stone. At dawn the boy went, and after a few blows the rock split as the tree had done. People went to see the wonderful feats which Agbo had performed, and said to Obassi, "What is the matter with this son? The most difficult tasks he does easily."

Next Obassi showed him a very great lake and said, "To-morrow dive within it, and pick up a heavy stone which lies at the bottom."

Again the boy complained to his mother of this new task.

When night came the woman went and slipped into the water. She found the stone, bore it to the edge, and laid it down by the brink. At daybreak the lad went and brought it back to his father.

Also Obassi said, "To-morrow go to Nsann, the Thunder town, and ask for my elephant tusk which is there. Do not come into my presence again unless you bring it."

At dawn his mother cooked plantains and gave him, saying, "Go with good courage. I will make the way safe before you."

On the road was a woman named Ita Ebat Ane (the Chief of the ghost people) bathing in a spring. She was full of boils, her whole body stank, and her hands had become useless because

---

* Witches are supposed to be able to "suck out 'the inside of things, such as trees, rocks, and even the hearts of human beings See p. 192

of the sores. For this reason she was not able to wash herself well, and asked Agbo to help her.

The latter did so, and bade her lean on him as she came up from the spring. He showed her a place to sit down, and gave her some of his plantains to eat. A bird flew by; he turned for a moment to watch it, and when he looked back the woman was gone.

The youth walked on till he came to the side of a river. There he saw the same woman, who again asked him to help her wash her body. He did as before, and again gave her his plantains. She said to him, "Do you know where you are standing?" He answered, "Yes, in the middle of the bush." She said to him, "Nay, this is not the bush at all." Again she asked, "Do you know who has played a trick upon you?" He answered "No." So she said, "I will tell you something. I know that your father does not like you at all, and has sent you on this journey that you may die."

She knocked upon her belly,* and at the stroke the bush became a town; also her sores disappeared, and she became very beautiful. She said to him, "I wish to help you." So she washed him all over in the river, and turned him up and down. Then she said, "I will tell you where the tusks are, for which your father has sent. There is the road to the ghost town, and here is a piece of chalk.† When you reach the town and they cook chop for you, touch none of it, but throw it on the ground, and see what will happen. Only eat of your plantains and this piece of chalk. When night comes and they ask you where you will sleep, say you will sleep among the goats, but, when all the people are asleep, leave the place quietly, and just choose a manger. You will see what the ghost people will try to do."

Before he left her, the woman asked Mfut, the Red Fly, to go with him. She then said, "Here is a guide who will lead you. Follow him. When Mfut enters the Egbo shed, you will see a

---

* To strike upon the belly in Ekoi legends produces the same effect as the stroke of a magic wand in European fairy tales

† The word used means chalk, but from the explanation given, probably a kind of edible clay or "steinbutter" is meant here Chalk is a great Juju, and marks are made with it on the bodies of men, women, and children to bring them good luck.

very small old chief. When the fly goes near and settles on him, kneel down and beg his protection, or the ghosts will kill you."

To the fly she said, "Do not forget or fail to carry out my message."

To Agbo she said further, "You will see several tusks in the Egbo house. Among them there is a very long one which points toward the town. That is the one your father means. Should they be moved from their place, wait until you see on which one Mfut will settle."

When Agbo reached the town, they brought him chop, but he said:

"I never eat from out the calabash."* So they brought a plate, and put the chop upon it.

He took this round to the back yard, threw it on the ground, and saw that the grass withered where the chop was thrown.

When night came, they asked, "Where will you sleep?" He said, "I will sleep among the goats."

When they had all entered their houses and closed the doors, he went softly out, and slept in the manger with the cows. In the middle of the night, they sent a thunderbolt to kill him. It fell among the goats, and struck many of them. In the morning, very early, he went back and lay among the dead goats.

When the people came to see what had happened, they saw the mark in the ground which the thunderbolt had made, and the dead goats and other damage, but Agbo sat there without a hurt.

During all the time of his stay in the town, he did not eat their chop, but only that which he had with him.

At length the townspeople grew tired and said, "We will try now to send the boy back with his father's tusk."

They brought all the tusks from the Egbo shed and laid them down before him, saying, "Choose"

Agbo stood there with Mfut his guide, and the fly settled on one of them. He caught hold of this and lifted it up. All the people clapped their hands, because he had chosen rightly.

---

* Some chiefs may not eat from calabashes, and for some plates are forbidden In many cases a carved wooden dish is used with a lid which slides up and down on a plaited handle. These are kept suspended from the roof of the house, and only taken down and used on the arrival of visitors, for whom other utensils are tabu. See p. 219.

They "dashed" him two women slaves and three cows, and appointed three men to guide him home.

He returned to the friend who had helped him on his way to the ghost people. She asked him, ". Where is the piece of chalk?" He said, " I have eaten it all."

The woman said, " Rest here to-night; to-morrow I will give you a matchet with which you can cut a thunderbolt in two. When you see one of them coming, do this, then put the half in your bag. When you see bees coming towards you, you can cut these also in pieces." She added, " These three guides may now go back. Take your wives and your cows. When you arrive near your father's town, take the half thunderbolt from your bag and send it before you to kill your father, who is your enemy."

On the boy's return, those townsfolk who were his friends came out to meet him, uttering joyful cries, and beating upon their mouths with their hands.* His mother heard the noise also ran to greet him.

When he saw her he said, "Do not come near me till you have told me one thing. Of us two, which do you choose, your husband or me?" She answered, " I choose you." So he said, " Pass me and stand behind."

Oru his brother also came, and Agbo said to him, " Here is the elephant's tusk for which I was sent. Go and give it to our father."

Oru took the tusk, and went back with it. Then Agbo stood before the town and said :

"My father tried to kill me. Therefore he sent me to Nsann, the Thunder town, see now what I am about to do." On that, he opened his bag, and took out half of the thunderbolt which he had cleft in two as the Queen of the Ghosts had ordered. He sent this before him into the town. It killed his father and all the people, save those who had come out to welcome him.

About two miles from Nsan is the town of Obung. This had formerly been further off, but according to the statement of one of the inhabitants, the town had now " walked forward in

* The Ekoi sign of welcome.

order to dwell nearer to the D. C." The old town had been small and in bad repair, while the greater part of the people lived in scattered farms. The new town is one of the best in the District, large and clean, with broad well-kept streets, and plenty of space between the compounds.

Many years ago the jar containing the Eja medicine, which belonged to the town, was accidentally broken. In terror as to the consequences, the inhabitants scattered in the bush, hoping if they kept apart, and well hidden, to escape the vengeance of the Juju. This, it seemed to them, might not take the trouble to search out and strike down each family, though it would surely have avenged itself, could this have been brought about by one fell stroke. Now that so long a time had elapsed, the people of Obung thought the danger might have blown over, and had gathered together once more to form a town. They had bought a new pot of Eja medicine, and seemed to be in a very flourishing condition.

During one visit the rain came down in torrents; it poured through the roof of the little Egbo shed, and as this had no walls, the floor soon became like a pond. The head chief invited us into his compound, where there was a picturesquely arranged Juju. While my wife was sketching this, and I was busy hearing a complaint brought by some of the townspeople, my rifle suddenly went off with a tremendous report within about a yard of us. The gunboy had been too interested in the proceedings to pay attention to his charge, and the curiosity of one of the spectators in the new type of weapon proved too strong for discretion. While examining it the little safety catch became displaced, and, considering the crowded state of the room, it was almost miraculous that no one was harmed.

Beyond Nsan, the next place of importance is Netim, a town about 4 miles off which had at first been disinclined to submit to white rule, but like all others, soon made up its mind to accept the inevitable with good grace. It is the largest town in the District, and the only pure Ekoi one, the inhabitants of which live in their bush farms during the greater part of the year, and only return to their town houses in the dry season, and on special occasions. It was once necessary

Rest-House, Nsan.

Egbo House, Netim.

to pay a visit to this place, while staying at Nsan, in order to inquire into the complaint of a man who was too ill to come over to plead his own cause. Soon after starting, the rain began to come down in sheets. It continued in a steady downpour during our visit and on the way back. When about two miles from Nsan, a rushing roaring sound made itself heard, growing momentarily louder and louder, much like an approaching express train. We had crossed no river on our way to Netim, only some small streams; but one of these, which had been a mere trickle flowing between steep, wide banks, had now become a torrent, more than 60 feet broad at our crossing place, and over 100 feet a little further down. A foot or so from the bank the water was up to my shoulders, and the current tearing down like a mill race, put swimming out of the question.

While we were trying to make a bridge of some sort, the Netim children, on their way back home from Nsan school, appeared on the opposite bank. Ropes of tie-tie were thrown over to them and they were shown how to fasten these to some of the trees, but this contrivance broke under the strain of the mass of water, tearing against the body of the man who tried to cross by its means. A way had to be cut through the bush by the water-side, to search for some place where a crossing would be possible. After some time the trunk of a tree was found which had fallen half across from the opposite bank. Another was felled so that it almost joined the first, and by this means we managed to reach the other side, and were able to get the children over in the same way.

From Netim to Ibum the march leads through the midst of the Forest Reserve, a stretch of land nearly 400 square miles in extent, which has been set aside by the wish of Government as a sanctuary for all wild bush things. Here one evening we came upon a great herd of elephants, which melted silently into the shadows on our approach. One cow, however, bolder or more friendly than the rest, paused a moment to wag its tail before disappearing in the wake of its companions.

Once too, on pitching camp, the arrival of the carriers disturbed a leopard, which was busily eating an antelope. The meal was hardly begun, however, and the men were delighted at this welcome addition to their larder.

The inhabitants of Ibum itself are far more enterprising and hard-working than their kin below. Farms stretch for miles in every direction, and one of these shows a really remarkable amount of energy; for, in order to make it, the whole surface of a small hill had to be cleared. From the top a panoramic view may be gained to the feet of a great circle of mountains, by which the landscape is shut in on all sides. Standing in the midst of this natural amphitheatre, the place has much the appearance of a huge crater.

Ibianshi peak, near Ibum, divides the sources of the Calabar and Kwa rivers. From its summit, which can only be reached by a stiff climb up the bare face of the rock, a magnificent view can be obtained of the mass of hills in the middle of the Forest Reserve. These, with their sharply defined outlines of every conceivable shape, seem so closely huddled together that it looks almost as if they had been suddenly dropped in a heap by some Titan grown weary of carrying them further. It was on this peak that the beautiful specimen of Napoleona was found, which is not only a new variety of this interesting group, but shows an inflorescence hitherto unknown. I have ventured to call it Egertoni, after the former Governor of Southern Nigeria, who managed somehow, amid all his work, to keep track with, and encourage, every effort of his subordinates, even in so small a matter as a botany collection. Another has been named after the Provincial Commissioner, Mr. Widenham Fosbery, C.M.G. It is impossible adequately to express my thanks to both for the help and encouragement so generously extended. A third has been called Alexandri, after my friend and former leader Boyd Alexander. The whole family bears the name of his hero, Napoleon, so it seems fitting that one of them should also bear his own.

From Ibum the way is steep and difficult, almost untouched by the hand of man, and very beautiful; though, as my companions had to be lowered down huge boulders, or occasionally thrown upward to be clutched and pulled into safety by someone stationed above, it was not unnatural that they should express a preference for the humbler beauties of lowlier paths.

New Anacardiacee. Cauliflorous Tree, with fruit like colossal bunches of scarlet grapes.

Napoleona Alexandri (Named after Boyd Alexander).

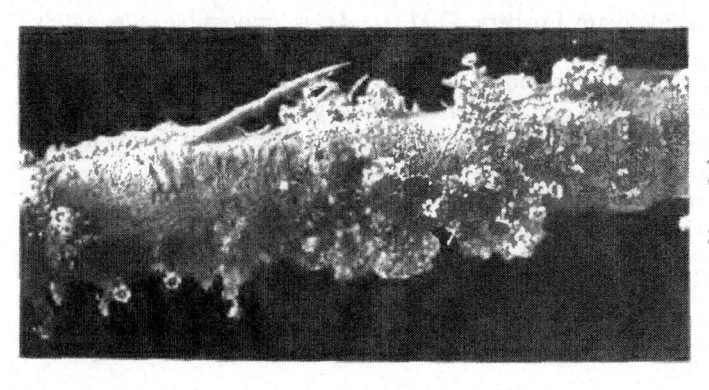

New Cola.

The road often leads down the faces of small cataracts which dash from the steep hill-sides to the rivers below, one of the most important of which is the River Ukpon. As we wished to explore this, we waded, on one occasion, for a considerable distance up its shallow bed. After a while the water deepened; a great tree trunk jutted out of the bank at a convenient angle, and my companions elected to rest there while I went on. I was just turning to leave them, when the orderly, after saluting with great punctiliousness, very slowly and respectfully begged leave to inform us that beneath that particular tree was the home of a crocodile, the eggs of which the carriers had just discovered and were taking home for supper.

In less time than it takes to write, my companions had left their seat and reached shallow water, nearly a quarter of a mile down stream!

Some of the people of Ibum have now migrated to the 12-mile-distant town of Etara, for, as the chief explained sadly, bachelors were growing scarce in his town, and the young and beautiful women did not find sufficient choice of wooers, so wished to descend to the larger town below.

In many of the houses of Etara elaborate graves are to be seen. These usually take the form of a low divan made of mud, 8 to 10 feet long, 3 feet wide, and about 1½ feet high. All along the edge plates and dishes have been pressed into the mud when soft. These were first broken, as is always done with the property of the dead, but the hardening mud acts as cement to hold them together. In the case of a rich man, a fresh coating of mud is plastered over the wall behind the grave, and in this more plates and dishes are fixed in a rough design.

CHAPTER XX

Ekoi of the Cross River

THE first town beyond the Oban-Ikom boundary is Abijang. Here the Ekoi have intermarried to a considerable extent with their neighbours in the twin town of Akam, which came over

Egbo House.

from Obubra and settled so close to Abijang that at first sight the two towns seem to form only one.

The decoration of some of the compounds, and of the Egbo house, is different to that in most Ekoi towns, though a little later we came on a particularly beautiful example of this style made by an Oban man. Instead of the pattern being moulded in relief on the surface of the wall, after the latter has been roughly mudded to form a background, the design here is first marked on the surface, which is then dug out between the lines, so as to leave the pattern raised. This is afterwards picked out in white paint, and over all raised figures are sometimes added, in the same manner as those of other parts. The figures shown in the drawing were variously explained as Obassi Osaw, his wife and Nimm (Snake), Obassi Osaw and Nimm in her three shapes (woman, snake, and crocodile), Obassi Osaw and Obassi Nsi with Nimm.

The clay near this part of the Cross River is specially suitable for pottery, and particularly beautiful examples are therefore to be found in the neighbourhood.

The head chief of Abijang has literally dozens of skulls embedded in the mud before the entrance to his room, and also in the ends and sides of the mud couches along the walls. The atmosphere of this apartment is singularly evil-smelling, even for this part of the world, owing to a small pool of fermenting palm wine before the entrance.

In one corner of the room was a very old, roughly-carved, wooden figure, holding its pointed beard with its right hand. The type of head is curiously like some ancient Egyptian burial masks discovered by my late brother-in-law, Dr. Hugh Baker, in the sand of the Egyptian oasis of Kharga.

At Nchofan, the next place of importance on the river, where the people are practically pure Ekoi, a wonderful variety of designs was to be found.

Here the children came to give a very charming " play." The performers numbered about fifty boys and girls, dressed in gay-coloured cloth and chains of beads, with ceintures, to which were attached little bunches of brass bells, or tiny rattles, made from the seeds of the "Agara" tree, with three big pods brightly painted in red and white, caught together by strings and tied just below each knee. In their right hands they bore thin play-swords of white wood, decorated with Nsibidi writing, with long fringes of palm fibre dyed red.

The drum belonging to the club was a wonderful example of its kind. It was cut from a solid piece of wood, trough-shaped, and with a roll of soft cloth fastened on its edge. This was held in place by nails, which also served to separate from one another rough slabs of cork wood, which were laid across it, much in the manner of a xylophone. At either end sat a carved figure, male to the right, female to the left, and to the right hand of the latter, raised on a post, was Tortoise. These again were explained to us in two ways. First, as the three principal personages in the well-known story, "How Obassi Osaw proved the Wisdom of Tortoise"; and secondly, as Obassi Osaw, Obassi Nsi and Tortoise, representing certain attributes of the latter, much in the same way as in the worship of Aphrodite Hestiæa.

Two performers sat facing each other, at different ends of the instrument, beating out the songs of the club, real "Lieder ohne Worte,"—for this society, unlike most others, has no song which can be put into words and sung. The subject of drum songs will be found treated more fully in Chapter XXVII.

On this occasion the songs beaten upon the drum were—

"Makara araw ba, kun abonn akam asum.
(If) white man come not, then the children would become slaves."

The second referred to the coming of the first white women to Insofan—

"Nkanang oiyenn ntuk nji, njum nji 'me nyenn A
(I) never saw such as this, a thing as this I saw not."

The head chief of Insofan possessed a particularly elaborate example of a "chief's dish," which he unfortunately declined to sell at any price, though he was delighted with the "dash" of tobacco leaves, which were given him for allowing it to be drawn. These dishes are carved, lid and all, from solid blocks of wood, and are suspended, by a string passing through base and lid, from the roofs of the houses of head chiefs, till a neighbouring chief, of equal or superior position, comes on a visit. The dish is then taken down and in it the visitor's food is served.

Another object of interest in the same room was a drum-shaped box of antelope and leopard skin, in which were kept the caps worn by the principal chiefs of Insofan for many generations.

Before the entrance was a little pool for ghost libations, like the one already described at Abijang, but surrounded by a crowd of objects, old bronze bracelets and anklets, Nimm stones of varying sizes, long stones roughly cubical, and human thigh bones.

On first entering one of the compounds, with the idea of purchasing typical examples of pottery, &c., the women rushed, in a state of panic, to hide their treasures, but no sooner did they understand that we wished to take away nothing that they did not want to sell, and at a price for which they were willing to exchange, than we were almost mobbed by would-be sellers.

Chief's Dish.

A march of 13 miles took us once more across the Oban border, to the ruined town of Mkpott. On the way thither a deserted farm was passed, close to the overgrown road of Itaka. Here, before the abandoned Juju tree, one of the pointed stones was found roughly sugar loaf in shape, which might have been a fragment of the larger piece afterwards discovered before the Egbo house at Mkpott. Within the latter building, just in front of the mud base in which the great end pillar is embedded, a splendid example of the "Etai Ngbe" was to be found, the sides of which were absolutely clear cut and four square (see p. 172).

Hat Box.

In the lowest circle of this base was a Nimm stone, which served to close up a small hole in which was concealed "medicine" to ensure the birth of many children to the townsfolk.

The former inhabitants of this once large and flourishing town have now divided, and formed several smaller ones, each under the leadership of its particular chief or group of chiefs.

In one of the deserted houses the "treasure chamber" remains intact, and is a really beautiful specimen of native ornamentation. No colour is employed; the whole is made of clay, with a surface smooth as that of pottery. The pattern, of conventionalised leaves, is left in relief by the depression of the background, like those already described at Abijang.

At the next stopping place, Ewaw-Offong, a curious little custom came to our notice. As usual, on arriving in a town, a stand was built for the cases of botanical specimens. So soon as this was finished the carriers brought logs and lighted a fire beneath. The spot chosen was under the sheltering eaves of a house. We had found it better to have the little erections built outside rather than within the compounds, and quite near to our own quarters, for it was thus easier to see that the fires were not allowed to die out.

In the centre of the open space before the Egbo house a Juju tree is to be seen, springing from a heap of small stones brought as offerings. Round this again a circle of larger stones is laid, to serve as seats for head men when special rites are being performed.

After dark had fallen, a bright light suddenly sprang out from the edge of the heap of stones. So brilliant was it that every leaf and flower on the Juju tree stood out against the night. The fire rose into a great flare, which flickered and wavered over a semi-circle of men who had silently gathered in the background, then settled down to a clear steady flame. Investigation showed this to be caused by a resin which exudes from the Njaii Asung cactus.

The reason for the ceremony proved to be that, in this town as in all which possess the Juju Ngbe Abum Obbaw, it is unlawful for a fire to be lit outside the compound walls. Should this rule be infringed, according to old tradition, the Juju which protects the town from leopards will no longer avail. The very night after the offending fire has been lighted one of these beasts will break through and carry off some of the goats or sheep. Only by means of the rite described above can the power of the outraged Juju be restored.

CHAPTER XXI

Funeral Ceremonies

In December, 1907, the head chief of Oban, Itorok by name, died. The funeral was typical of those of the more important members of his race, so an account of it may not be without interest.

First, water was heated, and the body washed. It was then clothed in the best robes which had been owned by the dead man, and enveloped in a broad native mat of plaited reed. Pieces of new cloth were wound round this, and then three more mats were added fastened with tie-tie.

The body was then carried into the bush, about 100 yards from the town, and laid on the ground, while a grave 6 feet by 6 feet was dug in the presence of all the chiefs.

When the grave was ready, Agbashan, the dead man's chief representative, approached, with two bottles, one containing rum and the other Juju "medicine." He had smeared red and yellow powder over his face, and poured out the spirit as a libation, while he took some of the "medicine" into his mouth, and spat it out near the head of the corpse. Next he placed two dishes in the grave where the feet would lie, and a cup and spoon by the head.

A net was then brought, and divided into three pieces, which were placed under the body, and, by means of these, six of the dead man's "members" lowered the corpse into the grave. While this was being done Chief Itaban took a Juju spear and struck it twenty-five times against the heart, counting each stroke. Each time that he touched the body all those present called out "Owe." All this time three young men were beating drums, very softly, and a sound was heard, the origin of which was difficult to locate. This was said to be the voice of the invisible Egbo, lamenting over the dead chief. It was unfortunately impossible to ascertain the actual cause of the sound, but it was produced by something quite different to the bull-roarer.

The nets were next drawn up, another cloth was spread over the body, and three calabashes filled with earth were placed upon it. Then the grave was filled in.

After this a brass pan was brought, holes were made in it, and it was set at the head of the mound. A sapling was taken from one of the Juju trees and planted close by.

The burial took place in the bush instead of within the house, as is usual with persons of distinction, because the deceased had died of dysentery and cough, which are considered very infectious.

All this time the women, who are never allowed to attend the funeral of a chief, sat in the house of the dead man, naked save for loin cloths, and weeping by an empty coffin, which, when the real burial was over, was let down into a hole in a small inner room. After this the house was cleared of all inhabitants, and young palm leaves were tied against the lintels as a sign that none might enter, as well as to keep out bad ghosts and spirits.

On the eighth day the door was opened, and a goat and cow were sacrificed. The former was placed with an offering of plantains under the Juju Obassi Nsi, in the courtyard. The latter was killed, as is always the case under such circumstances, by suffocation, through having its mouth and nostrils tightly bound round. Then the various Clubs to which the dead man had belonged came and gave plays, during which all the performers had yellow powder rubbed over their faces. At all funeral dances free men carry a spear in both hands, while those not free are only allowed to hold one in the right hand.

A wake was held more or less continuously for several months, especially when relays of kinsfolk arrived from long distances. Had it not been that Government had already taken over the District, the six members who lowered the coffin would probably have been murdered, and buried in their master's grave. By ancient custom this was always done, so that a chief might not arrive servantless in the spirit world.

The Egbo was supposed to have fled from the town after the

"Image" of the Igumi Club.

death of Itorok, so during February a hunt was instituted, in the course of which it was reported to be discovered and captured, and was then conducted back in great triumph.

Two years after the funeral above described, the head men of Oban came up to the station to invite us to be present at a great play which was to be held in honour of the same chief, and act as a *finale* to the long burial rites.

In the principal compounds stands had been dressed, much like the stalls of a country fair. These were spread with blankets or other bright cloths, and hung round with gay handkerchiefs and gaudy prints. On them was set out an array of china, from beautiful old Dutch pieces—brought by early traders—and groups of "cottage" figures, down to the crudest and coarsest examples of present-day earthenware.

The Ekoi happened to be very pleased with me, as my efforts to procure gunpowder with which to protect their farms from the ravages of buffalo and elephant, and their cattle from those of leopard and wild cat, had just been successful. They well knew my interest in all their old customs, and it was to a child-like wish to do something to show gratitude for my efforts in their behalf, that I put down the fact that two figures which here, at any rate, never before had shown themselves to a white man, suddenly appeared before us.

The first, a dark mask covered with skin, and with a ridiculous snake-like nose, was called Igumi, the name of a tree with tiny inconspicuous flowers, and a leaf much like that of Virginia Creeper. This tree has a bad name among the natives, partly because its hollow stems harbour innumerable ants, and partly for supposed occult properties. The Club had originally been formed to wage war on the neighbouring town of Aking, and the curious head adopted as its standard or device.

Roars of laughter greeted the image, and were redoubled as the other figure sprang forward, and came bobbing and dancing in our direction. This, Ojjen by name, was a sight, which for actual grisly horror would be hard to beat. On its head it bore a human skull, or rather dried head, the mouth of which was fixed open in a ghastly grin. The parched skin was wrinkled round the eye-holes in a way which produced the effect of ghoulish merriment. Words can give but a feeble impression of the loathsome horror of this apparition, as it mopped and mowed in the brilliant sunlight, among the gay dresses and gayer laughter of the delighted multitude. The accompanying photograph gives no idea of the ghastliness of its appearance. As in so many cases, the camera has utterly failed to catch the spirit of the thing.

The skull is a great Juju. It was brought by the Ekoi when they trekked down from their old home near Mkpott, and now forms the chief treasure of the "company" "Etim Ngbe" or "Ojjen." Its present-day use is interesting enough. On the marriage of a member of the club, or of any man rich enough to pay for the privilege, it is carried to the door of the bride-chamber. There it remains, a grim sentinel on the threshold, till the company come to fetch it again at dawn. It is thought that this will ensure fidelity on the part of the wife, for, should she attempt to leave her husband, the horrible head would follow her through the night, and, if necessary, summon to its aid countless hordes of dim mowing shapes from the ghost towns, which would throng around and block the way to the house of another lover.

The "customs" now to be described are typical of those carried out at the funeral of every woman of importance.

On the death of Adet Awaw, one of the chief women of Oban, the friends and relatives, who had gathered round her bed, remained for a short time bewailing their loss. Then water was heated, and the women washed the corpse. New clothes were placed upon it, and the hair was elaborately arranged in tufts. By ancient custom no coffin was provided, but in this case one was brought. It was lined with new cloths, and on these four pillows were laid, one for the feet, one for the head, and one under each elbow. The hands were folded across the breast, and, after the coffin had been nailed down, a new cloth was spread upon it. The women now accompanied it outside the house, and a goat and cow were sacrificed while the men dug a grave, 6 feet deep, in one of the rooms. When all was ready the coffin was carried back, and gently lowered. Then the earth was filled in again, and smoothed over.

Various men's societies of which the dead woman had been

an honorary member, came to play, and the women's society, Ekkpa, gave a performance. This is the same as the one called "Oóm" at Big Kwa town, and its rites are always held on the death of a member. About January, when the bush is cut for farms, and in the new yam season, September to October, Ekkpa plays are also given. By some people this society is thought so powerful as to take for women the place of the men's Egbo. The Juju is strong enough to kill a man, and can ward off sickness—especially small-pox—from family or town.

On the occasion of the death of Adet Awaw the members of Ekkpa ran maenad-like round the town in a nearly naked state, many brandished guns and swords, and all looked fierce and wild. The men kept carefully out of sight, though their presence is not absolutely forbidden in daylight, but after dark no man must show his face. The women dance stark naked the whole night through, and, should any man attempt so much as a glance at these mysteries, his strength will ebb away, and all his vital powers shrivel up for ever.

Men may join the cult on payment of four "wires" and 3d. worth of spirit, but they can only be regarded as outside members, and have no part in the ceremonies.

While the "plays" were being given in honour of Adet, the animals offered for sacrifice were divided. When this had been done the Head of the House arose, and took four small pieces of goat's flesh, and some boiled plantains. He called on the names of his principal ancestors, and said:

"Listen, my family! Here is the goat we have killed for our sister who has just died Here is your portion." On this he threw the meat into the middle of the court, crying, "It is time for us to eat."

The men and women gathered together in separate groups, and sat down, and the meat was divided between them. Next the sister of Adet Awaw stood up, and gave a small quantity of spirit to all. Then the Head of the House poured out upon the ground what was left, so that the ghosts might also drink, calling, "Here is rum for you." After this the people left the compound, but a wake lasting several weeks was held in the dead woman's honour.

A goat is always sacrificed at funerals, and in explanation of this custom the following story is told:—

Why a Goat is Sacrificed at every Funeral.

One day the ghost of a woman came back to earth. With her she brought a magic cloth, which she laid down by the side of the road near a town, before entering.

A boy saw the cloth by the wayside, and took it up. He ran away, and when the ghost came back for it, lo! it was gone

She went back into the town, crying, "Who has taken my property?" The cloth itself answered, and said, "A live person took me. Here I am tied round this boy's loins." The boy feared greatly. He ran away, and said to himself, "How is it that a cloth can talk like a human being?" He took it off and threw it over a he-goat. The goat tied it round his middle. The Ghost Woman still cried, and the cloth answered her. Then He-goat also said, "Strange! I never before saw a lifeless thing that could talk!" He ran and buried himself in the earth, but left one hoof above ground

When the ghost passed by, this foot trembled. She chopped at it with a matchet, and saw blood running out. Then she took hold and pulled, till out came the goat with the cloth still tied round him. She cried aloud, and at her call other ghosts came. They spat upon the goat, and threw foul things upon his body, because he had taken the cloth. That is the reason why he-goats smell. Also they said, "From to-day, whenever anyone dies, they may sacrifice you." That is the reason why native people always kill a goat at funeral ceremonies.

The final rites are carried out at no special date, but at any time when the relatives have got together enough money and food. Should the ceremonies be delayed for more than two or three years, the townspeople would talk behind the back of the man responsible, and say, "Look how long it is since the death of his relative, and he has never yet given a play!"

The dread of being looked down upon for such a reason causes survivors to use every effort to carry out the rites of their dead kin with as little delay as possible, and with almost incredible lavishness.

* * * * *

When a stranger dies he is not buried in the bush, but on the road by which he entered the town, so that his spirit may easily find the path back to his own place, or at least see the way to his home, and listen and watch for the coming of friends.

Certain burial customs are illustrated by the following story:

Why Chiefs are Buried in their Houses.

Once a woman had a son. He prepared his goods to carry them to market in a far-off town. The mother said, "Do not leave me, because I am old now, and near to my death" The son answered, "I go, but will soon come back." He went to the trading place and began to sell his wares. Then he thought of his mother and looked within himself, and saw that she could only live for two more days; so started back home. When he was only about 11 miles off he again looked within himself, and saw, and said, "My old mother, only one day left for her!" When he reached home the woman cried, "O my son, you have come!" She looked at him with great gladness, and that same day, before the sun sank, she died.

At midnight the townspeople chose a few of their number to go and dig a grave, but the son thought within himself, "I will bury my old mother without the knowledge of anyone." He went alone to the small inner room of his house and there dug a grave. The coffin he made with his own hands, and at midnight buried his mother alone.

Afterwards he made another coffin and placed it outside, so that all who entered the compound should see it. In the morning he called together his "age class" and that of his mother. He feasted them, and at eight o'clock they started to carry the coffin into the bush where the grave had been dug. There they laid it down and opened it, but lo! there was nothing within save some stones. So they buried it, full of wonder, and went away.

Now among them was one old woman. She said to herself,

"I must know what has become of the body." So she went home and brought out palm wine and food, which she set ready for the boy on his return. When he had eaten and drunk, she said to him, "Tell me now what you have done with the body of your mother, and why did you bury her without the knowledge of anyone in the town?"

Then the boy took her to the small inner room and showed the place where he had laid his mother. When the old woman saw what he had done she said, "You are a good son. Now I give you a distinct order. When I die, bury me as you have buried your mother." To this the boy agreed.

Three days later the father sent for his son and said, "Prepare to go to market once more." The boy answered, "There is an old woman named Anyin, who gave me distinct orders to bury her as I buried my mother. She might die any day. How can I bury her if I am away at the market when she dies?"

The father said, "Anyhow, you must go." He would listen to no further excuse. The boy thought, "There is only one way to keep my promise." He therefore went to the old woman and said, "My father wants me to go to market. Will you die to-day that I may bury you before I set out?"

The woman answered, "If I had known there would be such a hurry about it, I would not have given you the order. I did this because I saw that you were a dutiful son, and I have no child to bury me.'

The boy still told her that she had better die at once. She denied the necessity, but he entered into the small room of her compound and dug the grave. When all was ready he called a meeting of the townspeople. He related all that had passed between himself and Anyin, and asked what should be done.

The Head Chief got up and said: "The woman gave a distinct order. Agreements never change, save with the consent of both parties. She is old, and may as well die to-day, so that the boy can bury her."

Anyin still refused. Therefore the boy killed her and buried her at midnight as he had promised.

Afterwards he went to market.

That is the reason why, when Ekoi people die, they are buried that same night. Before this time all people had been

FUNERAL CEREMONIES

buried in the bush, but, from the day that the boy buried his mother in the house, the custom arose to bury all chief people in their dwellings, save when they died of some very bad thing.

According to Ekoi belief, in the beginning of the world when men died, they were carried in a sort of dream to the dwelling-place of Obassi Osaw. If Obassi thought it would be a good thing he would bid the dead man wake, and stand up before him. Then he would make him alive again and send him back to earth, but such men on their return could never tell what had happened to them.

One day Obassi thought, "Men fear to die. They do not know that perhaps they may come to life again. I will tell them that sometimes such a thing may happen, then they will have less dread of death." So he stood up in his house in the sky, and called a frog and a duck before him. To the first he said, "Go to earth and say to the people, When a man dies, it is the end of all things; he shall never live again." To the second he said, "Go tell the earth folk that if a man dies he may come to life again." He led them a little way, and showed them the road, saying, "Take my message. Duck, you may go to the left hand. Frog, keep to the right."

Frog kept on till he came to earth. He told the first people who met him the message which Obassi had sent. In course of time the duck also reached earth. She came to the place where they had been making palm oil and began to gobble it up. So eager was she, that she forgot all about the message, and thus men never heard the good news which Obassi had sent.

That is the reason why, when a man dies, we cannot see him again, because Duck lost the message, and we must go according to the one which Frog brought us.

CHAPTER XXII

Ghosts

NTUANTO, the word which is sometimes used for a ghost, really denotes the soul or spirit of a person. It is in some way connected with the breath, and leaves the body on the wings of the last outbreathing. While within the form of a living man, it is a small thing, and dwells in his breast, but, once set free, it expands and rarefies, till it reaches the size and shape of the body in which it used to dwell. It is intangible like air, though, to those who have the "four eyes" and can see spirits, it looks just like a man. This gift of "second sight" or "Eénna" is not confined to human beings. Dogs have it, and so has the little Ise, as has previously been mentioned. Two eyes they use in the day time, and two others at night. These latter, according to all Ekoi, may be seen when the animal is killed: they lie at the back of the other two, beneath the eyebrows.

The word in common use for Ghost is "Akaba-Nsi "—*i.e.*, One-who-cannot-come-back-to-earth. There are bad and good ghosts, but it is very seldom that evil ones are allowed to roam alone. Usually a good spirit accompanies a malevolent one, in order to prevent it from doing harm to the living. Should a man, without the "four eyes," meet a bad spirit alone in the way, the ghost will not step aside, but waits till the man reaches him, then stretches forth an invisible hand and deals a blow on the face. This produces lock-jaw, from which death always follows.

With reference to this superstition, it is somewhat singular that the Buduma assured me that the Djinns of Lake Chad bring death in exactly the same way on any of the race who are unfortunate enough to meet them in the night time. The Djinn strikes the man across the face with his long thin hand, and it is well

GHOSTS

known that death must come before moon and stars have climbed next night to the same place in the sky. The Genii of the great Baobab trees of Bornu, too, kill any against whom they have a grudge by a blow across the face.

To return to Ekoi beliefs. Ghosts can be kept from entering a room or compound during the night by burning spices or tobacco, by keeping lamps alight, or by wearing amulets. Some magicians can make a preparation, which ghosts dread, for washing the face and body; bad spirits will never appear to anyone protected in this way. Should a man meet a ghost without such safeguard, he will probably fall sick, and must go to the Diviner to find out why he should have been thus visited.

The soul is the real man, and can never be destroyed, while the body is something inferior and temporary, and rots away when no longer needed. The shadow cast by a live man is really the shape of the soul which is within him, though compressed, for the time, into a small space.

Sometimes the soul leaves the body, and then returns. Living beings, more often women, can pass into a kind of trance, in which their souls fly away. While absent they can see what is taking place in other worlds, much as some people do in dreams.

Once during my absence from Oban, a Nimm woman was thought to have died, and was therefore buried with the usual rites. Some weeks afterwards her spirit is said to have appeared to one of the initiates, and have complained of premature burial: "It was a great pity that my kin were in such a hurry to lay me in the grave," the ghost is reported to have said, "for my soul had but gone away for a time, and I only died after its return, because I could no longer breathe in the earth."

A man has two minds, a good one and a bad one, but these are only connected with the body, and die with it. He has only one soul.

With regard to dreams, the Ekoi may be divided into two classes—those whose dreams come true, like the visions which in the Odyssey pass earthwards through the portals of shining horn; and those whose dreams go by contrary. Should the latter dream of a wedding, it is the sign of a funeral; while to dream of a new-born babe means a death in the house.

Everything which exists has a soul of its own, from trees and rocks down to weapons, and the commonest of household goods, and it is their astral forms which are visible in dreams.

Wraiths of dead friends often come in visions of the night, to give warnings of dangers, or ask for offerings. Should a man unwittingly eat food which has been laid out for the ghosts, no harm will happen, but should he do so knowingly, some ill is sure to befall him. Food is always thrown upon the graves, and, though seeming to suffer no change, the spirits can feed upon it by sucking out the essence, and leaving only the shell of the offering.

Many beliefs which the Ekoi hold in common with Brahmins and Shintoists, seem to point to the probable easterly origin of this people. After death, the spirits who have lived a full earth life, or have no particular reason for staying, are supposed to go right away to another world, and only come back in exceptional cases. Others, who have died a violent death or are held back by some special cause, wander about in this world and trouble people until the time comes when they are set free to join those who have gone before. Such unhappy wanderers usually stay near their graves, and only come into the towns between midnight and 3 a.m. If anyone passes through a burial place at this time therefore, he will take no ill, for all the ghosts are away in the town.

Should a wraith be called up by a Diviner, he is always in a great hurry, and cannot be persuaded to answer many questions He never tells you that he is dead, and, if a man with the "four eyes" meets such an one, there is nothing to show that it is not an ordinary man whom he has met.

*   *   *   *   *

Akunane, the head priest of the Juju Ofiri, was talking about ghosts one day:

"I do not know," he said, "if ghosts can do harm to the living, but I always sacrifice yams and plantains to my father's spirit, so that I may not fall sick, and to ask him to protect my farms. About once a year too, generally when it it is time to cut 'bush' for our farms, I sacrifice to my mother, for we know that ghosts are hungry just as we are."

* * * * *

The reason why living men no longer visit the ghost town is given as follows :—

Why Living Men can no longer see the Road to the Ghost Town.

By Ndum of Nsan.

There was once a man with two wives. One day they went down to the stream to bathe and fill their water-pots. While they were standing in the water, the younger one cried out. The other looked at her and saw that a child was about to be born. At once this cruel woman picked up her pot and ran back home, leaving her poor companion alone and helpless.

The young wife still cried for aid, and a witch named Ngbe Eing (Leopard-tooth) heard and ran towards her. No sooner was the child born, than the monster said to the mother, " We will cut the babe into equal shares and devour him, you and I."

The poor woman did not know what to do, for she was too weak to defend her child, but fortunately at that moment Ise, the little grey duiker, ran up and said :

" It is quite right that Eing should claim half the child, only first she must go down the stream till she comes to the deep part and search for a large flat stone which lies there. This she must bring back, for it is only on such a stone that the child may be laid to be killed."

Eing was so pleased that Ise had said she was right in her demand, that she never saw the trick, but went dancing gaily down stream in full confidence that she would find the stone. The way she had to go was about three times as far as to the house of the terrified woman, and no sooner was she out of sight, than Ise told the latter to make all haste to her home

When Eing came back with the stone, and found that her prey had escaped, and Ise also, she was very angry. She followed hard in pursuit, but could not overtake the poor mother. When the monster reached the town, and found it nearly empty, for all the men had gone out hunting, she forced her way right into the compound where the woman had taken refuge.

Now Ngbe Eing was one of the most rapacious monsters ever seen. For days she sat watching the poor woman, thinking that the latter must fall asleep some time, but night and day the mother lay guarding her babe.

One day the monster was thirsty, and left the house to go down to the spring. While she was away, the husband came back and his wife at once told him all that had happened, and begged him to hide so that he might see Eing on her return. The husband caught up an Ejimm which belonged to his other wife, and then hid himself to watch. Now the thing he took is the sharp-pointed iron, used to spear lumps of meat from out a boiling pot, and, when the wicked intruder returned, he sprang out upon her, and drove it into her eye with such vigour that it ran right through her head. Nevertheless, she did not die at once, for her magic helped her. She ran screaming from the town, and fell dead as soon as she reached her home. There the people drew out the Ejimm from her eye and buried her, mourning over her, for they were witches like herself.

Unfortunately the Ejimm was the property of the second wife, as has been said, and the latter had ill-will toward the fruitful woman, because she herself was barren. When therefore she learned what had happened, she said that she would take nothing in exchange and no excuse, but that her fellow wife must set out at once and recover the property.

Very sadly the poor woman gave her babe to a friend, and set out to consult Porcupine as to what she must do

The latter consulted the charm, and said that she would be successful unless she offended someone whom she should meet on the road.

The woman therefore set out on her way, while all the townspeople stood weeping for fear lest she might never return. She went on and on, till at last, at a stream near the ghost town, she saw a woman bathing. The latter was a terrible sight, for she was covered with sores. Her left side was quite eaten away, and from it maggots were falling as rain-drops drip from the eaves. This poor woman called in a feeble voice and said, "Will you please pick up some sticks and scrub my back, because I am not strong enough to do it myself."

The newcomer answered gently, "I will wash you with my hands, for they will be softer, and it is always good to help those in pain."

The answer pleased the old woman, who all at once grew sound and well. "You will succeed in your adventure, whatever it may be," said she, "for I am the Chieftainess of all the ghosts." At these words hope flowed into the heart of the mother, and she related where she was going, and on what errand. "Do not fear," said the Chieftainess, "for I will tell you how you can easily obtain what you seek, and will also shorten the road before you When you meet anyone in our country which is called Mfam Akabansi (Ghost town), you must say that the dead person was your elder sister, then go along singing:

"'Atone ngam njum ayui 'ne ama
Show me thing (which) kills person mine'

"The people will flock round you, and dance and be pleased with your singing, and, when you stop, they will ask you the name of your dead, and you must say that it is Ngbe Eing. They will at once fetch what killed her, and allow you to go freely away with it, by my order."

This encouraged the young mother still more, and as she neared the town, she began to sing in a strong voice the words of the song. All the people came out and surrounded her, dancing and asking why she had come. She said what the Ghost Woman bade her, "Ngbe Eing was my elder sister; I have come, by your good will, to fetch the thing that killed her." All the ghost people were very pleased at this modest way of speaking. They went and fetched the Ejimm iron, and gave it to their visitor She thanked them, and walked away well pleased.

When the town was already some way behind, the young mother began to hasten her steps, for she thought of her babe.

All at once she heard someone calling. She looked back and saw that it was her friend the Chieftainess, who had at first appeared to her as a feeble old woman. The latter bore a basket in which were seven Ochitt fruits (Egg Plant). These she gave to the stranger saying, "Take these fruits to your town, and divide them up among all the people to whom you wish to do good; only be careful not to let any single person have more than half a fruit, so that the happiness they bring may be shared among as many people as possible." The woman thanked her and hastened onward.

When the townsfolk, who were watching, saw the young wife drawing near, they rejoiced greatly, and, when she gave back the iron to her fellow wife, they praised her much for her courage. Her husband also gave her great gifts for being so brave. Her child meanwhile had almost cried itself to death, for she had been away four days, but it looked up and smiled when she took it once more in her arms.

After she had rested, the woman cut up the Ochitt fruits and distributed them to as many as possible of the townsfolk. Half of one she gave to her fellow wife, the owner of the Ejimm, who had forced her to undertake such a dangerous journey. For herself she kept only a quarter of a fruit, and even this she did not eat, but laid it down on the Nju Aupp, the little mound on which the water-pots are set. Then she told her elder child to look after the babe and the house while she herself went down to the stream to draw water. Hardly had she left before the barren wife came in, saw the piece of fruit lying upon the mound, snatched it up and ate it.

When the younger wife returned from the spring she wished to eat her fruit, but could not find it. She asked her child if she had taken it, and, while questioning her, the other wife came into the room.

"You need not ask your daughter," said she, "for it was I who ate the piece of Nchitt." *

On this the younger woman went out and called the townsfolk together. When all were assembled, she said to them:

"One day, when our husband was away hunting, my fellow-wife and I went down to the spring. She saw that my child

* Singular of Ochitt.

GHOSTS

was about to be born, but went away and left me mournfully calling for help. All of a sudden, out came Ngbe Eing and aided me, but demanded that half my babe should be given her to devour. I was glad when Ise ran up, but sad when he decided that Eing must have what she claimed as the price of her aid. Soon, however, I saw that he was only deceiving the monster, so that I might gain time to reach home. Thither Eing tracked me, and sat waiting to devour my child, but my husband returned while she had gone to the spring, and killed her with the pot-hook which belonged to his other wife. When the latter heard all that had chanced, she would accept nothing in exchange for the iron, but demanded that I myself should fetch it from the ghost town, thinking that I should die on the way, and that my new-born babe would perish for lack of me. Judge now, all ye people, whether this proves hatred and ill will?"

"It is hate, strong hate," shouted all the people.

The woman continued, "Please listen further. After having had more of the joy-giving Nchitt than I kept for myself, this woman stole the one piece which was left in my house, so that nothing remains for me of all that I brought from Mfam Akabansi. What punishment does she deserve for this?"

"No other," answered all the people in a great shout, "than to go to the ghost town, and fetch you your Nchitt from the chief of the ghosts."

The husband tried to plead that his wife might be forgiven, but she herself stepped forth proudly and stopped him. "I will accept no favour," she said, "and am willing to go to Mfam Akabansi and fetch the Nchitt."

Just as the first had done, this woman also went to Porcupine to question the charm, and the answer was unfavourable. Yet she started out.

On reaching the same stream, the second wife saw the woman covered with sores. At the sight, she held her nose and began to spit as though she had tasted gall. The poor old creature begged her to stop doing this and to take a stick with which to scrub her back, as she was not fit to do this for herself.

The elder wife took a long stick, stood as far off as possible still holding her nose, and, instead of rubbing the poor old dame, only poked at the sores. The old woman begged her to stop, but she poked the more, saying, "You asked for scrubbing, and shall get such an one as to last you once for all!" No entreaties could touch her, but suddenly the old woman sprang out of the water, and stood before her, young, beautiful and richly robed. Then the wicked wife was frightened and begged to be forgiven. The Chieftainess answered, "I will do you no harm. Go on your way"

When the visitor entered the town she would not look at the old and sick people, and, when a man barred her path, and asked where she was going, she bade him be off out of her sight, for she had come to get Ochitt from the Chief of the ghosts, and not to answer questions from such as he.

This answer angered the man, who struck out with his club and felled her to the earth, so that she died at once.

All the ghosts gathered round, and ate up the body. Afterwards the Chieftainess gave orders that no live person should ever again come to Mfam Akabansi, and, from that day, hid the road from mortal eyes.

Days, weeks, months and years went by, but the wicked wife returned no more. The younger woman lived happily with her husband till the end of her life, in spite of the fact that she did not get the Nchitt; for she was kind and sweet tempered to all.

When a man dies he can see the road to the ghost town, but while alive he can find it no more.

Not only egg plants, but native tomatoes, are also thought to have come from the ghost town, as related in the following story.—

How the First Tomatoes came on Earth.

There once lived a man named Effa, and his wife named Akat. When the husband's mother died they sent round to all the neighbouring towns to invite the people to come and "play" for her death. The spirit of the dead woman went to a ghost town, which was as far off from that where her son dwelt as is Niaji from Nkami. One of the ghosts, named Echi, who in life had dwelt near them, thought that he would like to attend the play for the old woman's death, so he started out to go to Effa's town.

At the first place he came to, the Chief asked him, "What is your name?" He answered, "I am called Egut when I travel," and begged them to lend him a hand. This they did. At the next town he asked some of the people to give him a neck. This also they granted. The third town gave him a second hand, the fourth a belly, the fifth loins, and the sixth and seventh each provided a foot. At the next town he begged for a matchet, and for a gun at the one after that.

At the tenth town the people were all away save one woman. She came to the door of her compound to look at the stranger. So beautiful was he with all his borrowed limbs that she fell in love with him, and begged him to stay with her for a few days. She also was very beautiful, so he agreed, and when she asked for his name he said to her, "My name is Nopp Amba."

After he left her he went straight to the town where they were "playing" for the dead woman. All the people rejoiced at the coming of so handsome a stranger, and to them he said, "My real name is Echi." Then they all fell to singing and dancing, but in both arts the ghost man excelled them

A woman named Atem marked the grace of his dancing and the sweetness of his voice, and fell in love with him. He in turn noticed how kind were her glances when they rested upon him, and said to her as he had done to the other woman:

"My name is Nopp Amba. Will you take me for your husband while I stay in the town?" To this Atem agreed.

When they had finished "playing" for the dead woman, Echi prepared to go back home. Atem begged to be taken with him, but he refused, and said to her. "I am not able to keep two wives."

A meeting of the whole town was called, and the matter laid before them. They said, "You have married the woman, and it must be as she chooses." So, as she still persisted, the couple started back together. At the towns from which he had borrowed them, the husband returned the gun and the matchet. At the next places he gave up those parts of his body which had been lent him there.

When the woman saw him do this she began to weep, and said .

"Had I known what manner of man you were I would never

have taken you for my husband." But he still went on, and at each town his body grew less.

At length Atem refused to go any further, and would have returned to her own home, but the ghost said, "Of your own will you came, and now there is no turning back for you."

After the last town was passed only a skull remained to him When they entered the ghost town the inhabitants flocked out to welcome them, and one woman ghost saw Echi's wife, and recognised her at once. She said:

"This woman is my sister. Let her come to my house."

When night came, all the ghost people gathered together. and wanted to kill Atem, so that they might eat her. The sister, however, hid her, and said:

"Listen to me, and I will save you Touch nothing which they shall give you to eat, for if you eat of their chop you will die. They cannot harm you if you eat only what I give you." She then hid her sister in a secret place, and gave her tomatoes on which to stay her hunger.

So soon as all was safe she took Atem by the hand and set her on the homeward road. At parting she said to her:

"When you get home tell no one of what you have seen here."

So Atem left her sister, and hastened back to her town.

When she reached her house she felt very ill, so she went to Nyopp (Porcupine) and asked him to practise the charm for her:

Porcupine did so, and said:

"Throw the tomatoes which still remain to you into some soft earth at the back of your house, then go to the entrance of the town, make a sacrifice, and lay seven leaves on the ground."

This Atem did, and when the ghosts who had pursued her came and found them, they began to count the leaves. 1, 2, 3, 4, 5, 6, they counted, but could not add 7. So they ate the sacrifice, and went their way.

Up till this time, when ghosts were hungry, they came into the towns, and into the houses, and would not leave till the owners had given them whatever they asked. Since the sacrifice of the seven leaves was made, they do not do this any more. That is the reason why you see ghost sacrifices hung up before the town. There were also no native tomatoes till Atem brought them from her sister Affion at the ghost town. Those which she threw, by command of Porcupine, into the earth at the back of her house, sprang up and flourished, and it is from them that all native tomatoes come.

CHAPTER XXIII

Beyond Netim

THREE miles beyond Netim flows the Calabar River, which is the boundary between the land of the Ekoi, and that of the Ojo and Uyanga tribes.

A few yards from the bank lies a great oval-shaped stone, half embedded in the ground. Behind it a Juju tree has been planted, and in front a heap of leaves is piled, similar to that near the River of Good Fortune. The stone is one of the altars of Nimm, and well it is to seek her protection before entering the water, for the river has a sinister reputation, and is here over 300 feet wide and very rapid. The Ekoi have a little song about it, which, in all save name, is the counterpart of our

> "River of Dart, River of Dart
> Every year thou claimest a heart"

To ensure safety in crossing, leaves should be plucked and rubbed on the forehead, over the pineal gland, with the following prayer:

"'Me   eyange,   eyange, nkiji ka njimm   aiya 'ni
(May) I (be) free from danger, from danger, I go to other side water in,
     kpe   njum ebi nkaien!
may (I) thing evil not see!"

The leaves are then thrown upon the heap, with this invocation:

"Nkupba   aiya oiyange, kpe   nyipp   aserre   echi!
I am coming river across, may crocodile lay down (his) head!"

At the time of the new yams no prayer is made, as everyone knows that it would be unheard, for just as the Kwa is the dwelling-place of Nimm, so the Calabar is the special home of the Efumi of crocodiles and elephants, many of whom have their homes in its deep places.

Nimm Stone, Calabar River.

At one Ekoi town, a little lower down, where all the inhabitants are supposed to be "Efumi" of crocodiles, they give notice that for seven days during the new yam festival all traffic should be stopped, for if any man enter the water during that time he would never gain the further bank. The Efumi are holding their great festival to the Juju "Animm" (plural of Nimm), and to this, anyone rash enough to enter the water, or unfortunate enough to be caught and dragged down from the bank, must be sacrificed. Nimm will hear no prayer, as she longs for offerings, in return for which she makes fruitful the farms of her worshippers. At this time too each crocodile soul leaves the body which it has inhabited during the last year, and chooses another in which to dwell during the next twelve moons.

Early in 1911 the towns of Nsan, Obung, and Netim begged me to send up a hunter to drive away the herds of wild animals which were devastating their farms. The same request had come in from so many towns, however, that it was not until late in the year that I could send my hunter to that part of the District He seemed reluctant to go, but this might have been due to the fact that he had no friends there, so I did not give the matter further thought. The reason for his unwillingness was however explained, when, a little later, circumstances made it necessary for me to visit the neighbourhood.

One morning a boy of about fifteen ran into my office in the last stage of terror and exhaustion. According to his story, two men named Tambe and Wanchi hired him at Calabar, to go with them to the interior. They did not allow him to enter towns on the way, but sent him through the bush, giving as an excuse that there was something in his load which they did not wish seen, but really because they feared that questions might be asked on their return without the boy. Just before reaching Ojo Nkonmba food ran short, so they stopped at one of the towns to buy more. At Ojo, Ongwaw, the son of one of the chiefs, asked the boy what country he came from; afterwards he was taken by his masters to the house of Chief Ikum, where they arranged to sell him for £20. Next day he was left with Ikum, while Tambe and Wanchi went back to Calabar. Soon after they had left, a cage formed of iron rods was brought out, 4 feet by 4 feet by 2 feet, such as was only used for human sacrifice to the Jujus. The Chief wanted to make the boy drink rum, but he would not do so, for one of the women cried out that they were going to kill him. Ikum himself ate and drank, then tied his hunting knife round his waist One of his wives, named Ekungbe, called out and said, " Do not kill the boy " Ikum was very angry and struck her. The chief stood by the door. The boy stated, "It was night time, and I was on the other side of the compound by the head wife. She said to me, ' I am sorry for you, because you are a good boy. You brought firewood and helped with other work in my house If you could get away, perhaps you might reach "white man."' I slipped behind her and ran into the bush. People came out with lanterns to seek for me, but I hid away from them. I dared not follow the road lest men from other towns might be warned of my escape, and catch me and give me up again to the people of Ojo. On the third day I saw Forest-guard Okore, so I ran to him, and begged him to help me to get to white man."

Under these circumstances it was necessary to visit the town concerned, both to inquire into the story and to ensure the safety of the friendly woman.

After crossing the Calabar River, the road leads through beautiful and comparatively easy country, over streams, many of which are, during the dry season, mere strings of tiny waterfalls, dashing down between fern-fringed banks, but, in the rains, swell into torrents, which tear down from the mountains, bearing all before them.

Just before Ojo Nkonmba, we came upon a little river, on the banks of which, by the ford, grew a great clump of ground orchids, allied to Horsmanni, but with some points of difference. The flowers, shading from palest mauve to deepest purple, were borne on stems 4 to 5 feet high. The whole clump stood out from its dark background with the lustre of dew-drenched amethysts, and was mirrored again, narcissus-like, in the clear stream below

The native name for the inhabitants of Ojo Nkonmba and their neighbours of Ojo Akangba is "Kabila," but they are

Ikum, Head Chief of Ojo Nkonmba.

generally known by their Efik name—"Ojo." They belong to the same race as the people of Ekuri, whom we shall mention later on, but separated from them many years ago. Even in a comparatively short space of time, and although a certain amount of communication has been kept up, the language has considerably altered Like all other tribes in this neighbourhood, they have gradually come down from the North.

The old chief is an object of great reverence to his people On a former visit, when he came up to welcome us, he was wearing a gorgeous cap of scarlet cloth, cut somewhat after the Phrygian style, and decorated round the base with two double rows of leopards' claws By old custom he is never supposed to be seen bareheaded, and is the object of several interesting tabu

In a country like this, where the black population outnumbers the white by about 4,000 to 1, it is a matter of absolute necessity that certain signs of respect should be shown to the ruling race. Had the chief been allowed to continue covered, it would not only have meant that white rule would have fallen into discredit in his town and for many miles round, but that he himself would have had no respect for those who did not exact this token of it from him. He was therefore told that the hat must be removed while addressing the white man, and after some little trouble consented. His submission had one curious result. An elderly woman, with hair once bright red, but now tinged with grey, came up, positively capering with joy, which she made no effort to hide. She brought us a present of the largest yam we had ever seen, and explained that she was the head wife of the chief who had just had a lesson in manners. Her evident delight, because of her husband's discomfiture, puzzled us until we found out that he had been annoying her for years by airs and graces, invented to enhance his importance among his people, beside those tabu imposed on him by reason of his position as head priest of Akillinga, such as the rule of eating alone.

When we reached the town to inquire into the boy's story, we found it divided against itself. The townsfolk had decided to remove to another site, and the women, the young men and "members" were strongly opposed to that which the head men had chosen. The former pleaded that they did not wish to leave the main road and go right into the " bush," and also that there was no good water near the new site. When I visited this next morning, the reason both for the objection of the people and the choice of the chiefs became perfectly clear. The latter had chosen a spot where they hoped to be less visited by Government officials, or any person likely to carry reports to the white man. It was a long distance from the main road, along a difficult track, and, as the opposition party had stated, the only water within easy reach was a stream which dried up during the dry season. The new town, however, would have been close to the place where the head chief had built this compound, within which was the shrine of the great Juju Akillinga.

No wonder that the women, the young men and the " members" feared to leave the main road, where there was always a chance that some passer-by might hear cries for help or appear on the scene in time to make the chiefs afraid to sacrifice them to the Juju, lest news of their doings should be carried to those who would exact a swift vengeance.

Akillinga has, even in this land, the reputation of being a particularly cruel Juju. Before it, up to quite recent times, enemies were admittedly sacrificed, and cannibal rites carried out, though at present such practices are disclaimed with great energy. The relief of those of the community, from among whom sacrificial victims would naturally be chosen, was so obvious on my pronouncing against the site favoured by the chiefs, that the cause of their objection was clear to the most unobservant.

The people of Ojo Nkonmba, and their neighbours of Ojo Akangba, all of whom have now agreed to join together to form one town, believe that their souls are "Efumi" of elephants. Their farms are unravaged, and not a single uprooted palm tree was to be seen, though, only a few miles off, in Ekuri territory, the people were complaining of starvation from the depredations of vast herds.

The day before our visit, my hunter, Okun Omin, had tracked two wounded beasts down to the brink of the Calabar River, but when he saw them take to the water, he

Source of the Calabar River.

dared not follow, as the people of Netim, who accompanied him, said that these were two of the Ojo who had gone down to their houses in the bed of the river, there to take on human forms and tend their wounds. It was about the time of the new yams, and he dared not risk the peril of being seized by these uncanny river-folk, and offered to Animm.

One evening, not long after, the talk turned on the Efumi of elephants, and the following story was told :—

ADA THE FOREST DEMON.
BY NDUM OF NSAN.

Awsang Atikawt was a great hunter. So skilled was he that he never gave up the chase of any animal whose trail he had once started to follow. One day he was sitting with some friends when they began complaining of the way in which their farms were being destroyed by elephants. Atikawt asked why they did not at once follow the tracks of the beasts and kill them. They answered that they were afraid to do this, lest they themselves should be killed by the elephants. Atikawt said that they were cowards, and that he himself would not rest till he had destroyed every elephant which might dare to leave its mark upon his farm.

Now among those present were two men who were Efumi of elephants. One of these Efumi stood up and said to Atikawt, " Ka kpe awkame. Ojjokk kun oyi ebin eja awsem " (" Boast no more. Elephants may eat your farm and go free ").

But Atikawt answered steadily, " Ofu ojjokk awgae, tik oyen ngam " (" The day elephants try, they will see me ")

When they heard this, the two Efumi men looked sharply at one another. Then they arranged to go and destroy the farm and see what would happen.

Not long after, Atikawt's wives brought him news that their farm had been ruined by elephants. At once he began to get provisions together, and having filled his hunting bag, set out well armed for the chase. He soon got on the trail of the beasts and followed them till dark. All night he rested, leaning against a tree, and started again as soon as the dawn rose On and on he went till it was dark once more. Then he climbed into a great tree to pass the night, and next day overtook the elephants by a stream. At once when they saw him with his gun loaded ready to fire, they changed into human form, and begged him to spare them. He knew them for his friends the two Efumi, with whom he had conversed a few days before, so bade them watch while he shot at the trunk of a very tall tree. When the men saw how great a piece was blown away by the shot, they grew still more fearful, and begged Atikawt not to harm them, and they would repay him for all the damage they had done. To this he agreed, and turned to go home by the way he had come.

No sooner was he out of sight than the men once more assumed their elephant forms. Then they performed a great Juju and caused a heavy rain to fall, so that the whole road was blotted out Atikawt could not find his way home, and wandered in the woods till he was completely lost. After many hours he found himself in a part of the bush where he had never been before. When the rain stopped, he saw that he was close to a house the like of which he had never seen, it was so splendid. In it dwelt a "Forest Woman," and all around were heaps of human skulls and piles of bones.

The hunter gave himself up for lost, but suddenly he heard a call, "Awsang Atikawt" He answered, and saw a little lame girl creep out from a small side door. She came up to him and said how sorry she was that he had been so unlucky as to come to that place, for her mistress was a monster who killed and ate all who came near her palace, and by magic arts could overtake those who tried to flee. "Nevertheless," said the girl, "I may save you, and send you home safely if you will do as I say. Only you must not eat of any food which my mistress may offer you."

Awsang was thankful to hear this, and gladly promised to eat nothing save by the little maid's leave.

"Good," she said. "Then take this," and gave him a piece of edible clay. "Eat of it, and throw the food given you by my mistress to any animal which you may see, only do not let her know that you do this. In the night time you must beware, for she will take you to her chamber. When she seems to fall asleep, listen carefully. If her snores are only as loud as a tornado lie quite still, for she is awake, but when the sound of them shakes the house like the crash of thunder, you will know that she is asleep at last. Then creep from her room and come to me very softly. I will give you two kinds of magic plants which you must carry with you in your flight. Wring the juice of the first so that it falls on the gate, and it will fly open for you to pass out. Let the juice of the second fall into the river and it will dry up, so that you can cross over. When you are once on the other side do not turn round, but throw the 'medicine' leaves over your shoulder into the water, and the river will rise behind you and fill up the pass, so that you cannot be followed and recaptured."

Just then they heard the sound of the beating of drums, the blowing of horns and all kinds of music, borne on the evening breeze.

The little maid said that her mistress was coming, and that all the sounds came from her body. She bade the hunter stand still, while she hurried back to her hiding place.

Atikawt stood trembling with fear. No sooner had the Giantess drawn near than the music stopped She approached him quite gently, and told him not to fear, for she would take him for her husband, as she had been long without one.

When they had entered the palace she asked him to be seated. He sat down trembling, for indeed he was much afraid

" Monn-I-Mbuni " (Child of Lameness), she called to the little maid The latter came to her slowly, pretending that she had been sleeping. In her forest language the Giantess said, pointing to her guest, "To-morrow we shall have good meat for dinner.'

"Anaw" ("Just so"), answered the girl.

When the evening meal was ready, the monster dropped " medicine " into Atikawt's share. He, however, told her that in his country it was only lawful for a man like him to eat in the goat pen, so he was allowed to carry his food thither.

When he reached the place where the goats were, he spilt the ood on the ground so that the beasts might eat it. At the moment when it touched the ground, a flame sprang forth, but he sat, quietly watching, till the fire had gone out, and the goats ate all. Then he went back to the Forest Woman, and, after a short talk together, they went to bed

Before this the Giantess had put an iron instrument, sharply pointed, to heat in the fire. This she meant to thrust through Atikawt when he fell asleep. After a while she began to snore like a tornado, just as the little lame girl had said. He lay very quiet, and in a short time the snores grew so loud that the whole palace trembled.

Then the hunter crept out, took some pillows, and put them in the place where he had lain. Next he drew a cover over them, and, when all was arranged smoothly, went in search of his little lame friend, who gave him the promised "medicines."

When the first drops wrung from the magic herb fell upon the gate, it flew open before him, and, on crushing the leaves so that their juice fell into the river, this also held back the flow of its waters, and allowed him to cross. Just before he had reached the other side, however, he heard a sound as of thunder from the palace. "The Forest Woman is coming," thought he.

Once on shore he felt quite safe. He threw the "medicine" over his shoulder without looking round, and then turned to see what would happen. Immediately the river began to rise, and soon the whole pass was blocked by the swirling water, so that Atikawt could go on his way without fear of pursuit.

Meantime, about midnight, the Giantess awoke. She went to the fire and drew from it the sharp-pointed iron, which was now quite red. This she forced through the pillows which Atikawt had arranged. They at once caught fire. Judge if the monster was vexed or no! The fire raged all around, and the man, on whom she had intended to feast next day, had fled homeward!

She turned to follow in hot pursuit, but in her haste forgot to take with her the magic herbs which would cause the water to divide. Therefore when she came to the torrent she could not cross, so she stood on her side of the river and called to him on the other side:

"Ojjak anaw tik osiri se jen, Awsang Atikawt?" ("What will you say, where you go, Awsang Atikawt?")

"I will say," he answered, "that I have seen a woman who lives alone in the woods, who kills and eats all whom she entraps. A woman who has drums, blowing horns and even big guns in her belly. She is a danger to the whole human

Crossing a River.

An Oban Elephant.

race. The sooner she is killed the better for all hunters." Filled with fury at this, the Giantess went back to her palace, but Atikawt went on his way, and was received with the utmost joy.

A few days later a beautiful woman was seen coming towards the town. On her head she bore a calabash full of " chop," and her robes were richer than any there. She stopped to ask which was the house of Atikawt, and was at once led towards it. When the hunter came forward to welcome his guest and ask what she wished of him, she said that she came from a neighbouring town through which he had passed some time ago. She had seen him and at once fallen in love, but, though she had inquired from everyone as to his name and dwelling place, it was only that very day that she had at last found out. Awsang Atikawt listened to her flattering words, and never doubted that all was as she said.

Now one of the wives of Atikawt was a witch, and by her magic she found that the visitor was none other than Ada Etim Agbo Etum (Ada the Forest Ruler). So she called to her husband and warned him, saying, as plainly as possible, that the beautiful stranger was the very monster from whom he had lately escaped, the fiend woman, with the drums, bugles, guns and all manner of terrors in her belly.

Atikawt only laughed, and said that if his wife could see the Giantess, she would know at once how different was the latter from their visitor.

When evening came, the witch wife went to him again, and begged that now at least he would send the stranger away, for indeed she was the very monster about whose cruel deeds he had been so ready to talk a few days before. He, however, instead of consenting, only laughed the more, and told his wife that she was too jealous by far.

At night when he was going to rest by the side of the beautiful stranger, his wife again called him aside, and begged yet more earnestly that at least he would not sleep with their guest, lest she should kill him, for she was indeed none other than the forest woman Ada Etim Agbo Etum. When he remained obstinate, the woman saw that warnings were useless, but determined to do what she could to save him, for she was too anxious on his account to sleep unheeding. She went to the place where her husband's hunting dogs were, and pretended to be looking on the ground for something she had lost. Meantime she singled out two of the fiercest, and, while patting and fondling them, managed to whisper that they must keep wide awake all night and guard their master, otherwise the strange woman would kill him. Now both of these dogs were witch dogs, as the woman very well knew, and when she had gone sadly to her room, though, alas! not to sleep, they rose and crept to the place where their master lay by the stranger's side.

When some hours had passed, and all was still, Ada Etim Agbo Etum, for indeed it was she, disguised as a beautiful woman, thought that now it would be quite safe to kill Atikawt. She therefore struck her belly, and lo! out of it sprang the sharp-pointed iron, red hot. She prepared to drive this into the man by her side and kill him while he slept; but at the first movement up sprang the dogs, barking their loudest, and threw themselves upon her.

Atikawt awoke at once, and Ada, full of vexation, struck her belly once more, whereon the red-hot iron sprang within and was hidden. She then pretended that she also had been disturbed by the dogs, and said that she could not sleep if they stayed in the room. He therefore got up, took a stick, and soundly beat the poor dogs who had saved his life. Afterwards he chained them up on the verandah, and went back to his guest once more.

No sooner had he entered and closed the door than the witch wife crept out of her room, unchained the dogs, and whispered to them to keep as wide awake as before.

When Ada saw the hunter once more sleeping, she got up again, and hit her belly, whereon the red-hot iron reappeared. In sprang the dogs through the window, and attacked her, barking as loudly as before, so that Atikawt was awakened again. Just at that moment the cock crowed.

Ada sprang up at the sound, and told Atikawt that she must at once set out homeward. She begged him to chain up his dogs, and himself lead her on her way.

So foolish was the man that he not only did as she asked,

but took the keys with him, so that it should be impossible for anyone to free the dogs after he had left.

On the way the stranger told Atikawt to walk in front of her, but he refused her request, and said that he would rather she should go before him. This was the first and quite necessary opposition offered to his guest by Atikawt. His refusal, however, warned her that he might be growing aware of her true nature. She waited her chance, and often turned round to look at him, but could do nothing since she was before him, and he could see everything which she tried to do.

In a short time she hit upon a plan by which she thought she could rid herself of him for a while. Near the road grew a tree, which was covered by a climber. On this hung ripe fruits of a kind called Nsebbe by the Ekoi, though the Efik people call it Eting Keni. She asked the hunter to climb this tree and gather fruits for her. No sooner had he obeyed, than, by her magic, she caused it to grow, till it was taller than any tree in the whole world. Then, when she saw that Atikawt was safely held so far above her that he could not get back to prevent anything she might do, she struck her belly once more. About twenty men sprang out fully armed. They surrounded the tree, and called up tauntingly to the hunter, " Now fly " Ada also began to boast and to speak thus :

"'We oyen, okkpe oyen se oyen njum ebi.
If you look, (and) again look you can say you see a bad thing "

When Atikawt heard this, he thought of all his wife's warnings, and burst into tears. Also he understood the true reason why his dogs had barked in the night. From the top of the tree, where he clung, he could see his native town. He thought of the dogs whom he had chained up, and began to call for them, and to weep for his own folly.

Ada meanwhile ordered her men to cut down the tree with the axes which they carried. They began to do this, and, while the blows fell, a parrot flew by. He saw what had happened and bore to Atikawt's house news of the wretched plight of its master. He told them to loose the dogs at once, or one who had gone forth that morning would never come home. The keys could not be found, and the other people would have given up in despair, but the witch wife saw by her vision that the tree was near falling, and that only if the dogs were set free at once could they reach their master in time. So she got a stone, with it beat the chains till they broke, and then told the dogs where to go. These had not got half way, however, before the tree fell, but, happily for Atikawt, it was caught by another tree, and so could not come to the ground. Then Ada gave orders that the second tree should be cut through, so that Atikawt might at length fall into her power.

At the moment when this tree also came crashing down, the dogs reached the spot. Now one of them was called Oro Njaw. He was the fiercest of them all, and at once darted on the Forest Woman, while the others attacked her men and put them to flight. Many of these were killed, but some escaped. Ada herself was torn in pieces.

Thus ends the story of Awsang Atikawt, the famous hunter, and Ada Etim Agbo Etum, the terrible Forest Woman, who had within her belly all the music of all the world, and also all weapons which have ever been made

So we see that the plot made by the two Efumi of elephants to destroy this hunter's farm brought about a great advantage to us, namely, the death of Ada Etim Agbo Etum, the Forest Woman. A famous hunter must Atikawt indeed have been to have freed the bush from so cruel a monster !

Type of Uyanga.

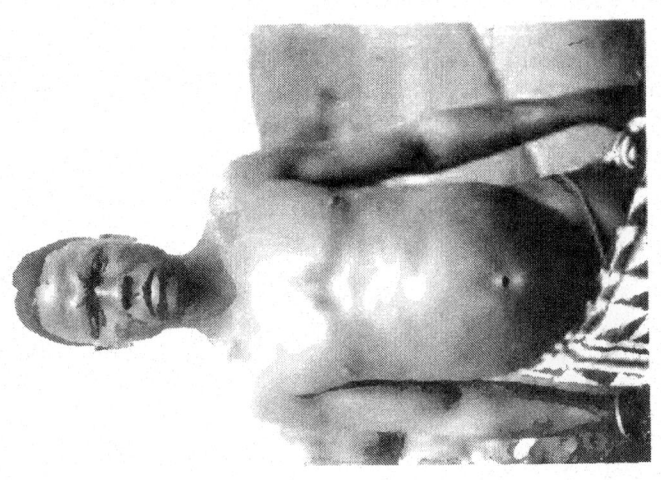

Type of Ekuri.

CHAPTER XXIV

Uyanga and Ekuri

To the north of the Ojo people live a small tribe called the Uyanga, who have settled at Ifunkpa, Owai Ifunkpa, and the three Iko towns. They are renowned all over this part of the country for their knowledge of medicine and magic. According to an article written by the Rev. J. K. MacGregor, in the *Journal of the Royal Anthropological Institute*, June, 1909, they are supposed to have learned the greater part of their magic lore, and also their knowledge of Nsibidi—the secret primitive writing already mentioned—from monkeys who came and sat round their camp fires. Unfortunately, it has not been possible to find a trace of this interesting legend among the people themselves. Perhaps it is allowable to mention here that the Ekoi claim to have originated this script, of which several hundred characters and a considerable number of complete stories were collected during our stay.*

Up to fifty years ago, the whole Uyanga tribe lived together by the River Tegott, north of Owai Ifunkpa, but separated about that time and founded the different towns in which they now dwell Early in 1909 the tribe was in a state of great excitement. They had heard that a force was marching against them, to arrest the persons concerned in the maltreatment of a Court Messenger. Some Native Court Clerk had sent in a highly picturesque account of their habits. Among other pleasing details he wrote that the houses were all "occupied with skulls." Up to this time, the people had been dwelling on more or less debatable land, as the country was not yet mapped, so it was not certain to which District they belonged.

It was somewhat difficult to obtain a guide, owing to the

* See Nsibidi, Chapter XXVIII.

sinister reputation of the people, but when Owai Ifunkpa was reached, white rags were seen fluttering from bamboo poles, to act as flags of truce. The Juju trees and stones had been freshly smeared with blood, or in some cases red and yellow paint, in order to propitiate the Genii and ensure protection from any danger which their white visitors might be bringing upon them.

Iko Akperem is only about 8 miles from Owai Ifunkpa. No white man had been through this part of the country before, and everywhere in the bush Juju offerings were to be seen, overhead, underfoot, and at each side of the road. Here, as at all non-Ekoi towns in the District, the people were away at their bush farms. They only come into the towns during the rainy season, or on special occasions, for, unlike the Ekoi, they have not, as yet, reached the sociable "town" stage. The difference is very clearly marked in their manners, which are not nearly so polite or friendly as those of the Ekoi. Some of the Iko chiefs were in the town, but from their behaviour it was evident that their feelings were far from friendly This was quite explained when we heard, on our return, that not many miles off vigorous hostilities were proceeding between two tribes, one of which was allied to the people of Iko. A Government force was at the moment employed in restoring order, which was attended with considerable difficulty, as the warring tribes had provided themselves with rifle pits and similar luxuries.

About 20 miles from Owai Ifunkpa lies Ekuri Owai. The road leads through difficult, hilly country, and is crossed by innumerable streams and rivers. It is in this part of the district that that rare and beautiful tree, the *Baikiea Insignis*, is to be found, with its creamy white petals over half a foot in length and velvety buds of dark golden brown

On first visiting the place, nothing but a bush track was to be found, and men with matchets had to go on ahead to clear a path for the carriers, who could not march at the rate of more than a mile an hour The inhabitants are called Ekuri by Efik and Ekoi, but "Nkokolle" is the name they give themselves.

While dining in the Egbo shed, loud cries were heard, and people were seen rushing round the town in a great state of

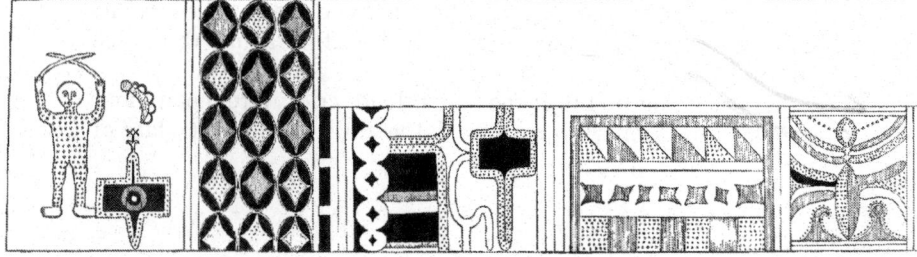

Note Chameleon. Open spaces represent windows. (Heraldic colouring.)

excitement. On sending out to find the cause of this, it was discovered that a "war party" had come in from Oburekkpe. When questioned, they quieted down, and explained that they had come to inform Ekuri that "war" had broken out in some neighbouring towns. Later, it transpired that they themselves had started the fighting, and had been carrying round young palm leaves, on which were hung freshly killed human jaws, in token of victory. These gruesome trophies were

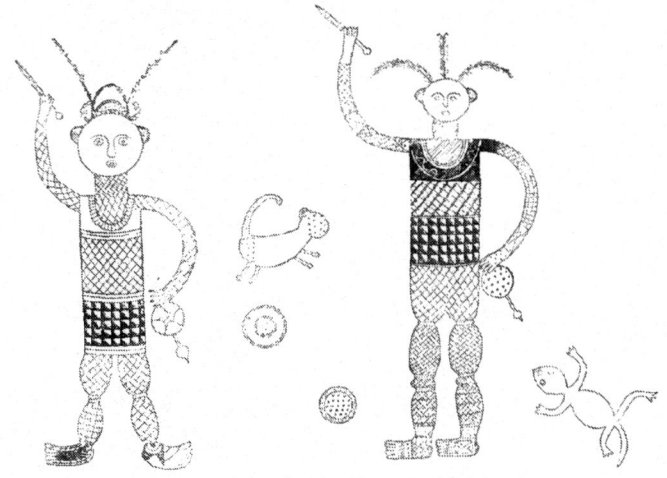

Figures at end of Egbo House, Ekuri Owai.

hidden on the first whisper of the arrival of a "white man," and information was not brought till too late to take action.

The Egbo house here is most elaborately painted. Indeed, the designs seemed remarkable enough to be worth copying, as it is the most ambitious colour scheme in the District.* Before the house stands a pillar which forms a ghastly monument to the state of affairs which is only just passing away. All over the country such relics exist, and a still worse example is to be found at Oburekkpe, where many skulls are fastened round the Juju post.

The chiefs of Ekuri Owai, who, like most others, have now grown very friendly, asked permission to remove their town to

* See p. 290.

a new site on the bank of the Ukpon River, just opposite Etara They gave as a reason that it was impossible for them to exist in their present town, because of the ravages caused by elephants in outlying farms, which the townsfolk were not numerous enough to protect. They described the bush around them as full of elephants, but, although I had come across a herd on a former visit, the statement on the present occasion seemed so exaggerated that I thought it possible that the chiefs were giving the rein to their fancy, in the hope that, by so doing, a few extra kegs of gunpowder might be obtained.

The statements were, however, completely corroborated during the march next day. Hardly had we left the outlying farms behind us before we saw the traces of great herds of elephants, and only a few miles had been traversed when a delighted exclamation broke from one of my companions. "Oh," she cried, "we have nearly reached camp! I can hear them cutting and hammering."

Almost at the same moment the chair-carrier, who was a little ahead, came rushing back, his face a picture of terror.

There was only time to beg my companions to take cover behind some big trees, and snatch my rifle. The sounds came nearer, and a great herd of dark forms was to be seen crashing through the bush in our direction. A few resounding blows on one of the tree trunks by the path was enough to turn them, however, and they headed away from us. Hardly had they disappeared than something must have startled them in another direction—possibly the voices of carriers descending the hill to the rear. Anyhow, they turned again, and this time seemed to be making a blind rush down upon us. A shot from my 470 turned them once more, and they made off determinedly through the bush to our right

One huge bull was hit in the forehead, and left a great trail of blood which it was easy enough to follow. About an hour's stalking led past a mud bath, which they had made for themselves, to a little clearing, where the wounded bull was found in company with four others, all fully grown and with splendid tusks. A further shot from my orderly settled the business. The bull fell as a tree falls, and lay as if sleeping, without so much as a twitching muscle, while his three com-

An Elephant Road.

panions made off after the main herd. Unfortunately he proved to have only one tusk, about a 33-pounder, the other had been broken off close in some fight. He was, however, a fine specimen in his way, well over 11 feet in height.

That night there was great rejoicing. Fires were lit to keep off unwelcome visitors, while, with the same object, lamps were hung from poles outside the tents.

A beautiful spot had been chosen for the camp, within the loop of a river, which encircled it on three sides During the night, several times, strange boomings and trumpetings were heard, and next morning, not 100 yards from the further bank, great five-toed indentations, only a few hours old, were found, to prove how near to us the herd had passed. I followed them up, and for hours they kept tantalisingly just ahead, but time did not allow of tracking them down. No matter how often one has been out after elephants, it yet remains a somewhat curious experience to follow, hour after hour, in the footsteps of these strange survivals from another world The very irresistibility of their onward march, crushing down, by sheer weight, all but the very greatest of obstacles, appeals curiously to the imagination. As if in contempt of danger, or indeed as a kind of challenge thrown down to possible pursuers, they leave records, often strangely intimate, of themselves and their doings, for him who cares to read One huge bull had stayed to sharpen his tusks upon a tree, which was scored again and again at least 14 feet from the ground. Countless palm trees were uprooted to enjoy the soft "cabbage," while in places regular slides had been made in the clayey banks down which the great beasts might glide, as on an inclined plane, to gambol in the baths below.

From Ekuri Owai the road leads through a region where ebony is so plentiful that almost all the houses are built of it. The Egbo house at Oburekkpe was so small that we decided to use it as a sitting-room only, and had our tents pitched near by to sleep in. I cannot say that we passed a very happy night. The side of our tent almost touched a little ebony hut built over a large and gruesome-looking pot, the sides of which were ornamented with iron hooks. Before this, about breast high, and the length of a man, was a kind of altar, made of stout ebony blocks. In front of our tent door was a tall carved pillar, ornamented with strings of human skulls. The people all had the filed teeth and thin shrunken appearance usually associated with cannibal rites, and, although one and all stoutly denied knowledge of anything of the kind, every one of our carriers said that not only was the pot in the little

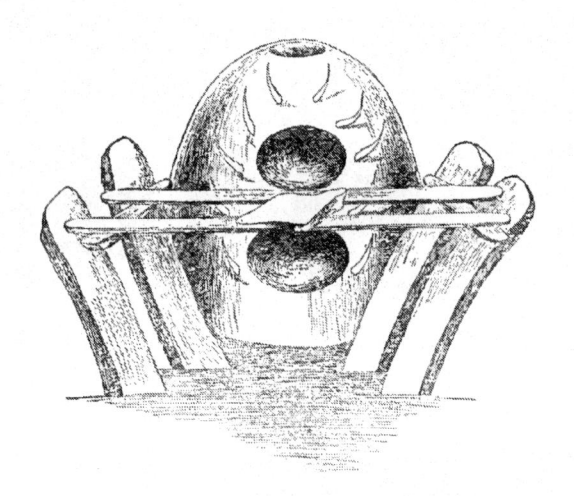

hut meant for the sacrifice of human victims, but the two hideous mud figures of a god and goddess in another shed on the further side of the carved pillar had had their heads worn away by constant libations of human blood poured over them.

The next place to be visited was Ekuri Eying, where the people of the two last-named towns first settled on coming down from the north. About sixty years ago they left to found Oburekkpe, whence, somewhat later, the people of Ekuri Owai again split off. On the road a rotting tree-trunk was passed, covered with Geasters, the first of this flower-like fungus to be discovered in Nigeria. Later, specimens of an unusually small kind were found on a peak near Oban, and in 1911 three more varieties of varying sizes were added to the collection.

To return to Ekuri Eying. This is a small town, now practically deserted, but with several points of interest.

One of the houses contains the shrine of a queer little god

Dancers with Juju Masks at Ekuri Eying.

Mourning Emblems at House of Dead Chief.

and goddess. The figures are seated on the ground, surrounded by offerings. The female has long, upstanding ears, which give her a rather rabbit-like appearance, while the male wears a false beard. In another house dwells a famous Juju man. Embedded in the mud before his door are three human skulls, before which human sacrifices used to be offered, and a very large number of these gruesome relics are displayed within In his possession were several ancient carved wooden heads of an unusual type, covered with human skin. With one of these he was induced to part. It bears a curious likeness to a fourteenth-century helmet.

In this part of the country, when a chief dies, it is customary to affix his coat and umbrella to the top of a tall palm stem, raised before his house.

On one occasion an old war dance was given in our honour. At the present day, mercifully, only wooden masks covered with skin are used, in lieu of the freshly killed heads of enemies formerly borne by the victors.

CHAPTER XXV

Conditions of Life in Peace and War

By old custom land can never be sold, but belongs to the heirs of the first settler, even if abandoned for hundreds of years. It is doubtful whether any part of the Ekoi country remains unowned at present, though there are great spaces, for instance, the Game and Forest Reserve, nearly 400 square miles in extent, which have been uninhabited for many years. A town, therefore, that wishes to remove to a fresh site must purchase the right of settlement, not ownership, from another. This is usually an affair of little difficulty, and the founding of Oban town on its present site, some fifty years ago, may be taken as typical.

The land belonged to the Ojuk people, who charged the newcomers:

One matchet, 1 sheep, 1 piece of iron, 1 hoe, and 7 iron hooks for the right to settle.

Forty pieces of dried meat for the hunting rights.

Fifteen baskets of fish for water rights; while, for forestry rights, 1 goat, 5 pieces of dried meat, and 500 pieces of ebony were exacted.

In addition, 3 pots of palm oil, 500 yams, 500 sleeping mats, and 10 bundles of corn were demanded in final settlement.

On starting a new town, a meeting is called, and after the site for the Egbo house has been agreed on, each family is apportioned its share of the new bush. As a rule, the first newcomer to explore a particular part has primary claim to it. The bush beyond the immediate vicinity is counted as belonging to the men who found it.

As already mentioned, the first ceremony of all is the choosing of the new site for the Egbo house. On this a little hut is erected, called "Ekpa Ntan" (the house without walls), and some Nimm stones laid where the Etai Ngbe will be raised later. Various sacrifices are then made to Obassi Osaw, Obassi Nsi and the ancestors.

The young men next clear bush, and erect temporary shelters, after which the actual planting is begun The head chief's compound is built, and gradually others, till dwellings have been provided for all

Special ceremonies are observed before the building of each homestead. The head chief, in company with the principal men of the town, hang up Antann leaves, and plant two young saplings of the Ibonn and Irun trees, where the little shrine will be set later. The name of Obassi is invoked, together with those of the chief ancestors. A libation of palm wine is then made, and other sacrifices offered.

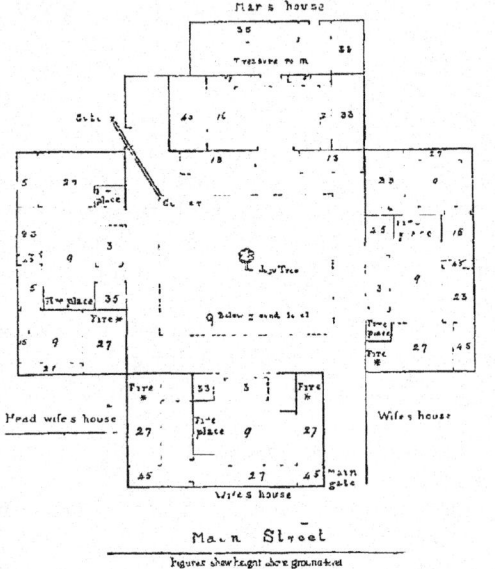

When the house is finished, the liane Mfinn is often laid right round it, without a break, so that no evil spirit can enter. The chief women of the town are then summoned, and palm oil and dried "Nsun" flesh offered to them, while the oldest of all lights the new fire upon the hearth.

Each compound is built much on the plan of a Roman house, with a central atrium, from which the living and sleeping rooms branch off. Even the mud couches, built against the walls of these rooms, are Roman in shape, while the red and black mural

264   IN THE SHADOW OF THE BUSH

decorations vividly recall in colour, though not in form, those of Pompeii.

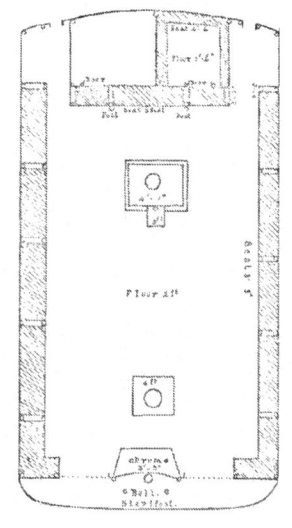

Here, too, as in old Rome, the head of each house is the priest of its particular Lares and Penates, though each Juju has in addition a head priest for the whole town.

As will be seen from the plan on p. 263, the four sides of a compound practically form four self-contained houses. One of these would be that of the husband, and each of the others would belong to one of his wives with her family, or to a married son. If the man is rich he would have an adjoining compound, on one side of which would be a hall to receive his guests, on another his sleeping room, and on a third his "treasure house."

Each compound is a little fortress in itself. A narrow door, which can easily be barricaded, at the back, and

Egbo House, NDEBBIJI
Figures shew height above ground level
Scale: ¼ inch = 8 feet.

Interior of Egbo House.

the front door, opening into the street, are the only means of ingress and egress. At night the animals were always driven into the central compound, as they still are in most towns, to ensure safety from leopards and other wild beasts. Should an enemy break into a compound, he would find it no easy matter to capture or kill the occupants, for the number of little secret chambers crammed into an Ekoi house is hardly believable.

As soon as the private dwellings are finished, the inhabitants set about building an Egbo house, nearly always on the plan given on the previous page.

This style of architecture is singularly well adapted to the conditions of the country. The open front, and many loop-holes, sheltered by overhanging eaves, provide the maximum of air with the minimum of glare—while complete protection is afforded against tornadoes.

Perhaps the most important part of the whole structure is the "Etai Ngbe," the long, cut stone, usually found standing before the second pillar. When this stone is first erected in a new town, every chief has to bring food in a calabash, and palm wine in an earthenware pot. A part is offered in sacrifice, and the rest eaten.

The stone is often transformed by rude painting into the rough semblance of a human being. A cap is made to fit the upper end, and iron in some form is always present, either in bars twisted round the stone, or laid below it.

Typical Pillar in Egbo House.

Women mud the walls, which they decorate after smoothing, but afterwards are never allowed to enter, save for cleaning purposes.

Near the Egbo house, and generally in front of it, is planted a young slip of the Isinn tree, brought from the one in the old town.

A village is usually composed of two rows of houses bordering the main road, which opens out into a broad space, where dances are held, before the Egbo house, then divides into two semi-circular arms, which surround the latter, and again join behind it. Sometimes several streets run parallel to the main one

To a certain extent the Ekoi may be termed an industrious people, and, with the exception of some turbulent spirits, both sexes have now become keen traders, though the greater share of this occupation naturally falls into the hands of the men. They have almost secured a monopoly of trade with the South-Western Cameroons, where they find a ready market for the salt, tobacco, cloth, and hardware from Calabar, which they themselves have purchased in exchange for fowls, dried meat, sleeping mats, rubber, and palm kernels. Owing to the improved roads and greater safety, trade has shown an extraordinary increase during

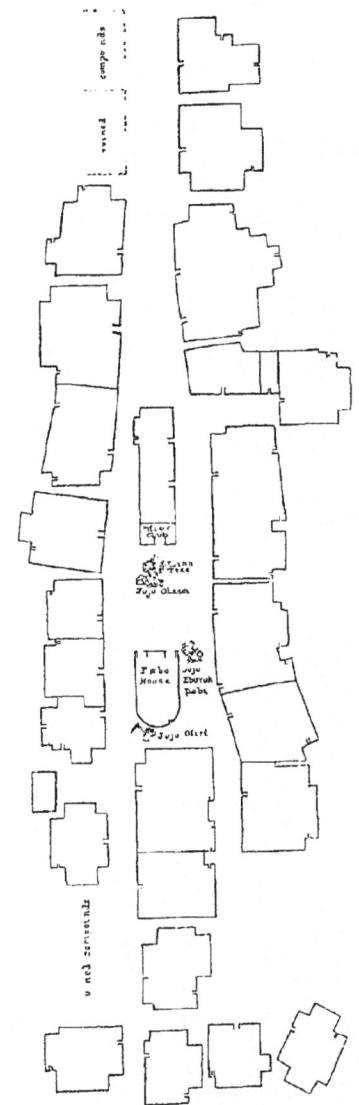

Plan of Aking
Scale ⅛ inch = 16 yards.

Juju Obassi Osaw.

Sacred Tree Always brought to a New Town from the Parent Tree in the Old Town.

the last four years. To take mats alone—where about fifty went down daily in 1907, over 500 are carried now.

In another direction also commerce is greatly increasing, for the Hausas have begun to come straight down from Northern Nigeria. Should the railway from Calabar to Ibi on the Benue, and thence through Bornu to Lake Chad, ever be laid it could hardly fail, with such a harbour for its base, and such a country to open up, to become one of the greatest trade arteries for Africa. There is but little doubt that such a line would attract the whole trade of the Central Sudan, and assurances have been given me from French sources that the project would be warmly welcomed.

It is somewhat curious that among a people where the instinct for trade is well developed, there should be no market-places throughout the length and breadth of the land. These are, however, constantly mentioned in the folk lore, which shows that, before dividing into small forest communities, the Ekoi were accustomed to such institutions. I have twice started markets at Oban. These were opened with solemn ritual, and for a week or two seemed to promise great success. Gradually, however, the inhabitants of other towns ceased to bring down their farm produce, as the ravages of elephants left them with less than enough for their own needs, while the three traders established at Oban supply the demand for European goods.

There are naturally some unruly members of the race who refuse to take up any money-earning occupation, and regret the old order of things, when town and tribal wars offered a quicker means for the strong to enrich themselves than is possible to-day. In the folk lore, descriptions are to be found, often naive enough, of the lawless state denoted by the Nsibidi sign shown at the right hand corner of the Nsibidi story No. 9, Appendix G, which stands for the condition of the country before the coming of "white" rule—"When there was no redress if a man hit you on the head." The following story is typical :—

Why Ntabe warred no more.

There once lived a man named Ntabe, who went about with his gun, and (contrary to the hero of Aristophanes' "Acharnians") made war for himself alone. He had a wife named Asim Eji. One day the latter went to visit a woman friend, who gave her the flesh of a newly roasted duiker to eat, and asked, "Where is your husband?" "He is always at war," said Asim Eji. "It is his only business. He never brings me meat from the bush like the husbands of other women."

When the unhappy wife reached home, she thought to herself "What can I do? I must try to stop my husband from such an occupation." She therefore cooked fu-fu and placed it in a calabash. In the midst she set a man's skull, but piled high the fu-fu, so that nothing else should be seen. Then she cooked soup and poured over all.

When the husband came in from his fighting he asked, "Where is my food?" She answered, "Before I bring it, call all the townspeople to come and dine with you, for I have made a great feast."

When the neighbours were gathered together, the woman set the table before them, and placed the food upon it. Next she put a knife into the hand of her husband, and said, "Will you cut the fu-fu?"

The man took the knife and tried to divide up the food, but every way he turned the blade he found it strike against something hard. So he dug down and found what lay beneath.

The people all wondered, and said to the woman, "Why did you do such a thing?" She answered, "I married him when I was a very young girl, and since our marriage he has never hunted for me as do other women's husbands, but his sole business is to kill men."

On hearing this, Ntabe got up and said, "I am not angry with what you have done to-day." He stood before the table and called to the townspeople, "That which my wife, Asim Eji, has done is but to advise me to give up the killing of men, and take to some other occupation, as the rest of the townsfolk do."

Then he went into a small inner room, and took down a large

calabash from the wall. In this he laid ten parcels of salt and spread two pieces of native cloth over all. This he brought and set down before Asim Eji, and said to all the people, "Here is a present for my wife. Will you kindly plead with her for me? I promise that I will war no more from this day."

Then the woman also stood forth and said, "Should my husband not take to some other way of life, according to this promise, I will divorce myself, and marry another man." To Ntabe she said, "Will you promise solemnly in the presence of all these people?"

He answered, "How can I promise more than I have already?"

She said, "Unless you get two kola nuts and bite a piece from one and give it to me to eat, and take also from me a piece which I have bitten off from the other, I will not believe you. Also you must take of my blood and of yours, so that we mix it together. Then I will believe that you will give up, and never war any more. Otherwise I will never believe you."

This the man did, and from that day he warred no more, but kept the faith which he had sworn on the kola nut.

The division of work between the sexes has been clearly laid down from time immemorial, and neither would dream of encroaching on that of the other. Indeed there would seem to be something indelicate and even impious in the mere thought of such a thing.

The chief occupations are hunting for men and farm work for the women, but it is the task of the former to cut bush in December and January for the new farms. This should be begun at the time of the new moon. The big trees, especially the cotton trees, are left standing, but all undergrowth is cleared away. The men help the women to plant yams and plantains, but coco-yams and corn are planted later by women alone. All weeding is done by the women, with the help of their "members."

The yams may be garnered in October, but, as has already been mentioned, are not eaten in towns where the rites of Eja or Mfuor are practised, until these have been performed. They can be stored for a whole year in racks built on the farms for the purpose.

Coco-yams ripen in September, and can be kept in heaps for nearly a year. They are looked on as women's food. Corn ripens in July, and can be kept till January, though it is usually eaten at once. Farms are left to lie fallow after one crop, save plantain farms, which can be used for two years.

It is interesting to note that Sir Walter Egerton pointed out in a recent speech that, with all our science, the Forestry Officers have as yet discovered no better way of farming the land.

Fishing again is looked on as almost exclusively woman's work. For this purpose they generally use one of the many varieties of vegetable poison. This they throw in the water. The fish rise stupefied and float on the surface, forming an easy prey.

Each woman is supposed to give her husband one big fish from her haul, generally the "Monn Aiya" (Child of the Big Water), and some to her father and mother. Before starting she usually rubs "lucky" leaves over her hand-net.

Save during June and July, when fish is in much request to eat with the new corn, most of the fishing is carried on during the dry season, which is counted by the Ekoi to begin from the flowering of the grass *Setaria Mauritana* (Sprengel), usually about October. This lasts till June, when the heavy rains begin.

The division of work is strictly maintained in building a house. The husband cuts down the necessary timber, and, with the help of his male friends, fixes all the posts into the earth and binds them with wattle. This forms the framework of the compound. The men also make the roof, usually by crossing over each other the stems of great palm leaves. They also make and fix in place the palm-leaf mats, which form a kind of thatch. There should be four thicknesses of these in a properly made roof.

It is the business of the women to spread mud over the walls and floors. They smooth these with wooden implements made for the purpose, and leave them to be baked hard by the heat of the sun. When dry, the cracks are filled in, and the whole smoothed over once more.

Men do all the fine plaited-work bags of coloured palm fibre, while the women make the coarser mats of plaited reed for the floor and sleeping mats of screw-pine, dyed and worked in various colours.

As has been mentioned, before the coming of "white" rule, fighting was one of the principal occupations of Ekoi men. The flint-lock gun, at present in use, displaced the spear, club and cross-bow, the latter of which is still used to shoot birds and as a child's plaything. As flint-locks increased in number, the old shields of plaited palm strips were discarded, but many men still alive have carried them into battle.

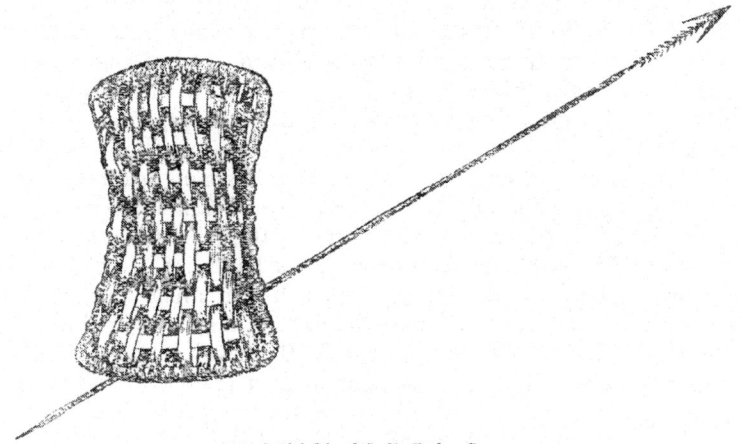

Ekoi Shield of Split Palm Stem.

Before setting out to attack an enemy, solemn sacrifices were made to the chief war Juju of the place. In Oban this was Oke Ewara. Every warrior drank from a vessel of "sacred" water and poured some over his body. Strips of palm leaf were tied round the neck of each.

Small parties were then organised to set out for the farms and watering-places of the enemy, there to lie in wait.

A slave, who fell into such an ambush, would either be shot on sight, or kept as a sacrifice to the war Juju of his captors, while a free-born man would probably be spared for the sake of ransom. Old women were sometimes killed, but young ones and children carried off as slaves.

Sometimes all the warriors of a place, with the exception of a small body left as guards, would sally forth in the night time and surround the enemy's town. Everyone who left the houses would be seized or killed, but apparently towns were never rushed nor compounds broken into.

The victorious party bore off the heads of all slain enemies in triumph to their town, where they laid the trophies before the Egbo house or the war Juju.

The "Egyuk" drum was beaten, and a great dance, in which only warriors might take part, held to celebrate the return of the victors. Each danced with his gun and matchet, or in older times, with shield, spears and cross-bow. The same dance is now given after the killing of an elephant. The chiefs and elders distributed the Nkundak's (Greater Plantain eater) feathers. To those who had slain an enemy, a long tail feather was given, to the rest only the smaller wing feathers.

The heads were first smoked, then plastered thickly with mud and dried again. In this state they could be kept for many years. A large number still exist and are used for Juju purposes. Some such, strangely pitiful in expression, as if still suffering behind their mask of clay, are to be seen, raised on little altars, in towns of the Interior. By some strange mental process, the spirit of the slain foe, represented by the head, has become the guardian of the slayers' hearths and homes, just as the slain leopard was invoked to aid the hunter (p. 142)

After a war dance the oldest man and woman present took palm oil, plantains and dried Nsun meat and offered them at the end of the town to their own ancestors, praying that these would not allow the ghosts of the dead enemies to enter the town to do harm. They also made a sacrifice to Obassi Osaw, and, at the same time, poured a libation of palm wine on the ground. Then they took gunpowder in the palms of their hands and scattered it in the air, so that the eyes of the ghosts, and those of their live enemies, might be filled with dust and thus blinded.

Any slave caught alive would then be taken to the altar, his throat cut, and the blood poured over the Juju. The body would be thrown away, but the head kept by the Juju and mummified as described above.

If either side wanted peace, a man from a neutral town, or one belonging by birth to both, would be sent, holding a palm leaf in his hand. Pourparlers then took place, and terms were settled.

The reason why the Nkundak's feathers were worn on such

an occasion as the dance just described is explained in the following manner.—

WHY NKUNDAKS FEATHERS MAY ONLY BE WORN BY A WARRIOR WHO HAS SLAIN A FOE

By NDUM OF NSAN.

Ekandem Obassi was the daughter of Obassi Nsi. She was as beautiful as the sun, and, when the time came for her to enter the fatting-house, she was asked in marriage by all the richest and noblest young men in the land. She said that as no one was her equal in beauty, she would not marry any of her suitors; and her father therefore troubled her no longer by asking her to look favourably on them.

Soon, however, the princess grew tired of living unsought; so she sent out her maid, a girl three years younger than herself, to the market-place with orders to try to find her a husband.

For two days the girl sought, but came back each evening and said that she had failed to find anyone worthy to become her mistress's husband. Ekandem was sorry, but asked her to try again a third time. To this the maid agreed, for, though a servant, she was also a faithful friend.

On the third morning, soon after arriving in the market-place, she saw a beautiful young man coming towards her. So handsome was he that all the people forgot their wares and sought neither to buy nor sell, but only gazed upon him. Except Princess Ekandem Obassi herself, no one had ever before been seen to compare with him in beauty or attractiveness.

The little maid ran at once to her mistress and told her that she had at last seen just such a suitor as she had been waiting for.

Ekandem ordered her to go back at once to the market and stand where the man must pass by; then, when he drew near, to tell him that her mistress was calling him, and to bring him back with her at once.

This the girl did, and led the willing youth to the fatting-room. What a merry party they were! The flesh of a duckling was made into a stew for them to eat with fu-fu. For a long time they sat at table, and then began to play sweethearts.

When morning dawned the man asked leave to go home, but the Princess said:

"If you go, I am coming with you."

"That you must not do," said her lover, "for I am a very bad man. My name is a terrible one, Ita 'Ne Echi (Chief man of Head (only)), and my home is as fearful as my name. Listen again, my country is called Mfam Ane Achi (Land of Men of Heads (only)). I am not worth staying with, or indeed looking at."

In answer to this warning Ekandem only said:

"I will never part from you. It is useless to try to put my heart off from you. I do not care whether you are bad or not. I am coming with you, and mean to stay with you until death. See how much I love you. My parents have gone to farm, but I do not care even to await their return to ask leave, or see them again before I go. I am ready to start with you now."

"I know," said the man, "how you love me. So do I also love you, but I am a bad man and am called Ita 'Ne Echi. If you come with me you will repent it."

Nevertheless she would not be put off, so they set out, together with the little maid.

On and on they went, and one after another the hands, feet, and other members departed from Ita 'Ne Echi, and went back to those from whom he had borrowed them in order to become an entrancing beauty. Ekandem noticed the wonderful sight, and began to wish to go back. At length only a skull was left, which bounded along the ground, making a noise like a cocoanut shell. Then, alas! she found out the truth of his words, for a skull is indeed not worth looking at, much less living with.

Now she would gladly have turned back, but with the beauty which her love had been forced to return to the proper owners, had gone his goodness and kindness also. He was now as wicked and cruel as any of the skull-people, and would no longer let her go back.

In vain she pleaded. He only said, "You ask uselessly. There is no going back for you any more. You will now come with me to the country of skulls. I never told you that I was better than I now am. You refused to take my warning, and must now abide by what you have chosen."

Poor Ekandem! What could she do? When she tried to turn back she found that the road closed up, and was dark behind her, though in front it was still bright and clear. So against her will, she must still go on. It was fearful to see, instead of her Love, a skull bounding and rolling by her side.

When they arrived at Mfam Ane Achi, both she and the little maid were very badly frightened by the way they were greeted. From every corner of the town the skulls rolled out. Up into the air they bounded, and then fell back on to the ground with a terrible crash. Some knocked against others so hard that it seemed to the lookers-on as though they must break. In the whole town there was not a single inhabitant save these bounding skulls. It was indeed a fearful sight!

Still worse did it seem to the two girls when the skulls began to thank Ita 'Ne Echi for bringing them such a feast of fresh meat! Poor Ekandem and her maid stood trembling for fear that they might be killed and eaten on the spot, while all the skulls shouted through the spaces where their noses should be, one calling this thing and one that.

Suddenly one of the skulls asked the rest to stop making such a noise, and said that the girls were far too beautiful to be killed and eaten, but should rather be given in marriage to Abia-Nkpaw, the king of the skull-people. To this they all agreed, and thanked him for having such a good thought.

Now Abia-Nkpaw is a giant. His bed is 70 feet long and his house 120 feet high. Terrible as he was, however, Ekandem preferred him to Ita 'Ne Echi; she was therefore willing and even glad to become his wife, and went to his house.

That night she sang as follows:

"Obassi, obod owo onnaw isöng,
Ekandem Obassi, angwan Abia-Nkpaw
Obassi, obod owo onnaw isöng'"*

"Obassi, when he made a person gave him land,
Ekandem Obassi, is now the wife of Abia-Nkpaw.
Obassi, when he made a person gave him land."

* Efik.

This song seemed to excite the skulls. It gave them a note to bubble about, and they started to tread a measure. A skull when dancing will often bound to a distance of a mile, and back again. Is this not curious ?

When Ekandem's parents returned from their farm in the evening, they could find neither their daughter nor her maid. They therefore began at once to seek for them, and promised great rewards to anyone who could give information as to their whereabouts. All was, however, in vain.

As the wife of King Abia-Nkpaw, Ekandem was now less afraid; she was allowed to go wherever she pleased in the town, for the skulls were quite sure that she could not find her way home.

One day she went with her little maid to fetch some water from the spring. As she drew near she heard a bird called Nkundak, whom she well knew to be a friend of her father's, crying " Kawkaw kawkawk kru kru kru kru kru kru kru." She called out, " Nkundak, Nkundak, where are you ? "

" Who are you who calls ? " asked the bird. " I am Ekandem Obassi, the daughter of your friend Obassi Nsi," she answered eagerly.

Down darted the bird, spread his wings above the two girls, and told them each to seize a wing and hold firmly.

Off it flew with them to its own house, where it left them, and went to tell the good news to Obassi Nsi.

Obassi was quite overcome with joy when he found his two lost children in Nkundak's house. He thanked the bird again and again, and told him to choose anything he liked out of the whole world, and it should become his as a reward for what he had done.

Nkundak begged that he should be given bravery of plumage beyond that of all other birds.

So Obassi painted his tail feathers with a bar of black on pale yellow. Breast and wings he dyed a glorious blue, and placed a beautiful crest on his head. Also he gave him a very strong voice, which might cause his enemies to fear when they heard it, " Kawkawk Kawkawk kru kru."

To this day the feathers of Nkundak worn in the hair by any man at a public dance are a sign of bravery, for no man dares

Ekoi Calf.

Leaf Men.

Momodo Mandara, my Bornuese Skinner.

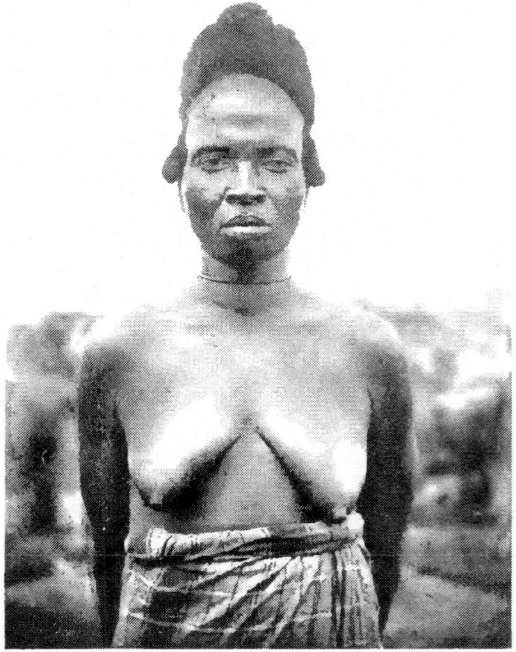

Woman Saved from being offered as a Sacrifice to Juju Mbor.

to wear them unless he has first killed an enemy, wilfully and challengingly. One tail feather only may be worn for each man slain. Of a truth Nkundak is a famous bird in the land of the Ekoi, and is well worth being seen by all people who come to this country.

* * * *

The monotony of bush life is described by most white men as among its greatest drawbacks. Curiously enough, it seemed to us almost overcrowded with incident. At the most unexpected times and places the silence would suddenly be broken by a cry for help, or a few steps lead us straight from the drowsy peace of the forest into the heart of a tragedy.

Once, for instance, we reached a town just as the Juju image was busy smelling out a "witchcraft," and, in defiance of all the proprieties, attended the ceremony. Had the proceedings been forbidden they would only have been delayed till our departure, and, besides an inborn interest in such matters, it was possible, by keeping on the alert, to see that no ill effects resulted. Not long after the supposed "magic" was unearthed, unmistakable sounds of a commotion brought us hurrying to the scene to find a wretched woman struggling in the grasp of her husband, who, eager to show zeal, was forcing her down on the ground, extremely rocky just there, before the accusing "image."

At sight of us she wrenched free, and, launching herself across the crowd, lay clutching my boots, every muscle twitching with terror. The onlookers drew back, their expressions of hatred changing to shame-faced submission, but none would approach the suspected witch, till at last one plucked up courage, and, kneeling down, folded the poor woman in her arms, and tried to soothe the sobs which were tearing her. It was the usual story. Several well-known men had died in the town, and the woman accused of bewitching them, a childless wife, who had come from a strange land, with no kin save one sister—was chosen as the most suitable victim. Both women followed us through the long trek, and are now happily settled under the eye of the white man."

CHAPTER XXVI

Life in Peace and War—*continued*

Medical

According to Ekoi beliefs, illness is usually sent by ancestors, as a reminder that offerings have been neglected, by some offended Juju, or by the malice of witch or wizard. When a man or woman falls sick, therefore, they go to the Diviner to discover the cause of the affliction, except in the case of some few illnesses, such as cough or dysentery, which are recognised as due to natural causes. For these, native doctors are consulted The latter possess considerable knowledge as to the curative properties of barks, leaves and roots, often gathered, as among the Leeches of the Middle Ages, at the time of the new moon. The luminary, now as then, is supposed to have great influence on disease. A sick man's malady increases with her waxing, and lessens as she wanes, while a madman has been noticed to grow more violent after she has passed her first quarter. The fat of snakes also holds an important place in the Ekoi pharmacopœia.

Most Jujus are supposed to inflict a special disease. For instance, Mfam and Onnuri give dropsy.

Ebangi—a split palm leaf, set up as a protection against farm thieves—gives pleurisy or pneumonia

Emenn, a large pod used for the same purpose as the last, produces sciatica or lumbago.

Etokk, a large round fruit, gives rheumatism and a pain in the ankle.

A simple sort of surgery is practised. For instance, a man gored in the abdomen by an elephant, replaced the bowels, which had been partially torn out, inserted a small calabash to keep them in place, then drew the skin over all and sewed it across. The shape of the calabash can be clearly seen, but he has quite recovered and is able to take his share of any hard labour, such as load work.

The most common diseases are malaria, dysentery, yaws, craw-craw, pneumonia, consumption, elephantiasis and beri-beri. Leprosy is rare, and to explain its origin the following story is told :—

How Leprosy came.

There was once a man of Nsan named Nsonn Agbe, who was a great wizard. All the people feared him for miles round, for it was well known that he had the power to kill men by his magic arts One day the townsfolk gathered together and said, " What can we do to rid us of Nsonn ? " The wizard heard and was very angry. He killed a man, drained his blood into a great calabash, and then went among all the people, sprinkling the blood to right and left. Wherever a drop fell, whether on man or woman, a leprous spot appeared. That was the first time that leprosy was seen in our country.

In old days a man could force a woman to wed him in payment for having nursed her through an illness, but this was forbidden many years ago. Doctors' fees, for cases requiring long attendance, were also fixed, as is related in the following tale :—

How Doctors' Fees were regulated.

Once there lived a doctor named Abia Ankokk. A woman named Adet was cutting firewood, when a small splinter flew into her eye, so she went to Abia to be tended. For about two weeks he looked after her, and then the woman recovered. She offered twenty pieces in payment for his services, but the man refused them, saying

" I wish to take you yourself either as wife or slave, and will accept nothing else."

Then the townsfolk held a meeting and asked, " Why do you refuse the twenty pieces ? " Abia answered ·

" Because I want the woman herself."

Then the people said:

"By our custom, if you are going to doctor a woman, you must first ask 'Have you any goods to give in payment?' If she answers 'I have none,' then you can take her for your wife or slave, but not if she offers you goods instead. From to-day, Doctors must keep this law, and not try to wed a patient against her will."

Then Abia made his own price and said, "When a man doctors anyone in a town the price is twenty pieces of cloth."

That rational ideas exist as to some causes of disease is shown by the next story:—

WHY DISEASE OFTEN COMES.

Once a husband had two wives. Both went with him to plant yams in the farm. When they came home, one woman had no water with which to cook, so she went and borrowed some from the other.

Next day the first woman sent her daughter to fetch water, that she might repay what she had taken. It was very hot, and when the daughter reached the stream, she found that it had all dried up. She went on and on, seeking for water, but could find none, so, after a while, when she came to a market-place, she sat down quietly, thinking, "Perhaps I may buy some water."

A ghost-man noticed the girl sitting among the stalls. He saw that she was very beautiful, and wished to have her for his wife, so he said, "Will you come home with me?" To this she agreed.

When they reached the man's house, his people asked the girl, "Where do you come from?" She answered, "My mother sent me to fetch water." Her lover said, "We will ask no questions at present Let us at once prepare the marriage feast."

No sooner was the wedding over than the girl heard a voice calling her, "Strange maiden, come hither to me." She looked up and saw the Lame Boy standing at the door of his house. She went to him at once, and he said:

"If your husband offers you food, you must not eat it. Put it on one side, and eat only what I give you." On that, he gave her a great piece of edible clay (or chalk) Next he warned her, "When your husband enters your room in the night time, say to him, 'I may not lie on a bed, but must sleep on the ashes of the hearth.' You will see that he has sores on his body, but be careful not to touch them. Allow no one to arrange your hair,* and when you go down to bathe in the morning, look at the bathing-place. You will see two springs gushing side by side from the rock, and falling into a shallow pool. One is of black water, and the other white and sparkling. Wash only in the black water and bring some of it home with you. Do not touch the clear water, nor let a single drop fall upon you, else your body will become full of disease. If you listen to all this, you may go safely home again, though the ghosts, who have caught you, wish to keep you among them; but if you do not do as I bid you, some great misfortune will happen" The girl thanked him and said that she would do all as he bade

One day at dawn she was sweeping up the house, which she always kept clean and sweet. She saw a piece of stale meat lying on the floor, and swept it up among the ashes, then threw all into the back-yard, where dead leaves lay, amid the other rubbish.

When it was time to go back to her mother, she began to arrange her hair. A woman ghost came and said, "Let me do it for you," but the girl refused. Another ghost came and said, "Let me," but she refused again. After this, she went for the last time down to the spring. When she came back the ghost people all said, "Are you ready to go home now?" She answered. "Yes," and went into the house to fetch a small box. They asked, "Is it yours?" She said, "It is mine," so they bade her adieu.

The husband accompanied her on the road towards her mother's town. When they had reached half way, he said:

"Of these two things, breeze and wind, which do you like best?" And she answered.

"I like 'breeze' best.

* This prohibition is probably connected with the hair Juju (see page 327) Cf the mediæval superstition by which hair thrown by sorcerers to the wind demons was capable of raising a storm—or a single lock offered to the powers of evil delivered the sacrificer into their hands, *vide* Sintram ünd seine Gefahrten

The husband said, "Now I am going back," but she said "No. First take me to the beginning of the town." So he took her on till they came to the nearest river. This was now full of water, so she filled her jar and took it home The husband went back, but, from that day, a gentle breeze followed the girl wherever she went. The mother and all her friends were very glad to see her again, and the water, which she brought, was given to the other wife to repay what had been borrowed so long before

One day when the dry season had come again the second woman came to borrow water. The mother was away from home, but the girl gave her all that there was in the house The second woman called her daughter to go and fetch water with which to repay what she had borrowed

This girl went straight to the market-place and sat down as the first had done. The same man came and took her home with him.

When the ghost town was reached, the Lame Boy called to the second girl as he had done to the first. "Will you come here? I have something to say to you." She went to him and he told her all that he had said before. This one, however, answered "No, I will eat whenever I see meat. Also, I do not fear to touch the body of my husband."

A woman came and offered to dress her hair, and she accepted at once, and when she went down to bathe she washed in the clean, white spring. Her body therefore grew full of disease, and at length she became as a leper.

When she prepared to go home, she went within the house and took a very large box This she filled with all the goods which she could lay hands on. The husband did not accompany her, as he had done in the first case, but asked, "Of these two things, wind and breeze, which do you like best?" She answered, "I like wind."

Then a strong wind arose, and blew the girl up and down and threw her against the trees, one after another. When she reached her home, no one knew her, for her face and body were so changed with disease and blows. Soon she died, and went back to the ghosts for evermore

The reason why disease often comes is because people will

eat bad meat, touch others who are diseased, and bathe in the white spring which should be left clean for drinking and cooking.

Also, when a woman leaves her husband, or when death has carried him away from her, she may not wash in the white water, but in black for purification.

Amusements

Life in an Ekoi village is more full of amusement and variety than might appear at first sight. There is a strong local feeling in every town, and the inhabitants are very jealous of its repute, whether for wealth, size, or the power of its Jujus. Social qualities are very highly developed—there is nothing more prized than popularity, or more dreaded than ridicule

On almost every day of the year some wedding or birth is celebrated, some girl leaves the fatting-house, some Juju gives a "play," or one of the many clubs or age-classes holds a feast. As has already been mentioned, these last-named associations, of which the Ekoi name is "Ekan" (plural "Nkan"), consists of all of one sex born within the same three years The age-class forms a kind of self-governing community, with power to watch over the conduct of its members, much in the same way as the experimental "Children's Republics" of the United States. Not long ago a case came under my notice of a small girl of seven who was fined by her age-class for having allowed too free behaviour on the part of a boy friend. When the members have reached the age of about fifteen years, they usually send a deputation to some man of influence in the town, and ask him to become their president. If he accepts he gives them a name, usually that of some former age-class which has now died out, and also the power to play the club drums and "Okankan." In return for all this they "cut" farm for him, and render other services. The age-class is then launched on its career, and its reputation depends on the energy and capabilities of its members.

Should a boy be of rich parentage, his admission fees to the Egbo and other clubs are paid while he is quite young. In such a case he is accounted an honorary member, but is not initiated into the mysteries till he reaches the age of discretion. If the mother be richer than the father, she pays the fees for her son.

Theoretically, all postulants are beaten before the mysteries of any club are unveiled to them. The more important the club the more painful the initiatory rites, but these may be commuted for a fine in the case of some clubs. In others, such as Ekkpo Njawhaw, no bribe can avail.

Most clubs hold their initiatory ceremonies and secret rites at some place in the bush, not far from the entrance to the town. This is approached by a winding path, cut through the thick bush, which gives almost the privacy of a yew hedge. Over this path, at intervals of about 10 to 20 feet, hang split palm leaves, held up at each end by thin posts. These arches are usually seven in number, and before each members are stationed, armed with whips or rods, for the flogging of postulants, who run through at topmost speed.

Before this ceremony the youth must have undergone circumcision, though this is usually performed a few weeks after birth, by some old woman of the town. Should the boy be sickly, the ceremony may be deferred till the age of eight or nine years, or even later, in which case he is afterwards confined in the fatting-house for three or four months.

In some clubs, the "Enyara Akum," the "dark things of the clubs," *i.e.*, bull-roarers, are used. These were formerly only played in secret; no woman was allowed to see them, or know the cause of the sound. My wife and her sister were the first women in this part of the world to whom the much-prized secret was disclosed.

Another carefully guarded mystery was the art of walking on stilts (Ekoi "Abia-Nkpaw" or "Abum-bum"), which no woman was allowed to see.

The origin of the custom was obligingly written down for me in the following words:—

"In the olding olding Oban town, there was once an old man named Awo Ntui Ane (Awo the Chief of Men). He been working in his farm, where he been plant the yams. One of the day, he find, the earth very hot with the sun, especially in the dry season. He cut a very piece of stick and put them in

A Stilt Dance.

Stilt Dance "Lame Boy" in Foreground.

his feet. One of his sons named Itafaha Egbise saw, and when they get home he called his friend named Itaneni, and said, 'Here what my father been doing to-day in his farm.'"

By these first stilts the feet were only raised a few inches from the ground, but the height was gradually increased, till now a good performer can walk on a level with the heads of the spectators.

On New Year's Day, 1910, a particularly interesting "stilt play" was given. There were four principal performers, each thickly veiled, among them one with only one stilt, very short, and bound round his right leg in such a way as to make him limp like a cripple. In him we recognised the "Lame Boy," the "Good Fairy" of Ekoi tales * The heads of several of the minor characters were bound with wreaths, from which depended, so as to cover the ears, leaves of the Piper plant, sacred to the ghosts. It is curious that the name for stilts, Abia-Nkpaw, is that of the giant King of the Skulls, mentioned on page 275. We gathered that the play was in honour of the ghosts, and that the other principal characters were Obassi Osaw and Obassi Nsi.

Next to their dances, the exercise which gives most delight to the people in general is undoubtedly that of wrestling. The style is Græco-Roman, and interesting enough to watch, for not only are the men surprisingly light on their feet, but they show a distinctly sporting feeling. It is seldom that the greatest strain overcomes the good humour of the combatants, but, at the least sign of anger or foul play, the bystanders rush in and stop the contest. Before and all through a wrestling match, the drums are beaten in the manner only used on such occasions. Before beginning each bout, both wrestlers bend before the drum and touch the earth with their hands. The monotonous tom-toming seems to go to the heads of performers and spectators alike, and produces intense excitement.

Among ball games, the most popular is perhaps Ukpe Ewaw, in which any number of men can join. Two unequal sides are chosen. The smallest party divides into two, and stands about 50 yards off. In between stand their opponents. The outside

* See pages 58, 370 etc.

men throw a piece of knotted cloth, made to serve as a ball, to their friends on the other side. This the inside men try to seize and charge back their opponents.

Another game is one in which the ball is never allowed to touch the ground.

As is to be expected in a primitive people, almost countless variations of "Ikomm" or Cat's-cradle are known to the Ekoi. Among playthings, tops, some made from round fruits, pierced by a pointed stick, and others roughly shaped from soft wood, are in use. The "Mancala" and a kind of chess-board are also in great favour.

CHAPTER XXVII

Art

THE belief has gradually grown upon me that among the Ekoi there exists the germ of a love of beauty almost Greek in character, though warped, and indeed all but overwhelmed by the introduction of blatantly hideous European wares, with which the country has been flooded.

That pure beauty does appeal to the race is shown by their surprising knowledge of flowers, and their delight in the form and colour of these, and even in the texture of leaves. On first coming among them it had seemed that they cared little for the wealth of blossoms strewn on every side, for one seldom finds flowers used for personal adornment, and never to decorate their homes. Closer study, however, has made it doubtful whether this is not due to other causes than want of appreciation. For the Ekoi, not only great trees, but the smallest plants possess a soul, and can feel pain when plucked. Very occasionally one sees a young girl with a single vivid flower twisted into her hair for purposes of adornment, but more usually, both among men and women, leaves or blossoms are only worn as signs, to express a definite message, such as the scarlet Akpanebesin, worn as a challenge behind the ear of a wrestler, or the little Ishut flower or leaf of Ekuri fern, which, worn in hair or cap, announces a death in the house of the man addressed by anyone so decorated.

Wherever suitable clay is to be found, infinite pains are taken to mould even the water-pots into beautiful shapes. None of these are used for house decoration, as would be the case with us, so that the time spent in moulding the many-handled, strangely graceful jars must be exacted by that indwelling love of beauty, which, debarred from expression on almost every side, finds an outlet in this one primitive art. There is

Ekoi pottery.

Ekoi pottery.

no market for the pottery, it is made solely for domestic use. Obviously a jar with slender neck from which spring three or four thin, outstanding handles is far more liable to break than the plainer pottery in general use among more civilised peoples—such indeed as the comparatively cultured inhabitants of Northern Nigeria.

In many cases both form and decorative pattern strike a curiously modern note, that indeed of "L'Art nouveau" itself. An example of this came to my notice among an even more primitive people, namely, the Banana of the Logone, the decorative lines on whose weapons might have been designed by Liberty.

In seeming contradiction to this feeling for beauty is the undeniable crudeness of the wall paintings. The most elaborate of these are naturally to be found in the Egbo houses, and typical examples are shown on the next page. Yet the designs painted on their foreheads, or clipped on their heads, show a sureness of drawing which few white people could equal. When the head chief of Ibum was questioned as to whether any of the younger people were taught to paint by their elders, or if some members of the community practised the art more than others, he answered that the women alone made the walls fine in this manner, and that they needed no teacher, save the good sense which Obassi had given them.* Although only capable of such rude expression, all Ekoi are quick to understand the meaning of drawing or painting. If, for instance, my wife wished for specimens of a flower which we had reason to believe grew in the neighbourhood, she had only to show what was wanted by a few rapid pencil strokes, or a brushful of colour, and delighted exclamations proclaimed its recognition. Search parties scattered in every direction, and not long afterwards some triumphant individual usually returned with the specimen, to be exchanged for leaves of another plant in great favour with the Ekoi, namely, tobacco.

As an instance of appreciation of pure line, apart from the attraction of colour generally supposed to be irresistible among black peoples, perhaps it may be not without interest to relate

* Cf the custom in Bohemia and Moravia, where the house walls are decorated each spring by the peasant women.

an incident which occurred after we had got back from a long tour. The chief men of Oban came up to congratulate us on our safe return from what seemed to them an almost incredibly long and dangerous journey. We had collected a good many objects of interest on the way, especially specimens of pottery made by a far-away branch of the Ekoi, and some musical instruments of a pattern unknown in these parts. The interpreter asked, on behalf of the chiefs, if they might be allowed to see the collection of "fine things" in my house. After examining these, they showed the most lively interest and admiration for the simple furniture and the few pictures and ornaments scattered around. I had just had framed for the office a couple of gaudy pictures of the King and Queen in their Coronation robes. These were shown to the visitors, and they expressed respectful interest, but no admiration. Suddenly we heard an exclamation of delight, and a moment after all our visitors were crowding round one of their number who happened to be a member of the highest grade of Egbo, and who had picked up a reproduction in black and white of Long's "India."

The man's face was alight with joy, and his hands kept moving up and down, following the folds of the drapery and the lines of the figure, in the same manner as one has seen employed over and over again by artists, whether Chinese, Japanese, or European, in explaining the beauty of some wonderful old painting. Several of the others caught fire from his enthusiasm, and his voice was positively unsteady with excitement, as he said:

"I never knew that white people could be so beautiful in shape, nor that they ever wore such long graceful robes. I thought white people always wore clothes like those they bring out here. Why are they so unkind as not to let us see things like this?"

If, too, as many people contend, with regard to the Greeks, colour phraseology is any test as to colour sense, the Ekoi are by no means backward in this respect.

The following terms are in common use:—

Ogokk-Ogokk, yellow, from Ogokk, the yellow powder used as dye (Adjectives are usually formed by doubling the noun. See Appendix E.)

Enyagha, black.
Ebarre, white.
Nkuyang-Nkuyang, red.
Ebu, brown
Enyaghe Awa, blue.
Awa-Awa, green.
Atong-Atong, grey   (From ashes)
Ebarre Ogokk, pale yellow.
Ebarre Awa, pale green

Thus roughly doubling the colour terms of Homer's days.

It is certain that white influence is to blame in many ways for vitiating the taste of the people. Even now, except at trading centres, one practically never sees any colour chosen for loin cloths or shoulder robes save dark blue, sometimes with a white, or paler blue pattern. This tint is, above all others, suited to bring out the warm brown skin tones and satisfy one's sense of colour.

The lines of the piece of cloth which, till a few years ago, was the ordinary women's wear, and which is still always worn for farm work, could hardly be bettered. The garment passes under the right arm, and falls from a knot on the left shoulder in free graceful folds which reach well below the knee. It is our influence, alas! which is changing the deep quiet tones of the old blue native dyes for the hideous reds, yellows, and greens, which have dazzled the untrained eyes, and are ruining the once true colour sense of the people. To the same cause is also due the hideous shape of the pinafore gowns, short in front and trained behind, often still further disfigured with common lace, or strips and yokes of cotton-backed velvet and satin, and sleeves which do their utmost to disguise the shape of the usually well-moulded arms. It is true that one garment is to be bought which is perhaps as little ugly as any of European make for the use of primitive peoples is likely to be. This is a simple little gown, cut something in the style of those made familiar by the drawings of Kate Greenaway, and with sleeves which only cover the arm 2 or 3 inches below the shoulder.*

* Since writing the above, I have read what Mr Morel says on the subject—"Nigeria its People and its Problems," page 219.

"Why cannot the Administration and the missionary societies combine in some practical, positive form, to combat this curse of alien dress? There is absolutely

It is in a great measure to freedom from the distorting influences of clothes that many of the Ekoi men owe their magnificent physique. Very young girls, too, are often beautifully shaped, but the constant walking over stony ground roughens their bare feet, as the farm work coarsens their hands. One undeniable charm, too, is possessed by almost every member of the race—men and women alike have noticeably long, exquisitely curved eyelashes.

The fatting-house was not originally instituted with the idea that mountains of flesh were beautiful, but because the treatment was supposed to strengthen the girl before and after any special drain on the system. Fat in daughter or wife grew to be desired as a token of strength and well-being, and at length, though not universally, as attractive in itself.

Two other great factors have helped the physique of the Ekoi, first the habit common to most primitive peoples of carrying great water jars, and other loads which need careful balancing, upon their heads; and second, but perhaps most important of all, their love of dancing, to which reference has already been made.

All other pastimes pale before the attractions of the dance, which, to the Ekoi, is one of the main occupations of life,

---

nothing to be said in its favour The West African looks better in African dress, the robe of the Mohammedan and of many pagan Africans It is much healthier for him It is preservative of his racial identity, and that is, perhaps, the most important of all pleas which can be put forward for its retention. With very slight modification—such as one sees among the native staff, and personal servants in many parts of Northern Nigeria—it can be made suitable for any form of labour, literary or otherwise Clad in his national dress, the African has a dignity which in most cases he loses almost entirely when he attires himself in a costume totally unfitted for the country, and hideous at best Nothing to my mind is more pitiable than to visit school after school in West Africa, filled with little boys and girls and big boys and girls in an alien dress, to see the denationalizing process going on day after day and nothing whatever done to stop it In the case of the women it is not only dignity and nationalism which are concerned, but decency as well The national dress of the women in West Africa is classical and graceful, and although leaving more of the body exposed than is usual at home (except in the ballroom) it lacks suggestiveness. It does not accentuate the figure It emphasizes that racial difference—not inequality, but *difference*—which it is so essential to emphasize With the substitution of European dress, especially of the prevailing fashion, the West African woman loses much of what she need never lose, and acquires that which is of no profit to her These things cannot be altered in a day, nor would it be possible in some cases for the present adult generation to go back to African costume But it would in many cases, and the reform could be at once taken in hand so far as the children are concerned."

and, as with the Greeks of old, provides an outlet for the dramatic instinct and religious fervour of the race. It affords the one means of expressing, as perfectly as possible, their otherwise inarticulate sense of the mystery of existence, the power of the supernatural influences which enfold them, the ecstasy of joy in life—of youth and strength and love—all the deeper and more poignant feelings so far beyond expression by mere words.

Every event, either in the life of the family or that of the community, is celebrated in this way. Occasions of rejoicing or grief, such as births, a girl's reappearance from the fatting-house, marriages, successful hunts, the entertainment of visitors, deaths, funeral rites, and the thousand and one religious observances—all have their special dances. No noon-day sun is too hot, no rain too heavy, to cause zeal to flag, or damp the ardour of the people. For hour after hour the performance continues, monotonous indeed to European eyes and ears, but capable of causing frenzied excitement in the dancers, and showing a feeling for true rhythmic motion which is little short of marvellous. Every atom of the body dances, but the point which distinguishes an accomplished dancer from others is the never-ceasing, wave-like ripple which runs down the muscles of the back, and along the arms to the finger-tips.

Though dancing is carried on during every hour of the day, and all seasons of the year, it is by the light of the full moon that the Ekoi most love to indulge in this pastime. On such occasions, when the people of some town in the interior have gathered together to give a series of dances, the scene possesses a weird beauty impossible to define or express, but which, like the monotonous chant and drumming of its accompaniment, vibrates on chords of being which more strictly beautiful performances fail to touch.

This is one point of view. That there is another is shown by the description sent home by my wife and sister-in-law soon after their arrival:—

"The dance was a maddening performance," they wrote, "and made all the more unendurable to us by P. A.'s attempts to draw our attention to the 'rhythmic harmony of the monotone' or some such appreciative expression. To our unmusical ears it sounded far more as if all the fiends had been let loose around us, and when, after hours of dancing, the performers broke into a new song, the refrain of which sounded exactly like 'hustling and bustling away,' but proved to be the prelude to a yet longer and more energetic series, it really seemed as if insult had been added to injury, in an almost unendurable degree"

It was not till months after their arrival that I discovered what terror these dances had at first caused my companions. During any such performance they sat smiling and apparently interested, and it never occurred to me that the sight of the brown figures painted with patterns in white, red, and yellow, dancing in and out of the fitful torchlight, could conjure up Fenimore-Cooper-like visions of frenzied savages working themselves up, by uncouth dance and song, to a sudden, treacherous attack. Only when a nearer knowledge had banished fear was the secret of this first terror confided to me.

Whatever may be the difference of opinion as to the merit of Ekoi dances from an æsthetic standpoint, there can be none as to their interest from an anthropological one. Some of the oldest hold enshrined within them traces of beliefs and fancies which have faded from every other record.

Such is "Ejame," a solemn dance, never given save during the funeral rites of very great chiefs.

Seven men dance in the centre of an immense circle formed by the other performers a long way off. Each of the seven must take care to leave a great space between himself and his neighbour on either hand, for should the " aura " of one of the seven, which on this occasion is thought to extend beyond its usual limits around his body, overlap that of any other present, both will die. It is forbidden for any of the principal performers to raise their eyes. From beginning to end of the dance, each must keep them fixed upon the earth at his feet. Three at least must wear rattles round the neck and bear spears. The songs sung during this dance are declared to be so old that their meaning has long since been forgotten.

Another peculiar dance is called "Okpata." When this is given, two little wooden fetishes are brought out from the back of the Egbo house, and placed upright upon a stone. Only one man dances, while another plays on a native harp. After a while the little fetishes begin to bend up and down, and appear to skip on the stone, in the manner of marionettes, though careful observation by broad daylight failed to show any mechanical contrivance by which this was brought about. None but those conversant with the mysteries of the dance are allowed to approach within several yards of the stone. The name Okpata is also given to the bundle of palm leaves set up in a farm to scare away thieves. Anyone who steals from a farm thus protected will fall sick, and will not recover unless the particular dance is given. The secret of Okpata has been handed down from father to son for many generations, in the family of Obassi Unaw of Oban.

. Another very old dance, already described (page 151), is the "Cat dance," now only practised at Niaji and Ekoneman.

There are many imitative dances, among the most graceful of which may be mentioned:—

"Fabi fabi ga ekum.
Fly fly like hawks."

And

"Ut ebbena ga nonn mfibba.
We dance as birds fly"

Many refrains are taken from incidents of everyday life, such as:—

"Ut efferk mba, ka mba arap aching
We are seeking a road, but the way is far too much"
"Aifpp aienn are ka mba ebbu akut ut kun ebikk echingum
A water great lies in (our) path, when (it) dries up we then can pass by
ejakk ka mbinn égira.
(and) go to farms our"

It should be remarked that in all dances, the movement is from left to right, never from right to left.

The children, too, have a charming series of action dances, one of which recalled the "King of the Castle" of our own childhood, though played more gently. All the time they kept up a chorus of "Ikpai, Ikpai: I conquer you." Another was not unlike musical chairs, and is danced to the accompaniment of a song, the translation of which runs "Three bottles of rum for a hundred men. Who will get some and who go without?"

Nothing could be more graceful than the waving arms and swaying limbs of the little brown forms, as they bent and moved always in perfect time to their song.

The musical faculty of this people is certainly wonderful, though developed along peculiar lines. They have a considerable number of musical instruments, but among these the drum reigns supreme. Of this there are many varieties, from the small boy's tom-tom, about 6 inches high, to the long drums almost the height of a man, and the great drum of the town, which is an object of reverence to the inhabitants, and in honour of

which many songs are composed. A typical one heard at Nkami ran :—

"Mfam are égina, akpatim egyuk.
The town belongs to thee, great drum."
"Mfam are égina, akpatim egyuk.
The town belongs to thee, great drum."

By old custom, when a stranger entered a town he asked for the head chief, that he might salute him. In the chief's absence, the visitor was expected to go straight to the Egbo house and salute the big drum "Egyuk." This he did by bending down before it, till the tips of his fingers touched the ground.

There is great rivalry among clubs as to which can procure drums with the most beautiful tone, for, to the Ekoi, the tone of a drum means almost as much as that of an old violin to us. Many a man has risked fine and imprisonment for playing on those which belonged to other men. It is not unusual for such cases to be brought before me. Summonses are even occasionally taken out before the Native Court, as for instance, that of the Nkum Enan Club of Okarara on July 5, 1909.

Obi Ekpe sworn, stated:

"Itoga came to our town. He was beating an old small drum in Mbi's compound. He asked, 'What about the good drums you use for dancing?' Mbi said, 'They are kept in Itayin's compound.' Itoga asked, 'Is any permission necessary before they may be played?' Then he went thither to beat them."

Mbi (sworn), "When Itoga went to Itayin's house, he began to beat the drums. The owners asked from whom he had authority. He answered that I myself had given it to him. At night the club members gathered themselves together and summoned Itoga before them. They pronounced him guilty of beating their drums. He told them that I was responsible, but I said, 'I am not a member of this club. How then could I give Itoga authority over the drums of others?'"

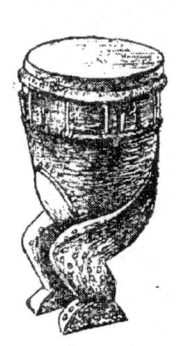

For this unauthorised performance the Club claimed goods to the value of 30s.

The study of the drum is well worth the attention of officials, as it is possible in this way not only to know what is going on in native towns round one—for every event has its different tune by which to summon the inhabitants, such as Egbo and Juju performances, wrestling bouts, &c.—but one is able to learn the drum language, and so interpret almost every secret message sent in warning to counteract one's orders or plans.

Two drums are generally beaten, of which the first leads while the second responds. In the transcription here attempted, the top line represents the notes of the first drum and the bottom one that of the second, usually lower in pitch. A dot represents the value of half a dash. When only one performer is available, he beats the two drums.

The combinations are so limitless that any attempt to do more than indicate the method employed would but weary my readers.

For instance, a white man travelling through the country

ART

will often hear, on his approach to a town, two drums beaten in the following manner :—

Which means

"Aba babapp ka mfam, ekum ekifari.
Come quickly to town, hawks are around"

This is used to summon the townsfolk from their outlying farms. The term "hawk" is employed to designate the white visitor.

"Nsan iburutu Nsum nyamm. Aigyut eriti babapp.
Nsan the brave. Monkey flesh (comes) Climb tree quickly."

This means "Men of Nsan, brave ones, another town is coming to attack us; return at once to your homes." The words "monkey flesh" were used instead of the name of the enemy, lest the women should be so terrified by the approaching danger as to lose their heads.

"Abakk 'ne oyue Mfonn mfam aiyuk eju.
Come man kill. Chief (or owner) (of) town has heard before."

I.e, Come to the town, we are killing a man. The Chief knows (or agrees).

Should a man be proved guilty of attempting to attract to himself the affection of a chief's wife, the following is played to warn all the townsfolk that no help or succour must be shown to the offender :—

"Ekum ekaw nkai eriti. Afabe aiye 'we akumi fan ?
Hawk marries woman (or wife) tree. Wings tired he sits down where ?"

I.e., Should a hawk marry the tree wife, where will he find a resting place when his wings are tired, as all trees would refuse him shelter.

The next is used to warn a friend to follow the course of a stream, as danger awaited him on the road :—

"Aiipp aiipp ebarre akatt. Ngun ojimm ajonge.
Water water white feet. Land walk thorns."

I.e., "If you walk along in the water, your feet will keep white (smooth and unhurt). If you walk on land, thorns (will pierce them)."

"Akai akare atui. Achott akare akukana.
Women give chiefs. Palaver give fatherless."

A chief may take a fatherless woman in marriage, though this is forbidden to others, as there is no one to provide a dowry. In the case of a chief, it will be provided by the women of the town.

The following drum songs, true " Lieder ohne Worte," were

played in our honour by the children's "Agara" Club of Nchofan (Insofan) :—

"A makara araw ba. Kun abonn akam asun.
If white man come not. Then children agree slaves."

"If the white man had not come to our country, the children would have no choice but to be seized as slaves."

The next was in honour of the first white woman to visit the town :—

"Nkang oiyenn ntuk nji. Njum nji 'me nyenna
Never saw I such (as) this Thing this I saw not."

The drum on which these songs were played has been described on page 217, but those in ordinary use are the great Egbo drum "Egyuk," and four varieties of that formed from a wooden cylinder covered at one end with antelope, or, more rarely, snake skin.

To call Oban people to a meeting the following is played :—

"Oban iburutu Aba nyaghe, nyaghe.
Oban (people) brave ones Come quickly, quickly."

Each man of importance in a town has his drum name, by which he can be summoned at any moment. For instance, should Ojong Egomm of Oban be at his farm when wanted, the townsfolk beat the following :—

"Awmenge ntemm etim. Kenn okubi ekubi ebi
Know friend inside. Then story talk bad."

To summon Itandak of Oban they play:—

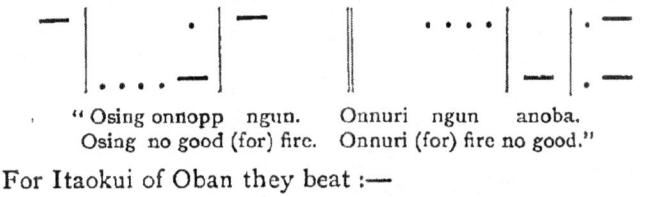

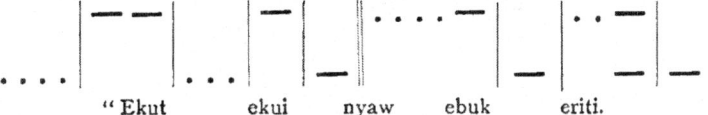

"Osing onnopp ngun. Onnuri ngun anoba.
Osing no good (for) fire. Onnuri (for) fire no good."

For Itaokui of Oban they beat:—

"Ekut ekui nyaw ebuk eriti.
Wood-pecker (with) strong mouth (makes) hole (in) tree."

At dawn, after the death of a great man, in the old days, the Egbo drum might always have been heard insistently beaten in a series of five equal strokes—

"Kran, kran, kran, kran, kran,
Kran, kran, kran, kran, kran."

While this sound boomed through the town, the people were seeking a victim to seize and offer up in sacrifice, and then to lay in the grave, beneath the swathed body of the dead chief. So soon as the strokes stopped, strangers approaching from a distance knew that they might enter the town in safety—the victim had already been found. In such a case he was usually put to death, near the Juju stone, by means of brass rods twisted round his throat. The body was thrown down before the great drum, which was then solemnly beaten once more.

Beside the drum, the principal musical instruments are the harp, okankan,* and rattle, but there are countless others, such as the one made from a palm mid-rib 3 to 4 feet long, of which

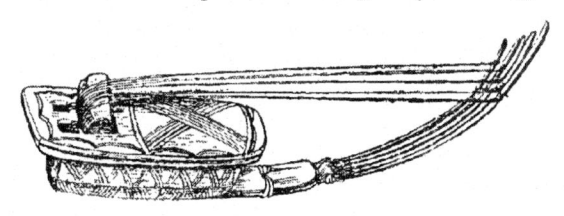

* See p. 54.

a strip of fibre has been loosened for the whole length save a couple of inches at either end, and then raised by two tiny "bridges" thrust beneath. This is played by a couple of performers, one of whom strikes the strings with two slender wooden sticks, and the other touches it here and there with a small closed calabash, with which he makes occasional "runs" by drawing sharply up and down.

CHAPTER XXVIII

Records

Records are usually kept by means of tallies of different kinds,—by dropping small stones or corn grains into a calabash, and by making strokes on walls.

The system of reckoning was to count first on the fingers, then on the toes, and, should the number exceed twenty, to lay down a small piece of grass, stick, or palm leaf for each five in excess, or, if large numbers were concerned, for each twenty. It was customary to begin with the little finger on the left hand.

To express numerals up to twenty, the following signs are employed.

1, 2, 3, and 4, the corresponding number of fingers are held out on one hand.

5, a closed fist is shown.

6, three fingers are held out on each hand

7, two fingers of the right hand are struck twice on to the palm of the left hand, or, four fingers of left hand and three fingers of right are held out.

8, four fingers of each hand are held out.

9, the left hand is held out, the fingers loosely closed, the right hand with the thumb against the palm is drawn from the left hand across the breast.—The old custom of shooting with the bow is clearly imitated.

10, two closed fists are held out.

15, the tips of the fingers of the right hand are bent over to touch the right shoulder.

20, the right hand is raised before the face, and then swung downward with the index finger extended.

Nsibidi

In 1905, Mr. T. D Maxwell, District Commissioner of Calabar, discovered the existence of a secret primitive writing in use among the Efiks. Twenty-four signs, the meaning of which he had succeeded in learning, were published in the Government Civil List of July, 1905. Later, a paper by the Rev. J. K. MacGregor appeared in the *Anthropological Journal* for 1909. In this paper its author states, first that Nsibidi originated among the Ibos, or alternatively among the Uyanga, who learned it from the monkeys which crowded round their camp fires. He says that he has been unable to learn of any trace of such a script in the Cameroons, and according to his opinion, it was unlikely that such should exist among peoples of the Bantu stock, but he adds a note to the effect that a work by Dr. Mansfeld—"Urwald Dokumente"—has since come under his notice in which some signs are given.

With regard to the Ibos, all of this nationality questioned by me deny the existence of any system of writing save that adopted from missionary sources, which has been modified to suit their convenience.

Among the Uyanga also it has unfortunately been impossible to find any trace of the interesting legend alluded to above, whereas, so far from a Bantu relationship offering any bar to the knowledge of the script, the Ekoi, who certainly have a strong Bantu strain, claim, and with what seems good grounds, to have originated the whole system. At the present day a greater variety of signs seems to exist among the Ekoi of the interior than amid any other tribe.

The script is certainly of considerable antiquity, and is to a large extent pictographic, but has become highly conventionalised in the course of years. The Ekoi explanation of the name Nsibidi, or more properly Nchibbidy, is that it is derived from the verb "Nchibbi," "to turn," and this has taken to itself the meaning of agility of mind, and therefore of cunning or double meaning.

One of the oldest clubs, which apparently existed before the inception of the Egbo, bears the same name. This was a powerful society to which chiefs alone could belong, and was charged with the execution of criminals.

On a small calabash, bought at Nkami, the record of a trial by the Nsibidi Club is to be found.

The circles show the Court-house, with verandah, round which, and the inner walls, the townsfolk are standing in order to hear the case. The five "Ts" are the Nsibidi executioners. No sooner was judgment pronounced against a man than these officials dragged him forth to death. They are said to have disguised themselves by covering their faces on the one side with a black dye made from ground charcoal and oil, and on the other with chalk. Over this background, signs in contrasting colours were painted. They used to rush upon their victim, bearing a buffalo horn in the left hand, and the "Isawm" or Juju knife in the right. According to Mr. Goldie (Efik Dictionary), an "Owo Nsibidi" in the neighbourhood of Calabar was in the habit of disguising himself in much the same way till quite recent days, before inflicting punishment or injury. The functions of the old Nsibidi Club are mentioned in the following story :—

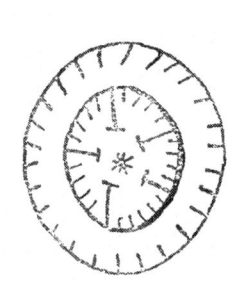

Lex Talionis.

By Atem Mbaiojonge of Ako.

Effion Obassi and all his people built a town. One day they went into the bush to cut palm leaves with which to make new roof-mats (Oka). The leaves were collected and brought back, and the townsfolk said, "We will sit in the Egbo house to make the mats." Before they entered, they made a law that no one should leave in the evening and go home before he had cleaned away all the palm leaves. If anyone should leave so much as a single piece in the Egbo house he should be put to death.

One day, after all had gone home, the man, whom Effion Obassi had chosen for his friend, but who was secretly very jealous because Effion was richer than he, got a piece of palm leaf and hid it under the floor-mat where Effion had been sitting. Next morning it was found there. Inquiry was made, and the townsfolk ordered everyone to sit in the place where he had been sitting the day before. They found that the piece of palm leaf was under the mat on which Effion had sat. So they said to him·

"You must die within twelve days according to the rule we have made." Obassi himself, however, answered, "My son shall not be killed at all."

When the days were over, all the town went to Obassi and said, "Give us your son that he may die."

Obassi replied, "I will give you a slave; take him instead of my son." This the townsfolk refused.

Now at that time there was a very powerful club called Nsibidi, to which only chiefs might belong. The seven "Images" of Nsibidi came out and demanded the son of Obassi. He could no longer refuse, so Effion Obassi was delivered up to them, and they cut off his head.

Obassi was very sad. He said, "This was the only son I had. I got plantains from him. From him I got yams and fresh water." One day he went into the bush. He saw a kola tree bearing three fruits. He said to himself, "If my son were here, I should send him to pick the nuts for me." He went home. He called to the man whom his son had chosen for friend, and said, "My son is dead. You who were his friend, will you pick the kola nuts for me in his stead?" The man said "Yes."

Both went into the bush. When the false friend had climbed the tree, Obassi called to it, "If this is the man who deceived my son, and gave him to be killed by the people, O tree! you may grow up very high, and throw him down to the ground, so that he dies. If he is guiltless, you may not grow."

Then the tree shot up into the sky, bearing the man with it. It shook its top and flung him down to the ground, so that he died.

Obassi went home for a time, but another day when he was hunting in the bush, he saw a porcupine run into its hole. He said to himself, "If my son were here, he would kill that animal for me. I will try to kill all those people who put my son to death."

On his return Obassi called to one of those who had helped to kill his son, and said, "Will you please go down that hole and fetch up porcupine for me?" The man did as he was asked, and, no sooner had he entered, than Obassi cried out, "If this man be guilty, O hole! cover him so that he dies. If he be guiltless, let him come out unharmed."

Another day Obassi called one of the men and said, "Go to Oremm and buy twenty yams for me, but take only one day on the journey, for, if you take more than this, Nsibidi shall kill you as it killed my son." The messenger went very hurriedly, but the road seemed to lengthen before him, and he spent two days on the journey. When he returned Obassi sent for the Nsibidi "Images," and they came and cut off the man's head.

Next Obassi called to one of the seven "Images" and sent him to the bush to pick native pears. When he climbed the tree Obassi spoke to it as he had done to the palm tree. It grew up high and flung the man to the earth, so that he died.

The fourth man was sent fishing, but the river had been ordered to kill him if he were in any way guilty of the death of Effion, so he was drawn under and drowned.

The fifth man was told to go and plant yams in the farm. There the farm Juju caught him. He cried, "I am sick, I am sick." Then he died.

To the sixth man Obassi said, "Now that my son is dead there is no one to sleep in the room with me. Will you come?" The man consented. In the middle of the night a great snake, which Obassi had brought, came and swallowed him up.

The seventh man was sent into the bush to collect firewood. There a tree fell on him, so that he died.

The wife of Obassi also said, "I, too, will do my best to kill those who injured my son." She also put Jujus upon some of them, so that they died.

The parents of all those dead men called a meeting in the town and said, "What is the cause of the deaths of our children?"

Then Obassi stood forth and said, "My son died through the deceit of one who pretended to be his friend. Therefore I also have killed those who had any part in his death. All the town was jealous of the wealth of my son, and wished that he should die, so that on my death my riches might be shared among you. Now your sons have died in payment for mine."

That is the reason why if anyone does you harm you try to do him harm also.

The rule about the palm leaves was only made so that the richest man might be killed, and his wealth be shared by the town.

For a long time messages have been sent in Nsibidi script, cut or painted on split palm stems.

The more interesting signs collected, each of which has been carefully verified, will be found in Appendix G.

CHAPTER XXIX

Government, Etc.

In old days each town was ruled by its council of elders—the Homeric "γερουσια"—and in most ways this still holds. Anyone, from the greatest chief to the smallest child, has the right to summon such a meeting and lay complaints before it. The greater number of the townspeople attend, but only the elders have the right to speak, others do so on sufferance. A powerful chief naturally would have more influence than a poor man on such occasions, but, should the case be clear against the former, the meeting would never decide in his favour.

In most ways the Ekoi are still ruled according to old custom, but appeal can always be made from the decision of the elders to that of the Native Court, and from the latter direct to the District Commissioner. The old "γερουσια" has no longer power to enforce punishments.

The Native Court is composed of representatives from different towns of the District, who sit in turns, usually under the presidency of the Commissioner. Should the latter unavoidably be absent, his place is taken by the principal chief present, but all decisions are inspected by the Commissioner on his return.

In this manner the people may be said to have almost complete self-government. Indeed, among races of a high type like the Ekoi, who have comparatively few customs repugnant to the English sense of justice, self-government is more truly a fact since the coming of the "white man" than before, when the rights of the poor, and those not free-born, were too often set aside.

The only serious crime prevalent among the Ekoi is that of poisoning, and this is more often directed against suspected magicians than private enemies. That it is all too prevalent, however, is proved by the fact that antidotes are kept close at hand, usually in the form of dried herbs hung from the roof. These are sometimes used as a lotion, and sometimes given as a drink.

It is usual to take an antidote before going to a meal, should there be any reason to suspect one's host of evil intentions. After this precaution, if poison be administered, the guest vomits at once and suffers no further ill-effects.

The only cases of deaths by violence known to me in the District were both committed by old "members" of alien race

The Ekoi custom with regard to the murder of a free man was to summon the head chiefs of the neighbouring towns, to inquire into the case. Judgment was given after seven days, and, if found guilty, the murderer was immediately put to death. No compensation was permitted, and the wealth or position of the guilty man was not allowed to weigh in the least.

Should the death have been proved due to accident, the slayer could ransom himself by the payment of one slave, or like value, for his own life, and one for each full brother, and two for each full sister possessed by himself, lest the blood guilt should fall upon them also.

The punishment for serious theft in the old days was to cut off ear, toe, or finger. For some time past, however, the procedure has been as follows :—

For the first offence the culprit was fined by the Egbo Club, for the second his "company" fined him more heavily, while for the third he was very heavily fined indeed. A cow was usually shot and he was obliged to refund the value to the owners. Next a bell was hung round his waist, he was painted over with black and white and driven round the town. The owner of the property taken was not allowed to inflict any punishment himself.

Most other offences were punished by fines A transgressor of the marriage laws would have to pay damages to the injured party. As far as possible, punishment was made to fit the crime, and, in the old days at least, a murderer was put to death in the same way as his victim.

Why a Murderer should Die in the same Way as his Victim.

There was once a man who had two wives. The name of the one was Nka Menge Njum (Know nothing) and of the other Menge Marri (Know all). After seven months the first woman bore a daughter, but the second wife remained barren.

The child grew up very quickly, and after five months could walk alone. One day she went to the house of Menge Marri, but the latter drove her away and said, "I want no children in my room." A second day the same thing happened.

Once the father went out hunting. Menge Njum said to herself, "I want to go to my farm and get food, firewood also is needed, but there is no one to take care of the child. If I could see anyone with whom to leave her, I would go at once."

On hearing this the daughter herself said, "If you do not fetch food, we shall die with hunger, so you must go. If Menge Marri were your friend, you could leave me with her; but she does not like you, so I am better alone."

The mother set out and collected all that was needed. On her return she found her daughter safe in the house. Nothing had happened to her. Next day, therefore, the woman went forth again to her farm.

This day, however, Menge Marri came to the house of her rival and said to the child, "Your mother is away. Let us go together to the bush. We will catch fish in the river."

To this the girl agreed, and, when they had gone some way, they came to a river in which there were many fish. Menge Marri took her little companion and flung her into the water, so as to form a dam. A high tree was growing by the side of the river, and on this sat a blue bird. He cried:—

"I never before saw any woman take the daughter of another and lay her across the water like this. If you want to dam the water, why do you not cut sticks?"

When the wicked wife heard this she picked up many stones, and threw them at the bird, but it flew away safely. She caught plenty of fish, and, after she had finished, drew the body of the drowned girl up from the water, and laid it across her back. On her head she bore a basket of fish, but when she found her load too heavy, she set down the fish, carried the body for some distance, and then set this down and returned for the fish. Thus she did till she reached home. When she arrived she put the dead body of the little one in the mother's room, then went to her own house and began to clean the fish.

When Menge Njum came back from farm she called to her daughter, "Come, help me down with my load, for it is very heavy. The child did not answer, so the mother let fall her load, and ran and caught hold of her. Then she began to weep bitterly.

A little time after, the father returned from hunting, and asked: "What is the matter? When I started I left my daughter without sickness. How is it possible that she can have died in two days?"

The blue bird flew down and settled on the roof.

"I never saw a woman take another woman's daughter and use to dam a river instead of sticks," sang he.

The father stopped his wife from weeping, and said, "Let us listen to the bird;" and the latter sang further.

"There is the woman who took your daughter and used her to dam a river." At that moment Menge Marri went by, but the man could not believe what the bird sang.

Next morning the wife said, "Our child is dead. Let us go and bury her" The man answered, "We will do as you say, but, if I live, I will find out who has killed her."

While they were burying their little one the bird flew down once more, and sang, "Menge Marri it is who took the child to the river to drown her, and afterwards carried the body back to the house She is the one who killed your daughter"

Then the parents called a meeting of the townsfolk, and accused Menge Marri of what she had done.

The latter stated, "The reason I killed their daughter is because I had none of my own."

On this the meeting gave judgment that she must die in the same way as she had killed the girl.

From that day a man who kills another must be put to death in the same way as his victim.

At death all property goes by right to the eldest brother of the deceased. Should the heir be a good man he would share with the dead man's children, but he cannot be forced to do this.

Any property given to a wife remains hers at the death of her husband, should she have children, but if childless it all goes to the elder brother.

A strict account as to property is kept between husband and wife. A rather amusing instance of this came up in Court soon after my arrival :—

A man had lent his wife goods to the value of fourteen pieces of cloth. She acknowledged the debt, and was anxious to repay it. As she could think of no other way in which to do so, she sallied forth in true Amazonian style, and annexed another woman, whom she brought back captive, and presented to her husband in full discharge of her own liabilities.

The practice of seizing free persons and converting them into slaves has naturally been forbidden throughout the land since the coming of white rule. So complaint was brought, with the result that the whole affair came into Court.

That this punctiliousness as to "Meum" and "Tuum" extends also to the children was proved, on one occasion, by a child of eight, who claimed damages against her father because he had used, without her permission, a cooking pot, which he had given her some time before. By native law she won her case. The father was condemned to return the pot, and pay compensation to his daughter for having made unauthorised use of her property.

Before entering into the next section of my subject, I should like to state that I myself do not touch intoxicants of any kind, and have the cause of temperance nearly at heart, while I yield to no member of the Native Races Committee in interest in the people among whom my lot is cast.

At all hours, without a moment's warning of our coming, native houses of every class of Ekoi have been open to us, as hundreds of sketches of interiors, type studies, &c., can testify. In the course of my life here, and the thousands of miles traversed, only two cases of natives the worse for drink have come under my notice. Neither was more than slightly intoxicated, and both lapses from virtue were due, not to imported liquor, but to palm wine, though in the last case about a teaspoonful of gin had been added.

The Ekoi are a thoroughly sober people, and, though a considerable amount of European spirit is brought to the District, a great part of this is used for libations or sacrificial purposes. The only native intoxicant is palm wine, of which there are two kinds. First, that obtained by climbing up the tree, making an incision at the top, and fixing a gourd or demi-john to catch the flow of sap. This is a troublesome process, owing to the height of the tree and its spiked leaves.

The wine thus obtained will keep for some time, but after the first few days it begins to grow heady. "Medicine" is then mixed with it, and it is used almost exclusively for Juju purposes.

The second kind of palm wine is obtained by felling the tree, cutting out the greater part of the "cabbage," and affixing some receptacle in much the way described above. The sap thus obtained must be drunk within thirty-six hours, and is no more intoxicating than cider. This method is discouraged by Government, as, if allowed, it would cause the destruction of many oil palms, the vast number of which now make Southern Nigeria the wealthiest of our Crown Colonies, and, if properly preserved, will form an inexhaustible source of trade with Great Britain, and the means of building up an ever-increasing market for her goods.

As has already been mentioned, an enormous amount of imported liquor is used for libations at funeral ceremonies, and at "plays" in honour of dead chiefs. At practically all sacrifices and religious ceremonies libations play an important part. Till we can educate the natives, not by book learning, but by gradual raising to a higher plane of thought, it is useless to attempt to keep them, by forcible legislation, from what they deem necessary to bring good fortune on themselves, and happiness to their dead kinsfolk. Spirits they will have, if only for the causes mentioned, and, if import is forbidden, not only will the palm trees be sacrificed to this end, but illicit distilleries will spring up on every hand, as has been repeatedly pointed out by the Press. In the dense bush which covers the greater part of the Protectorate, a whole army of officials would be unable to control this danger, and the consequent degradation of a people, at present law-abiding and sober, would lie at the door of those who, in mistaken zeal, are anxious to bring about at once what must need years of patient teaching.

Could those, who have the real good of the native races at heart, cast aside prejudice and come out to study the workings of the present administrative system, I venture to believe that they would go back to their own country to turn their zeal for temperance into channels which so badly need it. Centuries of education, backed by the whole strength of our police force, have not succeeded in rendering wife murder, due to drink, uncommon among us, while, amid the Ekoi, the murder of a woman is utterly unknown, with the exception of those offered up in sacrifice, or killed in time of war.

Surely, for very shame's sake, we should wait till at least such hideous crime was stamped out in our land before attempting to force our own unsuccessful experiments in the direction of temperance, on a people, who—to our utter disgrace be it said—are incomparably more sober than ourselves. When we can point to the self-conquest, whose outward unmistakable sign will be a sober England, there will no be need of temperance legislation for Southern Nigeria Its people, of whom the greater number are law-abiding and loyal to the core, if not forced into other courses by legislation which in their present state of evolution they could not but regard as a tyrannical abuse of power, would follow us upward in the disuse of harmful spirits, as surely as they are doing in the discarding of their old customs of ordeal and torture. Only these changes must be made gradually, as the evil of such thing can be brought home to them, and in this no amount of legislation can have the force of example.

Is it much to plead for a little patience—for a few years in which to bring about such vast changes—above all, for the charity of judgment, of which we all stand in need, to be extended to those at the head of the Administration, who have striven so nobly for the good of the people entrusted to their charge?

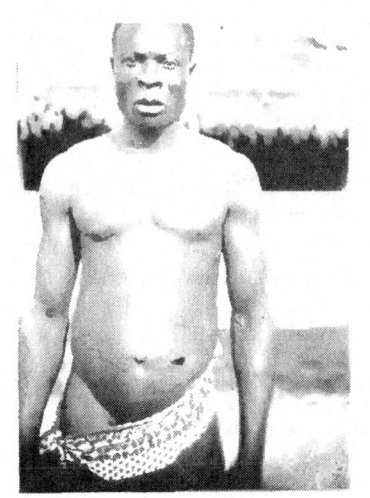

Type of Ekoi.

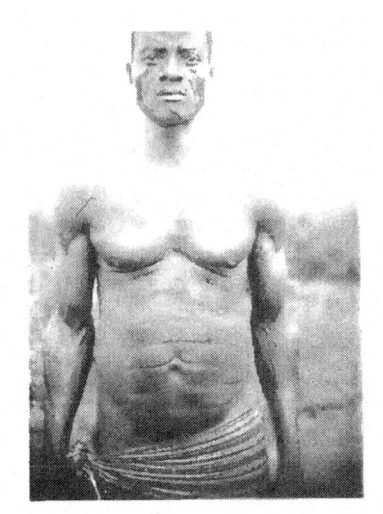

Ekoi Type.

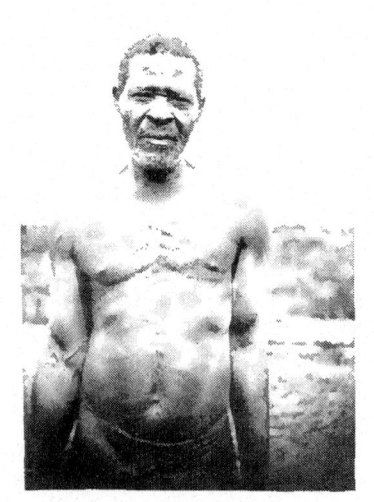

Type of "Member" from Slave Towns.

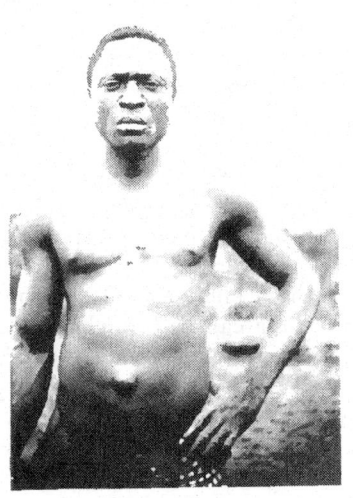

Type of Ekoi.

ORIGIN AND CHARACTERISTICS.

That the Ekoi are mainly of Bantu stock is shown both by their language and the shape of their heads. The latter point has been determined by Professor Keith, from skulls which he was good enough to work out for me.* Distinctly Himyaritic types are, however, still to be found

The original Bantu stock is now generally acknowledged to have arisen from a mixture of Hamitic and negro blood. The Ekoi were probably among the first of the races, so formed, to split off from the parent stem, and seem to have come straight from the lower end of the Nile valley There are many points about the Nsibidi writing,† which recall traces of the earliest Egyptian hieroglyphics. It is perhaps worth remarking, that with hardly any exceptions, buildings are represented in this script as circular,‡ a form generally considered peculiar to parkland peoples, and quite different to the rectangular houses of forest-folk.

That the Ekoi are descendants of a people living in large communities, swayed by powerful rulers, is shown by the fact that ancestor worship, practically unknown to tribes consisting of petty settlements, is still so strong. To the reasons already cited for believing that they have come down from the north-east, and probably from a land not so densely forested as Southern Nigeria, may be added the fact that, with hardly an exception, the former sites of all their towns are north of their present ones, and that the great "Nki" (lion) figures very largely in their early folk-lore. It is not impossible that this animal should occasionally leave its home in the grass country to the north, and pass the Cross river. More or less trustworthy authority is to be found for believing that it has actually penetrated as far south as Aking, but such incursions are certainly rare.

The salt springs which occur round the sacred lake Ijagham, and in other parts of Ekoi land, some indeed quite near to Oban station, were possibly a determining factor in the final

* See Appendix C
† See Appendix G
‡ See Story 4, Nsibidi Signs, Appendix G

choice of settlement, as the need for salt is strong among all tribes.

With the exception of a few towns near Obokum, all Ekoi now seem to have settled south of the Cross river. There are, roughly speaking, 20,000 in British territory, mostly in, or adjoining, the Oban district. Across the border of the Camerons, according to Dr. Mansfeld, they number less than 6,000, but if one includes the tribes called by him Keaka and Obang, with whom the Ekoi claim kinship, and who speak an almost identical language, the number would be raised to over 12,000. To the east of these are the Banjangs, a kindred tribe about 5,000 strong, whose speech is also very similar. Should the present rate of immigration into British territory, continue, however, the number of Ekoi in the Camerons will soon show great diminution.

The inhabitants of big Kwa town, near Calabar, claim to be the first Ekoi to have come down from the north, and were certainly there before the arrival of the Efiks, as the latter people obtained from them permission to mark out a site for their new settlement. The land within the bend of the Cross River was apparently uninhabited on the arrival of these pioneers, but other branches of the tribe soon followed, till practically the whole territory was settled.

The average height of the men is about 2 inches below that of Englishmen, while the women are still shorter in comparison with those of Teutonic races. So far from my experience of black peoples coinciding with that expressed by Mr. Northcote Thomas (p. 6 of Report on Edo-speaking Peoples, Part I), " Although the negro is able to carry loads for long distances, he must go at his own pace; even without a load his endurance is small when he is called upon to move faster than usual," I have found the negro show great powers of endurance over the whole extent of country covered by me in West and Central Africa, since 1902. Leaving on one side such splendid material as Mendis, Hausas, the inhabitants of the Tuburi marshes, &c.—to take the Ekoi alone—it is quite usual for them, when carrying for themselves, to bear a 100-lb. load over the 15-mile hilly road from Oban to Obutong, and return the same day. With regard to speed, it may be

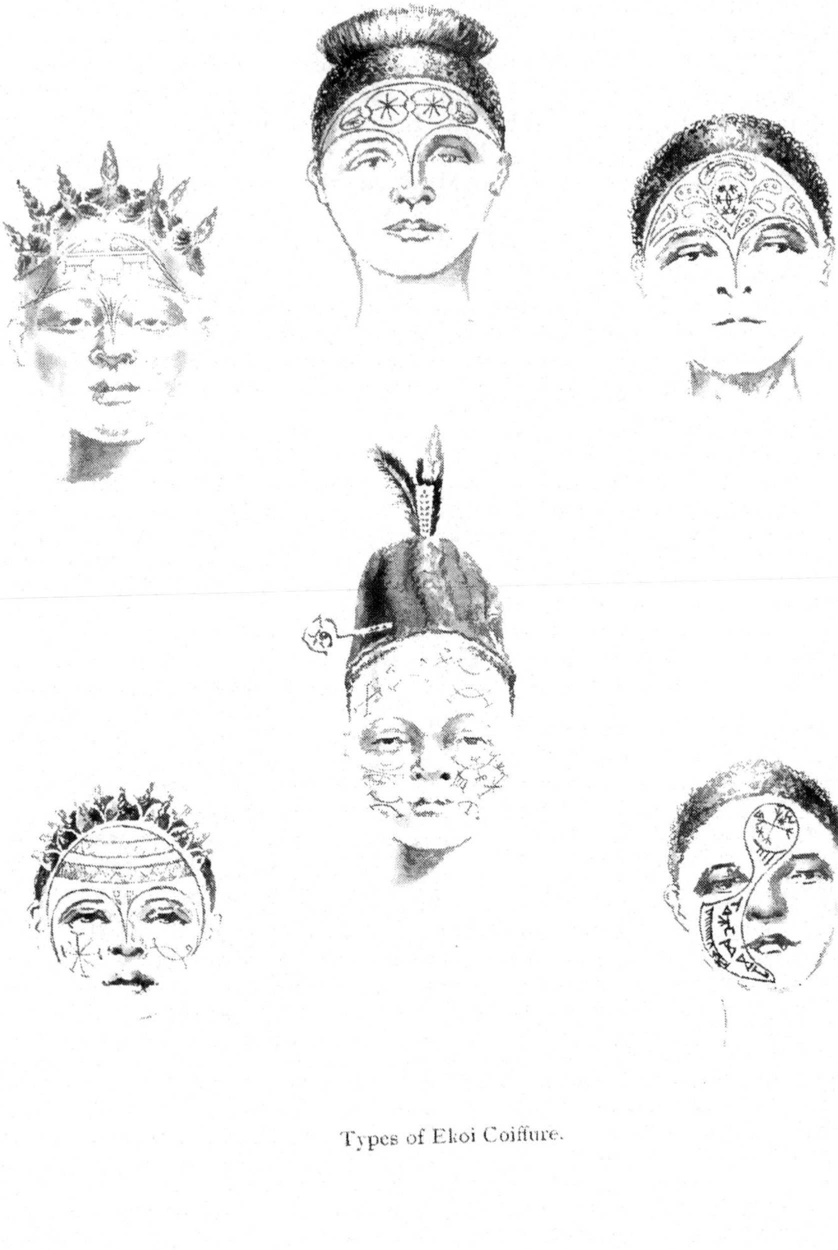

Types of Ekoi Coiffure.

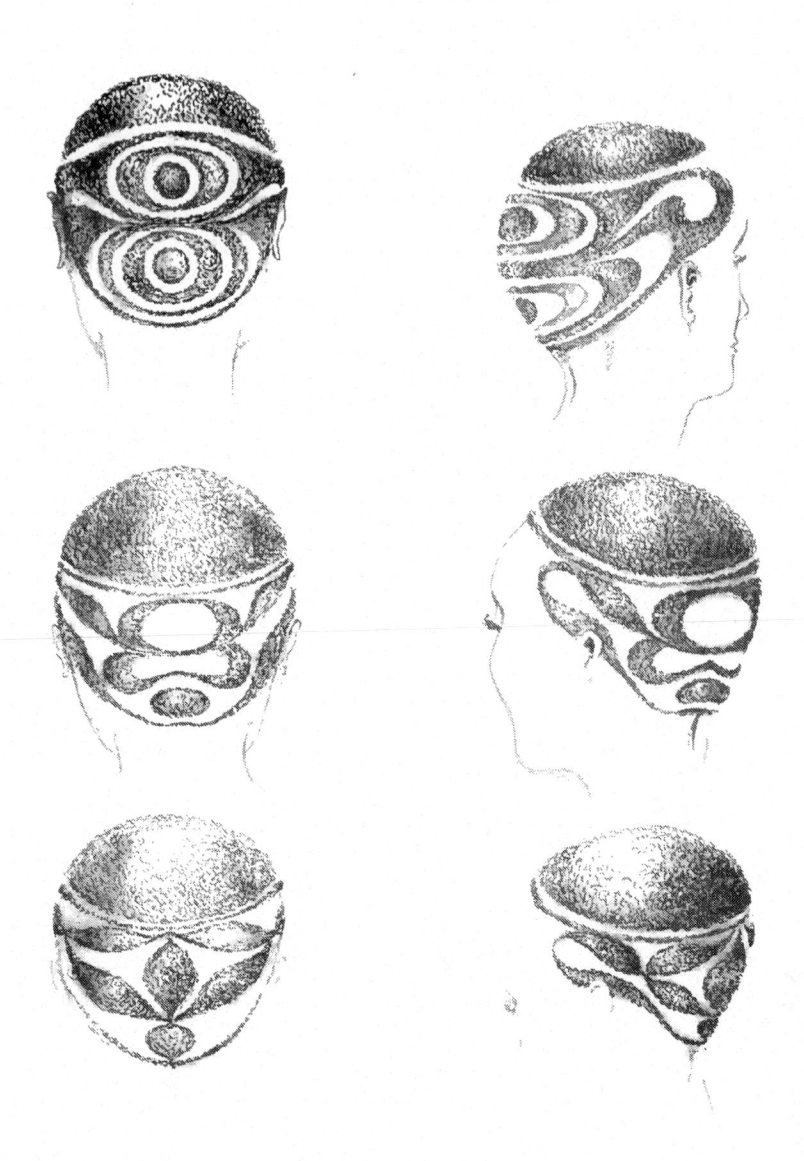

Types of Ekoi Coiffure.

mentioned that the ordinary mail-runners, sometimes with a load of 50 lb., do the 80 miles to Calabar and back in three days, though, unless they wish for any reason to come back at once, they usually wait a day or two for the return mail.

Like most hill tribes, the men prefer to carry heavy loads on their shoulders, kept in place by a strap round the forehead. Women and girls, however, carry everything on their heads, and their loads of firewood, &c., must often weigh over 60 lb. Like those of most tropical tribes, the women age quickly, though some keep their good looks till over forty. It is impossible to get accurate ages, as these are never known by the people themselves, but those over seventy seem rare, and I do not think it would be safe to put down any as more than ninety.

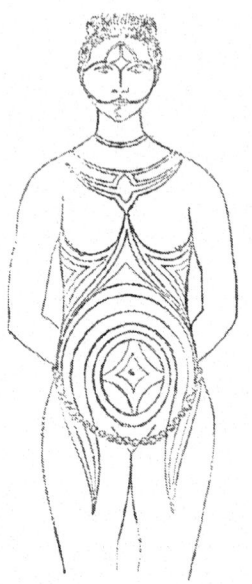

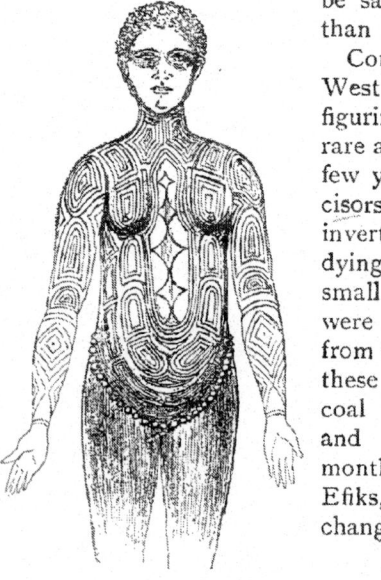

Contrary to the custom of many West African tribes, artificial disfiguring of face or body is extremely rare among this people. Up to a few years ago, the two front incisors were filed, so as to form an inverted V, but this custom is now dying out. In olden times, three small circles of concentric rings were cut at the side of the face from the temple downwards. Into these a mixture of ground charcoal and palm oil was rubbed and renewed about every six months. When the Ekoi met the Efiks, however, this race mark was changed to one larger circle, though some claim that they had made the alteration beforehand and the Efiks adopted it from them. This custom is also dying out, and since my arrival in the District, no child has been so marked.

In the interior, children and young girls still have their bodies painted with designs made by black vegetable dyes. The most usual of these is extracted from the rhizome of the little flower "Ibiri Nsi," much like a wild hyacinth. A small amount of tattooing is practised, and also the ghost marks described on p. 203. As regards coiffures, the variety of designs to be found among young girls and children is astonishing Usually they first shave the head, then, when the hair has grown to a uniform length of about a quarter of an inch, trace out with chalk an elaborate pattern, which is left standing against a clean-shaved background.

Young women and children are also fond of ornamenting their faces, especially their foreheads, with designs in various colours The absolute mastery of outline shown by these, as well as by those mentioned in the last paragraph, is far beyond the average to be expected from Europeans. The variety of such patterns is extraordinary. Several hundred sketches were made by my wife and her sister—indeed, the supply seemed inexhaustible. The outlines are often filled in with Nsibidi writing, and sometimes a girl's whole life-history is proclaimed in this manner. Such patterns are always traced by a female relative, usually the aunt of the person decorated.

The Ekoi are mentally an intelligent race, and though they have not the concentration of mind possessed by white people, they can undeniably fix their attention for hours at a time on any subject which interests them, while their memories are incomparably better, and their senses, at least those of sight, hearing and smell, are—as is to be expected—far keener than those of Europeans.

They are an eloquent people, and there are very few who cannot, at a moment's notice, discourse fluently on any topic of which they are conversant, or defend themselves ably enough on every occasion. Their points, though sometimes long drawn out, are well made in the end, the words accompanied by expressive tone and gesture. They have a keen sense of humour,

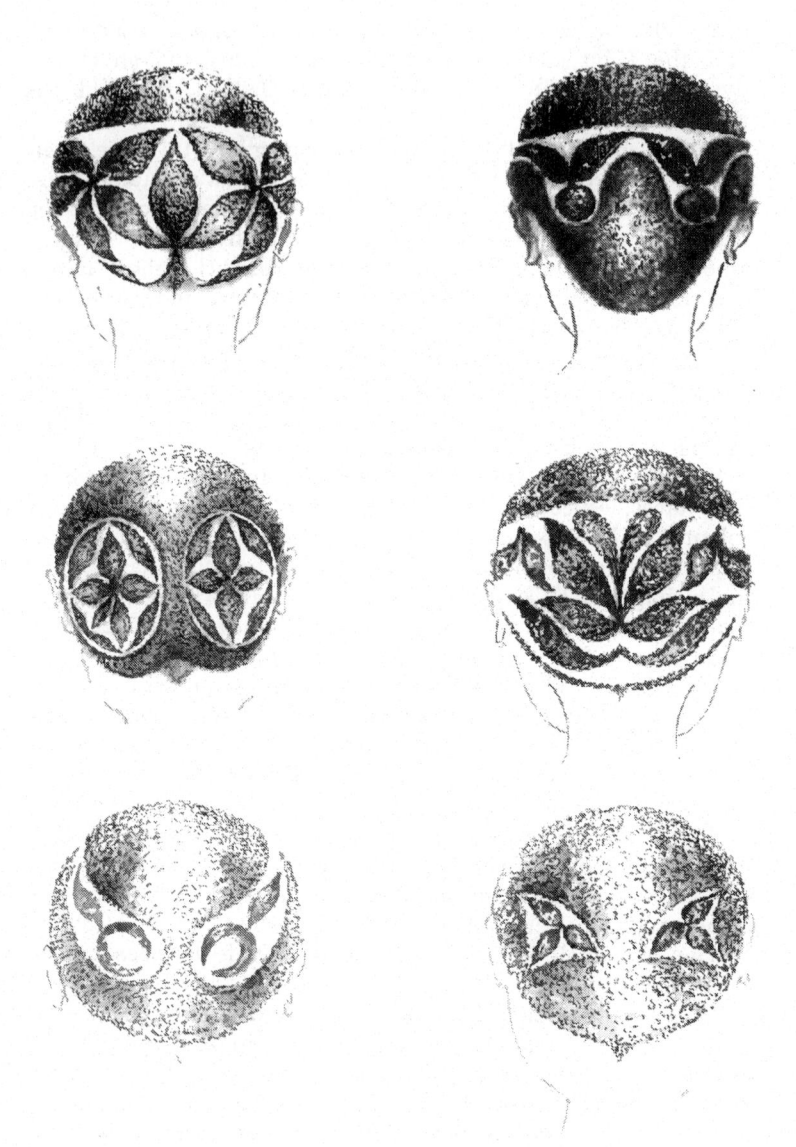

Types of Ekoi Coiffure.

Female. Types of Ekoi Coiffure. Male.

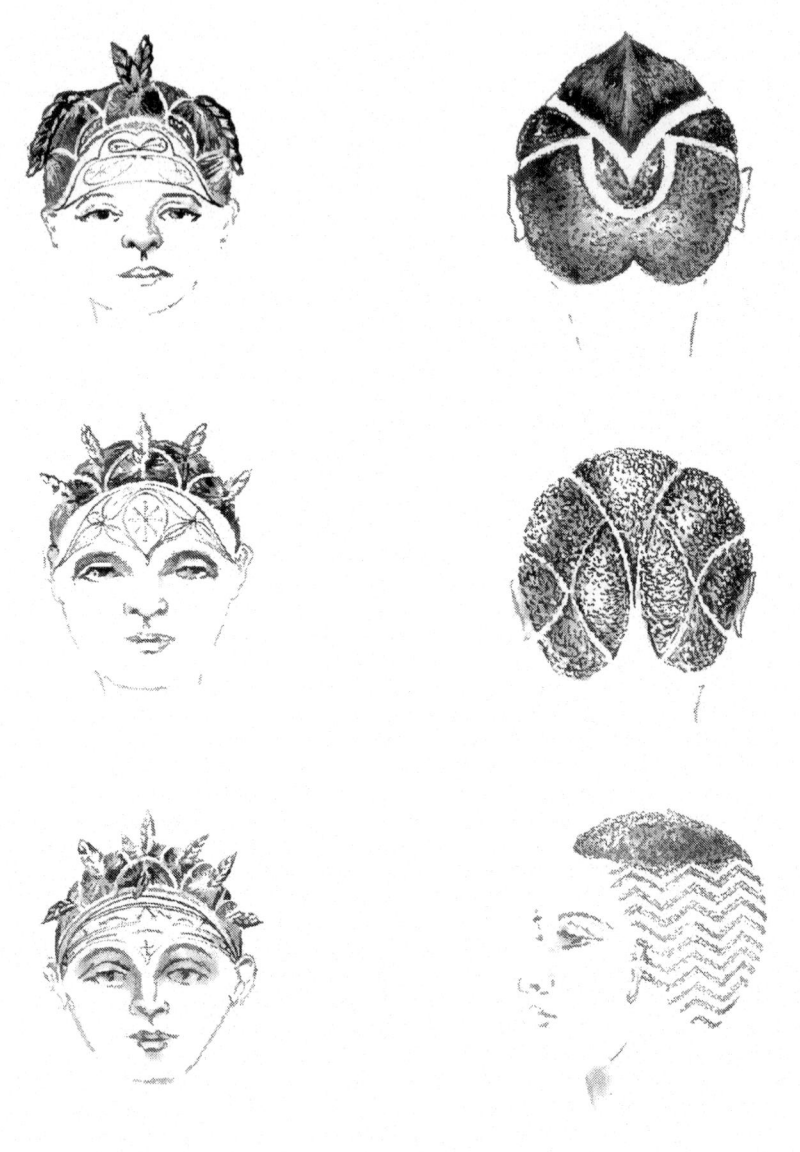

often disguised by a child-like guilelessness, and cropping up in the most unlikely times and places. Once a prisoner was brought before Court on the charge of having broken the prison rules by speaking to his wife without permission. When brought up by the Corporal, he pleaded "not guilty" in spite of the many witnesses against him.

He stated, "Among those who brought rations to the prison gate, I saw my wife with a basket of plantains. I would have liked to speak to her, but could not get permission, as the Corporal was busy. I thought to myself, 'Our Father the D. C. has forbidden us to speak with the townsfolk who come to sell us food, but never has he forbidden us to speak with the plantains.' Therefore I looked sadly upon those which lay in the basket and asked, 'O plantains! why are you so few? If more of you do not come quickly, I shall surely die of hunger!'" I swear to Your Worship that that was all. I said no word to anyone, save the plantains, and against conversing with them there is no law."

The simplest statements, too, often show a touch of unconscious poetry. Not long ago at Nsan we were visited by an old, old woman, who had come to present us with a small mat, made by her own hands.

She stood in the vivid sunshine leaning on her stick, shrunken and feeble, an image of extreme old age, but with eyes still bright, and a clear, kind voice.

"Each time D. C. came to our town," she said, "I thought, 'This time at least he will come to my compound, so that I shall learn to know him, for I am the oldest woman of Nsan.' Yet he never came to see me, so I have come to him that I may at last see the face of my Father."

We were very sorry that she had been unvisited for so long, but found that her house lay by itself in a little side street at the back of the main road. She took great pride in her age, and told how she had come, when already old enough to bear a small load for herself, from the old town of Nsan. We asked if any others of her "age class" were still alive, but she answered, "Of all those who were with me, dancing up and down in the moonlight or the sunshine, I alone remain. The others long since lie sleeping"

The two most noticeable qualities of the Ekoi are their reverence for age, and their love of children. The oldest man of the town is always its head chief, unless he has been so poor all his life as to have been debarred from entering any of the clubs. Only one case of harshness to a child has come to my notice during the whole time spent among them, and the spirit of indulgence, with which children are everywhere treated, shows its results in the independence and utter fearlessness of even the smallest.

One day at Nsan, while my wife and her sister were alone in the Rest-house, a mite of three invaded their room. He announced that he had come to see the "white man," and lay a complaint before him. They at once sent to request my return from the school play-ground, where a football match was in progress, and when I got back to interview the complainant, his tale was unfolded without delay. The small visitor declared that his father had not given him enough to eat, therefore he came to lay his "case" before "white man." His well-nourished little body looked as if any error of diet had lain in the contrary direction. Biscuits of various kinds proved inadequate to his needs, but at length he was made happy with a corn-cob, nearly as big as himself, and with this he toddled away.

On another occasion, when standing at the theodolite, I felt a touch at about the height of my shooting boot. Looking down, I saw a mite who could only just have learned to walk. In his upraised hands were some limes about the size of acorns.

He had come all alone, and quite on his own initiative, to "dash" the "white man," and had selected these diminutive limes as a suitable offering.

Everywhere the small children seem fond of playing at Juju processions, in imitation of their elders. A typical one was seen at Mfamosing.

The tiny "Okum" wore a long ragged garment of blue stuff, which had once formed part of his mother's gown. This trailed behind, but was held up in front by both small hands. He glided, courtesied and turned, in carefully studied imitation of "Akpambe." Before him marched a diminutive gnome-like mortal, solemnly tom-toming on one of our discarded coffee

Types of Ekoi Coiffure (Small Children).

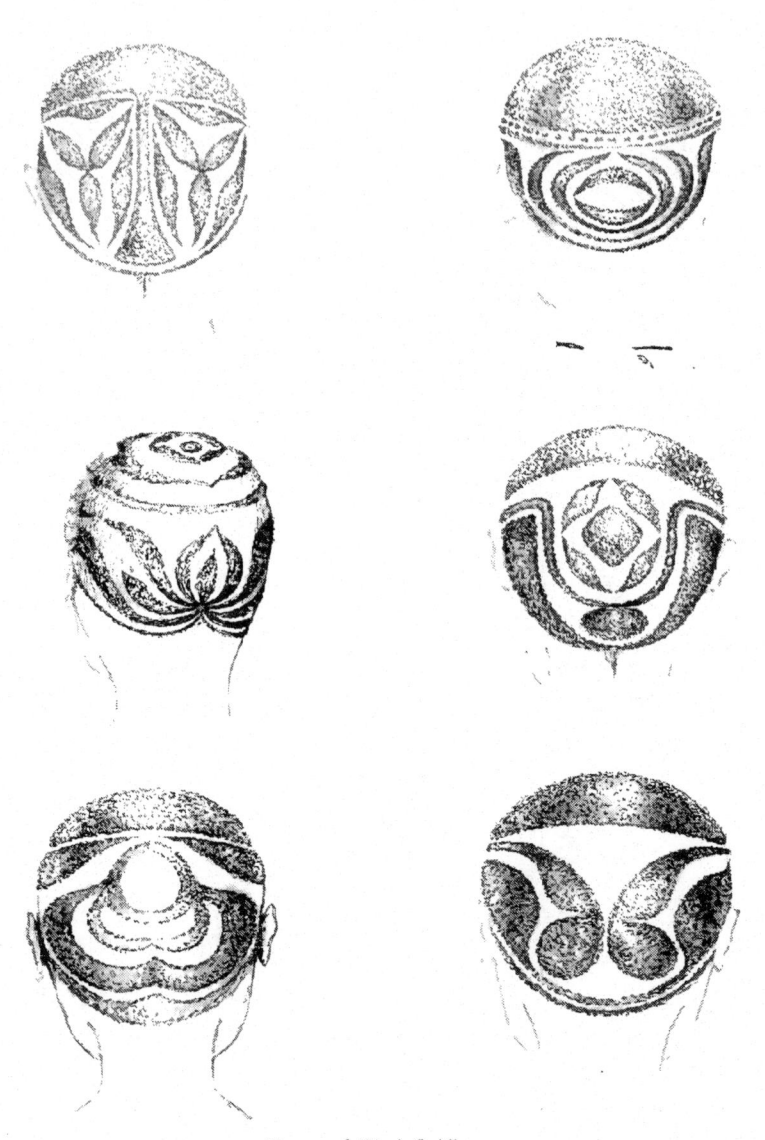

Types of Ekoi Coiffure.

tins, while behind, with an air of ineffable importance, walked a third midget carrying a wand. Later, two others, similarly weaponed, but with sticks about four times their own size, came to join the procession. Whether the superior height of the newcomers' wands struck terror or envy into the breast of small "Tom-tom" was not easy to tell, but he burst into floods of tears at sight of the new arrivals, and fled sobbing to his home.

Proverbs and Omens.

The language has an extensive vocabulary, and many phrases show unexpectedly poetical turns of thought. It is also rich in proverbs, some of which are apt enough, though many have little meaning for European ears.

The following are perhaps typical :—

" Eeti ejim ka mkpe aiya, mbuta anak amobikk etim.
Big tree stood on bank of great water, rain fell (but) could not cover (it) "

" Nse oa, nkpe oa, na akpawoi, odikk amitt amobikk etannum break."
Father your, mother your, if they die, crying (but) eyes cannot

i.e., A high tree grew by the side of a great water; the rain fell and fell, and the water rose, yet could not overflow the top of the tree.

If your father or mother should die, you weep and weep, yet grief cannot quite overwhelm you. Your eyes will brighten again some day.

"Ofung otue okett, ojokk otue okett, njinni ba ntue.
Buffaloes draw tired, elephants draw tired, small birds come draw "

i.e., What great folk failed to do, may sometimes be done by the small and weak.

"Ikum igbaw mfepp Chong obinn eye okaka eyuk
Firewood falls wind Go break to-day, don t sleep cold "

The firewood has been blown down by the wind. Go and break it up and carry it home to-day, so that you should not have to sleep cold to night; *i.e.*, Don't miss an opportunity.

Great attention is paid to any signs supposed to foretell the future, whether from outside or inside influences. Among the former, the cries and flights of birds hold an important place. There are five principle kinds with the gift of prophecy:

The Nkundak, or Greater Plantain-eater.

The Osaiiri, or Kingfisher.

The Aru,

and two varieties of Itott

In making a journey, it is a good omen if either of the first three of these birds cries on your left hand, but it foretells ill-luck should they be heard on the right. The Itott, on the other hand, brings good fortune if it crosses your path from right to left, but bad luck if in the contrary direction.

Of divination by feelings in different parts of the body :—

A twitching in the upper eyelid of the left eye denotes that one is about to see a bad thing, such as an ordeal by burning oil.

A twitching in the upper eyelid of the right eye, on the contrary, foretells a fine sight, such as a dance.

The same sensation in either of the bottom eyelids predicts coming cause for tears.

Should the twitching be felt in the top of the left arm before starting on a journey, it means that evil awaits you, and that the friendly powers are trying to hold you back. If this warning be disregarded, misfortune is sure to follow. Should the twitching be felt, however, in the top part of the right arm it is a good sign, and foretells that a friend's arm will soon lie within one's own.

If this sensation comes in the hollow of the elbow of the right arm, or the palm of the right hand, it means that you will be called on to pay a debt or give a gift; if in the left hand, that you are about to receive one, as in our own "Right hand ta'e, left hand pay."

A twitching above the heart means danger, trouble, or punishment, as also a tingling on the forehead or left thigh. On the right breast or thigh it means good luck. The same sensation below the elbow on either arm denotes that news of a death will soon reach you. On the sole of the right foot, it means that a strange man is coming to see you; on the left foot, that you will be visited by a strange woman.

When a meteor falls to the ground, it is a sign of a coming death in the neighbourhood, while a comet or a dark ring round the moon betokens the death of a chief.

People from the Interior waiting to welcome us at the nearest River to their Town.

Lowest Falls, Kwa River.

CHAPTER XXX

Treatment of "Members"

In the old days, Calabar and Bonny were rivals for pre-eminence among the slave ports of Africa, and few places in the world can have seen more misery. In this infamous traffic the Ekoi acted as "middle-men" for the greater part of the land to the north and north-east. Most of the victims were brought down from the "slave towns," as they are still called, *i.e.*, those lying between the Cross river and the Benue, and more especially near the line of the present Anglo-German frontier. The Ekoi did not usually travel far into the interior themselves, but the slaves were brought down and delivered into the hands of those living most to the north, and from these passed from town to town, till they reached the Calabar traders.

The abolition of slavery by England put a stop to all such export trade, but it still continued among the natives in out-of-the-way parts, such as the Ekoi country, which had not as yet been fully taken over by Government. For the first year after my arrival in 1907, one of my principal duties was to stamp it out.

The administration of Southern Nigeria is carried on to a large extent through the so-called "Heads of Houses." The word "House" includes not only the immediate family, but its retainers, freed slaves and their descendants—all, in fact, who recognise the authority of the Chief of the "sept." All, save blood relations, would perhaps be best described by the old Latin word "Clientes," and the reciprocal duties of the Roman noble and his retainers are closely paralleled by those of present-day Ekoi. The Head of the House now, as then, supports his "members" in infancy and sickness, sees to their general well-being, and in return receives their services, and exacts submission to his authority in all lawful ways.

This state of affairs has been recognised by the Government of Southern Nigeria, and, should either party not fulfil his part of the compact, there is a remedy at law. The one objection from a working point of view is that, in the mind of the people, there still exists a distinction between free-born "members" of such a house or clan, and those not free. They are beginning to grasp, however, that no such distinction exists before the law, and the difference will doubtless gradually die out. According to the unanimous opinion of those who have had experience in the governing of natives, it would be most inexpedient suddenly to deprive chiefs and heads of families of their hereditary authority. Such a course would reduce to anarchy that part of the Central and Eastern Provinces of South Nigeria near the coast, unless the number of officials were multiplied ten-fold and even then the natives would be less happy and contented than under the existing state of affairs. The necessity for slowness and caution in all changes is borne in from day to day with greater force upon all who have to do with ruling West African negroes. To change, at a stroke of the pen, the system of government evolved by the natives in the course of thousands of years, would have far-reaching ill results. By the present state of affairs at least no one is left uncared for, and beggars are unknown through the length and breadth of the Ekoi country.

The pledging of free-born persons for debt was common among the Ekoi, but this was a mild form of slavery. "Members" so pledged were specially well treated, and returned to freedom on payment of the debt. At death, also, they were buried like free-born men, not, as in the case of slaves, tied to bamboo poles, by means of which the bodies were borne to a distant part of the bush and there left unburied.

At the present day, a good "member" gives up from one-third to one-half of his time for the service of the Head of his House, mostly in farm work or hunting. Sometimes he trades, usually with capital supplied by the "Head," to whom the profits go, but a part is practically always returned to the "member." In the old days an idle slave was flogged, but, should the punishment be excessive, he could complain to the principal chief of the town. It is to be feared that such

TREATMENT OF "MEMBERS"

complaints were too often unheeded, in which case the slave usually ran away. If he were caught he was sometimes cruelly punished, but more often sold at Calabar.

To guard against attempts at escape, on first arrival in the house of a new master, the latter usually cut off a lock of hair and some nail parings, then took a piece of old cloth which the slave had worn. These were carried before the Juju and a prayer offered that death or recapture might follow any attempt to escape. After the ceremony the pieces were carefully kept in a secret place, and the slave believed that, should he run away, the Juju would infallibly "catch" him

Not long ago one of the wives of chief Nataba of Oberekkai ran away, and he brought an action in Court for her return. She was his "member" and accused him of having practised witchcraft against her, in that, seven years before, he had cut a strip from the hem of her gown and hung it up before the Juju. She is a light-skinned woman with some pretensions to beauty, and during the eighteen years in which they had been wedded, had not a single other act of unkindness to urge against her husband, or reason for wishing to leave him The old man pleaded pathetically that she should not be allowed to desert him, because all his other wives had quarrelled with him for loving her so much better than any of them, and giving her an unfair share of ornaments and presents of every kind. "Just lately," the old Chief said, "the Oberekkai women were dancing, so I dressed my wife full of native ornaments that she might go and dance with them. When the dance was over, she came and piled up outside my door all the property of her dead mother, who had been my 'member,' saying that by so doing she would free herself from me for ever."

Up till twenty years ago the ordinary price of a slave was:—

	£	s	d
7 pieces of cloth	1	15	0
1 keg gunpowder	0	5	0
1 gun	0	15	0
1 matchet	0	1	0
	£2	16	0

At the time of my arrival the price had risen to thirty pieces of cloth or one cow, *i.e.*, £7 10s. to £10.

As a general rule slaves were kindly treated, as are "members" at the present time, but cases of cruelty were not unknown, and are still occasionally brought before the Native Court.

Once at Nsan a man came up to beg that he might be allowed to settle down in the Oban District instead of having to stay with the master whose slave he had formerly been, and in whose house he still lived as a "member." He said that this man had lately returned from the funeral of a neighbouring chief, and had been overheard to say to his son, "Formerly when so great a chief died, slaves were sacrificed round the grave that they might serve him in the spirit world. Now it is the day of the white man's rule and we are no longer allowed to do this. Nevertheless I have thought what to do. One by one I will kill my 'members' as if by accident. Half I will leave alive for you. Some we will hold down in crossing a river, to others we will give poison and say they died of snake-bite and other things, then when I come to die will all be waiting to serve me, so that I should not be poor and unattended among the ghosts."

On another occasion, while at Niaji, a big Juju dance was given. The head priest, a man named Erim, feared on account of his magic by all the countryside, attended dressed in his full robes. Round his ankles he wore deep bands covered with little bells. In one hand he bore green boughs, which he kept waving before my eyes, and in the other his Juju staff, which he pointed almost ceaselessly in my direction. Both actions were performed with such peculiar intentness, that it would have been impossible not to suspect some serious motive. He was obviously trying to work a magic on the "white man," whose presence appeared to have a disturbing effect on him. Inquiries led to the following case coming before the native Court.—

Ekpiri Otu, who had once been a slave-wife of Erim's, after taking oath on the Juju "Mfam," said:

"Before I make my statement I beg that the D.C. will protect me, so that no man shall be able to hurt me because of what I may say

"Erim was my first husband; I know him well. His belly contains poison, and his body all round is poisonous. He is a great Juju man, and has a medicine which protects him, so that if anything happens like this, he can make favour for himself by magic, so that the Court shall decide for him.

"One of his wives reproached him for having married me, because she said that he should not have wedded a slave. He therefore divorced me in the name of his wife. In the month of February, at night time, the woman came and told me that a tree had fallen down in the farm. Next day Erim found me working there, and said I was to give up work and go away Next morning, when the day broke, they went and cut off part of my farm and gave it to a small boy. The big tree had fallen in the corner, and the owner of the next arm complained that it had spoilt her crops. She said, 'You are just like a small sister of Talbot's,' because whenever she called me 'wild animal' or anything like that I said 'I will go and complain to Talbot.' I answered her, 'If I were his small sister, this very day I would go and live near him; then you could harm me no more.' Then the woman, Ode by name, told her husband that I was going to take them to Court before Talbot. I was in the farm. They came and asked my daughter, 'Where is your mother?' She said, 'She has gone to farm.' Erim said before my three children that he would meet me in the road and kill me, that I might not take them down to Oban. He also said, 'I should like to die with my slaves. When Otu died, no one killed slaves to bury with him, as was formerly the custom with chiefs.' When I came back I found him in my house He called, 'Come here.' Then he caught hold of me, pushed me down on the floor, and began to kick and beat me. Our custom is that whenever a master beats a slave, the slave cannot touch the master. My children all cried out. He said, 'You cry because of your mother.' My daughter Omin was in the fatting-house, but he beat me so badly that she came out. He caught her and pushed her away. She clung to the roof ribs, but he shook her backwards and forwards, knocking her, and at length pushed her out of the house The accused's sister parted them, but he came back again and tore off my clothes and drove me naked into the town place. Chief Obun came up and said, ' Have you not heard of the " white man's " rule that no one must do such a thing as this? If your wife complains, why do you not wait till the people return from their farms ? ' To me he said, ' Go to your house and stay there till the evening.' When night fell the people came back, so they called and said, 'It is now time for the meeting.' They took me to the place where all the town was sitting The people asked me to make a statement, but I refused, saying, 'Let those who brought the complaint first make theirs.'

"This they did, and next I put my case, saying to the townspeople all that I am now telling the Court Erim then hit me hard on the head with his wife's staff. I cried out loudly. Ekuri San stood forth and said, ' I have often been to Court and heard about the ' white man's ' rules; also when I returned home I used to tell everything to you. Why do you do a thing like this?" I wept for the pain in my head, and kept on weeping as I went home. Ncha Echi, the daughter of Ode, met me and began to fight with me. My daughter came and parted us. It was night time. A woman named Magbo met me and said, ' You must not go home, Erim is waiting for you there.' I said to her, ' He and his daughter both beat me. What can I do? Must I sleep outside?' I said to myself, 'Erim has said " I will kill all my slaves to-day " I must run and hide in the bush,' but Ekuri San and Akimni caught me and prevented me from doing this. They said to me, 'Anyhow, we must prevent you from going to the bush The white man says, if people fight, the bystanders must part them' That same night, Ncha Echi, Ode's daughter, met my child and began to beat her. Omin did nothing, but only said to the Niaji people, ' You see what she does to me.' The husband of Ncha Echi said to her, ' You have a child on your back. Why do you fight with other people ? ' It was dark, Ode was hiding in the compound; but she came out, caught hold of Omin by her feet, knocked her down and jumped upon her, then caught her by the throat and crushed it against the ground. When Erim came, he saw Ode sitting on my daughter and beating her. He joined with his wife, and beat my child with his Juju ' Ekpiri Nkara.' His wife had told me before, as well as other people, that this Juju was most deadly, and that, if you took it in your hand and touched people with it, the person who was touched would surely die. As Erim beat my daughter, his hand touched Ode, and she cried out, 'Do you want to kill me because of the slave?' His hand only touched her by accident. One of my sons named Ekpe was present. After a while the people parted them and took my daughter home. Erim went again and said to her, 'Let us die to-day.'

"That same night the townspeople took me and my daughter and hid us, so that our master should not see us again. He got the Egbo drum and beat round the town against Ekuri San and Akimni, and said if they did not bring us out, he would fine them heavily by means of the Egbo. They said to him, 'We cannot give them back, lest we break the white man's rule.' I said to Ekuri San, 'Let me go outside, so that he can kill me,' but Ekuri said 'No, we will not let you go.' Erim did not sleep at all that night, but went all the time round the town with the Egbo drum. At daybreak I went back to my compound. My daughter's throat had swelled out, because of the beating by Ode and Erim, and her body was full of sores. Her breasts also pained her, for she was enceinte. When Ode, Erim, and Ncha Echi knocked her down, they crushed her body, and it was that that killed my daughter. This happened just before D. C. came to our town last time."

Once on a march, a man and woman stepped out of the bush, and stood waiting, hand in hand, in the middle of the road. When we reached them they first bent down and touched the ground with their finger-tips, in sign of supplication, then stood up and claimed the protection of their D. C. against several people who had wronged them. The case was tried next Court day, when Itita, the husband, stated on oath:

"Akot, my wife, told me one day that our master, Kako, had flogged her and wounded her with a matchet. The marks on her throat are still to be seen. In 1904 he made me swear by Osai, so that the Juju might catch me if I married a certain woman who was one of his 'members.' She kept following me, so Osai caught me, and I almost died. My master also grew ill, and Effion was sent to say that I had bewitched him. Several years ago he forced me and Akot, my wife, to swear by the Juju Mbian* that we would no longer keep together."

Akot stated on oath, "The accused wounded me with a matchet and said, ' You are not free-born, but no better than a wild animal. If D. C. Talbot were not always walking up and down through his District, you would long since have been offered up to the Juju.' Then he took up a knife and gashed my throat."

Cruelty was proved, the master was sent to prison for a long term, and the woman set free, but there was grave suspicion that on his release he avenged himself by poisoning her, though the case remained unproved.

Once a small boy of nine, a mere bag of skin and bone, ran into the office. He stated that he was bought from his parents only two years ago, but that his master dared not bring him into the town, because " Makara " (white man) has his eyes all around; he walks always up and down, and would say at once, " Who is this ' man '? It is a new face. I do not know him." So he kept me in the bush at a farm that he has. There he beat me often for no cause. Then I heard the other "members" say, " White man fears no one, not even great chiefs If the smallest slave goes to him he will see that justice is done." Then the others asked, "Shall we bring complaint of our master's cruelty before him?" But each one answered, "Nay, lest he kill us, when white man does not know " But I know that " white man " will not let him hurt me, so I come to bring my complaint."

Such, given in their own words, are the blackest cases brought by "members" against the Heads of their Houses. Now, the cases brought by the latter against " members " far outweigh in number those against themselves, and there is little doubt but that, at the present time, the pendulum is beginning to swing too far in the other direction. This is only natural, however, after the centuries of repression imposed by the free-born. That, even in the old days, these modern helots occasionally turn on their masters is shown by many legends,

---

* Juju, into the composition of which sea-water enters. Mostly used by coast people

TREATMENT OF "MEMBERS"

of which the one given on p. 27, "How the Slaves killed the Free-born with Gall," and the following are typical:—

How Slaves used to lie in wait to kill the Free-born.

By Eta Ndom of Niaji.

A woman named Ome once left her town to visit a friend who lived some way off. With her she took her daughter Ara, and a female slave called Ngonne. When they came to a shallow stream Ome said, "Let us bathe here;" but Ngonne answered, "The water is not good. Let us go further."

After a while they came to the banks of a river, where the water was deep in places, but shallow in others. Here the slave woman said, "The water is good; let us bathe."

While they washed, Ngonne said to her mistress, "Let me rub your back." No sooner had the other turned round than the slave pushed her into a deep hole where a crocodile was living. The beast rose and caught the woman, and Ngonne took the child and went back to the town whence they had come.

When they arrived the slave bore her mistress's child to the house of her own sweetheart. As they entered the compound the people saluted her, and said, "Welcome, Ngonne. Where is Ome?" To this she only answered through her nose, "Hong, Hong, Hong." (This is the noise made by Ngonne, a bird with a very long beak.)[*] Her sweetheart cooked, and brought the food for her to eat. Ara wanted to eat also, but the slave woman drove her away, and would give her no food save two pieces of plantain. For a long time Ngonne acted thus towards her mistress's daughter, eating all the good food herself and giving a very little of what was left over to the child.

One day birds were spoiling the beans in the farm, so the slave woman called Ara and bade her go thither and drive them away. All day the little maid wept in the farm, and a man who was cutting palm kernels came down from the tree to find out who it was who was crying so bitterly. He found no one, for she had wandered away from the farm, and came at

[*] Hornbill

length to the river where her mother had been lost. She sat down on the bank, weeping and calling her mother's name.

The woman heard the voice, and knew it for that of her daughter, so she begged Crocodile to let her come out of the water. When she saw the child she put her arms round her, and drew her head against her own breast. Then she parted her hair very tenderly, and after a while went down again into the river.

Ara went back to the house. When she got there Ngonne asked, "Who made that parting on your head?" The girl answered nothing.

Another day, when sent to scare birds in the farm, she sat down and wept again, and the same man heard her voice, and came to seek her. This time he found her, and asked, "What is the matter?" The girl told him all about her mother, and how cruelly the slave had treated her. He took her back to the town, and asked some people to go with them down to the river. To this they agreed, took their nets and went.

When the bank was reached Ara called to her mother. Ome came up to the surface, and the townsfolk caught her in their nets and brought her home, without letting Ngonne know.

Next time that the slave cooked chop, and began to eat, without giving any to Ara, the latter called out in a loud voice, "Why do you eat before me? Do you not know that you are my mother's slave?"

Ngonne replied, "You have not said such a thing as this for a very long time. I think that something must have happened."

At that moment Ome came out from her hiding place. In her hand was a sharp knife. She caught the slave and killed her.

At that time slaves were always seeking to kill their masters and hide the bodies. Since Ngonne tried to destroy her mistress, however, people have watched their slaves, lest they should do harm.

CHAPTER XXXI

Folk-lore

UNLIKE most primitive peoples, whose legends deal mostly with the terrible, there are many tender and gracious touches about Ekoi stories, while several show a distinct sense of humour In not a few, too, traces may be found, half understood, or wholly misapplied, of beliefs which have come down from ages so remote as to be forgotten save for such faint echoes. Some refer to times when snakes still possessed hands and feet*, and one, Oporopóotop, appears to be a relic of times when farms were actually subject to the ravages of dinosaurs and such-like monsters.

Much of the charm of these tales was doubtless due to the manner of their telling; for the Ekoi are wonderful story-tellers, and many, especially the young boys, relate their legends in a sort of dramatic recitative, chanting and crooning at times till the words almost fall into song.

Most of the tales recorded were taken down from sources never before brought into contact with white influence. Some, despite modern touches, show a close resemblance to well-known stories from the "Arabian Nights," for instance, "The Treasure House in the Bush." In some, again, I have fancied that echoes of Herodotus may still be traced. All have been taken down exactly as they were told, except the one given on p. 337, " How all Stories and all History came on Earth." The introduction to this was related by one man, and the bulk of the tale by another, but the *finale* so obviously belongs to that of which the first otherwise disjointed fragment, forms the beginning, that it seemed better, in this one case, to combine the two.

One of the most persistent characters in these tales is the

* See pp. 374-377.

Woman covered with Sores, who meets all travellers to the nether world, and helps to success, or dooms to failure, according to whether their goodness of heart is such as to pass her tests. In one case only (p. 62) is this personage of the male sex.

Another interesting and persistent character in Ekoi mythology is the "Lame Boy," already mentioned in the "Stilt Dances"* who plays the part of "Good Fairy" wherever he appears. As will be seen from the story "How Fire first came on Earth" he holds for the Ekoi much the position which Prometheus held among the Greeks. In one tale, "Ada, the Forest Demon," the character is feminine.

My knowledge of such things is unfortunately too limited for an opinion of mine to bear weight in the matter, yet I venture to think that the importance of the "Lame Boy," not among the Ekoi only, but in West African ritual generally, has not, as yet, been appreciated by Europeans, otherwise the significance of the lame man dragged round Benin would surely have been clear to Mr. Northcote Thomas; yet he passes it by with only the remark, "Another custom enjoined that once a year a lame man should be dragged round the city, and then as far as a place on the Enyai road called Adaneha. This was probably a ceremony of purification."†

Another point that may perhaps be worth mentioning is that, as in the case of Persephone, no visitor to the nether world may eat of food offered by the ghosts, else he will never return to the sunlight. Usually the necessary food is provided by the Lame Boy, or the Woman with Sores. In one case tomatoes were given by the ghost of a dead sister,‡ and those not eaten were brought back for planting in the upper world. In another case,§ egg plants were given by the Chieftainess of the Ghosts to the last visitor whom she allowed to return from her kingdom, on condition that they should be distributed among the living.

The constant recurrence of the number 7 in these stories,

---

* See p 285
† Report, "Edo-speaking Peoples," Part I, p 35
‡ See p 240
§ See p 236

Village on Cross River.

and the fact that ghosts can never make use of it when counting, is also worthy of note.

Sheep and tortoise are credited with cunning above all other animals, and hold in this respect somewhat the position of Brer Rabbit and Reincke Fuchs in the Folk-lore of other continents.

I would call attention to the length of these stories, unusual among those of primitive peoples Their cleanliness of tone is also noteworthy. Hardly a single unpleasant tale was taken down, and of those here recorded only one sentence—marked by dots in the text on p. 341—has been expurgated.

How all Stories and all History came among Men.
By Agra of Mbcban.

Mouse goes everywhere. Through rich men's houses she creeps, and visits even the poorest. At night, with her little bright eyes, she watches the doing of secret things, and no treasure-chamber is so safe but she can tunnel through and see what is hidden there.

In old days she wove a story-child from all that she saw, and to each of these she gave a gown of different colours—white, red, blue, or black. The stories became her children, and lived in her house and served her, because she had no children of her own.

*　　*　　*　　*　　*

Now in olden days a sheep and a leopard lived in the same town. In course of time Leopard became *enceinte* and Sheep also. Sheep bore a daughter and Leopard a son.

There was a famine in all the land, so Leopard went to Sheep and said, "Let us kill our children and eat them." Sheep thought, "If I do not agree, she may kill my child in spite of me," so she answered "Good."

Then Sheep went and hid her own babe, and took all that she had and sold for a little dried meat This she cooked and set before Leopard, and they both ate together. Leopard killed her own child, and ate that also.

In another year they both became *enceinte* once more. This

time again the townsfolk were hungry. Leopard came as before and said, "Let us kill these children also." Sheep agreed, but she took her second child and hid her in the little room where the first child was, then went out, and begged till someone gave her a few pieces of dried meat. These she cooked and set before Leopard as she had done before, in place of her babe. Leopard ate and said nothing.

Some years afterwards Leopard sent to Sheep and said, "Come; to-day you shall feast with me."

Sheep went, and found a great calabash on the table. She opened it, and found it full of food, and by it three spoons laid ready.

She was astonished and questioned Leopard. "Formerly we used two spoons, you and I. Why should there be three to-day?"

Leopard laughed, opened the door of the inner room, and called, "Come, daughter, let us eat." Her daughter came, and they all ate together. Then the mother said, "When my first child came, I killed and ate him because we were very hungry; but when I learned how you had saved your child, I thought, 'Next time I also will play such a trick on Sheep.' Therefore I saved my daughter alive."

After that Sheep went home, and tended her two children. Years passed by, and all the daughters began to grow up. Leopard put her child into the fatting-house. Then she went to Sheep and said, "Give me one of your daughters to stay with mine in the fatting-house. She is alone and cannot eat."

Now Sheep and both her daughters were quite black, but there were some young goats in the house which served them as slaves. These were white, so before Sheep sent her daughter to Leopard's house she rubbed her all over with white chalk, then dyed one of the young goats black, and sent them together.

When they both arrived at the house, Leopard thought that the goat was Sheep's daughter. All three of the young ones were placed in the fatting-house. During the night Leopard entered the room, took Goat and killed her, then cooked the meal and gave to her own daughter to eat, thinking it was the daughter of Sheep whom she had slain.

Next day Leopard went to Sheep and said, "Give me your other child, that our three daughters may be in the fatting-house together."

Sheep consented, but before this child went she advised her what to do.

When therefore the second lamb reached the fatting-house she took out a bottle of rum and gave it to Leopard's daughter, saying "Drink this. It is a present which my mother has sent you." So Leopard's child drank and fell asleep. The two young sheep kept awake until their companion slept. They then got up, carried her from her own bed, and laid her on one of those prepared for themselves.

It was very dark in the room, and, when Leopard came in to kill one of the young sheep, she killed her own daughter instead. She was pleased and thought, "Now I have finished with the children whom Sheep hid from me." Next morning, very early, she went out to the bush to get palm wine that she might drink it with her daughter while they feasted on the young sheep.

No sooner had she left the house than the two sheep ran out. One of them went home to her mother's house, but the other followed after Leopard. The latter was at the top of a high palm tree, so Sheep's child stopped some way off and called in a loud voice :

"Last night you tried to kill me as you did the young goat, but you made a mistake, and killed your own child instead."

No sooner had Leopard heard this than she jumped from the tree and ran after the young sheep.

The latter ran to the cross-roads, and when Leopard reached the place she could not tell which way Sheep had gone. After thinking a while she took the wrong road and ran on.

Now when Sheep had run a long way she met the Nimm woman walking along with her Juju round her waist. The woman looked as if she had come a long way, and Sheep said, " Let me carry your Juju for you "

To this the Nimm woman agreed. When they came to her house she was very tired and her head hurt her.

Sheep said, "Let me fetch water and firewood while you rest."

The Nimm woman was very thankful, and went into her house to lie down.

When the young Sheep had done as she promised, she went into the other part of the house where the Nimm shrine was. On it she saw the "medicine." This she took and rubbed over herself

Next day the Nimm woman said, "Will you go and fetch me my 'medicine' which stands on the shrine of Nimm?"

Sheep asked her, "Do you not know that I was 'born' into your medicine last night?"

At this the Nimm woman was very angry and sprang up. Sheep ran, and the Nimm woman followed her. In her hurry to escape, Sheep ran against the door of the house where Mouse lived The door was old and it broke, and all the stories on earth, and all the histories ran out. After that they never went back to dwell with Mouse any more, but remained running up and down over all the earth.

How the First Rain came.

By Okun Asere of Mfamosing.

Once, long ago, a daughter was born to Obassi Osaw, and a son to Obassi Nsi. When both had come to marriageable age, Nsi sent a message to say "Let us exchange children. I will send my son that he may wed one of your maidens. Send your daughter down to my town, that she may become my wife."

To this Obassi Osaw agreed. So the son of Nsi went up to the heavens carrying many fine gifts, and Ara, the sky maiden, came down to dwell on earth. With her came seven men-slaves and seven women-slaves, whom her father sent that they might work for her, so that she should not be called upon to do anything herself.

One day, very early in the morning, Obassi Nsi said to his new wife, "Go, work in my farm!" She answered, "My Father gave me the slaves so that they should work instead of me. Therefore send them." Obassi Nsi was very angry and said, "Did you not hear that I gave my orders to you. You yourself shall work in my farm. As for the slaves, I will tell them what to do."

The girl went, though very unwillingly, and when she returned at night, tired out, Nsi said to her:

"Go at once to the river and bring water for the household."

She answered, "I am weary with working in the farm; may not my slaves at least do this while I rest?"

Again Nsi refused, and drove her forth, so she went backward and forward many times, carrying the heavy jars. Night had fallen long before she had brought enough.

Next morning Nsi bade her do the most menial services, and all day long kept her at work, cooking, fetching water, and making fire. That night again she was very weary before she might lie down to rest. At dawn on the third morning he said, "Go and bring in much firewood." Now the girl was young and unused to work, so as she went she wept, and the tears were still falling when she came back carrying her heavy burden.

As soon as Nsi saw her enter he called to her, "Come here and lie down before me. . . . I wish to shame you in the presence of all my people. . . ." On that the girl wept still more bitterly.

No food was given her till midday on the morrow, and then not enough. When she had finished eating up all there was, Nsi said to her:

"Go out and bring in a great bundle of fish poison."

The girl went into the bush to seek for the plant, but as she walked through the thick undergrowth a thorn pierced her foot. She lay down alone. All day long she lay there in pain, but as the sun sank she began to feel better. She got up and managed to limp back to the house.

When she entered, Nsi said to her, "Early this morning I ordered you to go and collect fish poison. You have stayed away all day and done nothing." So he drove her into the goat pen, and said, "To-night you shall sleep with the goats; you shall not enter my house."

That night she ate nothing. Early next morning one of the slaves opened the door of the goat pen, and found the girl lying within, with her foot all swollen and sore. She could not walk so for five days she was left with the goats. After that her foot began to get better.

So soon as she could walk again at all, Nsi called her and said

"Here is a pot Take it to the river, and bring it back filled to the brim."

She set out, but when she reached the water-side, she sat down on the bank and dipped her foot in the cool stream. She said to herself, "I will never go back; it is better to stay here alone."

After a while one of the slaves came down to the river. He questioned her

"At dawn this morning you were sent to fetch water. Why have you not returned home?"

The girl said, "I will not come back."

When the slave had left her she thought, "Perhaps he will tell them, and they will be angered and may come and kill me. I had better go back after all." So she filled her pot and tried to raise it on to her head, but it was too heavy. Next she lifted it on to a tree trunk that lay by the side of the river, and, kneeling beneath, tried to draw it, in that way, on to her head, but the pot fell and broke, and in falling a sharp sherd cut off one of her ears. The blood poured down from the wound, and she began to weep again, but suddenly thought.

"My Father is alive, my mother is alive, I do not know why I stay here with Obassi Nsi. I will go back to my own Father"

Then she set out to find the road by which Obassi Osaw had sent her to earth. She came to a high tree, and from it saw a long rope hanging. She said to herself:

"This is the way by which my Father sent me."

She caught the rope and began to climb. Before she reached half-way she grew very weary, and her sighs and tears mounted up to the kingdom of Obassi Osaw. When she reached midway she stayed and rested a while. Afterwards she climbed on again

After a long time she reached the top of the rope, and found herself on the border of her Father's land. Here she sat down almost worn out with weariness, and still weeping.

Now, one of the slaves of Obassi Osaw had been sent out to

collect firewood. He chanced to stray on and on, and came to the place near where the girl was resting. He heard her sobs mixed with broken words, and ran back to the town, crying out, "I have heard the voice of Ara. She is weeping about a mile from here."

Obassi heard but could not believe, yet he said:

"Take twelve slaves, and, should you find my daughter as you say, bring her here."

When they reached the place they found that it was Ara for true. So they carried her home.

When her Father saw her coming he called out:

"Take her to the house of her mother."

There one of the lesser wives, Akun by name, heated water and bathed her. Then they prepared a bed, and covered her well with soft skins and fine cloths.

While she was resting, Obassi killed a young kid and sent it to Akun, bidding her prepare it for his daughter. Akun took it, and after she had washed it, cooked it whole in a pot Also Obassi sent a great bunch of plantains and other fruits, and these also they set, orderly upon a table before the girl. Next they poured water into a gourd, and brought palm wine in a native cup, bidding her drink.

After she had eaten and drunk, Obassi came with four slaves carrying a great chest made of ebony. He bade them set it before her, opened it and said, "Come here; choose anything you will from this box"

Ara chose two pieces of cloth, three gowns, four small loin cloths, four looking-glasses, four spoons, two pairs of shoes (at £1), four cooking pots, and four chains of beads.

After this Obassi Osaw's storekeeper, named Ekpenyon, came forward and brought her twelve anklets. Akun gave her two gowns, a fu-fu stick and a wooden knife.

Her own mother brought her five gowns, richer than all the rest, and five slaves to wait upon her.

After this Obassi Osaw said; "A house has been got ready for you, go there that you may be its mistress."

Next he went out and called together the members of the chief "club" of the town. This was named Angbu. He said to the men:

"Go; fetch the son of Obassi Nsi. Cut off both his ears and bring them to me. Then flog him and drive him down the road to his Father's town, with this message from me·

"I had built a great house up here in my town. In it I placed your son, and treated him kindly. Now that I know what you have done to my child, I send back your son to you earless, in payment for Ara's ear, and the sufferings which you put upon her."

When the Angbu Club had cut off the ears of the son of Obassi Nsi, they brought them before Obassi Osaw, and drove the lad back on the earthward road, as they had been ordered.

Osaw took the ears and made a great Juju, and by reason of this a strong wind arose, and drove the boy earthward On its wings it bore all the sufferings of Ara, and the tears which she had shed through the cruelty of Obassi Nsi. The boy stumbled along, half-blinded by the rain, and as he went he thought :

"Obassi Osaw may do to me what he chooses. He had never done any unkind thing before. It is only in return for my Father's cruelty that I must suffer all this."

So his tears mixed with those of Ara and fell earthward as rain.

Up till that time there had been no rain on the earth. It fell for the first time when Obassi Osaw made the great wind and drove forth the son of his enemy.

How the Moon first came into the Sky.

By Okun Asere of Mfamosing

In a certain town there lived Njomm Mbui (Juju sheep). He made great friends with Etuk (antelope), whose home was in the " bush "

When the two animals grew up they went out and cut farms. Njomm planted plantains in his, while Etuk set his with coco-yams.

When the time came round for the fruits to ripen, Njomm went to his farm and cut a bunch of plantains, while Etuk dug up some of his coco.

Each cleaned his food and put it in the pot to cook. When all was ready they sat down and ate.

Next morning Etuk said, " Let us change. I saw a bunch of plantains in your farm which I would like to get. Will you go instead to mine and take some coco ? "

This was arranged, and Etuk said to Njomm, "Try to beat up fu-fu." Njomm tried, and found it very good. He gave some to Etuk. The latter ate all he wanted, then took the bunch of plantains and hung it up in his house.

Next morning he found that the fruit had grown soft, so he did not care to eat it. He therefore took the plantains and threw them away in the bush.

During the day Mbui came along and smelt plantains. He looked round till he found them, then picked up one and began to eat. They were very sweet. He ate his fill, then went on, and later met a crowd of the Nshum people (apes). To them he said, " To-day I found a very sweet thing in the bush."

In course of time Etuk grew hungry again, and Njomm said to him, " If you are hungry, why don't you tell me ? "

He went to his farm and got four bunches of plantains. As he came back he met the monkey people. They begged for some of his fruit, so he gave it to them.

After they had eaten all there was, they in their turn went on, and met a herd of wild boars (Ngumi). To these they said, " There is very fine food to be got from Njomm and Etuk."

The Ngumi therefore came and questioned Etuk, "Where is coco to be had?" and Etuk answered, "The coco belongs to me."

The boars begged for some, so Etuk took a basket, filled it at his farm, and gave it to them.

After they were satisfied, they went on their way and next morning met Njokk (elephant).

To him they said, " Greetings, Lord ! Last night we got very good food from the farms over there."

Njokk at once ran and asked the two friends, " Whence do you get so much food?" They said, "Wait a little."

Njomm took his long matchet and went to his farm. He cut five great bunches of plantains and carried them back. Etuk also got five baskets full of coco, which he brought to

Elephant. After the latter had eaten all this, he thanked them and went away.

All the bush-beasts came in their turn and begged for food, and to each the two friends gave willingly of all that they had. Lastly also came Mfong (Bush-cow).

Now not far from the two farms there was a great river called Akarram (the One which goes round). In the midst of it, deep down, dwelt Crocodile. One day Mfong went down into the water to drink, and from him crocodile learned that much food was to be had near by.

On this crocodile came out of the water and began walking towards the farms. He went to Njomm and Etuk and said:

"I am dying of hunger, pray give me food."

Etuk said, "To the beasts who are my friends I will give all I have, but to you I will give nothing, for you are no friend of mine;" but Njomm said:

"I do not like you very much, yet I will give you one bunch of plantains."

Crocodile took them and said, "Do not close your door to-night when you lie down to sleep. I will come back and buy more food from you at a great price."

He then went back to the water and sought out a python, which dwelt there. To the latter he said:

"I have found two men on land, who have much food." Python said, "I too am hungry. Will you give me to eat?"

So crocodile gave him some of the plantains which he had brought. When Python had tasted he said, "How sweet it is! Will you go back again and bring more?" Crocodile said, "Will you give me something with which to buy?" and Python answered, "Yes. I will give you something with which you can buy the whole farm."

On this he took from within his head a shining stone and gave it to crocodile. The latter started to go back to the farm. As he went, night fell and all the road grew dark, but he held in his jaws the shining stone, and it made a light on his path, so that all the way was bright. When he neared the dwelling of the two friends he hid the stone and called:

"Come out and I will show you something which I have brought."

Climbing Palms.

Cascade.

It was very dark when they came to speak with him. Slowly the crocodile opened his claws, in which he held up the stone, and it began to glimmer between them. When he held it right out, the whole place became so bright that one could see to pick up a needle or any small thing. He said, "The price of this that I bring is one whole farm."

Etuk said, "I cannot buy. If I give my farm, nothing remains to me. What is the use of this great shining stone if I starve to death?" But Njomm said, "I will buy—oh, I will buy, for my farm full of plantains, for that which you bring fills the whole earth with light. Come let us go. I will show you my farm. From here to the water-side all round is my farm. Take it all, and do what you choose with it, only give me the great shining stone that, when darkness falls, the whole earth may still be light."

Crocodile said, "I agree."

Then Njomm went to his house with the stone, and Etuk went to his. Njomm placed it above the lintel, that it might shine for all the world; but Etuk closed his door and lay down to sleep.

In the morning Njomm was very hungry, but he had nothing to eat, because he had sold all his farm for the great white stone.

Next night and the night after he slept full of hunger, but on the third morning he went to Etuk and asked, "Will you give me a single coco-yam?" Etuk answered :

"I can give you nothing, for now you have nothing to give in exchange. It was not I who told you to buy the shining thing. To give something, when plenty remains, is good; but none but a fool would give his all, that a light may shine in the dark!"

Njomm was very sad. He said, "I have done nothing bad. Formerly no one could see in the night time. Now the python stone shines so that everyone can see to go wherever he chooses."

All that day Njomm still endured, though nearly dying of hunger, and at night time he crept down to the water, very weak and faint.

By the river-side he saw a palm tree, and on it a man trying to cut down clusters of ripe kernels ; but this was hard to do, because it had grown very dark.

Njomm said, " Who is there ? " and the man answered, " I am Effion Obassi."

The second time Njomm called, "What are you doing ? " and Effion replied ·

" I am trying to gather palm kernels, but I cannot do so, for it is very dark amid these great leaves."

Njomm said to him, " It is useless to try to do such a thing in the dark. Are you blind ? "

Effion answered, " I am not blind. Why do you ask ? "

Then Njomm said, " Good ; if you are not blind, I beg you to throw me down only one or two palm kernels, and in return I will show you a thing more bright and glorious than any you have seen before."

Effion replied, "Wait a minute, and I will try to throw a few down to you. Afterwards you shall show me the shining thing as you said."

He then threw down three palm kernels, which Njomm took, and stayed his hunger a little. The latter then called, "Please try to climb down. We will go together to my house."

Effion tried hard, and after some time he stood safely at the foot of the tree by the side of Njomm.

So soon as they got to his house, Njomm said, " Will you wait here a little while I go to question the townspeople ? "

First he went to Etuk and asked, " Will you not give me a single coco to eat ? See, the thing which I bought at the price of all that I had turns darkness to light for you, but for me, I die of hunger."

Etuk said, " I will give you nothing. Take back the thing for which you sold your all, and we will stay in our darkness as before."

Then Njomm begged of all the townsfolk that they would give him ever so little food in return for the light he had bought for them. Yet they all refused.

So Njomm went back to his house and took the shining stone, and gave it to Effion Obassi, saying :

" I love the earth folk, but they love not me. Now take the shining thing for which I gave my whole possessions. Go back to the place whence you came, for I know that you belong to the sky people, but when you reach your home in the heavens, hang up my stone in a place where all the earth folk may see its shining, and be glad."

Then Effion took the stone, and went back by the road he had come. He climbed up the palm tree, and the great leaves raised themselves upwards, pointing to the sky, and lifted him, till, from their points, he could climb into heaven.

When he reached his home, he sent and called all the Lords of the Sky and said, "I have brought back a thing to-day which can shine so that all the earth will be light. From now on everyone on earth or in heaven will be able to see at the darkest hour of the night."

The chiefs looked at the stone and wondered. Then they consulted together, and made a box. Effion said, "Make it so that the stone can shine out only from one side."

When the box was finished, he set the globe of fire within, and said, "Behold the stone is mine. From this time all the people must bring me food I will no longer go to seek any for myself."

For some time they brought him plenty, but after a while they grew tired. Then Effion covered the side of the box, so that the stone could not shine till they brought him more. That is the reason why the moon is sometimes dark, and people on earth say "It is the end of the month. The sky people have grown weary of bringing food to Effion Obassi, and he will not let his stone shine out till they bring a fresh supply."

How all the Stars came.

By Okun Asere of Mfamosing

Ebopp* and Mbaw† were making a tour in the bush. They looked for a good place to cut farm. When one was found they cut down the trees, and took two days to clear enough ground. After this they went back to the town where the other animals were living. Next morning Ebopp said, "Let

---

* The Lemur (*Galago talboti*).
† Dormouse (*Graphiurus hueti*).

us go back to our new farms and build a small house." This they did. Ebopp made his, and Mbaw his.

Now before a new town is begun, a little shed called Ekpa Ntan (House without Walls) is made where the Egbo house is to stand Ebopp and Mbaw accordingly set to work and built an Ekpa Ntan. Then they went back to their old town and rested for two days.

On the third day they went to work again. Ebopp worked on his farm, Mbaw on his. That night they slept in the huts they had built, and at dawn started to work once more. When night came, Ebopp lighted a lamp and said, "I do not want to sleep here. If we sleep here we shall sleep hungry. Let us go back to our old town."

When they got there their wives cooked for them. Ebopp said to Mbaw, "Come and join together with me in eating." So his friend came and ate with him.

Afterwards Mbaw said, "Let us go to my house and have food too." So they went thither.

After they had eaten up all that Mbaw had cooked, Ebopp went home.

Next morning he went to call his friend and said, "Go and get young plantains to plant in the farm.' Both of them collected a great basket full of these, and went to the place where the new farms were; Ebopp to his, and Mbaw to his.

Both worked hard. At midday Ebopp said, "Let us rest a little while, and eat the food we have brought." To this Mbaw agreed, but after some time they set to work again

About five o'clock Ebopp called, "Let us go back now to the old town, for it is very far off."

So they left off working and went back, but before they could get there night fell.

Next morning they took more young plantains, and again worked hard all day. When it was time to go back, Ebopp, asked, "How many remain to plant of the young plantains?" Mbaw answered "About forty." On which Ebopp said, "Of mine also there remain about forty"

At dawn next day they went to their old farms to get some more plantain cuttings. Then they went on to the new farms and began planting. So soon as he had finished, Ebopp said

"I have finished mine." To which Mbaw replied, "Mine also are finished."

Ebopp said, "My work is done, I need only come here for the hunting."

Then they both went back to the old town and told their wives:

"We have finished setting the plantains. We hope that you will go and plant coco-yams to-morrow. Try, both of you, to get baskets full of coco-yams for the planting."

To this the women agreed, and when they had collected as many as were necessary they set out for the new farms

When they arrived, Mbaw's wife asked the wife of Ebopp, "Do you think we can finish planting all these to-day?" Ebopp's wife answered, "Yes, we can do it"

All day they worked hard, and at night went home and said, "We have finished planting all the coco-yams." Ebopp said, "Good, you have done well."

Now his wife's name was Akpan Anwan (Akpan means firstborn). She and her sister Akandem were the daughters of Obassi Osaw. When she got home she started to cook the evening meal for her husband. When it was ready she placed it upon the table, set water also in a cup, and laid spoons near by.

They were eating together when a slave named Umaw ran in. He had just come from the town of Obassi Osaw. He said, "I would speak to Ebopp alone." When Akpan Anwan had left the room, the messenger said, "You are eating, but I bring you news that Akandem is dead"

Ebopp called out aloud in his grief, and sent a messenger to call his friend Mbaw.

So soon as the latter heard he came running and said, "What can we do? We are planting new farms and beginning to build a new town. There is hardly any food to be got. How then can we properly hold the funeral customs?"

Ebopp said, "Nevertheless, I must try my best." When Umaw got ready to return, Ebopp said:

"Say to Obassi Osaw 'Wait for me for six days, then I will surely come.'"

Next morning he said to Mbaw, "Come now, let us do our

utmost to collect what is necessary for the rites of my sister-in-law."

They went round the town and bought all the food which they could find. Then Ebopp went back and said to his wife, "I did not wish to tell you before about the death of your sister, but to-day I must tell you. Get ready. In five days' time I will take you back to your Father's town to hold the funeral feast."

Akpan Anwan was very grieved to hear of this and wept. Ebopp said to Mbaw, "We must get palm wine for the feast, also rum for libations. How can we get these? I have no money and you also have none." Mbaw said, "Go round among the townsfolk and see if any of them will lend you some."

Ebopp said "Good," and began to walk up and down, begging from all his friends, but none would give to him, though it was a big town. At last he went down to the place where they were making palm oil by the river. Near to this lived Iku (Water Cheviotain). Ebopp told his trouble and begged help, but Iku said, "I am very sorry for you, but I have nothing to give."

Ebopp was quite discouraged by now, and turned to go away full of sorrow. When Iku saw this he said, "Wait a minute, there is one thing I can do. You know that I have the 'four eyes.' I will give you two, and with them you can buy all that you need."

From out of his head he took the two eyes with which he used to see in the dark. They shone so brightly that Ebopp knew they were worth a great price. He took them home and showed them to his wife and his friend Mbaw

The latter said, "From to-day you are freed from all anxiety. With those you can buy all that is needed"

Next morning they gathered together all that had been collected, the plantains and the two shining eyes. Ebopp, Mbaw and Akpan carried the loads between them. They set out for the dwelling-place of Obassi Osaw.

When they got to the entrance of the town, Akpan Anwan began to weep bitterly. She threw down her burden, and ran to the spot where her sister lay buried. Then she lay down on the grave and would not rise again.

Ebopp carried his own load into the house where the dead woman had dwelt. Then he went back and got his wife's load which she had left behind.

The townsfolk said to Ebopp, "You have come to keep your sister-in-law's funeral customs to-day. Bring palm wine. Bring rum also for the libations, and let us hold the feast."

Ebopp said, "I have brought nothing but plantains. All else that is necessary I mean to buy here."

Now there was a famine in Obassi Osaw's town, so Ebopp put all his plantains in the Egbo house. Next day he sent to Obassi Osaw to bring his people, so that the food might be divided among them. Each man got one.

Then Osaw said, "All that you brought is eaten. If you can give us no more, you shall not take my daughter back with you to your country."

Ebopp went to find his friend, and told him what Obassi had said

"Shall I sell the two eyes?" he asked. "They are worth hundreds and hundreds of plantains, and many pieces of cloth, but if I sell them now, the people are so hungry, they will only give a small price."

Mbaw said, "Do not mind See, I will teach you how to get more sense."

"You hold one in your hand, and it is a big thing like a great shining stone, but if you put it in a mortar and grind it down, it will become, not one, but many, and some of the small pieces you can sell.'

This Ebopp did, and ground up the great bright stones which had been Iku's eyes till they became like shining sand.

Then they went and got a black cap, which they filled with the fragments.

Mbaw said, "Now go and look round the town till you find someone who can sell what we need."

Ebopp did so, and in the house of Effion Obassi he saw great stores hidden—food and palm wine, palm oil in jars, and rum for the sacrifice.

Ebopp said to Effion, "If you will sell all this to me I will give you in exchange something which will make all the townsfolk bow down before you."

S.B. A A

Effion said, "I will not sell all, but half of what I have I will sell you."

So Ebopp said, "Very well. I will take what you give me, only do not open the thing I shall leave in exchange till I have got back to my own country. When you do open it, as I said before, all the townsfolk will bow down before you."

So the funeral feast was made, and the people were satisfied.

When the rites were finished, Obassi said, "It is good. You can go away now with your wife."

So Ebopp said to Mbaw and Akpan Anwan, "Come, let us go back to our own town. We must not sleep here to-night."

When they had reached home once more, Ebopp sent a slave named Edet to Effion Obassi with the message:

"You can open the cap now. I have reached my town again." It was evening time, but Effion at once sent to call the townspeople and said, "I have a thing here which is worth a great price." They cried, "Let us see it." He answered, "My thing is a very good thing, such as you have never seen before."

He brought the cap outside and opened it before them. All the shining things fell out. As they fell a strong breeze came and caught them and blew them all over the town. They lay on the roads and on the floors of the compounds, each like a little star.

All the children came round and began picking them up. They gathered and gathered. In the daytime they could not see them, but every night they went out and sought for the shining things. Each one that they picked up they put in a box. At length many had been got together and shone like a little sun in the box. At the end of about a month nearly all had been collected. They could not shut down the lid, however, because the box was too full, so when a great breeze came by it blew all the shining things about again. That is why sometimes we have a small moon and plenty of stars shining round it, while sometimes we have a big moon and hardly any stars are to be seen. The children take a month to fill the box again.

When the sparkles were scattered about the town, Effion

sent a messenger to Ebopp to ask, "Can you see the things shining from your town?"

At that time earth and sky were all joined together, like a house with an upstairs.

Ebopp went out and looked upward to the blue roof overhead. There he saw the small things sparkling in the darkness.

Next day he went to Iku and said:

"Will you please go into a deep hole? I want to look at your eyes."

Iku went inside the hole. Ebopp looked at his eyes. They were very bright, just like the sparkles which shone in the sky.

The cause of all the stars is therefore Ebopp, who took Iku's eyes to Obassi's town.

Iku's eyes are like the stars.

The moon shines when all the fragments are gathered together. When he shines most brightly it is because the children have picked up nearly all the fragments and put them into the box

How the Two Biggest Stars came into the Sky.

Obassi Osaw had three sons. Two of these he loved, but Ndifemm, the third, he did not love.

One day the three brothers went out to see what had been caught in the traps they had set. The two favourite sons found nothing, but Ndifemm found an animal in each of his six traps. Four of the beasts he "dashed" between his two brothers, and the other two he took home to his father. Obassi refused them, but accepted from his other two sons those which Ndifemm had given them.

Another day Obassi ordered his three children each to dig a hole. They did so. He went and examined the work, and said "I find the two holes well done," but to Ndifemm he said, "Your hole is not deep enough."

The boy began to dig deeper, but one of his brothers went to him very softly and said, "Our father is attempting to kill you Will you go to consult the charm? That will tell you what you should do."

Ndifemm, therefore, went to Nyopp (Porcupine) and asked him to practise the charm.

Nyopp said, "Go and bring me a piece of yam and some palm oil."

Ndifemm fetched these and gave them to Porcupine. The latter practised the charm, and told him, " Go and ask the Dassie to dig a run from your mother's house to the hole you have made "

When all this was done, Obassi sent one day and said, " Go down into the hole you have dug."

Ndifemm obeyed, but so soon as he reached the bottom he passed through the little tunnel and reached his mother's house. Next Obassi ordered the people to throw stones into the hole. The pit was soon filled up by these, but Ndifemm was there no longer. After a time Obassi began to cry out for the mourning of his son, and called all the people together to make a great play for Ndifemm's death

On hearing this, the mother sent to her husband and said, " The Juju image will now come out." She dressed her son in the Egbo robes and took him before Obassi. Then she showed him that it was his own son whom he had thought dead. At that the father remained full of vexation.

One day Obassi called to his unloved son, and said, " Go to Nsann (the Thunder town) and bring me my cow from thence."

Ndifemm went to his mother and told her of this new order. She took a horn, and gave to her son saying, " When you get to Nsann town take this and blow upon it. You will see cows standing under a tree When one answers the sound of the horn you will know that that is the very one for which your father sent you."

Ndifemm set forth, and did all that she had said. In a few days he brought back the cow to his father.

Obassi thought within himself, " I sent this boy to Nsann town that he might die, but he has returned home full of life." He therefore took thought for a way in which he might surely kill his son.

Ndifemm saw that his father's heart was steadfastly set against him, so he went to his mother and said :

"I know that it is my time to die. Will you die with me?"

The woman answered, " My husband loves me no more. In

Tree Surrounded with Lattice Work Creeper which eventually kills it.

Type of Vegetation—Creepers Crushing Out of Life a Tree up which they Climb.

this world I have no one but you, therefore if you die I will die also."

Then, by cunning, Ndifemm made a hole in his father's eyes while the latter slept, and entered into them with his mother.

There they both died, and became stars in the sky.

Obassi opened his eyes, which are the heavens, and there they shone ! Those are the two biggest stars which you see in the sky. They are Ndifemm, son of Obassi, and his mother.

How the Sun came into the Sky.

By Okun Asere of Mfamosing

Once there lived a man named Agbo and his wife named Nchun. They had a daughter called Afion. When the latter was about fifteen years old, her father and mother agreed that it was time to put her in the fatting-house. So they sent for an old woman named Umaw, who was very wise in such matters, and told her to prepare everything She came and made all ready, and then said, "There is nothing more to be done I will go back to my own place."

The parents "dashed" her two bottles of palm oil and two pieces of dried meat. To the townsfolk also the father gave many demi-johns of palm wine. He took ten pieces of dried meat, cooked them and called all the people to a feast, because his daughter had entered the fatting-house that day.

After about four months the mother, Nchun, said to Afion, "You have stayed long enough You may come out to-morrow."

Then the father got together several demi-johns of palm wine, the kind that is drawn from the tops of the palm trees, and five pieces of dried meat. The mother also took the same amount of meat and drink The father announced to the townsfolk·

"My daughter is going to clean her face to-morrow. Let all men stay in the town." Next morning the parents cooked ten calabashes full of chop for the people, who feasted all that day.

In the evening the father took his daughter into the other

part of the house, and said to her, "To-day you have cleaned your face. From to-day if a man should call you into his house you can go."

Next morning the mother cooked for the girl. Then the parents went to their farm and left her with a small boy who was as yet too young to work.

Now at that time Eyo (the Sun) dwelt upon earth, in the place that lies towards the great water. His body was redder than fire. He was very tall and thin. He lay in the bush, so that all his body up to the waist was hidden by the bush trees, but he stretched out his head and arms right into the room where the fatting-girl was. He said to her:

"I want to keep sweethearts with you," but she answered:

"You are so tall, your head, hands and arms alone fill my room. I cannot keep friends with you."

When he heard this the Sun was very angry, and said, "If you are not willing to become my sweetheart I will take my length away, but first I will kill you and leave you here."

Afion said to him·

"I do not care so much if you kill me. I would rather die than wed such a terrible being as you."

As soon as Eyo heard this he stretched out his hands, and killed her for true.

All this time the small boy had hidden himself where he could see everything that happened. He watched the terrible visitor draw the body into the middle room. Next he saw him go into the inner place where Nchun kept the fine mats. He took four of these and covered the fatting-girl. Next he went into another place where the fine cloths were kept. Of these again he took four, with four blankets and two small loin cloths. All these he laid over the dead girl.

After this Eyo left the house and stood in the little courtyard at the back. He began to lift his body up to the sky. He was so long that, though he tried all day, six o'clock in the evening was come and he had not quite finished. Some of him was in the sky and some still stayed upon earth.

When Agbo and Nchun came back from their farm, the small boy crept out from his hiding place, and said to them:

"The man who killed your daughter is a very tall man."

Father and mother began to weep. They took the body and called all the townsfolk together for the burial

The people came with four guns. They wished to shoot the man who had killed the fatting-girl. At the back of the house they found him. They could not see all his body, but the feet only. With their four guns they shot at these. Then he gave a great spring and drew his feet up, after the rest of him, into the sky.

A fine house was standing there ready. Eyo entered and closed the door that he might be safe from the guns of the townsmen. In the morning, about six o'clock, he opened a window, and looked out a little way, very cautiously. When no one shot at him, he felt safer, and put his face right out. All day he looked down in case Afion should not be dead and he might see her once more. The people were busy away at their farms. At six o'clock they came back, so he drew in his face again, lest they should begin to shoot once more.

That is the reason why you only see the sun in the daytime. In the evening he draws back into his house and shuts the windows and doors

How Sun and Moon went up to the Sky.
By Ite Okonni of Aking.

Obassi Nsi had three sons, named Eyo (Sun), Ejirum (Darkness), and 'Mi (Moon). The first two he loved, but the last he did not love One day Nsi called to 'Mi and said:

"Go into the bush, catch a leopard, and bring him to me."

'Mi went sadly away, and as he reached the outskirts of the town began to weep. A man named Isse saw him and called "What is the matter?" 'Mi answered, "My father does not love me, and is sending me to catch a leopard in the bush, in order to destroy me."

The man said "Take comfort; I will give you a 'medicine' which will make you successful." He went away, but soon returned with what he had promised, and rubbed the "medicine" on the boy's hands.

'Mi went into the bush, and almost at once saw a leopard

lying down asleep. He cut strong lianes, and tied up the beast, so that it could not move, then dragged it along till he reached home once more, and stood before his father.

Nsi was astonished, but concealed his vexation, and said in a cunning way, "This my son is indeed a good son because he has done this thing."

Some time afterwards Nsi married another wife. Obassi Osaw came down to the wedding feast with his sons and daughters and a great retinue of sky people. These started to play with the earthfolk, who had also gathered together for the festival. After a while they took a cloth and tied it up in a bundle. To this a rope was fastened, and one of Nsi's sons caught the end, and began to draw it along the ground. All got sticks and tried to hit the bundle as it was dragged hither and thither. Ejirum also tried to hit it, but a splinter sprang from his stick as it struck the ground, and wounded the eye of one of Osaw's sons, so that the latter was blinded.

Osaw was angry, and said, "I myself will blind the eyes of Obassi Nsi."

The townspeople crowded round, and begged him to show mercy, but he would not relent. So they took Nsi and hid him away, where Osaw could not find him. After the latter had searched in vain he was still angry, and said:

"Now I am going back to my town, but Nsi will not escape me."

After two days he sent down ten men to fetch Obassi Nsi. They said, "We have been sent to bring you up," but the townsfolk said, "Here are great gifts of cows, bulls, and goats. Take them before your master, and perhaps he will not be angry any more."

When the men returned to the sky they said, "Here is a message from Obassi Nsi. He wants to beg you very much. He says, "It was not I who told anyone to hurt your son's eye."

Osaw would not listen, but sent down three other men, and said:

"Even if you yourself did not break my son's eye yet you must come up to me."

When Nsi heard this, he called his people together. To his son Eyo (Sun) he said:

"Here are forty pieces of cloth. Will you take them to Osaw and beg him for me?"

Eyo started on his journey, and had reached about half way when he saw five beautiful women standing at the entrance to a town. No sooner had he seen them, than he forgot all about his errand, and began to sell the cloth for plantains, palm oil and palm wine, with which he made a feast for the beautiful women. There he stayed for some weeks, then took what was left of the goods and went on a little further till he came to another town, where he found two more women, as beautiful as the first. For four years he stayed at one or other of the towns, journeying to and fro between them.

After four years, when Nsi found that Eyo did not come back nor send any message, he called to his son 'Mi and said:

"The case which I have before Obassi Osaw has taken a long time to finish. Go to Nsann (Thunder town) and fetch hence a cow which you will find. When you have brought it away take it as a gift to Obassi Osaw, and settle my case for me."

'Mi answered, "Very well;" and his mother called to him, and said:

"Do what you can for your father, who is guiltless as to Obassi Osaw, but take care for yourself when you reach Nsann town. Let no one know the place where you sleep, lest you should perish in the night time."

'Mi answered, "I will do what I can."

Next morning he set forth, and before evening had reached Nsann. The people asked him:

"Where will you sleep to-night?" He answered, "I will sleep among the goats." When all was still he left the goat pen in the darkness, and went to the Egbo house, where he lay down and slept.

At midnight a thunderbolt struck the shed where the goats were herded, and killed them all.

Early in the morning the people came together and opened the door. When they saw the dead goats, but could not find the boy they were much astonished. As they stood wondering 'Mi came forward and said:

"If I were not a smart boy, the bolt would have killed me. As it is, I have saved myself."

Everybody in the town was sorry for the lad, and said " Let us give him the cow to take to his father." So the boy set out homeward, well content.

When 'Mi reached his father's house and led the cow before him, Nsi said, very softly to himself, so that he thought no one could hear

" What can I do to kill this son of mine ? "

'Mi heard, and next morning took the gun which his mother had given him, and went into the bush to hunt. First he shot Ise, the little grey duiker, and next Ngumi (the wild boar). These he carried home, and brought before his father, but the latter said ·

" I will not eat of them."

So 'Mi took his kill away sadly, and gave it to his mother.

The woman cooked the meat in a delicate way, and then took it to her husband, who ate gladly of what he had before refused ; but when he learned what she had done, he said:

" From to-day take your son away from here. Neither of you shall live in my town any more."

When 'Mi learned this he also was very angry. He took his gun and his matchet and went to find his friend Isse, who had given him the " leopard medicine " years before. To his grief he heard that this good friend had died while he himself was away at Nsann. So he went sadly out into the bush to hunt, that his mother might not starve. After a while he saw an Ikomme (squirrel)* standing between the thick branches. He raised his gun to shoot, but in a moment all the place grew dark. A voice called behind him out of the darkness, "'Mi 'Mi, ' and he answered, " Who calls ? " The voice cried, " I am your dead friend. Tell me, now, which do you choose, to die or to live ? " 'Mi answered, " I am willing to die. Why should I live when my father seeks to kill me ? "

After he had spoken, a deep sleep fell upon him. When he awoke the whole place was clear of trees. The sun was shining brightly, and before him stood a long table, on which were set dried meat, biscuits, rum, and palm wine, and all kinds of gin. Then he saw Isse walking up and down as in life, and directing everything, while many people were busily working round about.

* *Funisciurus leucostigma talboti*

They worked hard, and as they worked more and more men came out of the bush, till in a little space the whole house was finished. Then Isse said

"This is your house, and all these are your people. Now, your father's case is a very long one. I will give you goods so that you may go and arrange it."

'Mi agreed, and next morning called together seven companions He gave them 300 pieces of cloth from the goods that Isse had provided, many heads of tobacco, and countless demi-johns of palm wine.

Then 'Mi himself set out at their head for Obassi's town

When he reached the entrance he called a meeting of the townsfolk, and said to them:

"I have come to try to settle my father's case, which has already been a very long one. I wish to hear from you how many goods I must pay."

The people said, "Let us see what you have brought."

So he showed them all, and they went before Obassi and begged him to take the gifts in payment, and settle the affair. Obassi answered, "Good I accept what you have brought. The case is finished"

Then 'Mi went back to his father's town to fetch his mother. He met her wandering about at the entrance to the town, and was about to lead her away, when Nsi himself came by.

"Whither are you going?" he asked.

'Mi answered, "I am leading my mother away to my own town, which is a long way from here, and is full of rich things."

On hearing this Nsi said, "I should like to see your town." So he followed his outcast wife and son till they came to that part of the bush where the new town stood

Nsi was amazed at what he saw, and still more so when he found that 'Mi had been to Obassi Osaw and arranged his case. On this he sent a great company of men to seize Eyo and bring the latter before him. When they returned Nsi called both his sons, and said

"From to-day you, Eyo, are my unloved son You are too hot; no one will like you any more You are careless sometimes, and burn up all tender plants in the farms" But to 'Mi he said.

"You, 'Mi, are my good son. In the night you can shine

softly, so that men may see to walk safely when they are away from home"

When Eyo heard this he thought, "Now my father will hate me as he used to hate 'Mi. Perhaps he will try to kill me also. I will not stay here on earth, but will go up to the sky to Osaw."

'Mi also thought, "Perhaps my father is deceiving me, or, at at any rate, he may grow to hate me again It is better to go up to the sky and stay with Obassi Osaw. From thence I can see what passes both in his land and in that of my father. Also I can shine the brighter on high, so that heaven and earth will be full of my light." Thus Nsi lost both of these sons, and remained on earth alone with his third boy, Ejirum (Darkness).

Why the Sunset is sometimes Red and Stormy.

In the beginning of things, Obassi Osaw and Obassi Nsi lived in towns some distance apart. The former had no sons, but the latter had three. The first of them was a great thief, the second was the same, and when they stole anything their Father had to pay for it.

Now Obassi had great farms and plantations outside the town. Sometimes cows ate his yams, so one day he came home and put powder in his gun but no shot, meaning to frighten the beasts away next time they came During his absence the two bad sons went and put shot in the gun. So when he fired at the cows one of them died.

Obassi Nsi cried out, and went back to the town. When he reached it he told the owner, "I shot your cow by accident;" but the man replied·

"Then I must kill you, just the same as my cow."

A meeting was held, and the townsfolk begged the man to accept another cow in exchange for the one he had lost, but he refused to do so, and still said that Obassi must die.

Next morning, therefore, Obassi said to his third son, "I have to die to-day;" but the latter cried

"How can you die. First son and second son are fully grown, but I am still small. Do not leave me till I am grown up."

Obassi said, "Here is a key. The room to which it belongs shall be your own, so that you have somewhere to run to, and be safe from your brothers."

In the evening he called the boy again, and said:

"Do no evil thing in the town, and when I am dead kill a cow and give it to the people." That night he died.

The third son killed the cow as he had been bidden, but the first and second sons were very angry, and beat him, and said, "The cow belonged to us." They took away the key of his room, so that small boy had nowhere to go, and they seized all the goods for themselves, so he was left penniless. After that they went away from their father's land.

The boy went out sadly and walked through the town. He met an old woman, who asked "Whither are you going?" He said, "I am the small son of Obassi Nsi, and I have nowhere to go."

The old woman answered, "Do not trouble. Stay here with me," and to this the boy agreed. One day he found an old knife in the ground; this he cleaned and sharpened till it became all right again. Next morning he went to the bush and set native traps. In one of these he caught an Iku (water chevrotain), which he brought home and gave to the old woman. She said, "I cannot eat this meat; perhaps you have stolen it;" but he answered, "No, I will take you to the place where the traps are set." She went with him, and saw that it was as he had said; so agreed to eat the meat.

Next morning the boy said, "I wish to go and clear my farm." When he got to the plantation he saw some slaves of Obassi Osaw coming towards him. When they arrived they said:

"We have come to take charge of the goods of Obassi Nsi." On this the boy answered, "They are not in my hands. First and second sons have taken everything." So the men returned empty-handed.

Next day six more came and asked the same thing, but the lad said, "Wait a minute and I will see what can be done." Then he went to the old woman and told her what had happened. She said, "Go to Porcupine, and get him to practise the charm."

When this was done the Diviner said, "Go to the middle compound of your father's town, and under the floor of the inner room you will find what will content the messengers."

The boy did as he was told, dug up the goods and gave them to the men to carry to Obassi Osaw.

When Obassi saw that his slaves brought back the goods, but not the boy, he was angry and said, "I told you to bring me the young son also. Why have you not done this?"

Next day, therefore, two more men were sent to bring the boy. No sooner did he arrive than the sky people brought him fruits, and all kinds of rich gifts, together with some very beautiful slaves. In spite of all that Osaw could do, however, the boy was not happy, but said, "I wish I could go back to earth once more."

Then Obassi Osaw was vexed, and his eyes began to glow, and from their gleam the sky grew red and stormy That is the reason why we see Tornado sunsets. Obassi grows angry and his eyes become red. The storm always follows, for Tornados are the sound of the wrath of Obassi Osaw.

How all the Rivers first came on Earth.
By Okun Asere of Mfamosing

In the very, very, very olden time, an old man named Etim 'Ne (old person) came down from the sky; he alone with his old wife Ejaw (wild cat). At that time there were no people on the earth. This old couple were the very first to go down to dwell there.

Now up to this time all water was kept in the kingdom of Obassi Osaw. On earth there was not a single drop.

Etim 'Ne and his wife stayed for seven days, and during that time they had only the juice of plantain stems to drink or cook with.

At the end of that time the old man said to his old wife, "I will go back to Obassi Osaw's town and ask him to give us a little water."

When he arrived at the old town where they used to dwell, he went to the house of Obassi and said

"Since we went down to earth we have had no water, only

Native Tree-bridge.

the juice which we sucked from the plantain stems. For three nights I will sleep in your town, then when I return to earth I hope that you will give me some water to take with me. Should my wife have children they will be glad for the water, and what they offer to you in thanksgiving I myself will bring up to your town."

On the third morning, very early, Obassi Osaw put the water charm in a calabash, and bound it firmly with tie-tie. Then he gave it to Etim 'Ne, and said, " When you wish to loose this, let no one be present Open it, and you will find seven good gifts inside Wherever you want water, take out one of these and throw it on the ground."

Etim 'Ne thanked Lord Obassi, and set out on his way earthward. Just before he came to the place where he had begun to cut farm, he opened the calabash, and found within seven stones, clear as water. He made a small hole and laid one of the stones within it. Soon a little stream began to well out, then more and more, till it became a broad lake, great as from here to Ako.

Etim 'Ne went on and told his wife. They both rejoiced greatly, but he thought, " How is this ? Can a man be truly happy, yet have no child ? "

After two days his wife came to him and said, " Obassi is sending us yet another gift. Soon we shall be no longer alone on earth, you and I."

When the due months were passed, she bore him seven children, all at one time. They were all sons Later she became *enceinte* again, and this time bore seven daughters. After that she was tired, and never bore any more children.

In course of time the girls were all sent to the fatting-house. While they were there Etim 'Ne pointed out to his seven sons where he would like them to build their compounds. When these were finished, he gave a daughter to each son and said, " Do not care that she is your sister. Just marry her. There is no one else who can become your wife."

The eldest son dwelt by the first water which Etim 'Ne had made, but to each of the others he gave a lake or river—seven in all.

After one year, all the girls became *enceinte* Each of them had seven children, three girls and four boys. Etim 'Ne said, "It is good." He was very happy. As the children grew up he sent them to other places

Now the seven sons were all hunters. Three of them were good, and brought some of their kill to give to their father, but four were very bad, and hid all the meat, so that they might keep everything for themselves.

When Etim 'Ne saw this, he left the rivers near the farms of his three good sons, but took them away from the four bad boys. These latter were very sad when they found their water gone, so they consulted together and went and got palm wine. This they carried before their father and said :

"We are seven, your children. First you gave the water to all. Now you have taken it away from us four. What have we done ?"

Etim 'Ne answered, "Of all the meat you killed in the bush you brought none to me Therefore I took away your rivers. Because you have come to beg me I will forgive you, and will give you four good streams. As your children grow and multiply I will give you many."

After another year the sons had children again When the latter grew up they went to different places and built their houses.

When these were ready Etim 'Ne sent for all the children and said, "At dawn to-morrow let each of you go down to the stream which flows by the farm of his father. Seek in its bed till you find seven smooth stones. Some must be small and some big like the palm of your hand. Let each one go in a different direction, and after walking about a mile, lay a stone upon the ground. Then walk on again and do the same, till all are finished. Where you set a big stone a river will come, and where you set a small stone a stream will come."

All the sons did as they were bidden, save one alone. He took a great basket and filled it with stones. Then he went to a place in the bush near his own farm. He thought, "Our father told us, if you throw a big stone a big river will come. If I throw down all my stones together, so great a water will come that it will surpass the waters of all my brothers." Then he emptied his basket of stones all in one place, and, behold!

water flowed from every side, so that all his farm, and all the land round about became covered with water. When he saw that it would not stop but threatened to overflow the whole earth he grew very much afraid. He saw his wife running, and called to her, "Let us go to my father." Then they both ran as hard as they could toward the house of Etim 'Ne.

Before they reached it the other children, who had been setting the smooth stones in the bush, as their father had told them, heard the sound of the coming of the waters. Great fear fell upon them, and they also dropped what remained and ran back to Etim 'Ne.

He also had heard the rushing of the water and knew what the bad son had done. He took the magic calabash in his hand and ran with his wife to a hill behind their farm. On this there grew many tall palm trees. Beneath the tallest of these he stood, while his children gathered round one after the other as they got back from the bush. Etim 'Ne held on high the calabash which Obassi had given him, and prayed:

"Lord Obassi, let not the good thing which you gave for our joy turn to our hurt."

As he prayed the water began to go down. It sought around till it found places where there had been no water. At each of these it made a bed for itself, great or small, some for broad rivers, and some for little streams. Only where the bad son had emptied his basket it did not go back, but remained in a great lake covering all his farm, so that he was very hungry, and had to beg from his brothers till the time came for the fruits to ripen in the new farm which he had to cut.

After many days Etim 'Ne called all his children around, and told them the names of all the rivers, and of every little stream. Then he said, "Let no one forget to remember me when I shall have left you, for I it was who gave water to all the earth, so that every one shall be glad."

Two days afterwards he died. In the beginning there were no people on the earth and no water. Etim 'Ne it was who first came down to dwell with his old wife Ejaw, and he it was who begged water from Obassi Osaw.

S B.   B B

How the Lame Boy brought Fire from Heaven.

By Okon Asere of Mfamosing.

In the beginning of the world, Obassi Osaw made everything, but he did not give fire to the people who were on earth

Etim 'Ne said to the Lame Boy, "What is the use of Obassi Osaw sending us here without any fire ? Go therefore and ask him to give us some" So the Lame Boy set out.

Obassi Osaw was very angry when he got the message, and sent the boy back quickly to earth to reprove Etim 'Ne for what he had asked. In those days the Lame Boy had not become lame, but could walk like other people.

When Etim 'Ne heard that he had angered Obassi Osaw, he set out himself for the latter's town and said:

"Please forgive me for what I did yesterday. It was by accident." Obassi would not pardon him, though he stayed for three days begging forgiveness. Then he went home.

When Etim reached his town the boy laughed at him. "Are you a chief," said he, "yet could get no fire ? I myself will go and bring it to you. If they will give me none I will steal it."

That very day the lad set out He reached the house of Obassi at evening time and found the people preparing food. He helped with the work, and when Obassi began to eat, knelt down humbly till the meal was ended

The master saw that the boy was useful and did not drive him out of the house. After he had served for several days, Obassi called to him and said, "Go to the house of my wives and ask them to send me a lamp"

The boy gladly did as he was bidden, for it was in the house of the wives that fire was kept. He touched nothing, but waited until the lamp was given him, then brought it back with all speed. Once, after he had stayed for many days among the servants, Obassi sent him again, and this time one of the wives said, "You can light the lamp at the fire." She went into her house and left him alone.

The boy took a brand and lighted the lamp, then he wrapped the brand in plantain leaves and tied it up in his cloth, carried the lamp to his master and said, " I wish to go out for a certain purpose." Obassi answered, " You can go "

The boy went to the bush outside the town where some dry wood was lying He laid the brand amongst it, and blew till it caught alight. Then he covered it with plantain stems and leaves to hide the smoke, and went back to the house. Obassi asked, " Why have you been so long ? " and the lad answered, " I did not feel well."

That night when all the people were sleeping, the thief tied his cloth together and crept to the end of the town where the fire was hidden. He found it burning, and took a glowing brand and some firewood and set out homeward.

When earth was reached once more the lad went to Etim and said.

" Here is the fire which I promised to bring you Send for some wood, and I will show you what we must do."

So the first fire was made on earth Obassi Osaw looked down from his house in the sky and saw the smoke rising. He said to his eldest son Akpan Obassi, " Go, ask the boy if it is he who has stolen the fire."

Akpan came down to earth, and asked as his father had bidden him. The lad confessed, " I was the one who stole the fire The reason why I hid it was because I feared "

Akpan replied, " I bring you a message Up till now you have been able to walk. From to-day you will not be able to do so any more."

That is the reason why the Lame Boy cannot walk. He it was who first brought fire to earth from Obassi's home in the sky.

Oporopóotop.

Tortoise and Ram were friends. One day they went to cut their farm, but only prepared a small bit Next day they went back to do more, but found the whole place cleaned. They wondered who had done all the work for them, but started to burn the ground with fire After this they went home to rest, and when they got back next day, lo! all the earth was ready tilled. They began planting yams, and next day found that this too had been finished while they slept. They wondered very much who had done this. It was a person named Oporopóotop.

Later the wives went and planted a few coco yams, and again, on their return, found the whole place set with these also. Next they started sowing corn, but could not cover much ground on the first day. The second day, however, a great space was found to have been planted.

When the corn grew ripe, the owners of the farm went to gather it. They took a very few cobs at first, but lo! next day all had been garnered, and so it was with the other vegetables. The two friends got a little for themselves and for their wives, but the rest disappeared mysteriously.

Tortoise said to Ram, "What can we do to find out who has stolen our fruits and vegetables?" Ram said, "Let us watch." So Tortoise went to his wife and said, "Will you go to-day and watch the farm?" She agreed, and after waiting a while in the little house they had built, heard something moving in the bush. It sounded like a wind among the trees, but was caused by the coming of Oporopóotop. He came to the hut and knocked at the door, crying in a loud voice, "Who is there?"

The woman answered, "I am the wife of Tortoise," and opened the door. The visitor entered and said to her, "Go and find some fruit in the farm, that we may eat." She answered, "Someone has stolen nearly all our fruit." She went, however, and found a few corn cobs, which she brought back and roasted over the fire.

When the meal was finished, Oporopóotop said, "Will you scratch the craw-craw on my body?" This the woman did, but he cried, "You scratch too hard!" and suddenly swallowed her up!

At daybreak, the husband came to fetch his wife, but found no trace of her. He said to himself, "What can have happened to my wife? I will stay here till I find out what has become of her." So he made a fire on the ground and waited.

At evening time again a sound was heard, like the going of a wind through the bush. It was Oporopóotop. The latter knocked at the door as before and said, "Who is within?"

Tortoise answered, "It is I," and opened. Oporopóotop entered and said, "Go and fetch some fruits that we may eat."

Tortoise went and collected what he could. He brought it back, cooked and gave to his visitor to eat. Again Oporopóotop said, "Scratch my craw-craw," but, while his host obeyed, exclaimed, "You scratch too hard!" and before the latter could answer, caught him and swallowed him up!

When daylight dawned Ram also came to the farm, but could find neither his friend nor the wife; so sat down to await their return. At evening time Ram heard the coming of Oporopóotop, just as the others had done. When the visitor asked, "Who is there?" Ram replied, "Why do you ask this? Does the whole earth belong to you?" And when the monster begged for food Ram refused, whereon they began to fight.

Now Oporopóotop was a fearful beast, bigger than all the animals on earth in our day. He was like a great lizard, but covered with hard shell, so that he could roll himself down from a high hill, yet take no hurt. His head and neck were very long, like those of some birds, so that he could reach up to eat from off the high trees. In colour he was mixed white and black. On his wings were claws, though he could not fly, and on his feet were terrible claws. It was with these that he usually fought.

Nevertheless, in spite of the huge size of the beast and his great strength, Ram was more cunning than he. For a long time they fought, but at length Ram struck down his enemy with his horns, and broke off his feet, so that he died.

Oporopóotop was a great king in the bush, and when people planted new farms he sent his servants to help them, so that he might eat of the first fruits when they were ripe. If Ram had not killed him, there would soon have been no more farms, as the people would all have died. How lucky it is that the bush is now free from such a monster!

How Palm Trees and Water came on Earth.

In the beginning of all things Obassi made a man and a woman and brought them down to earth. There for a while he left them, but came again a little later, and asked what they had found to eat and drink. They answered that they neither ate nor drank, so Obassi made a trench in the ground

Then from a fold of his robe he took out a vessel containing water, and poured it into the trench. This became a stream. Afterwards he took a palm kernel, and planted it. He then told the couple to use water for cooking their food, for washing and drinking. He also said they must carefully tend the palm tree which he had planted. When ripe clusters appeared upon it, they should cut these down, and take great care of them, for they would provide food as well as medicine. The outer cover or rind should be used as food, while the kernel makes good medicine.

How Pythons lost Hands and Feet.

There was once a Python, whose wife was about to bear him a child. One day, in coming through the bush, he saw some ripe Aju fruits, and plucked them, as he thought, "Perhaps my wife would like these."

The woman ate them with great delight, and from that day on, kept begging her husband to bring her some more. He went out to the bush to search, but could not find any. She, however, threatened that unless more were brought to her, she would break her pregnancy.

In those days Pythons had hands and feet like men, and could walk upright. When therefore he found no fruits in the bush with which to satisfy his wife's desire, Python went to the farm of a man, where an Aju tree stood, and each day plucked some of the fruit.

Now the owner of the tree had a son named Monn-akat-chang-obbaw-chang (Child-feet-not-hands-not), because he had neither hands nor feet. One day he complained to his father that someone was stealing their Aju, and begged that he should be carried to the foot of the tree, so that he might watch for the thief. To this the father consented.

When Nkimm (Python) came next day, he found the tree guarded by a wonderful boy without hands or feet. So soon as the latter saw the snake he called, "Are you the person who steals my father's Aju?" Nkimm denied his guilt, and said that this was the first time he had seen the tree, but begged the boy to give him a few of the fruits for his sick wife.

Akat Chang replied that he would do so with pleasure, had

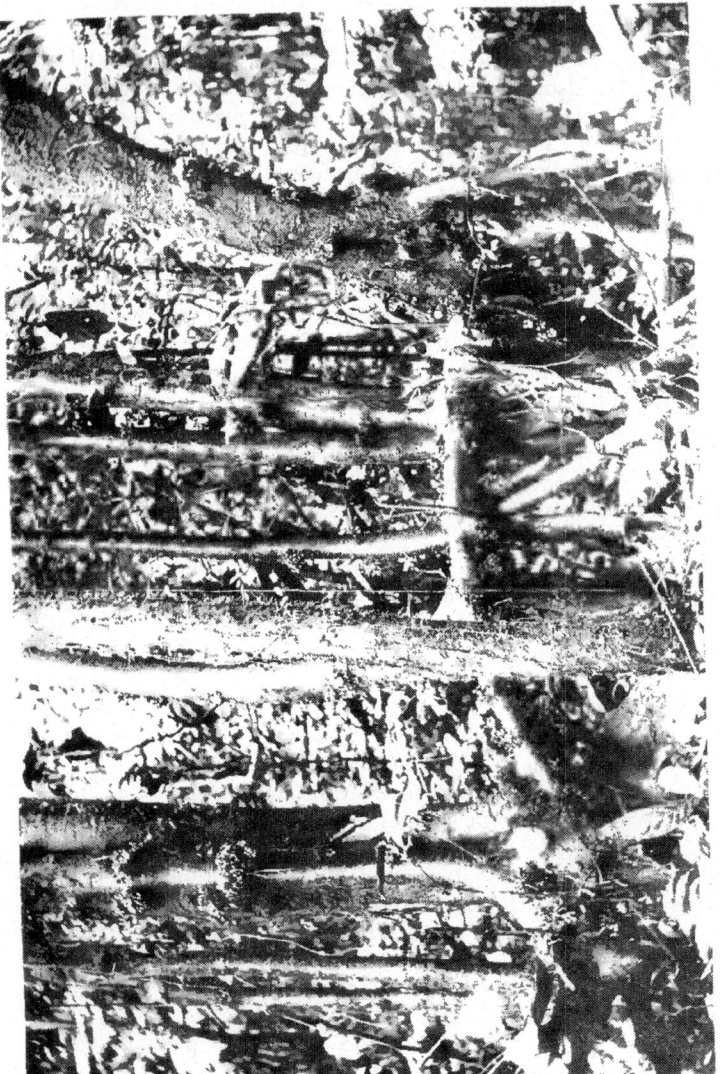

Cola Lepidota.

he but hands and feet with which to climb the tree, but, since he had not, this was impossible, as he could not allow any stranger to pluck his father's fruits.

Python offered to take off his own hands and feet and lend them to the boy, that he might be able to climb. This was done and the limbs bound on, after which the boy quickly went up into the tree, and threw down as many of the fruits as the visitor could carry away. He then came down again and returned the limbs to their owner, who thanked him and left with his load. When he reached his house he gave the Aju to his wife, who ate them with great delight.

Before it grew dark, the father of Akat Chang came to the tree to carry the boy home for the night. His son related how he had spent the time with the Aju thief, and enjoyed the advantage of using the latter's hands and feet.

Two days afterwards, Nkimm's wife had finished all the Aju, so told her husband that he must fetch her some more, again threatening to break her pregnancy if he did not do as she asked. So Python was obliged to set out once more for his well-known tree. There again he met his friend, the boy, who had been told by his mother to ask the thief to fix on the hands and feet very firmly. She bade him then climb into the tree, and stay there until his father came.

Once more Python took off his feet and hands and bound them strongly to the boy's body as the latter asked him to do What a loss to Nkimm!

Off went the boy up the tree, and did not cease from climbing till he reached the topmost branch. Then he began to sing:

" Sini sini mokkaw.   Sine sine mokkaw
           Oro obba
    Nta abe Aju, monn akat akpim
    (Lord plant Aju, child feet not get)
           Oro obba
    Nkimm atonn akat, akaw anam   Aju
    (Python has feet, take buy (with) Aju fruit).
           Oro obba
       Sini sini mokkaw   Sine sine mokkaw
           Oro obba "

(The narrator repeated the song very carefully as it had been taught him by his grandfather, but he had no idea of the meaning of the refrain. The latter appears to have some similarity to the Efut language.)

When the parents heard the singing, they ran towards their son. In his hands the father bore a great spear. When Nkimm saw this, he rushed off for his life in the opposite direction, throwing himself along the ground in the only way possible to him.

Since then, no man has been born without hands or feet and no Python or other snake with them.

Had it not been for this act of Monn-Akat-Chang, snakes would have continued to be footed animals instead of creepers, and man would sometimes have been born without feet or hands

Why Snake has neither Hands nor Feet.

By Itambo Asong of Oban

Obassi Nsi once made a farm. In it he put three animals, Mfong (cow), Mbui (goat), and Nyaw (snake) Cow and Goat were the gardeners, while Snake was ordered to collect the fruits and take them to the house of Obassi.

Before leaving them to their work, Obassi said, "Of all the fruits of this farm you may not eat Even should any plantains or other fruits fall down, you must not touch them."

One day some strangers came from a far town to visit Obassi; whereon the latter sent Snake to his farm to bring back a supply of food for them At that time Snake had hands and feet just like all other creatures. The first day he went quickly and brought back a plentiful supply, but the second day, when he went again, Cow asked, "Why does our master want so many plantains?" Snake said, "He is feeding the strangers who have come to stay with him."

Goat said, "I do not quite understand Do you mean that our master eats none of all these good things, but only gives them to strangers?" The three of them disputed the question, and it was late when Snake got back with his load. Obassi was angry and beat him because he was so long on the way.

Next time Snake was sent to the farm he said to Cow and Goat:

"I do not see why we should die of hunger while all the food is devoured by strangers. Why should not we ourselves enjoy the fruits of our labours?"

To this the others agreed, and Cow sent Goat to cut plantains. They were ripe, and when Cow divided them out, Goat said to him:

"You are the head man in the farm. You should eat first." On this Cow began to eat, and cried out, "Oh, very sweet plantains!" Then both the others joined him in eating.

Snake went and got yams. He came back and said to the others, "Do not tell anyone what I have done, for if my master heard, he would do something to me."

On his return, Obassi was more vexed than before. He said, "Why did you stay away so long? You already knew that there were strangers in the house."

Next day again Obassi sent the Snake, but this time he bade one of his daughters, named Afion Obassi, follow secretly, that she might learn why Snake stayed so long in the farm.

When Afion arrived, she found Cow and Goat eating. She said, "Who told you to eat the fruits in my father's farm?" They answered, "It was Snake who told us we might eat."

After the girl returned home, she told her father what she had seen. Obassi therefore sent for the three animals. When they stood before him he asked, "How is it that you ate the fruit in my farm, which I had forbidden you to touch?" They answered, "It was Snake who taught us to eat."

Obassi said, "Each of you must suffer for disobeying my orders." To Cow he said, "From now onward, when men pick plantains, they will keep the good part for themselves and throw only the rind to you." That is the reason why we always see Cow eating plantain skins. To Goat he said, "When people prepare their yams, the peelings only shall be your portion." That is why we see Goat eating up the yam parings.

Obassi seized Snake, pressed him and pulled off his hands and feet. That is the reason why he no longer has these, like other animals.

Why Lizard's Head is always moving up and down.

By Ojong Itaroga

In the old days, when all the beasts could speak like men, Obassi Nsi married many wives. These were the daughters of nearly all animals on earth, and each creature who gave his daughter in marriage to Obassi received a very rich gift in exchange.

Now Tortoise also wanted a gift like the rest, but he had only sons and no daughter. He took a long time to think over the matter; at length he made a plan. He called two of his sons and told them that he was about to give them to Obassi as wives, so they must take care never to let anyone see their nakedness. After warning them in this way, he dressed them in very rich robes, like girls, and they set forth.

When Tortoise and his two seeming daughters reached the hall where Obassi was sitting, he stood forth and said:

"I am the best of all your friends, for the rest have given you each a wife, but I alone bring two."

Obassi thanked him, and gave him in return twice as great riches as he had given to the others. "Lord," said Tortoise, "there is one thing which I must tell you. No one must see my daughters' nakedness, else they will die."

"What a thing to say!" answered Obassi. "It would be death to any man to see one of my wives unclothed."

"I spoke," said Tortoise, "of their fellow women."

"Fear not," answered Obassi, "since you have told me this, there is no danger of such a thing."

On this Tortoise went away, rejoicing in his success, while Obassi handed over the two new wives to his head wife that she might look after them, never thinking that they were boys.

Not long after, their mistress found out the true state of the case. She went secretly to Obassi and told him that the two girls whom Tortoise had given him in marriage possessed the masculine nakedness.

Obassi questioned the woman very earnestly if she meant

what she said, and when she assured him that it was true, he replied quietly:

"Do not speak of this any more, lest the two Tortoises should overhear and flee away to their father."

Obassi fixed a day on which to make known to all the trick which had been played upon him. He sent round to his fathers-in-law to tell them that he was about to give a great show, and that he expected all those who were invited to be present and in good time. By this invitation he meant to have Tortoise punished, and perhaps even killed, for his deceit.

The two sons of Tortoise suspected what was going on, so they sent for Lizard, and from her they borrowed the feminine nakedness. When, therefore, the day came round, and Obassi went very early in the morning to ascertain the fact that his two young wives were boys, he found them girls after all.

The guests came in great multitudes and sat down in companies, eager to see the wonders which Obassi had promised. The latter was very angry, and began scolding his head wife for lying to him, not knowing that all she had said was true. Then he went to the audience hall, and simply told the people that there would be no show, for his wife had disappointed him. So all departed with much discontent.

Three days later Lizard went to the boys to ask for the parts she had lent them, but they only asked her to take a seat and eat a few balls of fu-fu. Later they begged her to come again in a few days' time, when they would do as she asked.

Over and over again Lizard came, but each day she was put off in the same manner. At length one day she began to sing loudly, and her song was as follows:

"Ared   nkui, kumm 'me   ndipp   eyama
Ared Tortoise, give me secret parts mine.
Affion nkui, kumin 'me   ndipp   eyama
Affion Tortoise, give me secret parts mine
'Me nkpaw, 'me nkpaw, ka   ndipp   eyama
    I   die,   I   die, for secret parts mine.
Fenne, kpe nde mbitt, nde ka   ndipp   eyama
    Also, if I live life, I live for secret parts mine."

The people in the compound heard the singing, and ran to see who it was who could make such a song. Tortoise boys (now girls) begged Lizard to take a seat once more and eat a few fu-fu balls as usual. She sat down and began eating. One of them then said, "Let us each make fu-fu balls for the others to swallow," and all agreed to the fun. One of our well-known two then rolled a fine ball and secretly put some pricking fish-bones within it, dipped it in the soup-pot, and put it in poor Lizard's mouth. The latter tried to swallow it, but it stuck in her throat, where the pin-like bones held it fast. Lizard lay on the ground voicelessly stretching her neck, and trying in vain to swallow the ball or eject it.

This is the cause why Lizards are seen to raise and let fall their heads. They are still trying to get rid of the fu-fu ball given them by the sons of Tortoise.

That is the reason why Tortoise's trick has never been discovered up to this day, and thus it is that Lizard lost her voice and her "Ndipp," and only gained in exchange the habit of lifting her head up and down.

How Tortoise got the Cracks and Bumps on his Back.

By Effion Mkpat Okun of Niaji.

Once Nkui (Tortoise) was a great friend of Obassi Osaw. He went to visit Obassi and ate and drank in his house. Before he left he said, "Let us make a rule." Obassi asked, "How do you mean?" "I mean about the funeral 'play,'" said Nkui. "Whichever of us shall die first, the other must kill an elephant for the 'customs'" To this Obassi agreed, but when his friend had left, he ordered his people to build a house without doors or windows. There was only a hole in the roof. Through this Obassi let himself down with all his chop and his loving wife. He said to his eldest son, "Please go and tell Tortoise that I am dead." This the son did, and Tortoise started out to go to his friend's town. As he went along the road, he saw an Elephant feeding on some grass down by the water. Tortoise said:

"Lord, you are eating. They have sent to call me because my friend is dead. I am looking for someone who will be able

to dance at the funeral. Will you go with me for the dancing?
I think you could dance very finely indeed."

Next Tortoise got some pods of the Agara tree, which, when
shaken, make a noise like little bells. These he made into
anklets and tied them round the feet of Elephant. Then he
said, "Try, Lord, and see how you can dance." Elephant
danced, and Tortoise cried out, "In all the world there is no
such dancer! The ceremonies will be held next month. I
shall come along this road early in the morning and trust that I
may see you, so that we may go together to the dancing."

Now during all this time Obassi was inside the house, but
Tortoise was making a very strong rope all covered with the
little bell-like pods. When the new moon shone, Nkui took
the rope and went along the road as before. He called to
Elephant, "Lord, Lord, it is time now."

Elephant heard and came. Tortoise took the anklets and
tied them round the great feet. Next he took the rope and
threw it round Elephant's neck, saying, "Come, Lord, I will
lead you to the dance."

When the two reached Obassi's town all the people danced
with joy at the sight of them. Tortoise tied Elephant to the
Juju tree before the Egbo house. When he thought that his
prey was safely tied, he went away.

Two small children ran out and said, "Ho! here is the
Elephant which Nkui said he would kill for the burial of his
friend. Ho! Elephant will be killed very soon."

When Elephant heard this he knew that he had been deceived.
He was very angry, and strained at the rope till it broke. Then
he ran round seeking Nkui, who fled before him into the bush.
Elephant went round and round, but could not find whom he
sought, because Tortoise had hidden himself in a very cunning
place by the river. One day, as the latter sat in this new home,
he cooked plantains, then peeled them and threw the skins into
the water. They floated down stream till they came to the
place where Elephant was walking along the bank. He picked
them up with his trunk, and asked, "Where do you come
from?" They answered, "We come from Nkui's place." So
he begged them to guide him thither.

When Tortoise saw them coming, he called to his wife,

"Turn me over, and grind medicine upon my breast. Should Elephant ask for me, say that I am not at home."

When Elephant arrived he saw the wife of Nkui grinding medicine and asked, "Where is your husband?" She replied, "I have been very ill for a long time, and do not know where he has gone."

Elephant looked fixedly at the stone, and then said, "If you do not mind, I think that I had better throw away that stone."

She answered, "Do you not hear that I am very ill, and am grinding medicine for my sickness. Certainly you must not touch my stone."

On that Elephant laughed and turned the stone over with his foot. He saw Nkui and knew him. He placed his foot upon him, pressed him into the earth and broke all his shell. Up till that time Tortoise had had a smooth skin, but it has since been broken and humpy because Elephant smashed it up in punishment for his deceit.

Why there are no more Lions in the Bush

By Okun Asukwor of Ndebbji

A man named Etim married a wife. After a time she told him that a son was about to be born. He left home and went out hunting, but Nki (lion) sprang from out the bush and killed him.

The wife remained in charge of a brother of her late husband. When the babe was born, this man took care of both. One day when the boy was nearly grown up the uncle called to him, saying "My son." The lad answered, "Do not call me thus. I am no son of yours. My father was killed in the bush by Nki."

One day the boy went out and collected a great quantity of palm kernels. He took these to the white traders and exchanged them for guns. When he reached home, he went to the bush near the town and climbed up a tree. On this he made two seats, one high up and the other low down. He took his gun to the high place and left it there, while he went to call one of his sisters. Her he set in the lower place, with a small bell in her hand, and a horn with which to blow. He himself climbed up on high and lay in wait, and told his sister to ring the bell and blow the horn to call their enemy Nkí.

It was day time. The girl rang the bell and blew the horn as her brother had bidden. After a while the lion heard, and sent a poisonous snake to go and spy and bring him back word.

When Snake came the boy said, "I am not looking for you, but for my enemy Nkí. I could easily kill you with my matchet and would not need a gun." So Snake went back and reported what he had heard.

When he had gone, the girl again began to ring and blow the horn, and this time Lion sent Python to go and bring him back word.

When the boy saw Python he said, "You are big and long, yet I could cut you in pieces without a gun I wait here for my enemy Nkí."

Again the third time, the girl began to ring the bell and to blow, and this time Nkí sent Flame to report to him; but the boy called, "I could quench you with water. Go back and tell Nkí that I wait for him alone."

After this Nkí himself came "Who is it who keeps calling me?" he roared out.

The boy answered never a word, but raised his gun and fired, and Nkí fell down dead. For a while the two children did not dare to come down from the tree, for fear that their enemy still lived, and would harm them. A Parrot flew by, and the boy said, "Will you go down and cut off a finger from Lion for me?"

Parrot answered, "He is a very fearful animal; therefore I must refuse."

Just then Hawk flew past. To him also the boy called, and asked the same question. Hawk replied, "Give me a matchet." When this had been given, he flew down and cut off the middle finger from Nkí.

Then the boy came down and turned the dead lion round. From its breast he saw the head of his own dead father hanging. This he loosed and put it, together with the claw, in his hunting bag.

As the couple walked through the streets of their town,

the boy cried out, "I have killed a lion to-day." The people said, "We do not believe it," but the lad opened his bag and pulled out his father's head, and the claw of the lion, so that they might know. All clapped their hands and shouted. The boy said.

"We will keep my father's funeral customs"

He buried the head and gave a great "play." After this some of the people whose relations had also been devoured by the lion went and found these heads too hanging to the breast of the dead beast.

Up to that time no one could go into the bush alone for fear of the lions. Since the boy killed their chief, however, they have gone far away and left our bush free.

Why Bush Fowl (Ikpai) always calls up the Dawn.

By Ndum Agurimon of Nsan

A man once went into the bush with his wife to collect palm nuts. He saw a palm with ripe clusters upon it, and climbed up to get them. While he was trying to cut through the stems, a black fly named Njinn-I-Nyakk began to buzz round him, dash into his eyes, against his nose, and all over his face. He raised his hand to drive it away, and as he did so the knife fell from his grasp "Run, run," he called to his wife, who was just beneath the tree, for he feared that it might fall upon her. It was the time of the woman's seventh month, but she sprang aside so quickly that she was out of the way before the knife reached the ground. In her haste she jumped over a serpent called Nkimm. This startled him so that he dived down a brown rat's hole, and begged for a drink of water Rat handed him a calabash full, and he emptied it at one draught. Rat was so frightened at her visitor that she sprang past him out of the hole and ran up a tree, where she sat trembling. The place she had chosen was near Nkundak's (Greater Plantain-eater) nest. No sooner did the latter see her than she raised a war cry. This startled a monkey named Nyak-I-Mbuk (Black Monkey), who sallied out ready for a fight. In his haste to meet his enemy, Nyak sprang on to a ripe fruit of the tree called Ntun. This fell from its stalk on to the back of an elephant who was passing beneath. The latter rushed away so furiously, that he tore down, and carried off a flowering creeper called Mfinn, which caught round his neck.

The Mfinn in turn pulled over an ant heap, which fell on to Bush-fowl's nest, and completely destroyed her eggs.

Bush-fowl was so sad because of her loss, that she sat brooding over the crushed eggs, and forgot to call the dawn. For two days therefore the whole world was dark.

All the beasts wondered what could be the reason of this continued night, and at length Obassi summoned them before him to inquire into the matter.

When all were present Obassi asked Bush-fowl why it was now forty-eight hours since she had called for light. Then she stood forth and answered.

"My eggs were broken by Ekughi Nke (ant hill), which was pulled over by Mfinn, which was dragged down by Elephant, who was knocked by Ntun fruit, which was plucked by Monkey, who was challenged by Nkundak, who was startled by Rat, who was frightened by Serpent, who had been jumped over by a sick woman, who had been made to run by the fall of a knife, which had been dropped by her husband, who had been teased by a black fly. Through vexation, therefore, at the loss of my eggs, I refused to call the day."

Each thing and every beast was asked in turn to give the reason for the damage it had done, and each in turn gave the same long answer, till it came to the turn of Black Fly, who was the first cause of all the mischief. He, instead of answering properly, as the others had done, only said "Buzz, buzz." So Obassi commanded him to remain speechless for evermore, and to do nothing but buzz about and be present wherever a foul thing lies. To Bush-fowl he also gave judgment that she should call on the instant for the long-delayed dawn, and never again refuse to do so, whether her eggs were destroyed or not.

Were it not that Obassi had given strict orders to Bush-fowl, it might easily happen that one day or another she would again refuse to call, and then we should unawaredly enter on a long night, which might perhaps last for a week or more.

S.B.   C C

Why Frog and Snake never play together.

Frog had a son. Snake also had a son. Both children went out to play in the bush. They said, "We feel hungry; let us go home." When they arrived at home, each of them went to his mother's house. Mrs. Frog asked her son, "Where have you been this morning?" He said, "I was in the bush playing with Snake-child." His mother said, "Don't you know that the Snake family are bad people? They have poison."

Also, when the little Snake went home, his mother asked, "Who was your playmate?" Snake-child said, "Frog was my playmate." Mrs. Snake said, "What foolishness is this to come and tell me you feel hungry! Don't you know that it is the custom of our house to eat frogs? Next time you play with him, catch him and eat him."

Snake-child therefore went to call Frog to play with him again, but the latter refused. Snake-child then said:

"Evidently your mother has given you instructions. My mother also has given me instructions."

From that day Frog and Snake never played together again.

How the First Hippopotami came.

Once, long ago, Elephant had a beautiful daughter, whom all the beasts wished to wed. Now at that time a very great fish named Njokk Mbonn (Elephant fish) dwelt in the river, and one evening he came to Elephant and said, "I should like to marry your daughter."

Next morning Leopard came too, and said, "Do not let anyone marry the girl but me." When he heard that the King of the fishes had also asked her in marriage he was very angry, and went home to call all his family together to fight. Nsun (antelope) happened to pass by while they were arranging the matter, and he went at once and said to Fish:

"Listen to what I have heard to-day. Leopard and all his people are coming to fight you."

When Njokk Mbonn heard this he said nothing, but only took a yam and roasted it. When it was ready he ate part, and put the rest on one side. Just then he heard the sound of his enemies coming in the distance, and close at hand he saw Elephant also with his daughter.

Then Fish went down into the water. By magic he made a big wave rise up and overflow the bank. As this ebbed it drew Elephant and his daughter down to the depths beneath, where Fish lay waiting.

When the other animals saw what had happened they all fled, crying to one another:

"If we try to fight with Njokk Mbonn he will kill us all. Let us go back at once."

Fish thought to himself, "I must kill Leopard, or he will come back again some day."

At dawn, therefore, he came up to the bank, and lay there cleaning his teeth, which were very white and shining.

When Leopard came along he stood looking at his enemy and thought, "My teeth are not so fine as his. What can I do?" So he said, "Will you kindly clean my teeth also?"

When Fish heard this he answered, "Very well, but I cannot do it unless you will lie down. If you are willing to do this I will clean your mouth."

Leopard lay down, Fish sent his wave once more, and swept his enemy down to the depths of the river. Instead of finding a fine house there, as Elephant and his daughter had done, Leopard found only a strong prison, where he soon died.

Njokk Mbonn married the daughter of Elephant, and they lived happily for many years. Their children were the Water-Elephants (*i.e.*, Hippopotami). If Fish had not wedded this wife there would have been no Hippo in our rivers.

How Black and White Men came on Earth.

By Ojong of Oban.

In the beginning of things, Obassi had only one wife. These two were the first of all people. Before them neither man nor woman had ever been.

In course of time the woman bore four children to her husband Two were white and two black.

One day, when the children were yet young, the father called the two boys, and sent them out hunting, while the mother told both girls to go and fish.

Now when the white girl had been for a little time down by the river she saw a bird catching fish, and noticed that it had already thrown down several on the bank. These she took and ran quickly home to give them to her mother, but the black girl still went on slowly fishing with her nets in the river.

Meantime the white boy thought, "Why should I trouble to go hunting?" So he took his mother's goat and skinned it. Then he brought it to his father and said, "Here is an antelope which I have just killed in the bush."

When the black girl returned with the fish that she had caught, her mother said, "The white girl has brought me all that I want, and to her I have given the recompense which I promised to both of you."

After a time the black boy came back with a fine antelope (Nsun) which he had killed, but, when he laid it down before his father, the latter said:

"I have already accepted enough fresh meat from my white son, and to him have I given the hunter's reward."

In course of time the children grew up and thought of marriage. When this had taken place Obassi sent the black son and daughter into the bush, to live afar off, but the white children he kept with him always.

When some years had gone by, the white son and daughter came to their father and said, "Where are our black brother and sister?" To which Obassi answered, "I have sent them a long way off."

Another day they came again, and said, "We wish to see our brother and sister." But again they were answered, "I have made a very high fence in the road, and hewed down many trees so that the way is quite blocked up. You cannot go by to visit them."

Again a third time they pleaded, but once more Obassi answered, "I have already told you, you cannot pass by and come to their town without my order."

One day the white boy's son was playing down by the river. He fastened a long piece of tie-tie round his toy, and threw it into the water. He held the end fast, and the wind took the toy, and blew it along the water as if it were a kite. So pleased was he with the new game he had made that he came next day to play again in the same way. When the men of the town saw what he was doing, they went to watch, and said to one another, "It is a strange game for a small boy to play all alone. Come, let us help him."

Now this second day, the boy had taken an old nest, and fastened it to his tie-tie. The wind blew it to the other side of the river. Each time when it had crossed over, the boy pulled it back to him.

When Obassi saw what the child had done, he called his son and daughter before him, and said, "If you want to go to the place where your brother and sister live, you must make a canoe out of wood. Come, and I will show you how the thing should be done."

When the boat was ready, Obassi said, "Get in, but take your guns and matchets with you, for I think that when your black brother first sees you, he will wonder greatly and perhaps think that you come to bring some misfortune upon him."

The white children did as they were bidden, and their canoe bore them a long way down stream till they came to the creek where their black brother had built his town

The Treasure House in the Bush.

By Ojong Akpan of Mfamosing.

Obassi Osaw had two sons. The name of the first was Oro, and of the second Agbo. When their father died, Oro took all the property, while Agbo remained in the sky as a poor washerman. One day the latter said to his wife, "There is no food either for you or me. I must go into the bush and hunt, that we may not die of hunger." He went along a road which brought him down to earth, and led him at length to a part of the bush where a house was standing by itself. He wondered whose it might be, and crept round behind some bushes to watch unseen.

Soon some white people came through the bush close to where the hunter was hidden. He saw them open the door, carry forth a great treasure, and then lock up again.

When they had gone, Agbo crept out from his hiding place, found a way to enter the house, and took from it as much treasure as he could carry. This he bore off to the sky. When his wife saw what he had brought she said, "Where did you get all this?" He answered, "From a house in the bush where white people keep it."

Some days later the hunter went down again, and once more brought back a great load of treasure. When he had secured as much as he wanted, he went to his elder brother and said:

"Please lend me a basket, I wish to measure my money."

Oro did as he was asked, but one of his wives thought, "I should like to know how this poor man can suddenly have become rich." She followed Agbo, and, when they reached his house, offered to help him measure the money.

It took seven days to measure, and, when at last all was ended, the woman went back and told her husband how rich his brother had grown. On learning this Oro went straight to the latter's house and said, "Open the door and let me see what you have got."

Agbo replied, "Why should I show it? I am but a very small man compared to you." His wife however said, "Open the door and let him see." So at length it was opened.

When Oro saw what was stored within he asked, "Where did you get all this?" Agbo replied, "It came from the Treasure House of the white people, which I found in the bush." Then the elder brother began to beg the younger to show him the place, and the latter said, "To-morrow I will not go; but if you will come for me the day after, we will set out." This they did, and when they reached the house, entered and carried off a load.

Another day Oro said, "I want to go again;" but Agbo replied, "You must go alone. I will go no more." This time, therefore, the elder brother set off by himself. When he reached the Treasure House, he crept in by the way his brother had made, but instead of quickly gathering together some of the treasure, he saw rich robes lying in a heap on one side, and began trying them on. One after another he tried, and each seemed to him more gorgeous than the last. While he was still robing himself, the owners came in. They bound him, cut him in pieces and laid the fragments on the threshold.

When night came, Agbo grew anxious because his brother did not return. All night he waited, and, when day dawned, set out by the way which Oro had taken. On and on he went till he came to the house in the bush. There, oh, terrible sight! he found the fragments of his brother's body lying before the door. He collected every bit, and carried them sadly away. After a while he sought out a tailor and said, "Here is the body of a man who got cut to pieces in the bush. Can you sew it together again? If you will do this for me I will pay you richly." The tailor answered, "I will try what I can do."

When the owner of the treasure returned and found all the pieces gone he was very angry. He thought, "Who can have carried away the dead man's body, and what can have been done with it?" In his turn he also went to the tailor and asked, "Has anyone brought you pieces to mend?" The tailor replied, "Yes, a man named Agbo brought some."

The owner asked, "Who is Agbo? I do not know him." One of his servants answered, "I know who he is, and can find out all about him."

One day therefore this boy sought out Agbo and said, "I want to be your friend."

Agbo was willing, and cooked chop for his guest, but his son said, "My father, do not be friends with this boy, for he will go and tell his master all that you have done, and then they will come and kill you."

The servant went back to earth and told everything. In the night time he came again with some white paint, and painted all the posts of Agbo's house. After this he returned and told his master, "The place where the man lives who has wronged you will be easy to find, for I have marked it with white paint. In the morning, therefore, you can go with a large following and kill him, with all who dwell in his compound." Now a bright moon had been shining while the servant worked, and the son of Agbo had seen what was done. So he also got white paint and ran hastily round and painted all the houses in the town in the same way.

When the white man came early in the morning with a great following, he found the whole town painted alike, so he could not find the house which he sought, and was forced to return home without doing anything. He blamed his servant because the latter had failed to keep his promise, but the boy said.

"If you will lend me some of your war men, you shall not only be avenged of your enemy, but recover all that he has stolen." To this the master agreed, and called together some of his bravest fighters. The boy collected a lot of empty casks. These they rolled along till they neared the entrance to Agbo's town. There the servant said to twelve of the war men who were strong above their fellows, "I beg that you will now get into the casks." When they had entered and the covers were replaced, the others rolled them along till they came to Agbo's door.

Then the boy called out, "Agbo, Agbo. I am your friend, come back with a great gift See, here are many puncheons of palm oil."

Agbo was very pleased, but his son said, "I think that there are men hidden in those casks." The father answered, "How can you be so suspicious? There is nothing but oil." After that he made a great feast for his friend, and, when night came, prepared a bed for him in a room near to his own.

When all was quiet, the son got up and boiled much water. First he took a sharp knife and cut the throat of his father's guest. Next he went, very softly, to the casks, and made a small hole in each Through this he poured in the boiling water till all were nearly full.

Next morning when Agbo came out of his room he called to his friend, but no answer came. He went to the side of the bed and found him lying with his throat cut. When he saw this he gave a great cry and called.

"Who has killed my friend?" His son answered, "It is I"

On this Agbo caught the boy, chained him, and dragged him before the Judge, and there accused him of having killed their guest.

The Judge asked, "Is it true that you have done this thing?" and the boy answered "Yes" Then he asked, "Why did you do it?" and he answered, "To save my father's life, for his friend tried to kill him."

Then the son told of the casks which had been brought to the house with soldiers inside. The Judge sent to fetch them, and when they were brought it was found to be even as the boy had said, for the boiling water had killed all the men.

The Judge said to Agbo, "I cannot blame your son, for he has saved your life." So they decided to send the lad away free with rich gifts.

When home was reached, Agbo let his son into the place where his treasure was kept, and said to him, "The half of this I give to you now. When I die, all that I have will be yours, for you have been a good son and have saved my life. Fathers should take care of their sons, and sons should always help fathers."

Further he gave the lad seven slaves.

WHY THE OTHER MEMBERS MUST SERVE BELLY.
BY OKAM NTEM OF NDEBBIJI (*Girl just out of fatting-house*).

There was once a man named Effiong who had many children. One of these was named Hand, one Foot, a third Back, a fourth Head, and the fifth Belly. He loved all his children, save the last. Foot was useful for travelling, Back for carrying loads, and Hand for work. Head was also useful for some loads, but he did not like Belly at all.

One day Obassi heard Effiong scolding the unloved son, so he came down and called all the children before him, together with their father, and asked them to state what work they did. Belly said, "My father gives me nothing, so there is nothing I can do. I only remain empty." On this Obassi said to Effiong:

"Do you not know that Belly is a very important part?" To Foot he said, "For ever you must walk up and down, crushing the earth and soiling yourself as you go." To Hand he said, "You must always keep washing to make yourself clean." To Back he continued, "You also must wash once or even twice a day." But to Belly he said, "I make you head man among the children You are the eldest son, and shall be served three times a day."

That is the reason why the other members must serve Belly three times a day for evermore.

How Human Beings got Knee-caps.

Once, long ago, a woman named Nka Yenge went fishing in the river. With her were many other women. They all went into the water, some down stream and some up. Now deep down in one of the pools a smooth white stone was lying, something like a Nimm stone. As the women went by, several of them said, " What a beautiful stone ! " but when Nka Yenge came, she stood looking at it for a long time and said, " I wish I could get that stone ! " When she came back she said the same thing, and as she passed a third time she said :

" I must have that stone."

Suddenly the stone sprang out of the water and struck against her knee. There it stayed and she could not loosen it ; so she went home weeping with pain. On the way thither, she met a man, who asked, " Why do you weep ? "

The woman could not speak for tears, but the stone answered, " I was lying in the water. When the woman passed up and down, she said that she wished to have me. Her wish was so strong that it drew me up out of the water. Now I have joined myself to her, and shall never leave her again "

The man was very sorry, and called to the woman, " Come here. We will go to my house, and I will try what I can do." When they reached his house, he got a strong knife and tried to chop off the stone, but it was no use. The stone had gone inside.

That is the reason why we have knee-caps. Formerly we did not have any.

Hair's Revenge.

By Ntui Obassi of Mbeban

In the olden times, Stomach and Hair lived in the same town. Hair went trading, and left his wives alone in the house. While he was away, Stomach came and made love to them all.

When Hair returned, he called to his wives and asked them to make a bed ready for him, but they refused and said.

"If you will cook us a big calabash of food, and give us some fine clothes from those you have bought, we will tell you what has been happening in the house."

Hair did as he was asked, and the wives said, "Now we will tell you all, according to promise. While you were away, Stomach came to the house and made love to us all."

Hair was very angry. He went alone to his room and there talked to himself "To-morrow I will do this and that thing."

Now Rat was in his hole, and when he heard what Hair was saying, he ran to Stomach and said, "Get ready, you must not stay here. Hair is coming to punish you for what you have done to his wives."

Next morning, very early, Stomach left his house and set out to try to escape from his enemy He had not gone far before he heard Hair running after him. He ran on as fast as he could, and at length overtook a man on the road. To the latter he said, "Will you please open your mouth?"

The man did as he was asked, and Stomach went inside.

When Hair came up, he asked the man:

"Have you seen Stomach go by?"

The man answered, "No. What is the matter?"

Hair told him all that had happened, and the man answered·

"Ah, ha! That is why Stomach was so anxious to hide. He has now gone inside my body."

Hair said, "I do not believe you." Nevertheless he bent down his head and put his ear to the man's belly. He heard it shaking with fear, and then knew that his enemy was inside for true.

Then Hair took teeth, and set them all round the man's mouth. To these he said.

"If my enemy tries to come out this way, bite him, but do not let him escape."

He himself settled in the man's nose, and round both eyes, so that his enemy might not pass out thence, and also above the mouth in a moustache, that he might watch over Teeth.

From that time forward, if a single hair gets into a man's food and is swallowed, he vomits it at once. Hair and Stomach have not made up their quarrel to this day, and therefore do not agree.

How Obassi Osaw proved the Wisdom of Tortoise.

By Anjong Ntui Animbun of Nsan

Obassi Osaw married many wives. Among these was the daughter of Tortoise. She was so proud of her father that she annoyed Obassi by exclaiming, "Oh, my father, you have more sense than any other person!" whenever the least thing happened, even if she only knocked her foot or felt surprised.

Obassi determined to find out for himself if Tortoise was really so very wise. He therefore built a room without doors or windows. Into this he secretly let down eight persons, and sent to Tortoise to come at once and tell him what was within.

Tortoise sent back a message that he would certainly come next day, but in such a way that no one should see him enter, for he was surely the wisest of men, and none could know how he came. Obassi was still more displeased when he heard this.

Now the daughter went and told Tortoise that her husband was annoyed with her for constantly praising her father's wisdom. "Perhaps," said she, "it is to prove this that he has sent for you." Tortoise answered, "It is well."

Next morning Obassi sent other messengers to bid his father-in-law hasten, but, when the men arrived, Tortoise was nowhere to be found. His wife said that he had gone hunting, so the messengers had better not wait. They agreed to this, and set out once more. The woman ran after them with a parcel and said, "Will you please take this to my daughter?"

This the men promised, and gave the parcel to the girl, not knowing that it was Tortoise whom they carried. She bore the packet before Obassi, set it on the ground and unfastened the tie-tie, when out stepped—what? Tortoise himself.

Obassi was very much surprised, and bade the guest go and stay in his daughter's house till next morning. So they went off together.

At night, when all was quiet, Tortoise made a small hole in

the wall of the room which Obassi had built. Then he took a stick and dipped it into some foul-smelling stuff. The men who were inside noticed the bad odour, and began calling to each other by name, asking its cause.

In this way Tortoise heard that there were eight men in the secret room, and also learned their names. He was very careful to fill up the little hole which he had made, and afterwards went back to bed.

Next morning a great company was gathered together to witness the shame of Tortoise when he should fail to answer the question of their Lord.

Obassi stood in the middle of the audience room and said very loudly that Tortoise must now tell him what was hidden in the windowless house, or suffer death if he could not do so.

Then Tortoise rose and said that there were eight men shut up within, and, to the surprise of all the people, he repeated their names, thus proving himself to be wiser than all his fellows, just as his daughter had said.

Obassi was so vexed that he ordered his men to seize Tortoise, sharpen a stick, and drive it through this overwise creature, so as to fasten him to the ground at a place where cross-roads meet. He also ordered that the beast should be fixed upright, so as to look at his judge on high. Obassi decreed further that, whenever a man wished to make him a sacrifice, Tortoise should be offered in this way. That is why we often see Tortoise impaled before Jujus, or at cross-roads.

Why Nki[*] lives in the Tops of Palm Trees.

A new piece of land had been cleared by the people of a certain town. Next morning, when they went thither to work, they found the place befouled. Inquiry was made, but the offender was not to be found. The head chief therefore gave a gun to Ise and set him to watch.

When night fell, Ejaw[†] crept out of the bush, and began to befoul the place as before. Ise took aim and shot him, then ran and told the people what he had done.

---

[*] Small Dormouse (*Graphiurus C dorotheæ talboti*)
[†] Civet cat

At daybreak they all went forth and brought in the body. They cut up the flesh, and asked Ise to dry it in the smoke of the fire that they might feast upon it next day. Ise did as he was bidden, and, when he had laid the pieces in order upon the drying shelf, sat down to watch by the hearth.

Now Nki loved fresh meat, and thought of a way by which he alone might feast upon the kill. He took a great jar of palm wine, and went to visit Ise. The latter was very thirsty, so he drank a deep draught and then lay down and fell asleep. While he slept Nki stole all the meat, then, when dawn broke, before the theft could be discovered, this treacherous animal took a drum and stood in the open space before the Egbo house playing:

"Ofu awche, kpa kun edingi ane aba
Day breaks, now we may know each other
Mbana nyamm aba kare nyamm.
Drier of meat come give meat"

Ise awoke and found all the flesh gone, so he cried out

"A thief has taken all the meat which was given me to guard. Take my flesh instead that the town may feast"

On this the people said, "It is just," so they killed Ise and gave his body to Etuk,* that it might be smoked before the fire

Nki did as before, stole the meat, and at daybreak beat upon the summoning drum. So Etuk lost his life as Ise had done, and his flesh was entrusted to Nkongam.†

On him Nki played the same trick, with the result that he also was slain, and his body given in charge to Ngumi.‡ This latter also fell a victim to Nki in exactly the same manner as the other beasts, and this time Mbaw § was chosen to smoke the meat.

Now the latter is a very cunning animal, and no sooner had he reached his house than he laid the flesh upon the drying shelf, and spread over it great lumps of rubber. Next he piled high the fire, so that the rubber grew soft, and sat down to wait for the thief.

After a while Nki appeared as before, but Mbaw only pretended

---

* Bay duiker
† Yellow-backed duiker
‡ Boar
§ Large dormouse (*Graphiurus huetii*)

to drink the palm wine, and poured it away little by little when his visitor was not looking. At length he too lay down as if overcome by sleep.

Nki called, " Mbaw, Mbaw, are you awake ? " but the latter did not answer.

The thief thought that all was now safe, so he rose up softly, and laid his hand upon the meat. At once the rubber caught him and held him fast. Nki was angry and cried, " Let go of me, whoever you are, or I will punch your head." Still the rubber held fast Then Nki drove his own head against the place where his hand was held, thinking to force back his enemy, but the rubber caught his hair and held that also. In vain he struggled and fought, threatening his unseen foe all the while. Rubber answered nothing, but only held the tighter.

At dawn Mbaw went out and beat upon the summoning drum, " Day breaks now, we may know each other; drier of meat come and give meat."

The people came together, and found the thief caught fast. They debated as to how he could best be punished for the deaths of all those beasts who had died through his fault.

While they talked together, each proposing some more cruel fate than the other, Nki began to wring his hands and to weep. With each new suggestion he heartily agreed, adding always, " Yes, yes, kill me in any of these ways, only do not fix spears in the ground, and throw me up so that I may fall upon their points."

The people were so angry that they shouted, " Since he dreads this death above all others, it is by this that he shall die." They got spears, and fixed them firmly in the earth, points upward. Then they freed Nki from the rubber which had held him till now, and placed him before the spears. Six of the strongest men advanced to seize him and fling him into the air, but to the surprise of everyone, he himself gave a great leap, and sprang up a palm tree which stood near.

At once the people got axes, and cut down the tree, but before it fell, Nki sprang to another. Then they said.

" If we follow this man, we shall ruin all the palm trees. It is better to leave him alone."

That is why Nki always stays in the tops of palm trees. Up to that time he had lived on earth like all other animals, but since he caused the death of so many creatures, no one will be his friend, and he cannot come back to dwell among them any more.

The Lord of the Bush.

In the beginning of things, Nkimm (Python) and Njokk (Elephant) were Lords of the Bush. They disputed together as to which was the strongest. One said, "The bush belongs to me." The other answered, "Nay, it is mine." Osian (the black ants) listened and said, "In seven days' time, let us all fight, then he who shall beat the others shall be called Lord of the Bush." The two great beasts laughed, because the ants are so small, but they agreed, and from that time the latter gathered together over every tree and rock When the seventh day came they began to fight. First, they saw Iku. Him they surrounded and bit so badly that he ran to the river and was drowned. Next they sought out Nkimm, whom they found with his young ones. They came in such thousands that the great snake had to take his children and flee to the water, where they escaped. Next the ants pursued the monkeys, many of whom they killed, while the rest sprang up very high trees, calling out, "We leave the ground to you"

After this the Osian gathered themselves together in vast, numbers, and set out to fight with Njokk, but the latter only laughed. For several days they fought, but could not prevail, and at length sent a message to their king that the battle went against them, and that they would all be trampled to death beneath the great feet of their enemy if help were not sent.

Then the King of all the ants called together his people, even to the last one, and they came in such numbers that the whole earth was dark with them. Into Elephant's mouth they poured and into his eyes, his nose and his belly, till he could no longer stand against them, but fled to the water for refuge as the other beasts had done. When the bush creatures saw him fleeing they knew for true that the ants were lords of the bush So they called a meeting and brought out a great chair. The

Macrolobium lamprophyllum Harms.

Group of pale Duck's-egg blue Fungi.

King of the ants came and sat upon it, and all the animals stood before him, holding out their hands and saying:

"From to-day you are our lord. The land is yours, the bush is yours, and we will obey your orders."

During this time the monkeys were still amid the tree tops. The other beasts called to them and said, "Will you come down?" but they answered:

"No, we will make our homes in the branches." From that time onward the Ant King has been Lord of the Bush.

Why a Murderer must Die.

There was once a woman named Ukpong Ma, who had only one daughter. Just before it was time to put the girl into the fatting-house the mother died.

One day the husband, whose name was Uponnsoraw, set out for market. On his way he passed through a neighbouring town, where he saw a beautiful woman, and persuaded her to return with him as his wife.

When the couple reached the man's house, his daughter came out to salute them, and the new wife saw that in a little while her step-daughter would be more beautiful than she. So she hated the girl, and thought how she might destroy her.

One day, therefore, when the husband went out to hunt, the new wife called to her step-child and said, "Take the great water-pot, and go to the far river for water. Do not bring home any from the streams near by."

So soon as the girl had set out, the new wife killed a goat, ate the best part of the meat herself, and hid what was left over.

As the girl came back from the river it began to grow dark. Rain fell and she felt cold. When she reached home she went to the fireside to warm herself. Some water fell down on her, and she said to the new wife, "Where does it come from?" and the latter answered, "The roof leaks."

When Uponnsoraw came back from the hunt, he could not see the goat, so he called to his daughter and asked where it was. She answered, "Your new wife sent me to the river for water. I have only just come back, and do not know what has been happening at home."

At this the cruel step-mother came out of her room and said:
"Let us practise the charm to find who has stolen the goat."

They sent for the Diviner, and he came with a very long rope and said:

"We will go down to the river where the girl filled the jar."

Now the new wife was a great witch, so she secretly made a strong charm. Then, when they came to the river and threw the rope across, she stood on the brink and called.

"If I have stolen the goat may the rope break and let me fall into the river. If I am guiltless may I walk over safely"

She put her foot upon the rope, but the charm held, and she crossed without mishap.

The young girl stood by the river-side and said the same words. Then she walked on the rope as far as mid-stream. There the charm which the witch had made caused it to break, and the girl fell into the water. A great crocodile came up to the surface and caught her as she fell. Then all the people said, "She it was who stole the goat." Only her father said:

"My daughter never stole anything. I must find out the reason of her death."

A palm tree grew by the river-side, just by the place where the girl was lost, and one day a man climbed up this to collect palm wine.

Now beneath the water was the house of a were-crocodile, and she it was who had seized the girl, and kept her all this while as a slave. When the man began to climb the palm tree the crocodile was angry. So she took an axe and put it into the girl's hand and said:

"Go up to the top of the water and throw this axe at the man, that he may leave my palm tree and go back whence he came."

The girl did as she was bidden, but threw the axe so as not to hit the man. As it struck the tree the climber looked down and saw her. He therefore went back to his town with all haste, and told her father what had happened

The latter wondered, and went before the chief and said:

"This man says that he saw my daughter who died two years ago in the great river."

The chief was angry because he thought that the man was lying. So he ordered that chains should be brought and put upon him. The man, however, begged that they would take him to the place where he had seen the girl, and watch while he climbed the palm tree. To this the chief consented, and sent him, with three men, to the river. With them also went Uponnsoraw. The man climbed the tree and struck it with his matchet. No sooner did the girl hear than she rose to the surface, covered with ornaments, but sank down again almost at once. On this all the men ran back to the chief to tell him that the man had spoken truth, for they also had seen the girl.

The whole town set forth to fetch the Diviner, and asked him to practise the charm. This he did, and told them they must bring a black cock, an egg, a piece of white cloth, a ball of red cam wood dye. and some of the yellow "ogokk" powder; also they must bring the great nets which are used in hunting. All these things, save the red powder, they must sacrifice to the crocodile, but the nets they must hold ready in their hands.

As soon as they threw the offering into the river the girl rose to the surface. When she appeared they cast the nets and caught her like a fish Then they drew her to land and washed her with the red powder and with sand, and carried her in triumph to the house of the chief.

The cruel witch-wife came out to salute her, but no sooner did the girl hear her voice than she said:

"I will not see her at all. Crocodile told me a story about her. It was she who stole the goat." Then she said to her father, "Call all the people. I wish to say something."

When the townsfolk had come together they carried the girl before the Egbo house, where she stood up and said:

"Here I am. It was the new wife of my father who stole the goat that she might destroy me, lest I should be counted more beautiful than herself. Then she made a strong magic, so that the rope might bear her across the river, but break when I tried to pass over. Therefore all the people thought that I was guilty of the theft. Judge now, oh ye people, between her and me."

Then the Head Chief said, "Let the town give judgment"; and they cried in a great shout:

"The witch shall die for her crime." Then they set up two

great posts, and from these hanged the woman by the very cord which by her magic she had caused to break beneath the feet of the innocent girl. Thus died the witch in the sight of all men.

From that day forward a law was made, "If anyone is proved guilty of the death of another, he shall surely die."

That is the reason why if anyone kills another they must hang.

L'ENVOIE

SITTING as now, in the very heart of the Bush—writing, regretfully enough, the last words of what, to me, has been a work of pure pleasure, however weary a task it may have proved to those who made fair copies of my illegible manuscripts—I can but feel how powerless are mere words to express, even faintly, the charm of such a land. At best, one can but give, as it were, the dry bones of a country, which for sheer beauty can hardly be surpassed. Green as if carved from the heart of an emerald, flushed by opal dawns and sunsets, watered by streams of crystal clearness, and gleaming with the flash of countless waterfalls, it may be called, like the famous orchid, " Beautiful as the seven deadly sins." Yet all its loveliness cannot quite hide the deadliness that lurks beneath, and even on the strongest and most energetic, the strain of the climate must tell after a while. Government has done wonders as regards improved drainage, and so forth, but many years and an enormous expenditure will be necessary before the country can become habitable for white men for more than short terms of service.

There are occasions when the beauty around one fails to soothe the sting of hordes of sandflies and mosquitoes, which, when one stands at the theodolite, seem determined to leave no pin-point of face or hands unmarked; nor does it allay the torture of prickly heat as one toils painfully up some hill in the course of the almost ceaseless journeys necessary for the maintenance of law and order. Yet, even at the worst of times, when one is tempted to ask with Mary Kingsley, " Why did I come to Africa ? " one has but to let one's eyes wander over the loveliness around to answer like her, " Why! Who would not come to its twin-brother Hell itself, for all the beauty and the charm of it ? "

LIST OF APPENDICES.

		PAGE
A	Tabus	407
B.	Clubs	410
C.	Anthropometry	414
D	Orthography	415
E	Grammar	417
F.	Vocabularies	424
G	Nsibidi Signs	447
H	Botany	462
	(1) Fungi	462
	(2) Lichens	463
I.	Zoology	465
	(1) Mammals	465
	(2) Birds	469
	(3) Fish, Reptiles, etc	470
	(4) Insects, etc	470
	(5) Arachnida, etc	471
	(6) Crabs	473
	(7) Mollusca	473
J.	Mineralogy	474
K	Meteorology	476
L.	Geographical Survey	478

APPENDIX A.

Tabus.

There are many strict laws and tabus (Ntubi) which regulate the distribution of animals killed in the chase.

After a town hunt, one fore and one hind leg of each beast killed must be given to the townsfolk. The neck becomes the property of the man who stood nearest during the kill, the tail belongs to the mother of the hunter, one leg and the back to the father or the head of his house, while the head and remaining fore leg are left to the actual slayer.

When a man hunts alone or with one companion, the rules vary according to the animal killed.

In the case of a boar, the tail is given to the mother, the two legs and trotters to the father or head of the house, but he usually returns the latter. The cheeks and jaws must be cooked for the hunter's age class; half of the head and the stomach is given to the wife, and the other half-head to the companion; leaving the two fore legs to the man himself.

Both water chevrotain and bay duiker must be taken whole before the head of the house, who returns all except the two hind legs. Much the same rule applies to Ogilby's duiker, except that this is always taken to the hunter's father. Should the latter be dead, there is no obligation to offer it to the head of the house.

The rules about porcupine, blue duikerbok, and monitor flesh are similar, but not so strictly kept.

Elephant, buffalo, yellow-backed duiker, pangolin, civet cat, and genet must also be brought before the head of the house.

Should these rules be infringed, a Juju will catch the hunter and give him a sickness, from which he will not recover except by confession and sacrifice. In the case of a genet, the illness is supposed to take the form of elephantiasis.

APPENDIX A

The tabu on harnessed antelope has been described on p. 142

Should a man keep to himself a male drill ape or chimpanzee, certain death is supposed to follow, and an illness from which recovery is unlikely, if the kill be female.

When a leopard or python is killed, the heart and gall are cut out, buried in a deep hole, and the earth beaten over them. Anyone eating of these would die (see p 27). Only slaves eat leopards; for free men they are tabu.

Of birds, the Monkey-killing Eagle and the Greater Plantain-eater must be taken to the head of the house.

Neither man nor woman may feed on any scavenger bird, such as the vulture, nor on the owl, because it is a witch's familiar If killed, the latter must be offered up on two posts at the entrance to the town. The Kingfisher also is forbidden food. When killed its skull is dried, powdered, mixed with leaves and given as cough medicine.

Members of the Juju Mfam are forbidden to eat the bird called "Aru"

Many persons may not eat the fish called Ecchan or Mbonn, the heads of which are ground up and used as "medicine."

Of tabus for men alone, the principal ones are—the fish Eddokk, of which, should a hunter eat, he will be killed in the bush, and crab, "The Father of all Jujus," the eating of which would cut a man off from partaking in any ceremonies.

A woman may not eat (a) nandinia binotata, as a child born afterwards would surely die;

(b) Wild cat, lest she should become barren.

(c) Anything killed by leopard or wild cat, otherwise her child would be still-born.

(d) Crocodile, as her child would be born with a scaly skin and die.

(e) The Greater Plantain-eater.

(f) The first thing caught in her husband's new trap (see story p. 114).

The greater number of these tabus probably arose from totemic causes, others from sanitary reasons, and some, obviously, from the desire of the old men to obtain a full share of what was killed by their juniors.

APPENDIX A

Tabu on Fish for Men, Flesh for Women

One day Obassi Nsi called all the people on earth together. He said, " I make a law concerning the food which is proper for you. Of the fruits of the earth you may eat, both men and women, but of living creatures women alone may eat fish, and men only may eat the flesh of animals."

Now there was a woman named Aiya Ita, who had a husband named Atu Utup (Efik word for hunter). One day each of them went out, she to the river, and he to the bush. After she had been fishing for a little while she caught a fine fish. This she took home and boiled in her pot. When it was done, she ate some of it, and some she left for the morrow.

In the evening Atu Utup came home. He had hunted all day but killed nothing, and was very hungry. He saw the fish which his wife had left, and he took a piece and ate it.

Now a bird came out of the bush, and settled on the branch of a tree which grew close to the house. Through a small hole in the wall he saw what the man had done. At once he flew away to Obassi Nsi, and told what he had seen.

Obassi sent for the hunter and said, " You have gone against the rule which I made, that no man should eat fish. Therefore you must die."

After the man was dead, Obassi thought " The rule that I had made is too hard for my people." So he sent and called them again before him, and said:

" From to-day I remove the law. Men may eat fish. Women may eat meat. Only let no woman eat the genitals of any animal slain by a hunter. Should she do so, the hunter will never be able to kill again, unless he finds out from the charm who it is who has transgressed my law and makes due sacrifice, that the curse may be taken off him."

APPENDIX B.

CLUBS (OKUM, PL. AKUM).

The Oban Clubs may be taken as typical of those in most Ekoi towns. They may be roughly divided into (A) those only resuscitated for special occasions, and (B) those in constant use.

A.

The following are ancient institutions revived under special circumstances, for instance on the death of a member of the club, an important chief, or the funeral customs of such :—

1. "Oshum njum ka etemm. Oba eku ka nju,
    "Draw thing in bush. Come die in house.
    Owomm okpaw"
    Want die."

i.e., When a hunter shoots animals in the bush, he only comes to his house to die, if he fails to satisfy the inhabitants. The meaning is that members of his household would want to share in his kill, and would probably poison him if he did not content them.

This was originally a club for avenging the murder of its members, and was a very powerful association in olden days. When a dance is given, big rattles are worn, and should a member put on an Okum dress, without the permission of the President, the superstition is that the dress would stick to him and could not be laid aside until the old men had made sacrifices in atonement.

2. "Ewaw ekabomm 'ne."
    "(Name of Okum) not cut a person."

When the dance proper to this is given, an old man must get water, mix medicine in it, and pour it over the bodies of the members, while repeating the above words. The Okum bears a large cane erection on his head. The fine of a ram is levied on anyone who should cross in front of the dancers.

3.   "Okpe   etuma."
            "(Name of Okum) jumps."

This club is so called because the Okum must never stand still. He is always accompanied by two girl attendants, bearing looking glasses. One goes before and one behind.

4.   "Orui.   Achibbi wa njimm."
            "Go.   Turn   to   back."

"Go and come back." These words are said to a member who, after breaking a rule, is sent to fetch the fine ordained as punishment. The name has also a secondary meaning of "back-biting" during the man's absence.

5. "Ikadum." The Okum wears a skull. This club gave war dances, especially when its members came back with the heads of enemies. Meetings are never held in the town, but in the bush near-by. At all celebrations guns are fired.

6. "Ayunga." On the death of a member, his family must pay one goat, 20 yams and 4 bottles of palm-wine to the club. The eldest son is elected in his father's place. This society used formerly to serve as executioners for those condemned to death by the γερουσια.

7. "Esere Ise." No one could be found who was willing to explain the meaning of this, but the words appear to point to the practise of enforcing the trial by ordeal. Its functions were only given as those of a dancing club.

8 "Ukwa." This is the lodge of a Calabar club. Members dance with long swords to the accompaniment of two large drums.

9.   "Adia.   Akere   idemm."
            "Eat.   Think of yourself."

A dining club. The name signifies that, while being entertained in another man's house, you must remember that it will soon be your turn to act as host.

10. "Erong-Isonn" (Efik). "Knee earth." This is a dancing club. When plays are given, rattles are worn above the knee.

11.   "Ukai   ke isonn obio, Oban " (Efik).
           "Difficult on earth   town, Oban."

. A dancing club, started by an age class whose members had got into trouble with the Chiefs of Oban, and were heavily fined in consequence.

12.   " Nchibbi   achi ebai."
        "(Name of Okum) heads two."

The Okum wears a large two-faced head, one side male and the other female, decorated with the feathers of the Greater Plantain-eater. The dancers hold matchets and guns and fire the latter at intervals.

No woman can belong to any of these clubs, and none save the free-born, after passing middle age, to any except the last mentioned.

B.

The following are those most prominent at the present day. Any man, free-born, or "member," can join them, while to the first women may also belong.

1. "Ikkpai," Whip. At dances every member carries a whip. The Okum wears two white feathers above a carved head. This association was formerly more powerful than now.

2. "Utap-Anam." "Touch take from," *i.e.*, Should you injure our club, we will fine you.

This was originally started by two age classes. Women may neither join in the dances nor see the instruments proper to the club. These are long hollow pieces of wood, which, when rubbed together, produce a loud harsh sound. Juju worship is connected with the rites.

3. "Ekang." When the Okum comes out, a young palm leaf and other prickly leaves are tied about him. Should he meet a non-member, he catches hold of the man, so that the leaves should scratch and hurt him.

4. "Ekkpo Njawhaw" (Efik). "Ghosts break," a lodge of an Ibibio club. A common plan to increase membership of this society is to take the Okum to the house of a friend who is a non-member. Should the latter be unprepared to provide entertainment without notice for so large a number of guests, his plates and calabashes are broken by the club. To this proceeding the association probably owes its name, as the damaged property looks as if broken to lay on a grave for the use of the ghosts.

5. "Obbonn" (Efik and Ekoi). "Chief." This club dances at night, and no woman may be present.

APPENDIX B

6. "Itiatt Obbonn." "Stones of the Chief." Connected with the last-named society. Only old men can become members, and a considerable amount of Juju worship is mixed up with its rites. There is no dancing

7. "Angbo." It is impossible to learn the meaning of this word. Every town has a lodge. In many none but adults are allowed to join. Dances are always given at night, and no woman may be present.

8. "Nsikpe." A new and powerful club brought from Onun, near Calabar. The Okum wears a tall cane erection on his head, and much Juju is connected with its rites.

9 "Mfuor." This is specially devoted to the worship of the great Juju "Asunga." It is very powerful in some towns.

10. "Ekkpa." This is a powerful club in which the worship of Nimm Asam is very strong. It differs from the others in being a woman's club (see p. 225).

"Members" have many clubs of their own. The mysteries of one of these, named "Kpifonn," may be witnessed by no freeborn man nor by any woman.

All clubs have different tunes and peculiar ways of beating the drums, so that even at a distance it is easy to tell which of the many societies is holding a celebration.

APPENDIX C.

ANTHROPOMETRY.

BELOW is given an abstract of the more important measurements of inhabitants of the Oban District. Fuller information will be found in an article entitled "On certain Physical Characters of the Negroes of the Congo Free State and Nigeria," in the *Journal of the Royal Anthropological Institute*, January to June, 1911, in which Professor Keith, M.D., kindly subjected my measurements to an exhaustive analysis; except those of the Ekuri, which will be published in a later number of the *Journal* :—

No.	Tribe.	Head. L.	Head. B.	Head. Ind.	Face. L.	Face. B.	Face. Ind.	Nose. —	Nose. —	Nose. —	Stat.	Span.	Ind.
24	Ekoi	191	146	76·2	61	139	43·5	45	43	95·9	1687	1761	74
10	Kabila (Ojo)	195	144	74·0	64	143	44·7	47	46	99·2	1717	1765	48
20	Ekuri	194	145	74·6	59	141	41·9	43	47	108·3	1654	1722	68
17	Korawp (Ododop)	195	146	74·9	61	138	44·3	45	45	99·3	1644	1754	110
4	Uyanga	194	145	75·2	54	139	38·8	45	46	101·3	1658	1702	44
2	Efik	193	148	76·4	56	124	43·5	42	42	101·6	1702	1753	51
1	Ibibio	190	153	80·5	57	133	42·9	44	45	102·2	1753	1804	51
2	Ibo	190	145	76·1	64	135	47·9	47	46	88·5	1676	1740	64

APPENDIX D.
ORTHOGRAPHY.

The system of orthography employed in this book, with the few exceptions mentioned below, is that laid down by the Royal Geographical Society and fully explained in " Hints to Travellers." As stated therein, the broad features of the system are :—

(a) " That vowels are pronounced as in Italian and consonants as in English.

(b) Every letter is pronounced, and no redundant letters are introduced.

(c) Two accents only are used:

1. The acute, to denote the syllable on which stress is laid."

2. The sign ˘ used by me over the short and open u, a, i, and o, when followed by ng, to avoid the more awkward nng.

To express the different sounds of the vowel u three ways are used :—

(a) When pronounced as in "up" or "lull," the following consonant is doubled, as usual, or the sign ˘ is employed;

(β) For the sound as in "pull" or "full," no alteration is made;

(γ) While for the u sounded as in "flute," a long mark is placed over the vowel, thus ū.

Before some consonants a sound like a rough breathing may be heard, which, in the case of m or n, sometimes produces the effect of doubling the consonant. This sound has been marked with a rough breathing as "'Mi" moon.

At least two distinct tones are prevalent in the language, and serve to differentiate words spelt in the same way. Thus Nki on a high note means dormouse, on a low note, lion.

As with us, words spoken with a rising inflection denote

questions, *e g.*, "Akaba ? Is he coming ?" while without the raised tone, it merely states the fact, "He is coming."

Interrogation is often shown by the use of the word "na" at the beginning of each sentence.

As a rule equal stress is laid on all syllables.

The letters b and p, r, d and t, sh and ch are often interchangeable, as are also, though more rarely, l and r ; or it may be more accurate to say that sounds exist midway between these, not accurately represented by either. The same man, too, in repeating a word, will often interchange consonants.

A final vowel is elided when the following word begins with another vowel.

The detailed system of phonetics employed by some authorities does not seem applicable in the case of the tribes under consideration, since pronunciation varies considerably even in the same town.

APPENDIX E.

A SHORT GRAMMAR OF THE EKOI LANGUAGE.

Nouns.

Nouns are usually derived from verbs. The most common ways are :

1. By prefixing a vowel to the verb root, *e g.*,

    Kott, love (verb).   Okott, love (noun).
    Ji, go.   Eji, place.
    Siri, speak.   Esiri, story.

2. By prefixing a consonant, generally n or m, to the verb root, *e.g.*,

    Fonn, have.   Mfonni, possessor.
    Chott, to speak.   Nchott, speaker
    Berk, cut.   Mberk, cutter

3. By prefixing e and affixing m, um, umm, emm, or imm to the verb root, *e.g.*—

    Maghe, leave.   Emaghum, abandonment.
    Yimm, do.   Eyimmum, action.
    Fap, go.   Efapumm, departure.

Words formed in the latter way are verbal nouns, and may be used as infinitives.

Plurals are formed by changing the prefixes as follows:

Singular.	Plural.
O	A
M	A
E	M
N	O
N	A
M	O
E	A

&c. &c., &c.

Examples will be found in the vocabulary.

S.B.

Gender is shown in some few cases by the use of different words, *e.g.*,

   Nse, father.   Nyenn, mother.
   Ntemm, male friend. Nat, female friend,

but is usually denoted by

   Num (plural, arum), male.
   Nkai („ akai), female,

placed before the word qualified, *e.g.*,

   Num mfŏng, bull. Nkai mfŏng, cow.
   Num njaw, he dog. Nkai njaw, bitch,

except in the case of

   'Ne-num, man (plural, ane-arum),
   'Ne-nkai, woman („ ane-akai).

No trace of declension has been found.

ADJECTIVES.

Adjectives agree in number with the substantive qualified, and form their plurals in the same way as the nouns, *e.g.*,

Singular.	Plural.
Eébi, bad.	Abi.
Enopp, good.	Anopp.
Ndam, long.	Adam or Aram.
Iiuk, small	Nduk.
Ibonne, little.	Mbonne,

with the exception of those formed, as is usual in the present day, by doubling the noun, *e g.*,

   Ewak, quickness.   Ewak-ewak, quick.
   Efebbum, cleverness. Efebbum-efebbum, clever.

These never change in the plural.

Degrees of comparison are expressed by the introduction of other words; the comparative by "Achinge," "surpasses," *e.g.*,

  "'We enopp achinge 'wa."

  " He good surpasses you," (*i.e.*, He is better than you), the superlative by Mfonne, very, Etimm, oldest or last, or by repetition of the word.

  Examples:— Mfonne nyenn, very good.
       Etimm eébi, very bad.
       Ndam-ndam, very long.
       Ngpuk-ngpuk, very short.

APPENDIX E

The rules for the position of adjectives are very complicated. Some always proceed the noun, while others must follow it. A third class comprises those placed either before or after, probably according to the Ekoi ideas of euphony.

PRONOUNS.

The personal pronouns are as follows:—

Singular.	Plural.
'Me, I.	Ut or ud, we.
'We, thou.*	Un, you.
'We, he, she, it.	Abaw, they,

when used as subject to the verb, and by themselves;

'Ngam, me.	Ut or ud, us.
'Wa, thee.	Un, you.
'We, him her, it.	Abaw, them,

when governed by a verb or preposition.

The interrogative pronouns Enne? who? Bagha? which? Jenn? what? do not change. The other pronouns vary according to the category, to which the word qualified belongs, as can be seen in the following list:—

CATEGORIES.†

Possessive Pronouns.

Meaning.		1	2	3	4	5	6	7
My, mine	(S)	Oma	Éama	Éjama	Ífima	Iima	Áwama	Áama
,, ,,	(P)	Ama	Áwama	Áama	Íima	Ama	Ama	Ama
		or		or		or	or	or
		Áama		Éama		Áama	Áama	Áama
Thy, thine	(S)	Oa	Ea	Eja	Ifa	Ima	Oba	Ama
,, ,,	(P)	Aba	Oba	Ama	Ima	Ama	Ama	Ama
His, her, hers, it, its	(S)	Oe	Egye	Eje	Ife	Ime	Obe	Ame
,, ,,	(P)	Abe	Ebe	Ame	Ime	Ame	Ame	Ame
			or					
			obe					
Our, ours	(S)	Ora	Egyira	Éjira	Ífira	Ímira	Óbira	Ámira
				or	or	or	or	or
				Éjara	Ífara	Ímara	Óbara	ámara

* ' 'We, thou,' is spoken in a high tone, " 'we, he," in a low tone
† See p 422.

420 APPENDIX E

Our, ours (P) Ábara Óbara Ámara Ímara Ámara Ámara Ámara
　　　　　　or　　　or　　　or
　　　　　　Áwara Ámara Ébıra
　　　　　　　　　　　　or
　　　　　　　　　　　　Égıra
Your, yours (S) Óana Égyına Éjına Ífina Imına Óbına Ámina
　　　　　　　　　　　　or
　　　　　　　　　　　　Éjana
　„　　„　(P) Ábına Óbına Égına Mıana Amına Ámina Amına
　　　　　　　or　　　or
　　　　　　　Ábana Ébina
Their, theirs (S) Abaw Abaw Abaw Abaw Abaw Abaw Abaw
　„　　„　(P) „　　„　　„　　„　　„　　„　　„

Relative Pronouns.

Who, which (S) Nyaw Nyı Njı Mfi Mı Mbı Ma
　„　　„　(P) Mba Mbı Ma Mı Ma Ma Ma

Demonstrative Pronouns.

This, the same as Who, Which
That　　(S) Anyaw Anyi Ajı Afi Amı Abı Ama
　„　　(P) Aba Abi Anyı Ami Ama Ama Ama
What kind of?
　　　　(S) Nyonn Nyınn Njenn Mfunn Munn Mbunn Munn
　„　　(P) „　　„　　„　　„　　„　　„　　„

The *Reflexive* Pronouns are:

Myself	(masc. or fem.) Ka-bıjı	éama.
Thyself	„　　„	eba
Himself, herself, itself	„　　„	ebe
Ourselves	„　　„	ébara.
Yourselves	„　　„	ébina.
Themselves	„　　„	abaw.

Pronouns follows the words to which they refer.

VERBS.

All verbs are conjugated in the same way as the example given below:—

I do, 'me nyımm. Thou dost, 'we oyımm. He, she, or it does, we ayımm We do, ut eyımm. You do, un oyımm. They do, abaw ayımm.

APPENDIX E

I do not: 'me nkayimm, 'we okai yimm, 'we akai yimm, ut ekai yimm, un okai yimm, abaw akai yimm.

I am doing. 'me nki yimm, 'we oki yimm, 'we aki yimm, ut eki yimm, un oki yimm, abaw aki yimm.

I am not doing: 'me nka yimm, 'we okai yimm, &c.

I have done. 'me ba nyimm, 'we ba oyimm, 'we ba ayimm, ut ba eyimm, un ba oyimm, abaw ba ayimm.

I have not done: 'me be nkai yimm, 'we be okai yimm, &c.

I have been doing · 'me na nyimmi, 'we na oyimmi, &c.

I have not been doing: 'me nka yimm, &c.

I had done: 'me nde nyimm, 'we ore oyimm, 'we are ayimm, ut ere eyim, un ore oyimm, abaw are ayimm.

I had not done. 'me ka ndaw nyimm, 'we ka oraw oyimm, 'we ka araw ayimm, &c.

I had been doing. 'me nde na nyimm, 'we ore na oyimm, &c.

I had not been doing: 'me are nkai yimm, 'we are okai yimm, 'we are akai yimm, &c.

I shall do · 'me tikk (or tukk) nyimm, 'we tikk oyimm, &c.

I shall not do: 'me tikk mawyimm, 'we tikk omawyimm, 'we tikk amawyimm, ut tikk emawyimm, un tikk omawyimm, abaw tikk amawyimm.

I am about to do. 'me njawe nyimm, 'we ojjawe oyimm, 'we ajawe ayimm, ut ejawe eyimm, un ojjawe oyimm, abaw ajawe ayimm.

I am not about to do. 'me mawjawe nyimm, 'we omawjawe oyimm, &c.

I shall be doing: 'me tikk njawe nyimm, 'we tikk ojjawe oyimm, &c.

I shall not be doing: 'me tikk mawjawe nyimm, 'we tikk omawjawe oyimm, &c.

I shall have done: 'me ta ba nyimm, 'we ta ba oyimm, &c

I shall not have done: 'me kpe nkai yimm, 'we kpe okai yimm, &c.

I would do: 'me kun nyimm, 'we kun oyimm, &c.

I would not do: 'me kun mawjawe nyimm, 'we kun omawjawe oyimm, &c.

I would be doing: 'me kun njawe nyimm, 'we kun ojjawe oyimm, &c.
I would not be doing: 'me kun mawjawe nyimm, &c.
I would have done: 'me kun ba nyimm, 'we kun ba oyimm, &c.
I would not have done: 'me kun nkai nyimm, &c.
I would have been doing: 'me kun ba njawe nyimm, &c.
I would not have been doing: 'me kun mawjawe nyimm, &c.

Imperative.

Do, yimm; Do ye, yimm un.

Infinitive and Verbal Noun.

To do or doing, eyimmum.

No sign of a passive voice has been discovered.

"A" is added to the verb when followed by a plural object, *e.g.*, 'Me nyimm njum, I do a thing; 'Me nyimma mbimm, I do things.

SYNTAX.

The construction of sentences is very simple, as may be seen from the interlined stories shortly to be published. Conjunctions are little used. The order of words closely resembles that of English.

NUMERALS.

The Ekoi divide all things into seven principal categories or classes. The first nine numerals are inflected according to the category to which the word they qualify belongs:—

CATEGORIES.

No.	1	2	3	4	5	6	7
1.	wat	yit	jutt	futt	mat	butt	mat or butt
2.	abai	ebai	ebai	mbai	abai	abai	abai
3.	asa	esa	esa	nsa	asa	asa	asa
4.	ani	eni	eni	ni	ani	ani	ani
5.	aronn	eronn	eronn	ndonn	aronn	aronn	aronn
6.	asáasa	esáesa	esáesa	nsansa	asáasa	asáasa	asáasa
7.	anighaasa	enighaesa	enighaesa	'nighansa	anighaasa	anighaasa	anighaasa
8.	anighani	enighaeni	enighaeni	'nighaani	anighaani	anighaani	anighaani
9.	aronnani	eronneni	eronneni	ndonneni	aronnani	aronnani	aronnani.

The remaining numerals are uninflected and will be found in the vocabulary. From these it will be seen that Ekoi and

APPENDIX E

Ododop, unlike neighbouring tribes, have built up their numerical system principally on groups of three and four.

There are no proper ordinals, but the following phrases are used.—

The first cow, ndagha-mba (the leader on the road) mfŏng.
The second cow, mfŏng ennyere (following).
The third cow, ennyere-ennyere mfŏng.
The fourth cow, mfŏng ennyere mfŏng esa.
The fifth cow, mfŏng ennyere mfŏng eni.

Numeral adverbs are formed by the word ntimm:—

Once, ntimm yit.
Twice, ntimm ebai.
Thrice, ntimm esa, &c.

APPENDIX F.

VOCABULARIES OF THE SIX TRIBES IN THE OBAN DISTRICT.

List of Words chosen by Sir Harry Johnston, G.C.M.G., K.C.B.

For Orthography, see Appendix D.

English.	Ekoi.	Kwa.	Efik.	Ekuri.	Ododop.	Uyanga.
Ant (black)	Nsiang, Nkung	Nsiang	Iyong	Unanaia	Ekkannakann (buwan) bū-kannakann	Awkokkoi
Plural	Osiang, Okung	Osiang	,,			Bawkokkoi
Ant (white)	Ngke	Nke	Nkakatt	—	Etenge	Ejja
Plural	Oke	Ake	,,	—	Būtenge	Boja
Antelope— Ogilby's duiker	Nsun	Nson	Okoyo	Inommi (antelope in general)	Enom	Ebin
Plural	Osun	Oson		Unommi	Punum	Bobinn
Harnessed antelope	Ngū	Ngo	Edopp	—	Iku	Adifan
Plural	Ogū	Ogo		—	Muku	Osboding
Bay duiker	Etuk	Etuk	Ebet-okoyo	—	Inemn	Metwina
Plural	,,	,,		—	Munenn	Baturna
Blue duikerbok	Ise	Ise	Oso	—	Yut	Etuba
Plural	Nse	Nse	—	—	Myut	Botuba
Yellow-backed duiker	Nkŏngam	—	—	—	Kiŏngaa	—
Plural	Awkŏngam	—	—	—	Biŏngaa	—
Ape (drill)	Nshum	—	Nsimbo	Edum	Etum	Eyum
Plural	Oshum	—	,,	Odum	Būtum	Boum
Ape (chimpanzee)	Nyokk	—	Idiokk	Ubani	Obinn	Ufurna
Plural	Oiyokk	—	,,	Abani	Bubinn	Bafurna

APPENDIX F

Arm .	Obbaw	Obbaw	Ubokk	Obaw	Ubaw	Obbaw
Plural	Abo	Abo	"	Obo	Ibaw	Babaw
Arrow .	Mbom	Mbawm	Idang	Lobuk	Katai	Gūna
Plural	Abom	Abawn	"	Labuk	Butai	Bagūna
Axe .	Efuk	Efok	Ekūri	Iban	Chuun	Ife
Plural	Mfuk	Afok	"	Uban	Ichun	Bufe
Baboon .	Monni Nshum	—	Ekpiri nsimbo	—	—	—
Plural	Abonn ojū	—				
Back .	Njmm	Ngyim	Edem	Lam	Inum	Eram
Plural	Ojmm	Ogyim	"	Lam abombe	Munum	Boram
Banana .	Nsūri	Egawme ebe	Mboro	Ekwom mokarara	Lundouni	Guama midikuri
Plural	Asūri	Agawme ebe	"	Okwom	Kundouni	Bōoma
Beard .	'Ngū ngeg (hair chin)	'Ngū eyat	Ntang-ebek	Ebomm	Arukanyan	Dūfem
Plural						
Bee .	Nkoni	Nkoni	Awkwawk	Nbomm	Ūwan	Dafem
Plural	Okkonn	Akkonn	"	Okwunkwana	Soi	Eyungkawna
				Akwunkwana	Soi keetchauwi	Bawyung-kawna
Belly .	Awya	Awa	Idibi	Ūtū	Būgūn	Dutū
Plural	Aiya	Aa	Inuen	Natū	Kommpawn	Dafū
Bird .	Innonn, enonn, nnonn	Inonn		Kononn	Itott	Odawn
Plural	Nnonn	Nnonn	Iynpp	Lanonn	Muntott	Badawn
Blood .	Aiyung	Aung		Kadji	Munkchi	Bu
Plural				Wadji	Mun ketchauwi	Labui
Body .	Biji	Begye	Idem	Mkpa	Beekett	Ekpa
Plural				Mkpa ebomm		Bokpa
Bone .	Ekipp	Ekipp	Awkpaw	Echankauo	Kūwi	Eyamn
Plural	Akipp	Akipp		Ochankauo	Būwi	Bawyamm
Bow .	Oik	Oik	Ūtiga	Unekk	Unkk	Fran
Plural	Aik	Aik		Lanekk	Nnekki	Boran
Brains .	Aronn	Aronn	Mfune	Kūjitokk	Munbopp	Dijawn
Plural	"	"				Tawawn

APPENDIX F

VOCABULARIES OF THE SIX TRIBES IN THE OBAN DISTRICT—*Continued*.

English.	Ekoi.	Kwa.	Efik.	Eturi.	Ododop.	Uyanga.
Breast	Ngang (chest or breast)	Ngang (chest or breast)	Ikpanesit	Lekonntū	Ikung	Etin
	Ebe (woman's, for suckling)	Ebe (woman's)	Eba (woman's)	—	—	—
Plural	Abe	Abe	—	Lakonntū	Mūkung	Botin
Brother	Monn-nyenn-i-ne-num (child, mother, person, male)	Monn-i-nyenn-i-nimm	Eyeneka erenn	Gwoban	Aminkai	Apawdijaw
Plural	Abonn-i-any-enn-ane-erum	Abonn-i-nyen-anaom	Nditaw eka irenn			
			Eyeneka erenn	Buoban	Baminkai	Otunadur
Buffalo	Mfung	Mfóng	Editim	—	—	—
Plural	Ofung	Ofóng	,,	—	—	—
Buttocks	Nkiggi ndipp (fresh meat of genitals)	'Nip	Etak	Lagaliba	Chabidisien	Ofukpai
Plural	Akiggi ndipp	Oup	,,	,,	Muncha-bidisien	Dafukpai
Canoe	Okpii	Okpee	Ubom	Ekpokk	Uwan	Okpūga
Plural	Akpii	Akpee	,,	Okpokk	Nwan	Bakpūga
Cat	Angwa	Angwa	Angwa	Anwa	Anwa	Anwa
Plural	,,	,,	,,	,,	Nanwa	Banwa
Chief	Ntui	Ntoe	Awbóng	Ogbun	Obonn	Ofor
Plural	Atui	Atoe	Mbóng	Agbun	Bobonn	Baforde
Child	Monn	Monn	Eyenn	Gogorra	Kweenn	Goe
Plural	Abonn	Abonn	Ndito	Boborru	Kwanabenn	Jaóe
Cloth	Effaw	Efaw	Oñóng	Lojello	Etta	Durba
Plural	Mfaw	Afaw	,,	Lijello	Ita	Deba
Cocoanut palm	Mbang-i-makara (white man)	Mbang-i-mawkara	Isip makara	Nkau-abashe	Chn-okat	Eyam okarara
Plural	Obbang amakara	Obbang amawkara	,,	—	Ichñ-okat	Boam ,,

APPENDIX F

Cold . . .		Edyuk	Euk	Tũep	Bisi	Payawe
Plural		,,	Mfam	Idut	Lūse	Lapyawa
Country . .		Mfam (town)	Offam	Me-idut	Nise	Wunta
Plural		Offam	Mfõng	Uman enang	Ewumm	Bowunta
Cow . . .		Mfõng	Offõng	—	Bũwumm	Ebawrn
Plural		Offõng	Nyipp	Effiom	Kũung	Bobawn
Crocodile .		Nyipp	Oyipp	,,	Biung	Etagaram
Plural		Oyipp				Botagaram
Date palm (none).						
Day . . .		Ofu	Ofo	Usenn	Deakwe	Ti
Plural		Mfinn	Mfen	—	Iakwe	Bati
Devil . . .		—	—	—	Erut	—
Plural					Burut	
Dog . . .		Njaw	Mbiaw	Ebũa	Ebbia	Appia
Plural		Ojjaw	Awbiaw	—	Bũbia	Bopia
Donkey (none)						
Door . . .		Mba	Nyaw mba	Enyinn usãng	Itun	Itam
Plural		Awba	Anyaw oba	—	Mutum	Botemm
Dream . .		Ndemm	Ndemm	Ndap	Durau	Itamofii
Plural		,,	,,	,,	Irau	Botamofii
Drum . .		Ekpiri, Awkam	Ekpera, Awkam	Ekawmaw, Ibit	Ikommo (small), Iuwum (large)	Ifunn, logbo (small, large)
Plural		Nkpiri, Nkam	Nkpera, Akam	—	Mukommo, niwum	Bofunn, dogbo
Sing. . .		Ichumi, Egyūk	—	Mbombo	Iban	—
Plural		Nchumi, Ngyūk	—	—	Abanbo	—
Ear . . .		Otung	Otõng	Utõng	Lũnung	Orung
Plural		Atung	Atõng	Nsenn	Inung	Dirung
Egg . . .		Eji	Egyi	Enenn	Essienn	Edunnti
Plural		Aji	Agyi	Enenn	Busienn	Badunnti
Elephant .		Njokk	Ngyokk	Ifuaw	Enyi	Idi
Plural		Ojjokk	Ogyokk	,,	Bunyi	Bodi
Excrement		Abung	Abing	—	Usienn	Definn
Plural		,,	,,		Nesienn	Dafinn

APPENDIX F

VOCABULARIES OF THE SIX TRIBES IN THE OBAN DISTRICT—*Continued.*

English.	Ekoi.	Kwa.	Efik.	Ekuri.	Ododop.	Uyanga.
Eye	Egyitt	Eitt	Enyinn	Ije	Neenn	Chien
Plural	Amitt	Amitt	—	Nye	Deenn	Dachiena
Face	Ochi	Osi	Iso	Lulo	Dunyaw	Ludi
Plural	,,	Asi	—	Lilo	Inyaw	Ladi
Fat	Afomm	Afomm	Isek, Ikpŏng, aran	Una	Mŭne	Baŭ
Plural	,,	,,	—	Echanuna	Nenne	,,
Father	Nse, Nta (old word)	Nse	Etc	Ata	Omona	Aüta
Plural	Ase	Ase	Mete	Ata gamibi	Bomona	Boita
Fear	Efup	Efop	Ndikk	Kegwunn	Bndiemm	Ebera
Plural	Iniri (or inira) obbaw	Inira awbaw	nuenubokk	Ogwunn	—	Bobera
Finger	'Niri (or 'nira) awbaw	Nira awbaw	—	Iuanai	Dawnaw	Edadoi
Plural	Ngun	Ngonn	—	Tinanai	Munonai	Bodadoi
Fire	Agun	Agonn	Ikaug	Ekkonn	Diun	Duun
Plural	Nsi	Nsi	—	Nkonn	Niun	Djuun
Fish	Osi	Osi	Iyakk	Iballe	Ekwenun	Ifurrdi
Plural	Ekatt	Ekat, Eyara	—	Uballe	Bŭkwemm	Bofurrdi
Foot	Akatt	Akat, Ayara	Ukut	Loonnkill	Iwan	Obawn
Plural	Eékui (primeval) Eétinm	Ekoeya	Akai Ikott (primeval)	Laonnkill	Bŭkpat	Ebawn
Forest	Akui, Atimm	Akoeya	—	Lelang	Urum	Etam
Plural	Nkokk	Nkokk	—	Lalang	—	Botam
Fowl	Okkokk	Okkokk	Unen	Hononn	Unonn	Oddawn
Plural	Esang	Nsang	—	Lanonn	Nononn	Dadawn
Frog	Nsang	Awsang	Ikwott	Ikpawpaw	Ansang	Ikpawpaw
Plural	Nkabansi	Nkimanse	—	Ukpawpaw	Nansang	Bokpawpaw
Ghost	Akabansi	Akimanse	Ekkpo	Ubŭ	Awkanni	Ubije
Plural			—	Abu	Bakanni	Babije

APPENDIX F

	Nkae-mbūi	Nkae-mbóe	Oman-ebutt	Ijennmian	Omanebun	Efonnaba
Goat (she)	Nkai-mbūi (female goat)	Akae-obóe	—	Ajanmian	Pamabaubun	Bofonnaba
Plural	Akai-obūi	Ninm-i-mbóe	—	Ujandam	Ikak	Obare
Goat (he)	Effam-i-mbūi	Aom-obóe	Okpo-ebutt	Ajandam	Munkak	Ebare
Plural	Arum-obūi					
God (Obassi)	Obassi	Obassi, Asi	Abassi	Eburukpabi	Obassi	Owase
Plural	„	„	„			Bobase
Grass	Ewangi	Anganga	Nyanyanga	Tiane	Karam	Ijeen
Plural	Awangi				Būram	Bugween
Ground	Nsi	Nse	Isōng	—	Būke	Etoii
Plural	Asi	Ase		Loshe		Botoii
Ground-nut	Ifut	Mbang-sang	Mbansang	Lishe		Afokpa
Plural	—	—	—	Afakpa (Aro)	(same as Efik)	Bafokpa
Guinea-fowl (none)						—
Gun	Ngun	Ngonn	Ikang	Ekkonn	Diun	Duun
Plural	Agun	Agonn	—	Nkonn	—	Dijuun
Hair	'Nyu, Anyott (on head),(on body)	'Nu, Amiott	Idett	Li	Ninn	Ding
Plural	—	—	—	—	—	—
Hand	Obbaw	Obbaw	Ubokk	Ebakonn	Ubaw	Boding
Plural	Abaw	Abaw	—	Nbakonn	Ibaw	Lapiada
Head	Echi	Esi	Ibul	Letū	Dono	Bafiada
Plural	Achi	Asi	—	Latū	Nono	Delo
Heart	Mbōngi	Mbīngi	Essitt	Lekonnduli	Erumsinn	Dalo
Plural	Obōngi	Obōngi	—	Lakonnduli	Munsinn	Etangam
Heel	Ndipp ekat (root leg)	'Nipp ekat	Nditing-ukott	Laanchann	Kan-kuwan	Botangam
	Adipp akat	Aup akat	Nditing-ikpat	Laanchano	—	Labano-cheen
Hide	Ngū (nyam = animal)	Ngo (nyamm)	Ikpa (unanm)	Echankpa	Kūup	Dabano-cheen
Plural	Ogū(onnyamm = animal)	Ago (onnyamm)	—	Nchankpa	Iyup	Iyum
						Bowawm

VOCABULARIES OF THE SIX TRIBES IN THE OBAN DISTRICT—*Continued*.

English.	Ekoi.	Kwa.	Efik.	Ekuri.	Ododop.	Uyanga.
Hippopotamus	Njokk aiipp (elephant river)	Ngyokk aa	Isantim	—	—	—
Plural	Ojiolkk aüpp	Ogyokk aa				
Honey	Akhu-okkonn	Aku-okkonn	Aran-ukwawk	Okwunkwana	Mune	Edone
Plural						eyungkawna
Horn	Inyekk	Imiekk	Inuk	Libije	Masũi	Bawdawm "
Plural	Anyekk	Amiekk		Labije	Duyikk	Dabi
Horse	Mfõng-i-	Mfõng-i-	Enang makara		Uyikk	
	makara	mawkara			Ewunm-okat	
Plural	(ox, white man)				(cow, white	
	Offõng	Offõng			man)	
	amakara	amawkara				
House	Nju	Ngyo	Ufokk	Etũo	Enawn	Erraw
Plural	Oju	Ogyo		Ntũo	Inawn	Borraw
Hunger	Njai	Ngyae	Mbiong	Ogwaw	Mungwo	Bujaw
Hyena (none)						
Iron	Esene	Etũna	Ukwak	Elamo	Kopũpũ	Aam
Plural	Asene	Atũna				Baam
Island	Isũo	Isũo	Isũo esikk			
Plural	Nsũo	Nsũo				
Ivory	Ibãng	Iban	Inuk (enen)	Innilala	Duyikk	Dejenn (tusks)
Plural	Abãng	Aban	'Nuk "	Unilalaje	Denyi	Dajenn
Knee	Erung	Erung	Edong	Udandau	Dorum	Debung
Plural	Arung	Arung		Ndandan	Norum	Dabung
Knife	Itimi	Itima	Ikwa (ekpri)	Olamogwaw	Erisi	Egwoi
			(small)			
Plural	Ntimi	Ntima	Mkpri ikwa	Alamogwaw	Burissi	Bogwoi

APPENDIX F

		Ekat	Idibi-Ukott	Hoonn	Uwan	Obbawn
Leg	Ekat (ankle to knee) Ichomme	Akat		Nwun	Iwan	Dibawn
Leopard	Akat	Mgbe	Ekkpe	Ekkpe (Efik)	Ekwe	Ekkpe
Plural	Ngbe	Oggbe		Nkpe	Bukwe	Bokpe
Leopard Plural	Ekpaghe nyaw Akpaghe nyaw	Ekpagha nyaw Akpagha nyaw	Ikpawk mua	Emakpai	Bnung Bnwa	—
Lips						
Plural	Oiye (Witchcraft)	Oyye, ebo	Ifott, idiong	Hunui	Irut	Eyuna
Magic	Ebu (divination)					
Maize	Aje, Ebu	Aye, ebo	Ibokpott	Lanui	Nurut	Bowuna
Plural	Nchamm	Nsamm		Nshamm	Nkwi	Ansam
Plural	„	Nsamm, Asamm		„		Arasham
Man	'Ne-num (person-male)	Ninimm	Erenn owo	Udumman	One - erum (person, male)	Otunadur, odur
Plural	Ane-erum (anarum)	Anaom	Irenn owo	Adamman		Batiemadur, badur
Meat	Nyamm	Nyamm	Unamm	Echan	Krapp	Eren
Plural	Onyamm	Onyamm		Nchan	Ikrapp	Boren
Milk	Aupp Ebe (water (of the) breast)	Aupp ebe	Mong eba	Leba	Mombai	Miburnm
Monkey	Aupp abe	Aupp abe				Mabumm
Plural	Mbuk	Mbokk	Ebokk			
Moon	Obuk	Obokk				
Plural	'M	'Mii	Offiong	Egwie	Oye	Ebi
Mother	Ami	Ami			Kaiye	Bobi
Plural	Nyenn	Nyenn	Eka	Aiya	Ama	Jagraam
Mountain	Anyenn	Anyenn	Meka	Auaban	Bama	Ojagaam
	Ndandam egui (high hill)	Erawrrawdaw igoe	Akwa obut	Hiilan	Giium	Ekpun
Plural	Adandam agui	Arawrawdaw ngoe	Ikpaw obut	Nlan	Myuum	Bokpun

APPENDIX F

VOCABULARIES OF THE SIX TRIBES IN THE OBAN DISTRICT—*Continued.*

English.	Ekoi.	Kwa.	Efik.	Ekuri.	Ododop.	Uyanga.
Mouth	Nyaw	Nyaw	Inūa	Ema	Inwa	Eba
Plural	Onnyaw	Onnyaw	—	Nma	Munwa	Boba
Nail (toe)	Enyare	Einiare	Mbara	Hinuonn	Konott	Ebbie
Plural	Anyare	Amiare	—	Unuonn	Bunott	Bobie
Name	Mbing	Mbeng	Enying	Lokwum	Diinn	Dũum
Plural	Obing	Obeng	—	Likwum	Niinn	,,
Navel	Etung	Etung esi aa	Ekup	Liko	Dũup	Deyum
	aiya					
Plural	Atung aiya	Atung asi aa	—	Lako	Nĩup	Dawum
Neck	Ntung	Ntung	Itong	Likill	Koawt	Dije
Plural	Otung	Otung	—	Lakill	Biawt	Dei
Night	Atũ	Atũ	Okineyo	Hilani	—	Deyinn
Plural	—	—	—	Olani	—	Iyinn
Nose	'Mi	'Mi	Ibũ	Nyamo	Ikyun	Suna
Plural	Omi	Omi	—	Lanyamo	Munyun	Ebomm-
Ox	Mfong	Mfong	Enang	Õonndum	Orun-ewunm	atawn
						Bobomm-
Plural	Offòng	Offòng	—	Õonnmarum	Borum-	atawn
					bewunm	
Paddle	Ekafi	Ekafi	Udeng	Nohopp	—	Edaam
Plural	Akafi	Akafi	—	Aõhopp	—	Bodaam
Palm-tree	Obi	Obi	Eyop	Otari	Okeikei	Dichi
Plural	Abi	Abi	'Min nteon	Ntan	Nakeikei	Dachi
Palm-wine	Awkemm	Awkemm	(up) 'min	Itawo	'Ntenn	Etara
			eyopp			
Plural	Akemm	—	—	Lato	Munuk	Botara
					mantenn	
Parrot	Egut	Egot	Inum	Ijinm	Irum	Bichan
Plural	Agut	Agot	—	Lajinm	Mundum	Bocham

… APPENDIX F 433

Penis	Ntını	Nda, ntını	Ekpawraw	Okpo	Lunumm	Lodaaw
Plural	Otını	Odda, otını	—	Laḳpo	Inumm	Ladaam
Pig	Ngūmı	Ngome	Edi	—	Inyennye	—
Pigeon (green)	Ogūmi	Ogome	—	—	Munyenne	—
Plural	Ishu	Ishu	Ibiom	Igñi	Inkwam	Bıḳpeyı
Place				Ugū	Munkam	Bokpeyı
Plural	Eji	E′gyı or begyı	Ebet, ıtıe	Ponkpoa	Okwum	Lıjeem
Rain	Ajı	—	—	Ponkpo	—	Boem
	Mbuta	Áıp	Edım	Itū	Mını	Burrm, burm (water)
Plural						
Rat	Mbe	Mbe	Ekū	Utū	Ekkpı	Iḳpı
Plural	Obbe	Obbe	—	Iḳpı	—	Boḳpı
River	Aıya (big)	Aa	Inyang, akpa (big)	Uḳpı	Okpa, lujı	Lojaaın, ejawalı
	Alıpp (small one)		Idımm (small)	Ada, Ojıkawa		
Plural	,,	,,		Wada, Ajıboborru	Nakpa, iyéennı	Lajaam, bojawalı
Road	Mba	Mba	Usung	Iyamm	Enenn	Itéenn
Plural	Oba	Obba	—	,, lebuomo	,,	Botéenn
Shame .	Nsóonn, ochi eyubum (face heavy)	Nsonn	Mbawm	Huḳpı	Itonn	Oḳpı
Plural	,,	,,		,, usan nan-nal-eyc		Boḳpı
Sheep	Njomm-mbuı	Ngyawmboe	Eröng	Ohamm	Ennamı	Eraam
Plural	Nkñı ,, enoḳk (garment? war)	Nkñı enoḳk or ebeta	Ofonidem	,, abomige	Bunamı	Boraam
Shield	Oḳhu enokk	Oku enokk or ebeta	ekong	—	—	—
Plural	Monn-nyenn-'ue-nkaı	Monn-nyenn-1-nng-kae	Eyen-eka-ang-wan	Gwobananan	Amınke-onatu (woman)	Apawdıjaw-mawyenn
Sister	Abonı enyenn-anakaı	Abonn-inyenn-anakæe	Ndıto-eka-iban	Bobananan	Bamınke-bo-batun	,, baıyenn
Plural						

S.B.   F F

APPENDIX F

VOCABULARIES OF THE SIX TRIBES OF THE OBAN DISTRICT—*Continued.*

English	Ekoi	Kwa	Efik	Ekuri	Ododop	Uyanga
Skin	Ngu	Ngo	Ikpa	Echankpa	Kiiup	Iyum
Plural	Ogu	Ogo		Nchankpa	Iyup	Bowawn
Sky	Ngŭribŭ, ngŭrogŭ	Ebonta	Ikpa enyong	Ligi	Ejung-arubut-obassi (air-wall-god)	Doforu ekpai
Plural	,,	,,		,,	,,	
Slave	Nsung	Nsun	Ofn	Utekk	Owan	Uyemm
Plural	Asung	Asung	Ifn	Atekk	Bawan	Bayemm
Sleep	Eyaw	Eyaw	Idap	Ndiamo	Dudau	Lotaam
Plural				,,		Detaam
Smoke	Atuk	Atuk	Nsung-ikang	Rishi	Kotaun	Ogweenn
Plural						Bogween
Snake	Nyaw	Nyaw	Uruk-Ikott (rope of bush)	Diiaw	Ennung	Shaw
Plural	Onnyaw	Onnyaw	Eyen-eren	Diiaw lokian	Ibunung	Lasbawa
Son	Monn-'ne-num (child-person-male)	Monn ninimm		Gwanagani	Kwenŏng-ne-erum	Gwotumadur
Plural	Aboin-ane-erum	Abonn-anaom	Nditaw-iren	Gwawa lebomo		Pematumadur
Song	Ekonn	Ekonn	Ikwaw	Okwanebŭ	Kawchŏng	Lugwawene
Plural	Nkonn	Nkonn		Anebakwanebŭ	,,	Bangwag-wawene
Spear	Osam	Osam	Eduat	Okonn	Osam	Bawonn
Plural	Asam	Asam		Lakonn	Nasam	Bawonna
Star	Irunandu	Irorando	Nian-ta-offiong (sand moon)	Ekwunkurni	Iyuyune	Ekwunkurni
Plural	Ndunandu	Ndorando	Ekpiri eto	,, abombe	Muyuyune	Bokwunkurni
Stick	Iti	Ete		Mkpun	Lufuun	Edi
Plural	Nti	Ate		Akpun		Bodi

APPENDIX F

Stone . .	Etai	Etae	Itiatt		Oran
Plural	Atai	Atae	—	Unan	Daran
Sun . .	Eyo	Eyu	Utinn	Nanan	Duawng
Plural	,,	,,	—	Lukwenn	Darung
Tail . .	Iki	Ike	Isim	Deikenn	Dian
Plural	Nki	Nke	,,	—	Dian
Tear . .	Abubbi	Abubi	Monn eyet	Munjenn	Esenn
Plural	Abubi	,,	Ekpawraw	—	Bosenn
Testicles	Ntini	Ntini, nda	,,	Munji-kun	Datat
Plural	Otini	Otini, awda	,,		,,
Thief . .	Nyagha-njü	Nyaghajü	Inaw	Ojii	Osumadur
Plural	Anyagha-njü	Anyaghau	Me inaw	—	Bosumadur
Thigh . .	Awta	Awta	Ifik-akut	Unau	Orawk
Plural	Ata	Ata	—	Nanau	Darawk
Thing . .	Njum	Nyom	Nkpaw	Bienn	Bobie
Plural	Mbimm	Mbiem	Nkukim	,,	,,
Thorn . .	Ejonge	Eyonga	—	Keigwe	Fuyi
Plural	Ajonge	Ayonga	Ungwong	Owana	Dafnya
Tobacco	Awene	Onngwana			Onnwawana
Plural	Auene				Enwawana
To-day . .	Egye	Ee	Mfinn	Ndeigwi	Itidi, pl. botidi
Toe . .	Iniri ekat	Inira ekat	Nten-ukut	Donaw-luan	Edadoi-ebawn
Plural	Oniri ekat	'nira akat		Munonnoi-	Ladadoi ,,
				mwan	
To-morrow	Ojaw	Obbiaw	Mkpong	Diyenn-ikwi	Ugweddi
Plural	—	—	—	—	—
Tongue	Edibi	Eebe	Edeme	Dara	Lata
Plural	Adibi	Aebe	—	Nenenn	,,
Tooth . .	Eing	Eing	Eddett	,,	Lejeenn-
					gwnadu
Plural					Lajeenn-
	Aming	Aming	—	,,	gwuadu
Town . .	Mfam	Mfam	Obio	Luse	Wunta
Plural	Offam	Offam	—	Nise	Bowunta

F F 2

APPENDIX F

VOCABULARIES OF THE SIX TRIBES IN THE OBAN DISTRICT—*Continued.*

English.	Ekoi.	Kwa.	Efik.	Ekuri.	Ododop.	Uyanga.
Tree	Eeti	Ete	Eto	Hechi	Kurni	Eri
Plural	Ati	Ate	—	Ochi-kelelan	Beni	Jari
Twins	Abonn-offat	Abonn-abiema	Nditaw-amaniba	Agbaha	Amanbawan	Okeotoga
Urine	Afighi	Afughi	Ikimm	Niyani	Ojangi-miange	Biyam
War	Enokk	Beta, ebeta, enokk	Ekŏng	Lekñ	Enokk	Deyung
Plural	Benokk	Benokk	—	—	—	Layung
Water	Aipp	Aipp	'Mŏng	,,	,,	Burm
White-man	Ebare 'ne	Ebara 'ne, Mawkara	Afia owo, *or* makara	Luji	Minni	Odnakura
Plural	Abare ane	Abara ane, *or* amawkara	Mfia owo	Okarara	Ambut-one	—
Wife	Nkai	Nkae 'ne	Ngwan owo	Hanagam	Atun-omi	Oiyenn
Plural	Akai	Anakae ane	Iban owo	Wanabam	Batun-bemi	Dayenn
Wind	Mfepp	Mfep	Ofinm	Ufefe	Ebepp	Efan
Plural	,,	,,	—	—	—	Bofan
Witch	Nje 'ne-nkai	Nye ningke	Ngwan ifott	Oliochiann	Busa	Utan
Plural	Aje anakai	Aye anakae	Iban ifott	Ayichano	Basa	Otan
Woman	'Ne-nkai	Ningkae	Ngwan	Hanan	One-atun	Oiyenn
Plural	Ane-akai, anakae	Anakae	Iban	Whanan	One-batun	Baiyenn
Womb	Oya 'nyenn (belly mother)	Awa nyenn	Idibi eka	Legal	Esienn	Dedinn
Plural	Aya anyenn	Aa anyenn	—	Lagal	Munsienn	Dadinn
Wood (for fire)	Nkun	Nkon	Ifia	Iman	Kemett	Ibidd
Plural	—	—	—	Hellong	Imett	Bubidd
Yam	Eyũ	Eo	Bia	Olong lebamo	Karaia	Emn
Plural	Ayũ	Ao	—	Di	Buria	Batun
Year	Eya	Eya	Isua	Di lebomije	Diett	Effenn
Plural	Nya	Nya	—		Niett	Bofenn

APPENDIX F

	Enyane	Enyene, enyane	Mkpong	Kingpū	Diyenn	Chinidi
Yesterday			Kiet, tiet			
One	Jitt, mat, fitt, git, futt, wat, mitt, b't	Yitt, fitt, mat, ut, mut, bat		Nagani	Buuni	Kurni
Two	Ebai, mbae, abai	Ebai, mbae, abai	Iba	Nawa	Buwan	Baban
Three	Esa, nsa, asa, essa	Esa, nsa, asa, essa	Ita	Nachili	Bunan	Baraa
Four	Eni, 'ni, ani	Enyie, 'ne, ame, ane	Inang	Nania	Bunai	Badau
Five	Eronn, ndonn, aronn	Eronn, ndonn, aronn	Ition	Nateo	Buneng	Baruon
Six	Essaasa, asaasa	Esaksesa, nsaksansa, asaksasa	Ituoket	Natinagani	Kasaasa	Baruon na baban kurni
Seven	Enighasa, 'nighansa, anighasa	Enyieghesa, 'neghansa, aneghasa	Itiaba	Natinawa	Bunai na bunan	Baruon na baban
Eight	Enghani	Enyieghenyie	Itiaita	Nati nachili	Changa-changa-nai	Baruon na baraa
Nine	Erionneni	Edonnenyie	Usuk-kiet	Nati nania	Buang-nabaanu	Baruon na badau
Ten	Offaw	Boffaw	Duop	Najo	Diu	Chiup
Eleven	Offaw-na-jitt	Boffaw-ya-gyitt, or Boffaw-a-gyitt	Duopekiet, duop-yet-kiet	Najo nagani	Diu na buuni	Chiup otenn ta kurni
Twenty	Esamm	Eti	Edipp	Lenau	Dakáanu	Dedáap
Thirty	Esamm na offaw, esamm n(a) offaw	Eti a boffaw eti ya boffaw	Edipeduop, edip-ye-duop	Lenau na najo	Dakáanu na diu	Dedáap te chiup
Forty	Nsamin ebai	Ati abae	Aba	Lenau nawa	Dakáanu nawan	Dedáap babaan

APPENDIX F

VOCABULARIES OF THE SIX TRIBES IN THE OBAN DISTRICT—*Continued*.

English.	Ekoi.	Kwa.	Efik.	Ekuri.	Ododop.	Uyanga.
Fifty	Nsamm ebai n(a) offaw	Ati abae a boffaw, ati abae ya boffaw	Aba ye duop	Lenau nawa na najo	Dakáanu nawan na din	Dedáap bahaan te chuup
Sixty	Nsamm esa	Ati asa	Ata	Lenau nachili	Dakáanu nanan	Dedáap baráa
Seventy	Nsamm esa n(a) offaw	Ati asa a boffaw, ati asa ye boffaw	Ata ye duop	Lenau nachili na najo	Dakáanu nanan na diu	Dedáap baraa te chuup
Eighty	Nsamm eni	Ati ane	Anang	Lenau nania na najo	Dakáanu nanai	Dedáap badaii te chuup
Ninety	Nsamm eni n(a) offaw	Ati ane a boffaw	Anang ye duop	Lenau nania na najo	Dakáanu nanai na diu	Dedáap badaii te chuup
Hundred	Nsamm eronn, *or* ikie futt	Ati adonn	Ikie	Lenau nateo	Dakáanu deneng	Dedáap baruon
Thousand	Loggodd ebai na nkie mbai, *or* nkie offaw	Ati eti abae	—	Ennoano	Dakáanu diu	Dogaw
1200	Na nsamm offaw	Ya boffaw	—	—	—	—
I, Me	'Me, 'Ngam	'Me, Kam	Ami, 'mi	Aam	'Mi	Aam
Thou	Te, 'we	'We	Afo	Aba	Ngn	Awawk
He	'We	'We	Enye	Ee	'Mawng	Ame
We	Ud, ut	Ud, ut	Nyinn	Aban	Ibun	Afar
You	Un	Un	Mbufo	Ananbu	'Mbe	Afe
They	Abaw	Abaw	'Maw	Abi	'Mbe	Afe
All	Kpekpe, sfii	Kpekpe, esenesen	Kupurru, fafap	Abanaigegi	Ibun	Kukwiya
This man	'ne nyaw	Ninimn nyaw	Eren, eren-owo emi	Onagani	One, *or* onne kwn	Oduruma
Plural	Ane mba	Anaom mba	Iren, iren-ow emi	—	—	—

APPENDIX F

That man	'Ne anyaw	Nmmm nyaw gaw	Eien oro, oko	Ukemaguu	One, *or* onne-kwaw	Madigou
Plural	Ane aba	Anaoui ba gaw	Ireu oro, oko	—	Kurmi-ki	Err-omani
This tree	Eeti nji	Eto emi	Eto emi	Hechi nshu	—	—
Plural	Ati ma	Ate ma	Ufokk mi	Etiiadam	Ennaw-emi	Erraw-ogwaam
My house	Njñ eyama	Ngyo ama	,,	—	—	—
Plural	Ojñ awama	Oyo awbama	Ufokk fo	Etiiadawghi	Ennaw-ngu	Erraw-ogwaw
Thy house	Njñ eya	Ngyo eya	,,	—	—	—
Plural	Ojñ awba	Oyo awba	Ufokk esic	Etiiadai	Ennaw- 'mawng	Erraw-gwame
His house	Njñ egye	Ngyo ee				
Plural	Ojñ obee	Oyo obe	Obio nymi	Léoni-ogban	Lũse-lubun	Dogon-gwafani
Our town	Mfam égyira	Mfam ira				
Plural	Offam óbura	Offam óbura	Obio nynn	Léoni-jaw	Lũse-lumbun	Dogon-lagwaani
You country	Mfam égyina	Mfaina ma				
Plural	Offam óbuni	Offam óbuna	Me obio mbuto	—	—	Baduruma
Their children	Abonn abaw	Abonn abaw	Nditaw naw	Boborro abi	Ben-bembe	Bobeshinshi
Bad	Eebi, echak	Esak	Idiokk, obukpo	Bawjenno	Obe	Bopashinshi
Plural	Abi, achak	Asak	Midiokk, inbukpo	Bobinia	—	
Black	Enyaghe	Eniagha	Obibitt	Awbange	Ambinn	Okeifurna
Plural	Anyaghe	Anjagha	Mbitibiil	Okpawbamge	Bambinne	Beeifurnafurn
Female	Nkai	Nkae	Uman	Kananagani	Oman	Doba
Plural	Akai	Akae	,,	Wanan	Baman	Deba
Fierce	Obi-obi, ofi	Efop-efop, eki eki	Uko-uko	Ogwanan	—	Ebéira
Plural	Efup-efup	Awgban-awgban	Idat-idat	Agwanan	—	Bobéira
Good	Enawe, ennopp	Ennaw	Eti, edifonn	Ejenn	Onomm	Bobereshéenn
Plural	Anawe, anopp	Annaw	Nti, me-cdifonn	Ujenn	Bonomm	Bopareshéenn

APPENDIX F

VOCABULARIES OF THE SIX TRIBES IN THE OBAN DISTRICT—*Continued.*

English.	Ekoi.	Kwa.	Efik.	Ekuri.	Ododop.	Uyanga.
Great	Ekpatim, etikpa	Ekpatim, etikpa ekawe	Akamba, akwa ikpaw	Abalige	Awkangi	Boberafara
Plural	Akpatim, atikpa	Akpatim, atikpa akawe	,, ,,	—	Bukangi	Boparafara
Little	Iruk, monni, ibonne	Iruk, imonna, monn, irik-irik	Ekpiri	Arechiane	Odiomi	Bobepapak-parre
Plural	Nduk, abonni, mbonne	Mbonna, nduk-nduk	Mkpri	—	Budiomi	Bopapapak-paare
Long	Ndam, ndandam	Edawrawdaw	Anyan	Orami	Buyiri	Uwerre
Plural	Adam, adandam	Adawrawdaw	Nyan	Aramibe	Oyiri	Awerre
Male	'Num	'Nimn	Ayara, eren, okop	Udannan	Odum	Otara
Plural	Arum	Aom	Nyara, irin, okop	Arinnan	Burun	Patara
Old	Eékui, etimn	Etim	Akani	Ntamia	Onum	Mitoma
Plural	Akui, atim	Atim	Nkani	Atamnan	Bonum	Bobutana
Red	Ebi ekui-ekui	Ekoe-ekoe	Ididuott	Awkilige Akilibe	Andun	Lekpenn Dakpenn
Plural	,, ,,	,, ,,	,, ,,	Ofanga	—	Okefama
Rotten	Aácha	Esaa, ekpawaw, ebawe	Ntagha, obukpo, mbumbu	Abamibe	Owan	Bibufama
Plural	Aácha	Asaa, akpawaw, abawe	Ntagha, mbumba, mbukpo	Uyo	Buwan	Bubinm
Sick	Emange	Emange-emange	Udawngaw	Laiyu	Omoka	Obangame
Plural	Amange	Amange-amange	—		Bumokk	

APPENDIX F

White .	Ebare	Ebara	Afia	Awgulli	Ambut	Ojokula
Plural	Abare	Abara	Mfia	Agulibe	Ambun	Badakyla
Above up	K(a) 'awsaw	Kawsaw	Ke eyong, kenyon	Kadu, lewi	Ejung	Aturofvt
Below .	Ka awsere, kawsere	Kawsera	Ke idak kidak	Boda olishe	Konan-kabuke	Ewñ
Behind .	Mba njimm	K(a) ebawgyim	Ke edem kedem	Odakilame	Ode	Urukulam
Plural	Awba Ojimm	Oba ogyimm	—	Auorige	—	—
Far Plural	Ndam-e-mba	Mba nda	Anyan	Auoribe	Anyirri-ninn	Ujurmiwila
Here .	Adam awba	Oba-oda	Nyan	Nwa	Mandi	Aa
In, inside	Mfa, nga	Mfa, nga	Mi, kenn	Hetuakonn	Oreting	Ulan
	K(e) etim	Kawtemm	Ke esitt, kesitt			
Outside	Njimm ere, mba ere, ke-ere	Ngyimm otung	Ka angwa, edem-angwa-angwa	Helibam	Orutung	Lebomm
Plural	Ojimm ere, awba ere, ke-ere	Ogyimm otung	Kc angwa, edem-angwa-angwa	—	—	—
Plenty .	Eti-oti, nti-nti	Awege (n)fim (adj)	Nwak-n-cdiwak ekese (adj)	Kalabam	Anjauo	Oyammo-yamm
There .	Afaw	Faw	Do, doe	Wani	Mando	Eenna
Where .	Fan, mba nyinn	Fan, kafan, ebat ngyinn (which part)	'Maung, ke mating	Wauidukk	'Mang	Ndaena
No, not	Ee, cháng	I-i, sung, eraw-asik	Baba, idigha	Nfiru	Nkawngani	Ee
I am .	'Me nki, 'me nde	Nde, 'me nde	Ami	Hanaa	'Mi	Aam
I bring	'Me nkaw mbak	'Me mankaw mba	Ami nda ndi	Ambandun	'Mi nbagwi	Aam tuagmu
Plural	Ut ckaw eba	Ud bikaw iba	Nyinn ida idi	—	—	—

APPENDIX F

VOCABULARIES OF THE SIX TRIBES IN THE OBAN DISTRICT—*Continued.*

English.	Ekoi.	Kwa.	Efik.	Ekuri.	Ododop.	Uyanga.
I come	'Me mba, me nkaba	'Me mamba	Ami medi, medi	Ndula	'Mi nkwi	Aam niwu
Plural	Ut aba, ut ekaba	Ud biba	Nyinn inedi	—	—	—
I come not	'Mo nkába	'Me nkaba	Ami ndighe	Mandul	'Mi kameni ukwi	Aam nivu
Plural	Ut ekába	Ud ikaba	Nyinn edighe	—	—	—
I dance	'Me mbinn	'Me mabinn	Ami menekk	Hudu	Mi joikojo	Menkuju
Plural	Ut ebinn	Ud bibinn	Nyinn imenekk	—	—	—
I drink	'Me ngwaw	'Me mangwaw	Ami mong-wong	Ngwawa	Mi njonn	Niwaw
Plural	Ut ewaw	Ud biwaw, biwaw	Nyinn imong-wong	—	—	—
I die	'Me mkpaw	'Me mangkpaw	Ami makpa	Mbeya	Mi nkwa	Nibi
Plural	Ut ckpaw	Ud bikpaw	Nyinn imakpa	—	—	—
I drank	'Me ngwaw	'Me mangwaw	Ami ma ngwông	Kim pufing waw	Mi njonn, or mi nchonn	Nwaw
Plural	Ut ewaw	Ud biwaw	Nyinn ima ingwông	—	—	—
I drank not	'Me nkawaw	'Me nka aw	Ami ngwongke	Magwo	Mi mbiri jonn	Niwaw
Plural	Ut ckawaw	Ud ika aw	Nyinn ing-wonke	—	—	—
I eat	'Me nyi	'Me manyi	Ami mata	Ndia	Mi ndia	Niji
Plural	Ut eyi	Ud bii	Nyinn imata, nyinn-inadia	—	—	—
I eat not	'Me nkayi	'Me nkayi	Ami ndiaha, ntaha	Madi	Mi mbiri ndia	Ndiane nji
Plural	Ut ekayi	Ud ikayi	Nyinn idiaha, itah	—	—	—
I give	'Me nkare	'Me mankare	Ami 'monnaw	Nshua	Mi njang	Angenn
Plural	Ut ekare	Ud bikare	Nyinn imonnaw	—	—	—

APPENDIX F

I give you	'Me nka-a,	'Me mankare-a	Ami 'monnaw fi	Amshugaw	Mi njăng ngu	Angenn awk
I give him	'Me nkare 'wa 'Me nka-e,	'Me mankare-e	Ami 'manaw enye	Amshure	Mi njăng aiye	Agenne ame
I go	Me nkare-'we					Nkaotönga
I went	'Me nji	'Me manye	Ami 'maka	Nshongoo	Mi nkekku	Martung
I kill them	'Me nji 'Me nyui abaw	'Me manye 'Me manyoe abaw	Ami 'ma nka Ami 'mowot maw	Kimpu ingbun Amwani	Mi nkun mbe	Nkagha emban.i
I know	'Me menge	'Me mamenge	Ami 'moffiokk	Njilla	Mi ndaw	Nkai-oshenn
I know not	Me nka menge	'Me nka menge	Ami 'mfiokka	Minjin	Mi ndaw ndawni	Amunshenn
Thou lovest him	We okkott	We bokkodde	Afo amana enye	Arerai	Ngu gasek-aiye	Lekanekpara
We make	(Ut) eyimm	Ud bujem	Nyinn ima nam	Abon lashali	Ibin isi	Afodjuma
We say to you	Ut echott na we	Ud isodd ya we	Nyinn iting ye afo	Abon lehila-nawo	Ibun ibekka na-ngu	Dıyiddina-awk
We say not	Ut eka chott	Ud ika sodd	Nyinn itingke	Abon welelino	Ibun ibiri bekk ndio	Adishoigu okei-tun
He stinks	(We) akiyu	We akiyu	Enye ketebe, ke etebe	Ano nenumi	Mawng arumi	
He steals	We aju eju	We bayu eyu	Enye eyipp inaw	Ukam gande	Mawng ojuju	Amu eshebba
They laugh	Abaw ayawe	Abaw aawe	'Maw esak	Akwellalala	Mbe besekk aiye	Afibekkparana
You weep	Un ori	Un bode	Mbutfo etua, mbufo emetua	Otulabu	Ngu awonga	Awawk keirun
Where art thou sleeping?	Jenn 'we awyaa, or awyaa jenn?	Esi ere gyenn 'we awaeya?	Nsi-namm afo edede?	Ogbanana olora?	Mawng-asi airat?	Orĕngu ngöoma arotam?
Where did he go?	'We aji fan?	'We aye fan?	Enye akaka inong?	Wa abun?	Mang onyi-man?	Ame madiloba?
Who comes in?	Ene (or bagha ne) ayekk abak?	Ene (or bane) ae bak?	Anie oduk edi?	Anarulo?	Men okwi ma?	Orung godu?

APPENDIX F

VOCABULARIES OF THE SIX TRIBES IN THE OBAN DISTRICT—*Continued.*

English.	Ekoi.	Kwa.	Efik.	Ekuri.	Ododop.	Uyanga.
What dost thou say?	'We se jenn? se jenn?	Se jenn? we se jenn?	Afo awdawhaw didie?	Oni atiyo?	Aning-ǵmu?	Adinangoebe?
How do you make palm wine?	Oyima na okemn nan?	Awem (we) nan awkem?	Anam didie minn ntenn?	Ojo-bobo awu lenobule itawo?	Ngasi ning mumuk mantenn?	Orufa awawk nafei etara?
What shall we drink?	Ut tikk ewaw jenn? Tikk ut ewaw jenn?	Ud tikk iwaw yenn? Tikk ud iwaw yenn?	Nyinn iding wong nso? N'soke nyinn idingwöng?	Bfiuna bfina agwaw?	Ibun nkamen mung?	Orufa makor?
When art thou coming?	We awba bagha ebu?	'We tikk awba ba erik?	Afo edi di ini ewe?	Ngalligñ awun?	Ngu akakwi adangi ngwini?	Ngwudibi afaumbarri?
Give me food	Kare ngam njun egyim	Kaam, *or* kare kam, nyom eyiam	Naw mi udia	Shon abundi	Njang ne daria	Tun agwam lucha
Cut me a small stick	Gbut iruk iti kunnu	Yawre ite kare kaam, *or* kaam	Sibe ekpri eto	Gami echia shuno	Yieng ini chang ne	Ere murde-penni jangam
I want a little stone	'Me nwawma iruk etai	Me nye monn-i-ntae	Ami nyenn eyenn itiatt	Ntaiabi hota-tairu	Nkwaka kwana unan	Amin nderbi oran akpapari
Which fowl will you give me?	'We tikk okunm bagha nkokk? *or* Ban nkokk we tikk okunm?	'We tikk awkaam nkokk nyinn?	Ewe ñnen ke afo erinaw?	Ngan bóonn etai nasuno?	Mung unonn anakaka njang ne?	Ngwoia donn afeingyam aam?
He is inside the house	Are ka nju?	'We ayikk ka etem-i-nyo?	Enye odu ke esit ufokk?	Oda we etuo	'Mawng are eteng ennaw	Ame osa erarifu erraw
The birds flew away	Nonn omfibi ndui	Nonn nam-fubi ndu	Inuen efe edaha	Lenonmo ogwia-ogwiamo	Itott ibebbe	Badawn obeinm

APPENDIX F

English						
He is taller than I	'Me adap achĭngi ngam, or 'Me adap achĭngum	'We bawdap asenge kam	Enye amana okŏng akan mi	Ora ma oda-wano	Mawng awyiddi okpai ne	Okaikaiya oshingum
The parrot screams	Egut egyũ̈	Egott bekokk	Inum efiori	Ijimm okwanebu	Kawjonn kurum	Bicham lugwaine
The rotten tree falls	Eekiu eéti eghaw	Ekuu ete begbaw	Obuĭkpo eto awduaw	Eche ofafang otuha	Awkanneke-ini anaw abuke	Ere mifefe okekponga
Can you see me?	Te obĭkk ngam eyenn a? or Obĭkk ngam eyennum ma?	Kam eyenam ekonn?	Afo emekeme ndikut mi?	Oloh naai?	Aka-kame-ne uni?	Okefeena aferrin ame?
No I cannot.	Eé' me nkabĭk	Ii, 'me mbegam, or Nkabck	Ii, ami nkemeke	Ha ma lon	Mi kame-ni ngŭ uni	Amaferrinam
	Spoken by the Ekoi tribe in the Oban District	Spoken by the Kwa people near Calabar.	Spoken by the Efiks at Calabar	Spoken by the Ekuri in the NW part of the Oban District.	Spoken by the Ododop in the SE of the Oban District and in the Cameroons, also a dialect by Okoyong	Spoken by the Uyanga in the Western part of the Oban District.

APPENDIX G.

NSIBIDI SIGNS.

Nsibidi

APPENDIX G

NSIBIDI SIGNS.

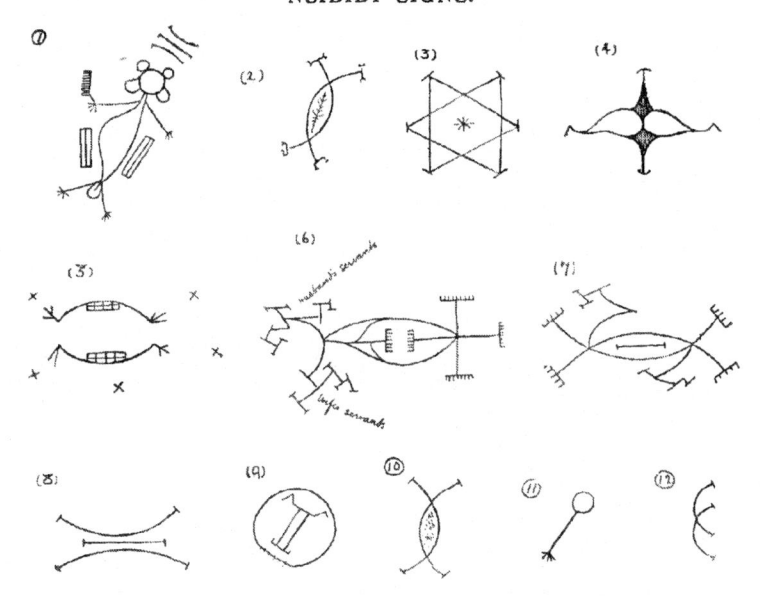

(1) Husband and wife love each other ardently. They like to put their arms round one another (shown by extended hands). They are rich, have three pillows and a table on each side. The wife holds a comb.

(2) Wedded pair belonging to Egbo Society. Shown by the Egbo feather.

(3) Very great love between husband and wife. The central "star" denotes a warm and loving heart.

(4) A husband cooks two calabashes of food to give to his wife.

(5) Man and wife with river between them. The latter is denoted by two "canoes." The crosses show that messages are always being sent from one to another.

(6) Another sign for ardent love between husband and wife. They have many servants.

(7) Man and wife lying with their "piccan" between them. The consorts lie with their heads in different directions.

(8) Quarrel between husband and wife. They turn their backs on one another and place a pillow between.

(9) A woman wants to marry a man, but her people object.

(10) A man wishes to leave his wife because she has craw-craw.

(11) The wife tries to hold back her husband by his loin-cloth. At the bottom of which her hand is to be seen.

(12) Woman who wishes to be rid of her husband.

APPENDIX G 449

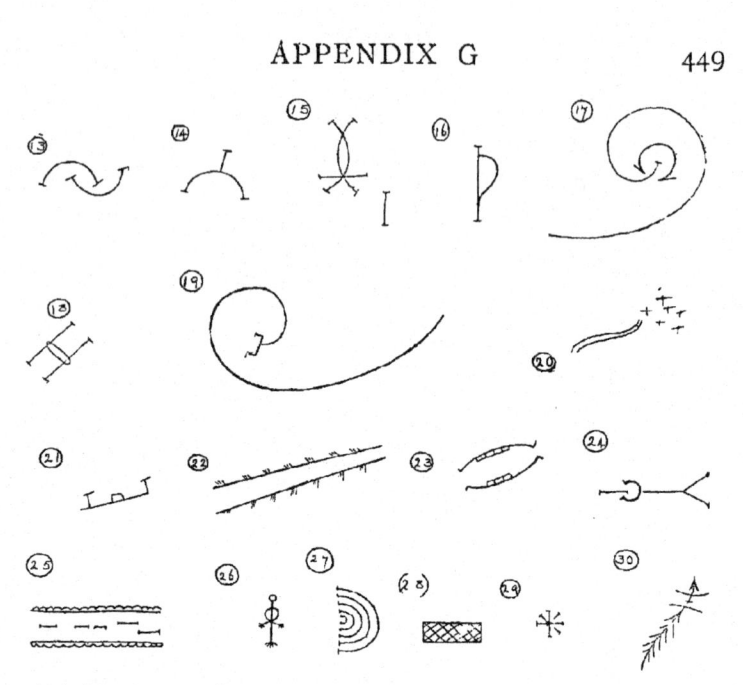

(13) An inconstant lover.
(14) A courtesan
(15) Man who tries to steal the affection of a married woman.
(16) A woman who is about to become a mother.
(17) A man has been in the habit of going along a certain road to visit his sweetheart.
(18) He comes to a place where a great tree lies across the road He holds both hands against his breast, and stands wondering (17) if the road has been blocked on purpose, and if so, why ?
(19) The woman stands waiting for her lover. Her hands are crossed on her breast—showing expectancy
(20) She sends a message telling the man to hurry.
(21) Two men accompany a third part of the way homeward.
(22) The " bush " road along which they walk
(23) They come to a river where they say " good-bye." The one crosses in a canoe, and the others return
(24) Trader bearing native money ↄ comes to forked roads
(25) Main road with much traffic
(26) Slave with hands tied together.
(27) Sign denoting plenty of money.
(28) Razor.
(29) Egbo sign
(30) Egbo feather.

S.B. G G

APPENDIX G

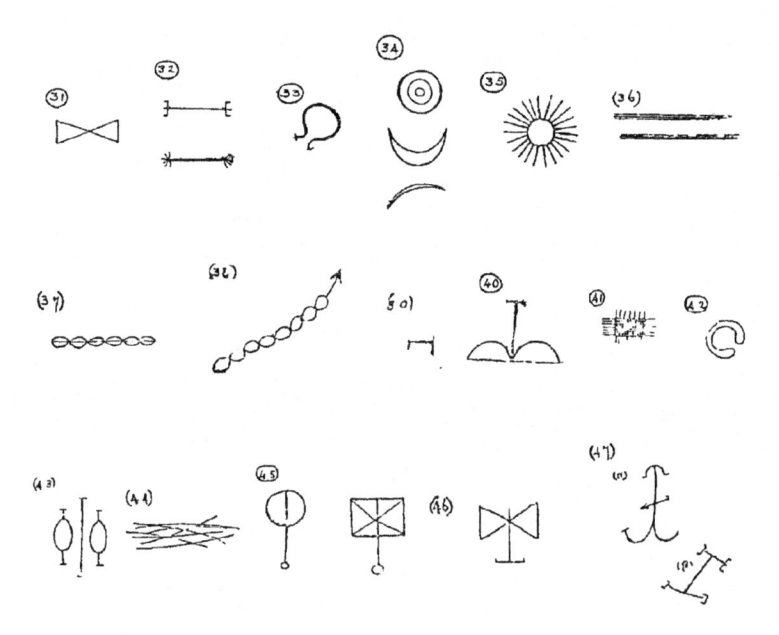

(31) Weaver's frame
(32) Two ways of drawing a dancer's rattle.
(33) Manilla, native money
(34) Moon in three phases.
(35) Sun
(36) Darkness
(37) A chain.
(38) A very heavy chain.
(39) Handcuffs
(40) Man fastened by leg-irons
(41) "Ghost-mat" offered to ancestors
(42) Ghost bracelet or anklet offered to ancestors
(43) Sign for little ant-hills "bush men" put up to keep danger from a house
(44) Sign for firewood
(45) Two hand glasses.
(46) Swing mirror to stand on table
(47) (a) Mirror standing on table ↝ denotes the metal "point" with which paitings are made (β) People who have come to arrange their hair at the mirror

APPENDIX G

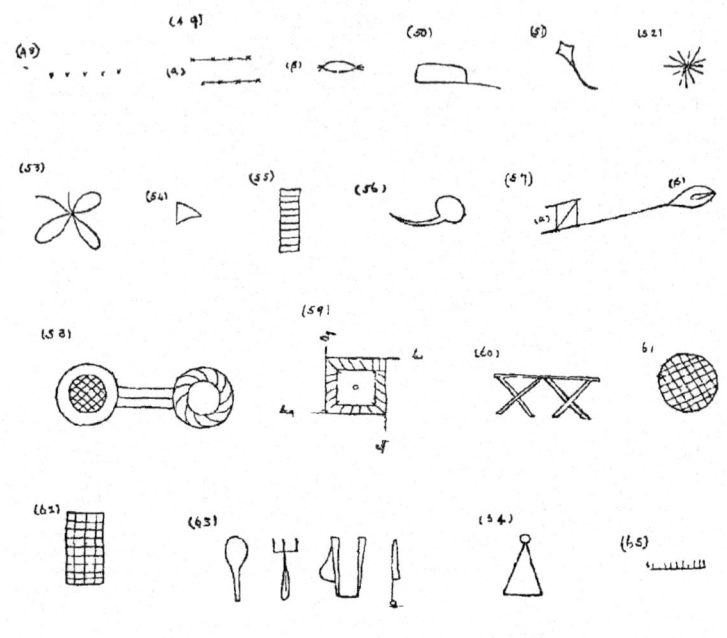

(48) Lizard tracks.
(49) (a) Wild cat tracks (β) Sign for genet or "bush" cat.
(50) Bird trap.
(51) Lizard.
(52) A spider's web
(53) A butterfly
(54) A parrot's beak.
(55) A canoe
(56) Gourd ladle, used for drinking
(57) (β) Calabash spoon (a) Cupboard in which spoon is kept
(58) Calabash laid open, strings between top and bottom
(59) Table with calabash of food in centre.
(60) Table with crossed legs
(61) Plate
(62) Bed
(63) Spoon, fork, mug, and knife
(64) Okankan (see p. 54)
(65) A native comb.

APPENDIX G

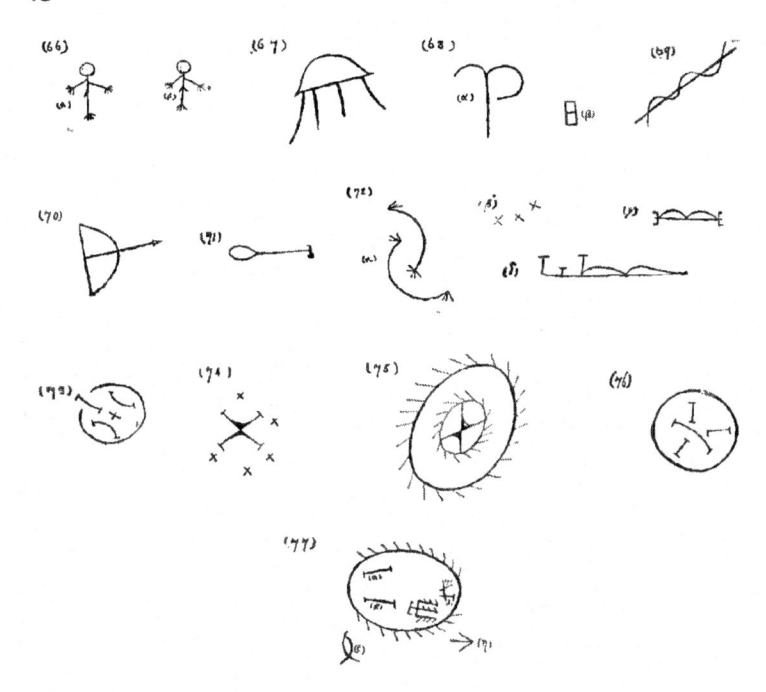

(66) Man (α) and woman (β) with small-pox.

(67) Crab.

(68) Signs for hunger. (α) The man is supposed to stand pointing to his stomach.

(69) Sign denoting the conflicting testimony of two witnesses. The first talks "straight," and the other tells a deceitful tale.

(70) Crossbow.

(71) Denotes: "I have no gunpowder—send some."

(72) (α) Two women quarrelling; (β) what they say; (γ) each threatens the other with leg-irons, and (δ) prison house.

(73) The husband enters the house, and tries to settle the quarrel.

(74) Sign denoting a talkative man.

(75) House where discussion is going on; people listen round inner wall, and in verandah.

(76) Sick man lying down in his house, with three visitors.

(77) A case in court: (α) and (β) two Chiefs sitting as judges; (γ) woman plaintiff (without hat); ( ) male defendant (with hat); (ε) two women friends who sit outside listening; ⇾ (η) three court "members" acting as jury.

Story (1).

In the top left hand corner, Head men and Head-women of the town are looking on from a Chief's House with verandah (m)
In the top right hand corner, children of both sexes stand watching the "play", but on the far side of the road
(k) rattle (used at dances)
A dead man lies on his house
He had only one wife
She sits at his feet.
They had three children
Two sons (α α) and a daughter (β)
The townsfolk come to play for the funeral
First the men
next the women
after these come three men with drums
and last the three Egbo 'images'
(k) rattle
Bench on which four old men sit looking on
Table on which stand three corked bottles
(e) sword
(e) sword

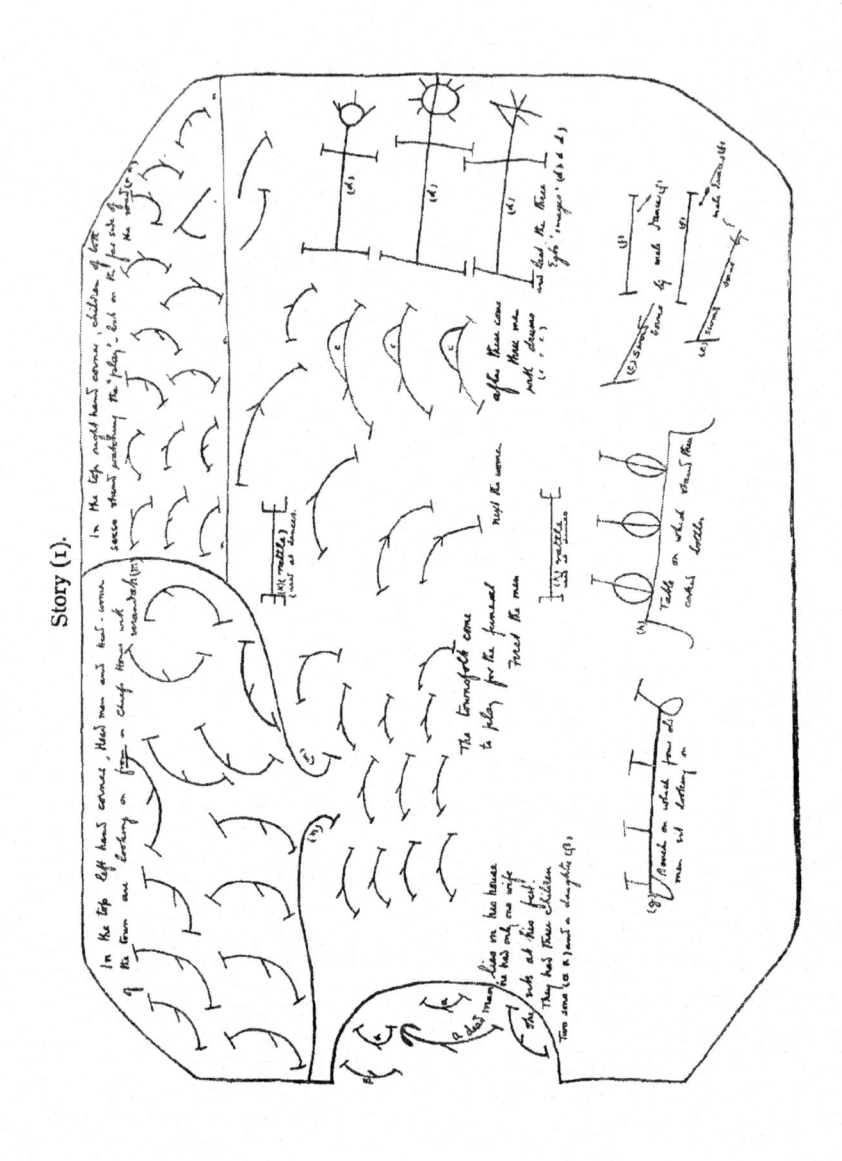

Story (2).

This is the house of a widow. You can see that she has no husband because it is so open
The house of an unmarried man, also open because he has no
The man thinks. 'I should like to marry the widow.' He calls one of his 'boys' (5)
and sends him with a message (6) to ask the widow to be his friend
When the boy reached the widow's house, (1) – he found her besieged by
So many men were eager to wed the widow. That the boy (5) had to go back and tell his master there was no chance for his suit.
The man (4) must therefore stay alone in his house, sleeping sadly with only a

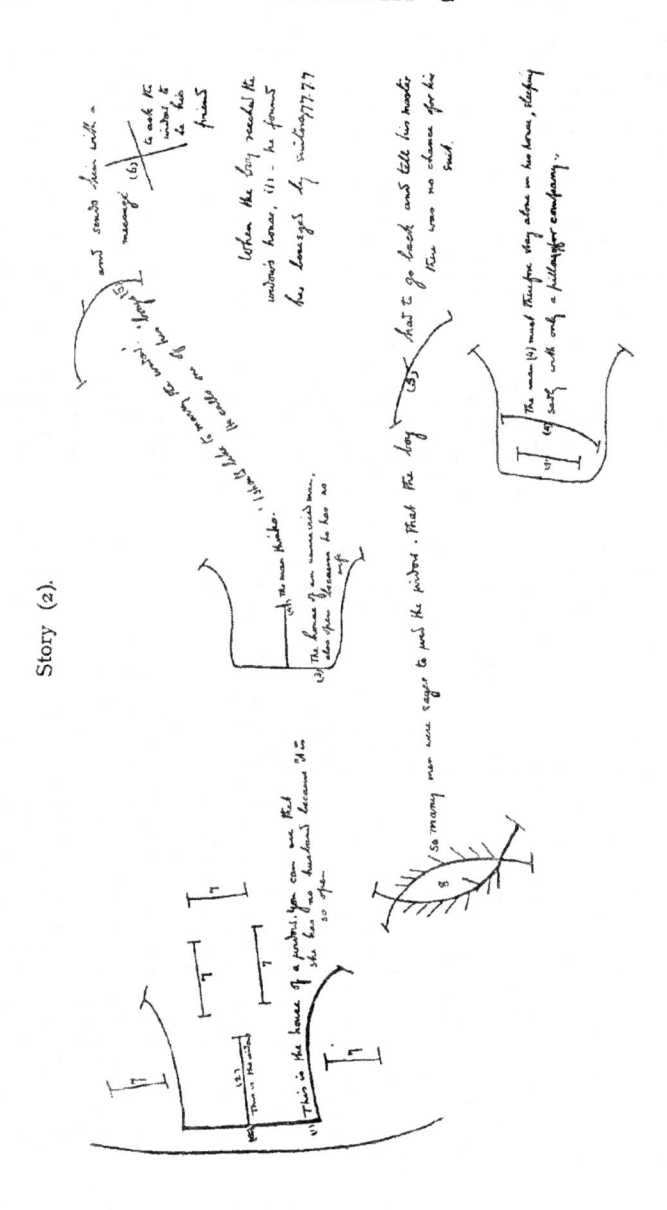

APPENDIX G

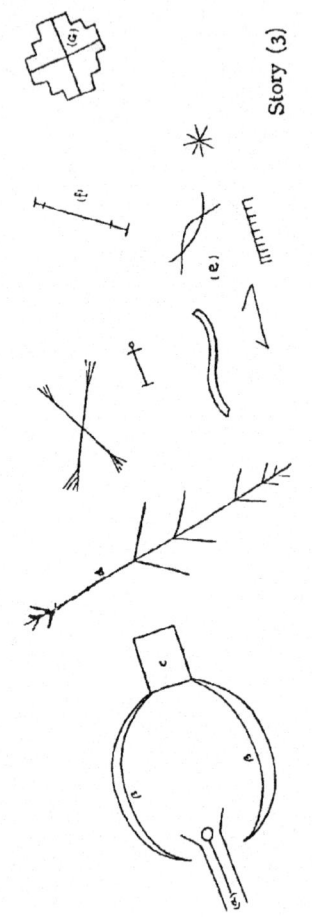

Story (3)

(a) A stranger enters a town. He walks up the main street between two rows of houses (β β) till he comes to the Egbo House (c).
(d) Is", a comet which has lately been seen by the townspeople
(e) Property is strewn about in disorder—denoting confusion.
(f) A seat before the Chief's house
(g) The arm-chair in which the body of the Head Chief has been set. His death was foretold by the comet
(hh) Two claimants to the office of Head Chief now vacant. The townsfolk have collected in the Egbo House to decide between the rivals.
N.B.—The rectangular shape of Egbo House should be remarked

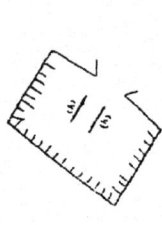

456   APPENDIX G

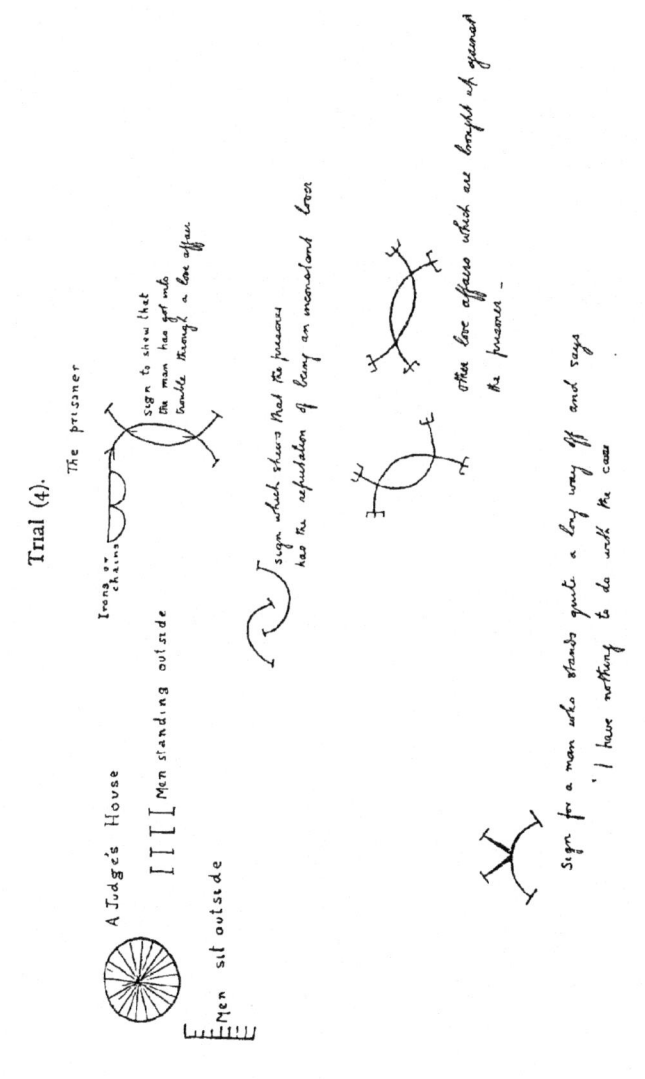

Trial (4).

The prisoner

A Judge's House

[[[[Men standing outside

⊕ (circle with spokes)

Men sit outside

Irons or chains

Sign to shew that the man has got into trouble through a love affair

Sign which shews that the prisoner has the reputation of being an incontinent lover

Other love affairs which are brought up against the prisoner.

Sign for a man who stands quite a long way off and says 'I have nothing to do with the case'

Story (5)

Trial (6).

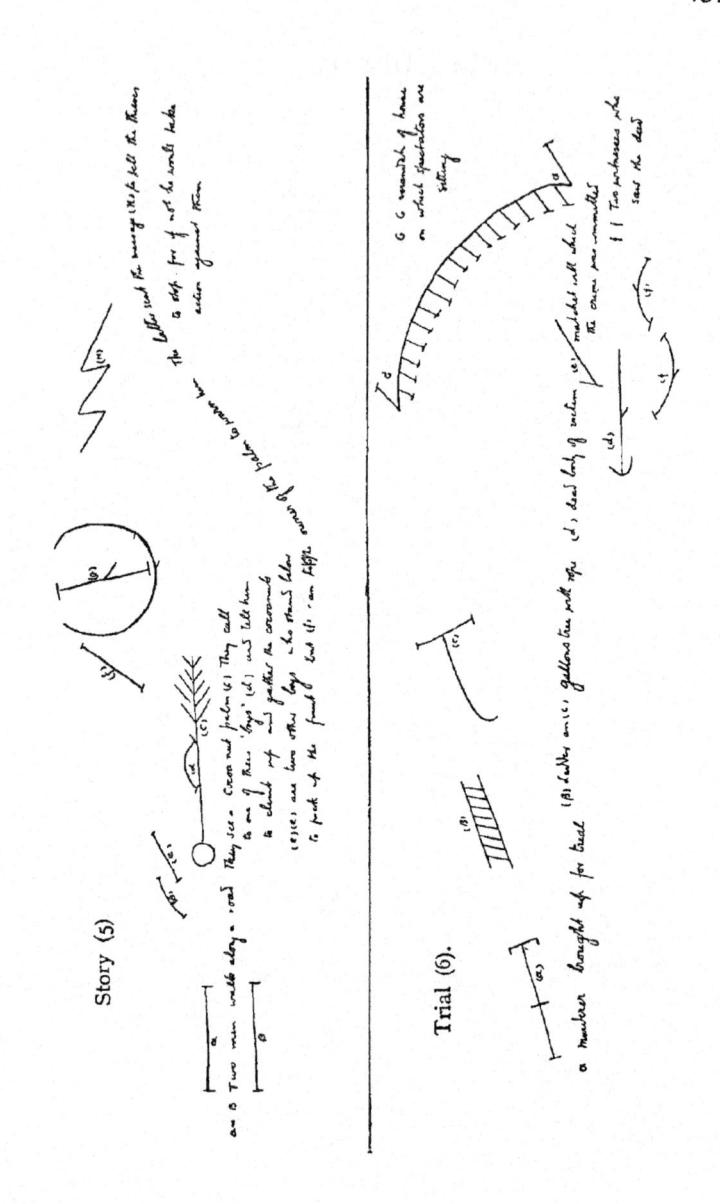

Story (7).

a woman was sitting in her house she is married, because it is closed up all round.
(1)
(2) She comes out with an egbo feather in her head.
a man (3) sees her and fell in love
He sent 'boy' (4) with a message (5) to beg the woman to be his 'friend'
6 6 6 are the husband's members. they hear the message and go and tell the husband (7)
The suitor (3) next sends for some rum (8) as a bribe.
The case in trial 9.9 are witnesses
The suitor tells a lie.
suitor taken into prison yard
(A) marries two wives B & C. C shares his room
The couple are very luxurious, for they have three pillows.
B sleeps in her own room alone, with only one pillow;

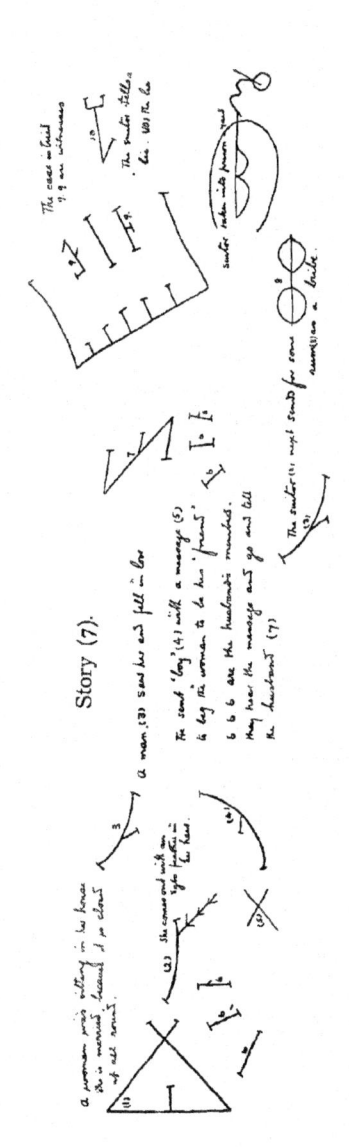

Story (8).

(Toy Juju Sword - Obam No 1)
Looking glass
calabash in which woman cooks food for man who is not her husband
She adorns herself for the visit of her lover
The husband
verandah
with people leaning against it listening & watching
palavers
loving couple
advise wife to give up her lover
Jury
Judge
Judge
correspondent
Respondent
Case brought to Court.
plaintiff.
young girls.
wifes contemporaries who come to advise her to give up her love
Mans father who comes.
hands with his hands on his knees - bending forward to ask for pardon for his son they have put chains.
people who the father brings to help him plead.
The son bound with neck ring and leg irons
Compound into which the son was taken
Men come into the Compound
and say to the man.
You are not unmarried but have your own wife at home!
Why then do you go to another mans wife. and take food from the calabash which belongs to another -
Both parties listen to the good advice.
They go for a last walk together. Then
say 'goodbye' - after which each goes a different way
The girl friends approve

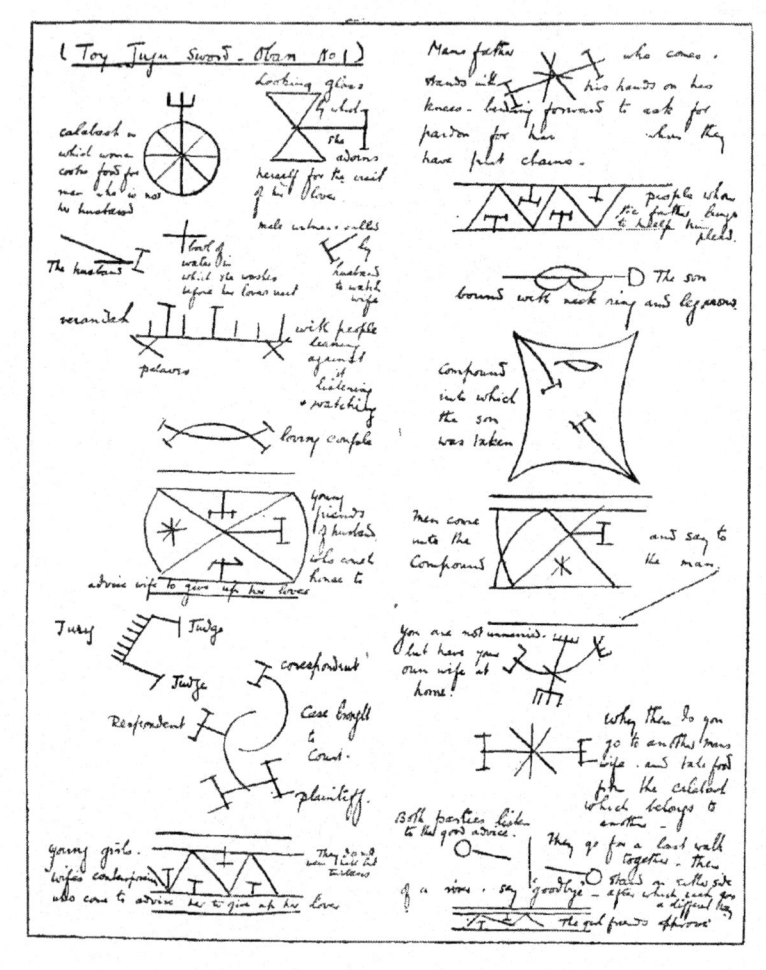

Story (9).

Oban No 2
The sign of carelessness before the coming of the white man - when there was no redress if a man hit you in the head
A woman has a lover
the two go off together
The husband sees
he stands with his hand to his face in an attitude expressing that he is considering what to do
he calls his five other wives - they come with his four children
the door
He says - I cannot well break down
He calls the townspeople and announces
I have my five wives whom I love and keep to
5 remaining wives
with their four children
the parting of the ways
separation from guilty wife
five remaining wives with their 4 children
The other one can go - I will have nothing further to do with her

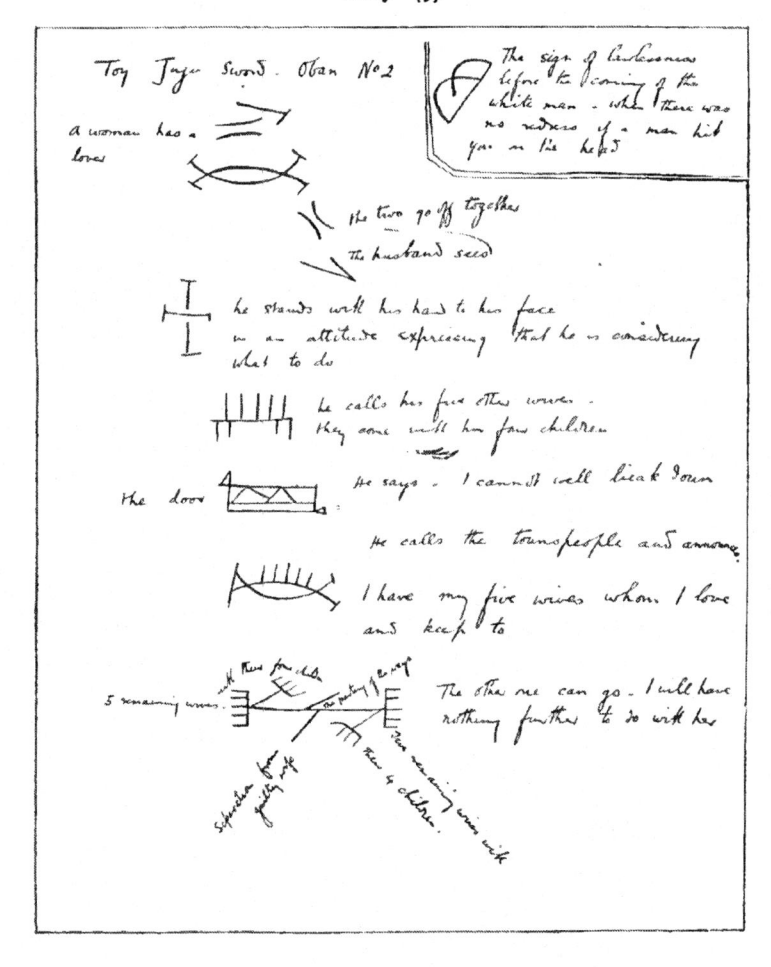

No. (10).—Record of Trial, taken from small triangular calabash. MFAMOSING.

APPENDIX H.

BOTANY.

The Oban District has a marvellous flora. Out of the 2,000 varieties collected by us in 1911-12, about 150 new genera and species have already been worked out by the authorities of the British Museum, Dr. Rendle, F.R.S., Mr. E. G. Baker, Mr. Spencer Moore, and Mr. H. F. Wernham, to whom we owe deep gratitude for the kind interest shown. 1,600 natural-size drawings, mostly in water-colour, have been made by my wife of new and rare species.

It would be impossible to give here any adequate idea of the flora of the country, but a descriptive catalogue of the collection is shortly to be published by the British Museum. It is also hoped to issue, a little later, a volume containing full descriptions, with coloured plates, of the new genera and species. In aid of this, the Royal Society has most kindly signified its intention of making a grant, subject to the approval of referees.

(1) FUNGI.

List kindly supplied by Mr. Massee, of the Royal Botanic Gardens, Kew.

Hypholoma Talboti, Massee (sp. nov.).

Hymenomycetes.

Marasmius ferrugineus B.
,, sp.
Lentinus velutinus Fr.
,, exilis. Klotzsch.
,, fasciatus Berk.
Lenzites pallida B.
Polyporus adustus (Willd.) Fr.
,, sp. (indeterminable).

HYMENOMYCETES—*continued*.
    Fomes rugosus Fr. (immature).
      ,,   lucidus Fr.
    Polystictus carneo-niger B.
        ,,   Malaiensis Cke. (prox.).
        ,,   xanthopus Fr.
        ,,   sp.
        ,,   sp.
        ,,   sp.
    Favolus brasiliensis Fr.
    Stereum elegans Fr.
      ,,   involutum Kl.
      ,,   lobatum Fr.
      ,,   versicolor (Sw.) Fr.
    Lachnocladium semivestitum B. et C.
      ,,   sp.
    Tremella fuciformis B.
DISCOMYCETES.
    Trichoscypha Hindsii B.
PYRENOMYCETES.
    Xylaria Wrightii B. et C.
      ,, sp. (immature)
    Hypoxylon coccineum Bull.

    Daldinia concentrica, Ces. et de Not.
    Panus sp.
    Phallus sp.
    Panus sp.

The last collections and those at the British Museum are not worked out as yet.

(2) LICHENS.

List kindly supplied by Miss Lorraine Smith, of the British Museum.

Parmelia Hildebrandtii Krempelh.
    ,,   melanothrix Wain.
    ,,   olivetorum var. esorediata Wain.
Ramalina leptosperma.

Usnea angulata Ach.
  ,, articulata.
  ,, arthroclada Fee.
  ,, dasypoga Fr.
  ,, florida Hoffm.
  ,,   ,, var. australis Wain.
  ,, rigida Wain.

APPENDIX I.

ZOOLOGY.

Information supplied through the kindness of Dr. Harmer, F.R.S., of the British Museum (Natural History).

(1) MAMMALS OF THE OBAN DISTRICT.

By Guy Dollman, Esq., of the British Museum.

N B.—Ekoi names in parentheses

Cercocebus collaris, Gray.—The white-collared Mangabey.

Cercopithecus mona, Schreb. (Mbuk).—The Mona Guenon.

Papio nigeriæ, Elliot (Monni Nshum).—The Nigerian Baboon. A skull from Oban.

Papio leucophæus, F. Cuv. (Nshum).—Drill Ape.

Two specimens ♂, Nos. 63 and 74.

In addition to the above-mentioned specimens (No. 74 being a very fine old male), Mr. Talbot also collected nine skulls of this rare Ape, these skulls being the first the Museum has ever received.

Andropopithecus troglodytes (Nyokk).—Chimpanzee.

Galago talboti, Dollm., sp. nov. (Ebopp).

This handsome *Galago*, originally described from a single specimen, is now represented by a fine series of skins and skulls, adult and immature. The young Pelage is rather greyer and less suffused, with the yellowish-buff tint so dominant in the adult phase.

On account of the great differences in colour, especially of the under parts, this Nigerian form must be considered quite distinct from *G elegantulus*, and deserving of specific rank. *G elegantulus pallidus*, Gray, is readily distinguished from this new species by its dull greyish under-surface, greyer back and much larger size.

A full description of this and other new mammals has been published in the " Annals and Magazine of Natural History."

Galago demidoffi, Fisch. (Monni Ebopp).

Unlike the larger forms, this small Lemur enjoys a very wide geographical distribution, specimens from the Gold Coast, Nigeria, Cameroons, and Congo all appearing to be representatives of the same species.

Hypsignathus monstrosus, H. Allen (Ekpangpang).

Both Mr Talbot's examples of this extraordinary Bat were male specimens; the unique development of the nasal region is well illustrated by these two individuals. This Bat is popularly known as the hammer-headed fruit bat.

Epomops franqueti strepitans, K. And.—A small species of Fruit-eating Bats.

Eidolon helvum, Kerr.—One of the commonest of the larger African Fruit Bats.

Rousettus ægyptiacus, E. Geoff.—A medium-sized Fruit-eating Bat.

Taphozous peli, Temminck.—The West African Tomb Bat.

Hipposidorus caffer.

Crocidura, sp. (Ifim Mbe).

It is impossible to accurately determine this Shrew, as the specimen is not quite mature.

Genetta æquatorialis (Nsimm).—West African Genet.

Nandinia binotata (Reinwardt), Gray (Mbai).

Viverra civetta, Schreb. (Ejaw).—Civet Cat.

Mungos naso, de Wint. (Ebi).—Long-nosed Mungoose.

Mungos paludinosus, G. Cuv. (Ebi).—Marsh Mungoose.

Crossarchus obscurus, F. Cuv. (Ifett).—Brown Cusimanse.

Crossarchus talboti, sp. nov. Thos.—Talbot's Cusimanse.

Bdeogale nigripes, Puch. (Obo Ebi) —The Four-toed Mungoose.

Lutra maculicollis, Licht. (Esimm Nsaw).—Otter.

Manis tricuspis (Njokk Ika).—Pangolin.

APPENDIX I

Anomalurus beecrofti argenteus, Sch. (Ebhagi).

Two specimens quite in agreement with Schwann's type which came from Abutshi, 150 miles from the coast, Niger River The general pale silvery-grey tint which is so dominant in the coloration of this Flying Squirrel readily distinguishes it from all the allied forms.

Sciurus poensis, Sm. (Isumm).

There would appear to be no great difference in general colour between these Nigerian specimens and individuals from Fernando Po, the type locality. Probably with the help of a larger series some racial differences would manifest themselves, but for the present it is best to regard these specimens as representing the Island species

Sciurus stangeri.
Helioscurus rufobrachiatus, Waterh. (Irun Ebange).

This would appear to be the commonest of all West African Squirrels. In general colouring this species shows a very considerable range of variation, chiefly due to the bleaching of the dark-brownish tints into a rich rusty red.

Funisciurus auriculatus oliviæ, Dollm., sp. nov. (Ebange).

This strikingly coloured Squirrel is now represented in the Museum collection by six specimens, all exhibiting the same beautiful colouring as described in the original diagnosis.

This handsome Squirrel is readily distinguished from the allied forms by the bright, yellowish coloration of the hind quarters and posterior back, the yellowish-olive neck, shoulders and limbs, the almost pure rufous-orange colour of the head, without any conspicuous black speckling, and by the pale buff tint of the entire ventral surface. *Funisciurus auriculatus, a. boydi*, and *a. beatus* are all much more rufous on the back, a great deal darker on the neck and shoulders, richer in colour on the ventral surface, and with the posterior portion of the head speckled with black or yellow and black

Funisciurus leucostigma talboti, sp. nov. Thos. (Ikomme).

This Squirrel was described by Mr. Thomas in a paper on "New African Squirrels" published in November, 1909; since that date further specimens of this interesting Squirrel have been collected by Mr. Talbot, and the form is now well represented in the Museum collection

Protoxerus stangeri eborivorus Du Ch. (Nchab Ebange).

These giant Squirrels appear all very much like each other, there being very little colour variation.

Epimys rattus, L. (Mbe).—The Black Rat.

Epimys tulbergi, Thos (Mbe).

Hybomys univittatus (Pet).—Striped Mouse

Cricetomys gambianus, Waterh. (Nku).—Giant Rat.

Atherura africana, Gray (Nyopp).—African Brush-tailed Porcupine.

Cephalophus sylvicultor, Afzel (Nkŏngam).—Yellow backed Duiker.

Cephalophus ogilbyi, Waterh. (Nsum).—Ogilby's Duiker.

Cephalophus dorsalis, Gray (Etuk).—Bay Duiker.

Cephalophus melanorrheus, Gray (Ise).—Blue Duikerbok.

Dorcatherium aquaticum (Iku).—Water Chevrotain.

Syncerus nanus, Lydekk (Mfŏng).—Congo Buffalo.

Dendrohyrax dorsalis, Fraser (Iting).—Tree Hyrax.

Potamochœrus porcus.

Procavia dorsalis (Ikpimm)—Dassie.

Graphiurus hueti.

Graphiurus crassicaudatus dorotheæ (Dollm.), sp. nov.

The type and one other specimen are the only known representatives of this interesting Dormouse. It appears closely allied to the Liberian *crassicaudatus*, and, at present, represents the eastern limit of that group. The cranial characters exhibited by these two forms are quite unlike those found in the "*murinus*" group, and the only approach to these conditions is found in the large *Graphiurus hueti*, which agrees with the *crassicaudatus* group as regards the broad cranial and interorbital regions and the narrow parallel-sided nasals. These cranial characters, considered together with the question of the distichous tail, appear to justify the conclusion that the *crassicaudatus* group are diminutive allies of the large West African Dormice belonging to the *hueti* group.

This handsome new form is named after Mrs. Talbot; it forms a most worthy addition to the long list of new and rare Nigerian mammals collected by Mr. Talbot, and presented by him to the National Collection.

(2) BIRDS.

FOUND IN THE OBAN DISTRICT, AND PREVIOUSLY UNKNOWN TO EXIST IN NIGERIA.

List kindly supplied by Mr. Ogilvie Grant, of the British Museum (Natural History).

Astur macroscelides
Lamprocolius splendidus
,, splendens
,, purpureiceps
Onychognathus hartlaubi
Nigrita canicapilla
Spermestes bicolor
Hyphantornis cucullatus
,, castaneofuscus
Malimbus nigerrimus
,, malambicus
,, nitens
,, scutatus
,, olachelliæ
,, racheliæ
,, ocutatus
Spermospiza guttata
Andropadus gracilis
Ixonotus guttatus
Bleda notata
,, indicator
Cinnyris batesi
Psalidoprocne nitens
Alseonax milanoptera

Muscicapa lugens
Turacus meriani
Chrysococcyx smaragdineus
Coracias abyssinicus
Eurystomus gularis
Astur castaniluis
Herodias alba
Hoplopterus coronatus
Glottis nebularius
Œdicnemus senegalensis
Galactochrysœa liberix
Porphrio alleni
Podica senegalensis
Francolinus lathami
Xenocichla notata
Totanus glottis
Lobivanellus albiceps
Ceryle rudis
Lophoceros communis
,, hartlaubi
Coccystes cafer
Centropus anselli
,, monachus
Scotornis climacurus

APPENDIX I

Bubo cinerascens
Haliætus vorcifer
Asturina monogrammica
Phalocrocorax africanus
Ardea purpurea

Pseudo-tantalus ibis
Ceratogymna atrata
Hoptopterus spinosus
Machetes pugnax

(3) FISH, REPTILES, Etc.

List kindly supplied by Dr. Boulenger, F.R.S, of the British Museum.

Among the most interesting are:—

SNAKES. Tropidonotus ferox
Causus lichtensteini.
Chlorophis heterodermus.
Bitis nasicornis.

CROCODILES. Crocodilus niloticus ? (egg).
Osteolemus tetraspis.

FROGS. Rana oxyrhynchus.
Arthrodeptis pœcilonotus.
Rappia tuberculatus.
Hylambatus rufus.
Cardioglossa leucornystax.

TOADS Bufo superciliaris.
„ latifrons.

FISHES. Marcusenius brachistius.
Barbus ablabes.
Haplochilus sexfasciatus.
Malopterurus electricus.

GECKO. Hemidactylius fasciatus.
CHAMELEONS. Chameleon cristatus.
Rhampoleon sputicus.

An eroded Cinixys from the District is now in the Zoological Gardens.

(4) INSECTS, Etc.

A large collection was made, but it has not yet been worked out. The authorities of the British Museum inform me, however, that it contains a considerable number of specimens new to science.

APPENDIX I

BUTTERFLIES.

Information kindly supplied by Mr. Heron, of the British Museum.

Within a few months in 1909 the following species were collected:—

Lycænidæ	14 species
Satyrinæ	7 ,,
Danainæ	4 ,,
Acrœinæ	11 ,,
Nymphalinæ	76 ,,
Papilionniæ	17 ,,
Pierinæ	16 ,,
Hesperidæ	4 ,,
	149

Some of these were new to the Museum.

E g., in Nymphalinæ.   Euryphene barombina. Standingeri. ♂ ♀
Harma reinholdi. Ploetz. ♀
Harma standingeri. Aurivillus. ♂ ♀
,,   Lycenidæ.   Phytata elais. Hewittus ♀

The genus Hypotimnas is well represented by five forms and varieties.

Conspicuous among the Papilionidæ are the sabre-winged Antimachus, the blue-green Salmoxis, and the large Meneothais and Hesperus; while Euxanthe Trajanus is the showiest of the Nymphalinæ. The Papilio (Drurya) Antimachus measured 9¼ inches

(5) ARACHNIDA, ETC.

From information kindly supplied by Mr. S Hirst, of the British Museum.

SPIDERS.

1. A new genus and species, not yet described, of the family Barychelidæ, allied to Cyphonisia, Sim., trap-door spider.

2. A new species. Hysterocrates. Mygale or bird-eating spider. (The natives have assured me that people have died

from a bite of this insect. Within my own experience the mother of one of my boys, Itamfum by name, nearly succumbed to a bite and was ill for weeks.)

3. Hysterocrates laticeps. Poc. Mygale or bird-eating spider.
4. Nephila lucasii. Sim. Large orb-web spider.
5. Nephila femoralis. Lucas. Large orb-web spider.
6. Nephila pilipes. Lucas.
7. Heteropoda regia. L. House spider.
8. Araneus sp. (immature).

HARVEST MEN.

Guruia talboti, n. sp. Roewer (*Archiv. für Naturgeschichte*, 1911. Supp. pp. 106, 3 pl.).

ACARI (MITES).

Hæmaphysalis leachi. Aud. Taken from a long-nosed Mungoose.
Hyalomma ægyptium. L.

MYRIOPODA.

Centipedes.

Ethmostigmus trigonopodus. Leach.
Scolopendra morsitans. L.

Millipedes.

Spirostreptus, sp. nov.
Odontopyge, sp. nov.
Trigoniulus, sp. nov.
Osircomulas, sp. nov.
Alloporus, sp. nov.
Oxydesmus granulosus. Palirot.
Cryptodesmus, sp.

Of the seven millipedes four are new species and one is remarkable for its length ($11\frac{1}{2}$ inches), which is greater than that of any millipede hitherto known.

Pedipalpi.

Damon johnstoni. Poc.

APPENDIX I

(6) CRABS.

Crabs exist in great numbers in the District, as might be guessed from the prominent part which they play in ritual and folk-lore. My collection has not yet been worked out, but according to Mr A. T. Calman, "Some appear to come near the species known as Potamon (Potamonautes) Pobeguini, but the group to which they belong is still very imperfectly known, and it is difficult to speak positively as to the identification."

(7) MOLLUSCA.

No shells new to science have been discovered in the District, but various points in the life-history of some of them have been noticed which were previously unknown.

The large Achatina Marginata, for instance, possesses the power of screaming. This fact is well known to the natives, who were much amused at my start of surprise when one of these Snails screamed on being taken into my hand. It is supposed that the noise is produced by the creature scraping against its shell. Anyhow, the sound is loud enough to prove distinctly startling on a first experience.

Another small land snail has the power of springing 3 to 4 feet.

Fine clusters of Œtheria are to be found in the beds of the rivers, especially in the Kwa.

APPENDIX J.

MINERALOGY.

Information supplied by courtesy of Dr. Prior.

Minerals are present throughout the District in very large quantities. As an example, the compositions of pannings from eleven rivers, kindly worked out for me by Mr. W. Campbell Smith, of the British Museum (Natural History), are given below :—

No.	Name of River.	No. of Pans.	Weight.	Remarks.
1	Mo, near Nkami	2	389 gms.	Fine grained. Consists mainly of ilmenite, with much magnetite. Zircon in microscopic colourless crystals is abundant. Some fragments of pink garnet. Rounded quartz grains.
2	Awa, near Nfunum	2	68 gms.	As above (1), but very rich in pink garnet in small crystals and fragments.
3	Akup, near Ojokk	1	32 gms.	Very fine grained. Magnetite much more plentiful than in any other sample. Zircons and garnets only occur as microscopic crystals, the latter being rather scarce.
4	Ekku, near Ako	2	116 gms.	Coarser grained. Ilmenite with very much magnetite. Zircons very abundant in colourless prisms with brilliant lustre, and often 1 mm. long. Pink garnets are also abundant. No cassiterite. Rounded grains of quartz.

APPENDIX J

MINERALOGY—*continued*.

No	Name of River.	No of Pans	Weight.	Remarks
5	Between Niaji and Ntebbashott	2	273 gms	Fine grained Ilmenite with some magnetite No cassiterite Garnets scarce Zircons much less abundant than in No 4.
6	Akpininni, near Oremm	2	300 gms	Fine grained As above (5), but zircons present as microscopic crystals. Garnet rather scarce
7	Between Oremm and Ntebbashott	2	103 gms.	Fine grained As above (6)
8	Ikpan, on Mfamosing-Ekkonnanakku Road	2	25 gms.	This is characterised by the presence of monazite in quantity sufficient to give a yellow colour to the sand, the monazite is, however, quite subordinate to the ilmenite. Pink garnet and quartz are both abundant Zircon is relatively scarce.
9	Okot-Ikpo, near Ekkonnanakku	2	150 gms	Again a large percentage of quartz has remained in the pan Garnet is abundant and in large fragments There is a very small amount of monazite The ilmenite, which forms the bulk of the sand, is very finely divided
10	Aripp Ainyakk, near Ekkonnanakku	2	350 gms.	A nearly pure ilmenite concentrate Quartz, garnet, and zircon are all present, but only in small percentages
11	Akwa Yafe, near Falls	2	42 gms	A very pink and white sand, containing much quartz and pink garnet. It contains a small amount of monazite and some brownish zircons This concentrate seems characterised by the presence of fragments of a green hornblende. Cassiterite seems to be entirely absent in all the pannings.

APPENDIX K.

METEOROLOGY.

Temperature.

Readings were taken during the rainy season from June to October, 1909, which is the coolest time of the year. Early in November the instruments were struck by lightning, and the records thus brought to a sudden end.

Temperature in the Shade.

Month.	Mean.	Highest.	Lowest.	Greatest Diurnal Variation.	Mean Max.	Mean Min.
June	77·7	89	64	19	83·3	72·1
July	76·5	89	69	18	81·7	71·3
August	77·2	90	69	23	84·3	70·1
September	77·9	92	69	23	84·9	70·9
October	79·9	95	68	27	89·8	70·0

Rainfall at Oban Station during 1911.

Month.	Total Rainfall per Month in Inches.	No. of Days per Month on which Rain fell.	Maximum Rain in any one Day in Inches.	Duration of Rainfall on Day of Maximum Rain.
January	3·22	7	1·65	7 hours
February	2·63	3	1·83	6 ,,
March	5·99	11	1·32	1 ,,
April	12·18	17	2·20	6 ,,
May	25·98	25	5·00	6 ,,
June	17·59	15	3·60	6 ,,
July	22·88	26	4·15	9 ,,
August	28·17	29	6·38	10 ,,
September	24·21	27	4·11	3 ,,
October	27·28	23	4·63	10 ,,
November	3·43	18	0·89	3 ,,
December	1·93	3	1·80	4 ,,
Total	175·49	204		

APPENDIX K

The rainfall during June to December in 1909 amounted to 116·83 inches, and that for the whole year 1910 to 144·10 inches. The latter was an exceptional year, and many streams dried up, which had never been known to fail previously. According to native reports the rainfall during 1911 was below the average.

APPENDIX L.

GEOGRAPHICAL SURVEY.

I.—Principal Positions.

The survey depends chiefly on latitude and azimuth base lines from Oban to Mt. Awsaw Ifogi and Oban to Ibianshi Peak, and three subsidiary measured bases at Oban, Ibum, and Nkami.

Longitude is reckoned from the position of Obutong, fixed by chronometrical differences from Calabar.

Place.	Latitude North.	Longitude East.	Height in Feet.	Remarks.
Oban Hill A .	5° 19' 37"	8° 33' 36"	1105	△ Cairn at N.W. point.
,, ,, A[1] .	5 19 31	8 33 40	1067	△ Easterly end.
,, Station .	5 19 22	8 34 30	408	In front of District House. Latitude by Observation.
Ibum Town .	5 38 18	8 28 59	1045	× Latitude by Observation.
Ibianshi Peak .	5 34 49	8 26 41	2880	△ ,, from Ibum Town.
A[5]	5 23 41	8 34 27	1619	× H.P.
D[3]	5 26 57	8 36 9	2487	× H.P.
Agamdugum Peak .	5 41 34	8 21 6	2348	× H.P.
D[1]	5 30 21	8 37 11	3147	× H.P.
K[4]	5 33 9	8 51 7	3731	× H.P.
K[5]	5 33 59	8 50 41	3573	× H.P.
K[1]	5 30 6	8 50 18	3162	× H.P.
G[1]	5 29 29	8 46 10	2697	× H.P.
G[2]	5 30 35	8 46 8	2287	× H.P.
G[3]	5 31 10	8 46 13	2081	× H.P.
G[4]	5 31 24	8 46 9	1959	× H.P.
M[1]	5 35 55	8 52 4	2031	× H.P. Dependent upon the position of Nkami.
M[2]	5 35 27	8 52 20	2181	Ditto ditto.
M[3]	5 35 13	8 51 27	2435	Ditto ditto.
Mt. Awsaw Ifogi .	5 30 11	8 49 14	3085	△ 6 feet East of single tree. Latitude from Niaji.
Niaji Town .	5 32 11	8 46 50	678	△ In front of Egbo House.
Ikpai .	5 32 23	8 47 12	652	In front of Egbo House. Fixed by Subtenses from Mt. Awsaw Ifogi.
Owum .	5 32 41	8 47 22	608	Ditto ditto.
Ibum Farm Hill, B[1]	5 38 47	8 28 58	906	H.P.
,, ,, B[2]	5 38 42	8 29 7	953	H.P.
K[8]	5 32 42	8 49 9	2237	H.P.
K[9]	5 33 5	8 48 29	1957	H.P.
N[5]	5 38 28	8 27 5	1830	H.P.
Pinnacle Peak, B[6] .	5 36 9	8 33 38	3280	H.P.
B[8] .	5 36 33	8 29 37	2331	H.P.
N[3] .	5 40 17	8 29 8	1110	H.P.
B[5] .	5 33 56	8 30 42	2784	H.P.
B[4] .	5 35 46	8 33 18	3501	H.P.
O[1] .	5 37 54	8 35 45	3024	H.P.
O[2] .	5 38 40	8 34 21	2888	H.P.
R .	5 16 13	8 40 45	1180	H.P.
R[1] .	5 14 19	8 38 20	1178	H.P.
D[2] .	5 26 41	8 33 36	1653	H.P.
P[1] .	5 29 3	8 26 56	1147	H.P.
D[4] .	5 29 12	8 37 2	3255	H.P.

APPENDIX L

Height from theodolite vertical angles (dependent upon the lowest step at Obutong Beach being 60 feet above sea level).

Heights are reckoned to ground level, except at intersected points, where the tallest tree has been observed.

H.P. = Highest Point.
Δ = Triangulation Station.
× = Triangulation Intersected Point.

II.—Secondary Positions.

Latitudes and longitudes by astronomical observations, the latter being determined by chronometric differences. Heights by aneroid.

Place	Latitude North	Longitude East.	No. of Independent Observations for Longitude	If Longitude checked by bearing to × at or near Town	Height in Feet	Remarks
Nkami	5° 36′ 51″	8° 52′ 8″	4	Yes	510	In front of Egbo House
Ndebbiji	5 35 9	8 49 29	4	,,	600	,, ,, ,,
Ekkonnanahku	5 6 24	8 40 9	2	No	320	,, Rest ,,
Obarekkai	5 5 57	8 26 6	4	,,	70	Eastern end of Town
Nsan	5 19 9	8 22 55	11	,,	490	In front of Rest House.
Mbarakpa	5 12 19	8 26 24	10	,,	390	,, ,, ,,
Netim	5 21 13	8 21 4	1	,,	430	,, Egbo ,,
Ekuri Owai	5 42 12	8 24 59	3	Yes	890	,, ,, ,,
Oburekkpe	5 49 20	8 23 12	2	,,	410	,, ,, ,,
Owai Ifunkpa	5 33 48	8 14 17	4	,,	480	,, ,, ,,
Ojo Nkonimba	5 25 53	8 16 16	2	No	460	,, ,, ,,
Etara	5 47 5	8 29 30	2	,,	510	,, ,, ,,
Iko Akperem	5 38 2	8 10 54	2	Yes	390	,, ,, ,,
Ako	5 27 49	8 43 12	8	No	500	,, Rest ,,
Okarara	5 22 8	8 42 5	4	,,	420	,, Egbo ,,
Aking	5 26 12	8 38 5	5	Yes	460	,, ,, ,,
Ebuugo	5 0 14	8 41 45	2	No.	100	,, Rest ,,
Nchofan (Insofan)	5 48 26	8 40 40	2	,,	—	,, ,, ,,

III.—Positions fixed by Obutong-Oban Theodolite Traverse.

Place	Latitude North	Longitude East	Height in Feet	Remarks
Oban Town	5° 19′ 4″	8° 34′ 22″	413	West end Juju Nchibbi
Ekong	5 16 29	8 33 31	478	In front of Egbo House
Ndingane	5 8 55	8 30 41	310	,, ,, ,,
Nwan's	5 8 14	8 29 38	281	,, ,, ,,
Obutong	5 8 19	8 29 12	236	,, Rest ,,
Top of Kwa Falls	5 8 36	8 29 12	162	Bench mark on Eastern bank
Bottom ,,	5 8 19	8 28 53	60	Lowest Step, beginning of Oban-Obutong Road
Obutong-Calabar Oban-Cross-Roads	5 8 35	8 30 21	286	———
Ekong Ndekke Obutong Cross-Roads	5 16 16	8 33 33	423	———

APPENDIX L

ADDITIONAL HEIGHTS FROM ANEROID READINGS.

Place	Height in Feet	Remarks
Ndekke	310	In front of Egbo House
Agbung Beach	50	
Hill North of Agbung	210	
Oknpedi	250	
Abbiati	350	Mbe Kako's Compound
R Donnya	420	On Netim-Ibum Road
R Ndiansha	750	,, ,, ,,

MAGNETIC VARIATION (1909).
MEAN VALUE OF NEEDLE REVERSED AND UNREVERSED.

Place.	Date	Latitude	Longitude	Variation	Remarks
Oban Stn	Dec 27, '08	5° 19' 22"	8° 34' 36"	12° 44' 37"	
,,	Dec 5, '09	,,	,,	12 39 35	
Oban Hill	Dec 6, '09	5 19 37	8 33 36	12 43 28	Not reversed 1105 feet high
Nkami	Oct 23, '09	5 36 51	8 52 8	12 18 25	Considerable local attraction
Mt Awaw Ifogi	Oct 28, '09	5 30 11	8 49 14	12 41 36	3085 feet high
Ibianshi Peak	Dec 12, '09	5 34 49	8 26 41	12 35 12	Not reversed 2880 feet high

T

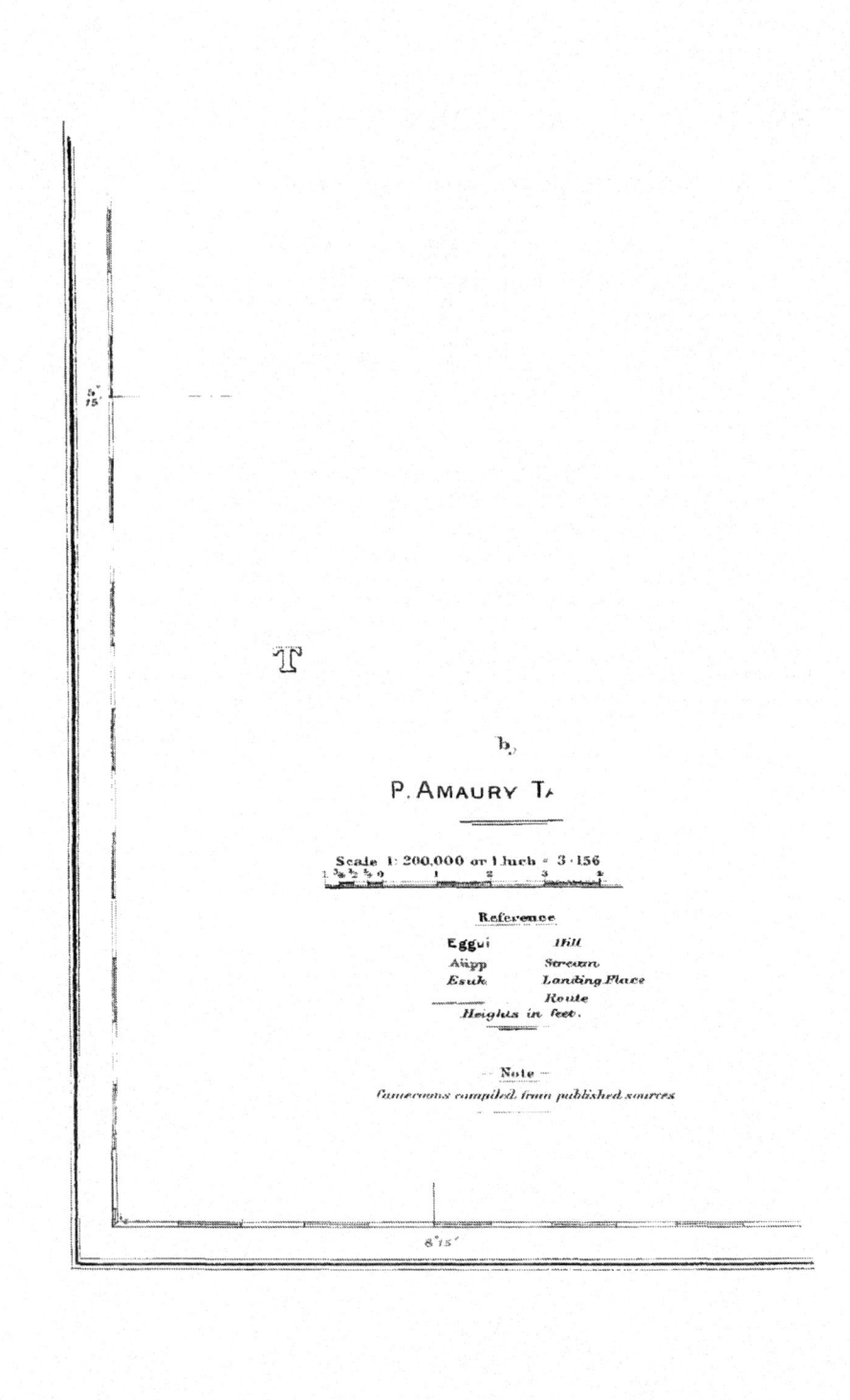

b,

P. AMAURY T

Scale 1: 200,000 or 1 Inch = 3·156

Reference

Eggui	Hill
Aüpp	Stream
Esuk	Landing Place
	Route

Heights in feet.

— Note —
Cameroons compiled from published sources

INDEX

ABBIATI, Egbo stone at, 171–2
Abiankpaw, giant king of Skull people, 275–6
Abijang, Ekoi-Akam inter-marriages at, 216
   Pool at, use of, 217, 218
   Skulls at Chief's house, 217
Abonn Ogbe, Egbo grade, 41
   Master of ceremonies of, 43
Ada, the Forest Demon, story of, 247, 336
Adet Awaw, Woman of position, Funeral of, 224–5
Adia Club, 411
Adonis, birth of, Ekoi analogies to, 132 et seq.
Adonis-Attis-Osiris worship, Ekoi parallels, 74–5
Æsculapius, staff of, symbolism of, 27
After-life (see also Ghosts), Ekoi ideas on, 17
Agara tree, pods, in Folk-tale, 381, seeds in decoration, 217
Agbashan, Chief, at Oban, Were-shape of, 82–3, 87
Age, Ekoi reverence for, 322
   Probable maximum, 319
Age-classes, 108, 112, 115 321, evolution, 48, nature, 283
Agegam, River, Bridge, and Cascades of, 152
Agriculture, Crop-rotation, 270
   Women's part in, 269
Akaba-Nsi, Ekoi word for Ghost, 230
Akam-Ekoi inter-marriages at Abijang, 216
Akillinga Juju, of the Ojo, 245–6
Aking, Children's Games and Songs at, 90
   Mediterranean type of Ornament from, 173
Ako, 90, 161
Akpambe Juju, 51, 52
   Amulets of votaries, 52
   Case of, 125
   Smelling-out of Witches by, 198
Akpanebesin flower, as Wrestler's challenge, 287

Akunane, head-priest of Juju Ofiri, on sacrifice to Ghosts, 232–3
Akwa, tribes near, Secret Society of, 37
Akwa Yafe river, 3, Falls of, Caves near, 162–3
Alexander, Lieut Boyd, Plant named after, 214
Ambushes, 271–2
Amulets, against Ghosts, 231
Amusements, 283–6
Ancestors, Diseases sent by, 278
   Ekoi cult of, 13
   Sacrifices to,
      at House-building, 263
      after War, 272
Angbo Club, 413
Animal forms assumed by Humans (see also Efumi), 80 et sqq, 195
   Life (see also Zoology), Kwa river, 1, 2
Animal Sacrifice, 9, 10, 19, 55, 222, 224, 225, story on, 226
   Crab's Claw in, 196, story on, 197–8
Animals in Folk-tales (see under Names), American Negro parallels, 337
   Second-sight of, 175, 230
   Speech of, The Man who Understood, story of, 99–101
Animm Juju, 50, human sacrifice at, 243–6
Antann leaves, ritual use of, 263
Antelopes (see also Duiker), 6, 142–3, 160, in Egbo art, 141, in Folk-tales, 314–9
Ant-hills in Eja Juju, 77–8
Anthropometry, Appendix C, 414
Antikka, Familiars exorcised from, 194–5
Ants, Lords of the Bush, story of, 401–2
   Black, in Folk-lore, 9, in "Medicine," 131
Anwan Nsibidi, site, and meaning of words, 157

INDEX

Ape People, why they no longer live in Towns, 78-9
Apes (*see also* Drill Ape), Anthropoid, Ekoi beliefs on, story on, 78-9
 Oban District, 465
 Why Hunter may not Eat Apes killed in the Bush, 143-4
Ara, the Sky-maiden, 340-4
Arachnida, &c, Oban District, 471-2
Aret Offiong's dowry, 106
Art, Ekoi, 287 *et sqq*
Aru bird, Omens from, 324, Tabu on, 410
Arums, Kwa river, 1
Assyria, Axe symbol from, 15
Astral forms of Things in Dreams, 232
Astronomical Myths, 344, 349, 355, 357
Asunga Juju, of Mfuor Club, 413
Ataiyo river, 11
Aura, personal, belief in, 295
Awa river, Bridge over, 151
 Were-crocodiles of, 81
Awaw Anjanna, Head Chief, of Ododop tribe, 84, 85, death of, in Were-beast form, 85-6
Axe (*see also* Double Axe), in Folk-tale, 402
 Symbol, Assyrian origin of, 15
Axe-Medicine, Ekuri Ibokk, features of, 45
Ayunga Club, 411

Babi, 157
Baboon, Oban District, 465
Baikiea insignis, 256
Ball games, 285-6
Banana people, Decorative art of, 290
Banjang tribe, Ekoi affinity of, 318
Bantu strain in Ekoi, 305, 317
Baobab trees, Bornu, Genii of, Death-blows from, 231
Barrenness, Ideas on, Jujus against, Stories on, and Tabu against, 123-6, 126-9, 132, 133 *et sqq*, 408
Bats, Oban District, 465
 Cave-dwelling, as delicacies, 162-3
 Hammer-headed, Death-messenger, 193, 466
Bavili Paint House, Ekoi analogy to, 108
Beasts, How they all came upon Earth, 149-50

Beasts, Birds, &c, Tabued as Food for Men, and for Women, 407, 408, story on, 409
Beating, Initiatory, 284
Beauty, Ekoi love of, 287 *et sqq.*
Bee, Ekoi name for, 20
Beggars, non-existent, 326
Bells, and Rattles, in Children's "Plays," 217
Belly, of Witch, music and weapons in, 249, 251, 254
 Striking on, 209 & *n* *, 252, 253
 Why other Members must serve, 393-4
Beri-beri, 279, ascribed to Witch-craft, 193
Berlinia, Kwa river, 1
Bigui Juju, tabu to Women, 21
Bini people, Osa, high god of, 13 *n*.
Bird and Tree worship, Minoan, Ekoi analogies, 14
Bird-eating Spider, n sp, Oban District, 471-2
Birds, *see under* Names,
 Dances imitating, 296
 in Folk-tales, 196, 312, 313, 409
 Found in Oban District, previously unknown to exist in Nigeria, 469-70
 Omen-giving, 324
 Sacred, 14
 Tabus on, 408
Birth customs, Ekoi, 31, 44, 120 *et sqq*
 Post-natal, 130 *et sqq.*
 Pre-natal, 130, 167, 183, 219, 408
Births, Multiple, in Folk-tale, 367-8
Bisexual character of Ekoi gods, 14 *et sqq*, 44, and Juju symbols, 67, 76
"Bitter leaf" plant, story of, 133-4
Black Fly, why he can only Buzz, 384, 385
Black Men and White, How they came on Earth, 387-9
Blood-bond, ceremony in, 201
Blood, Human, Libations of, 260, 272
Blood Juju, 109, procedure in, 201
Blow on Face from Ghost, Death from, 230-1
Blue bird, in Folk-tale, 312, 313
Boar, Wild, in Folk tale, 362, 398
 Hunting Tabu on, 407
Boat of Witches, 195
Body, borrowed, of Ghost, 239
Body-painting, 295, 320
Bonny, Slave trade (former), at, 325
Bornu, Baobab trees of, beliefs on, 231

INDEX

Botanical Notes, see Names of Plants, &c
Paintings, &c, by Mrs. P. Amaury Talbot, 462
Botany, Appendix H., 462-4
Bowel-repair, 278-9
Bowl, as Eja symbol, 76
Box, talking, 185-6
Boys, Age classes of, 283
 Initiation of, into Egbo and other Clubs, 284-5
Brahmin beliefs, and Ekoi parallels, 232
Breach of promise, 106, 107
Brer Rabbit and the Briar Patch, parallel tale to, 399
Bride-gifts, 60, 105-8, 111
Bridges, 204, 206, 213
British Museum authorities, help acknowledged from, 462-74
Broom Juju, 81-2
Buduma belief on Death from Djinn's blow, 230-1
Buffal-affinities of Ododop Chiefs, 86, 87
Buffalo, 6
 Hunting Tabu on, 407
 Ravages of, 223
 Congo, Oban District, 468
Bull-roarer, 222, 284
Burial (see also Death and Burial), premature, 231
Burial Masks, Egyptian, Ekoi parallel to, 217
Bush, Division of, near Towns, 262
 Lord of the, story of, 400-1
 Supernatural denizens of, 13
 Tours in, 290
 Treasure House in, story of, 389-93
Bush Animals, damage by, 6, 161, 223, 243
Bush-cow, devastations by, 161, in Folk-tales, 346
Bush Fowl, Egg of, in Divination, 175
 Why it always Calls up the Dawn, 384-5
"Bush men," see Ant-hills
Bush Soul, Animals possessed by, 80 et sqq
Butterflies, Kwa river, 2; Oban District, 471
 Black, as Witch's Familiar, 195

CACTUS, Resin from, 220
Cactus-juice, use of, 194

Calabar, Efiks of, Trade of, and Secret Society, 37
 Railway from, to Lake Chad, route for, 267
 Slave trade (former), at, 325
Calabar river, 3, affluents 11, source, 214
 Leaves heaped beside, 91, 242
 Tribes divided by, 242
 Were-animals in, 81-2, 242
Calabashes, Chiefs tabued from using, 210 & n
 Magic, 28, 367, 369
Cameroons, Ekoi in, 318
 Mountains of, 11
 Nigerian Boundary of, 1
 South, 151 et sqq
 Secret Society in, 37
Camp Life, 190-1
Cam-wood dye in Egbo ritual, 41
Cannibal rites, at Akillinga Juju, 246, aspect of those associated with, 260
Canoe-making, origin of, story, 389
Cap of Chief Ikum, 245
Cap-box of Chiefs of Insofan, 218
Carriers, Ceremony and Song of, 91
Carthaginian origin, possible, of Ekoi cut stones, 172-3
Carved Dishes, 210 n, 218
 Figure, Ekoi, 24
 Egyptian parallel to, 217
Cassava, 150
Cat Dance, 151, 296
Cat-worship, traces of, 151
Categories, Ekoi, 419-20, 422
Cats, why deified, 25
Cats'-cradle, 286
Cauliflorous growths, Kwa river, 205
Caves, Akwa Yafe river, 162-3; at Ekkonnanankku, 84-5
Chalk, White, ritual uses of, 24, 41, 94, 113, 121, 131, 209 & n
Chameleons, Oban District, 470, notions concerning, 91
Charms, see also Magic, Divination, & Witchcraft
 Against Ghosts and Leopards at entrances of Ekoi towns, story of, 7 et seq
 Witchcraft, 200
 Used on Drill Ape, 79
 to Ascertain Ghost preferences, 9
 in Divination, 174 et seq
Chastity, pre-marital and marital, 105
Chessboard, Ekoi, 286
Chiefs administration by and through, 325-6

Chiefs—*continued.*
  Death and Burial of, 221 *et sqq.*,
    261, 295, 315
    story on, 227
  Dishes of, 210 *n*, 218
Child-protecting *motif* in Folk-tales,
    337–40
Children, *see also* Birth Customs,
    Naming, &c
  Clubs, Dances, " Plays," &c , of,
    206, 217, 296–7, 322–3
  Ekoi love of, 322
  From Plants, &c , stories on, 132
    et sqq
  Wife's rights over, 97, story on,
    101–4
Chimpanzee, Oban District, 465
  Finger of, in " Medicine," 131
  Tabu on, 408
China owned by Ekoi, 141
Circles of unhewn Stone, Oban, rites
    performed at, at full and
    new Moon, 10
Circumcision of Boys, 284
Civet Cat, Oban District, 466
  Hunting Tabu on, 407
  in Folk-tale, 397
Classical analogies to Ekoi refrains,
    121
Clay, Edible, 209 *n* †, 248
Cloth, Magic, 180
Clubs and Secret Societies, *see*
    Dances, *see also* Egbo,
    and others *under* Names
  Ekoi, 13, Appendix B , 410–3
  Origin of, 37
  Women's, *see* Women
Clubs (weapons), 271, 272
Cobras, adventure with, 89–90 ,
    seven in one house, 4
Cock-crow, as affecting a Witch, 252
Cocks sacrificed in Juju rites, story
    on, 55 *et sqq*
Coco-yams, associated with Obassi
    Nsi, 21 , culture of, 269,
    270
Cocoa-culture, Native, 201–2
Cocoanut Palms as Lightning Con-
    ductors, 73
Coffins, Empty, in Chiefs' Funerals,
    222 , Women's, 224
Colours associated with Egbo Society's
    grades, 40–2
  Names for, 291–2
Comets, Omens from, 324
Commerce, Progress of, 266–7
Compounds, *see also* Houses,
  Building ritual, &c , of, 263, 270
  Ghost-exclusion from, 231

Compounds—*continued*
  Haunted, 6
  Plan of, and Roman analogies,
    263–5
Congo Buffalo, Oban District, 468
Congo Free State, Anthropometry
    of, 414
Consumption, 279, ascribed to
    Witchcraft, 193
Cook, A B , *cited* on " Cretan Axe
    Cult outside Crete," 15–16
Corn-cobs wedged into Tree-forks,
    161
Corn culture, 269, 270
Costume, Children's " Plays," 206,
    217 , Egbo Plays, 44–5, 52
Cotton trees, as Juju tree, 30 , over-
    thrown by Mfepp Juju,
    73 , sacrifice to, 34, 36
Councils, Native, 310
Counting methods (*see also* Seven),
    304, 422–3
Courts, Chiefs' position in, 84
Cows, in Folk-tales, 211, 361–2, 364,
    365, 376–7
  Sacrificed at Funerals, 222
Crabs, Oban District, 473
  Father of all Jujus, 408
  in Folk-tales, 144–6
  Claw of, in Ritual, 198
  Tabu on, 408
  Why Sacrificed, story, 197–8
  Why used in many Jujus,
    story, 62 *et sqq*
Cranial manipulation of members of
    Leopard Society, Sierra
    Leone, 38 *n*
  Measurements, Natives of Oban
    District, 414
Craw-craw disease, 279, 372
Creation beliefs, Ekoi, 70, 387–9,
    story on, 373–4
Criminals, Execution of, by Nsibidi
    Club, 306
Crocodile, Cult, Ekoi, 24 possible
    origin, 25
  Form of Nimm, 2
  Heads of Juju " Images," 53
  Honoured in Egypt, 28
  Mask, in Eko Juju, 45
Crocodiles in Folk-tales, 333, 334,
    346–7
  of Oban District, 470
  Tabu on, 408
  of various Rivers, &c , 1, 3, 24, 215
  Efumi of, 80, 81, 94, 95, 242–3,
    402
  Rain-making by, 71
Cross-bows, 271, 272

INDEX 485

Cross River, Ekoi settlements in relation to, 318
    Watershed and affluents of, 11, 154
Crossed-stick Juju, 112
Croton amabilis, the Mfam Juju tree, 139, leaves of, in Ekoi death ritual, 44
Cruelty, 328 *et sqq*, 332
Cry of Owl, 196
    of Snails, 473
    of Witches, 195
Cusimanse, Talbot's, n sp, 466
Custom, in Ekoi governance, 310

DANCES, 285, 293 *et seq*
    at Eja festivals, 74
    Cat-dance, 151
    Children's, 296-7
    of Egbo Society and other Clubs, 39, 41, 43 *n*, 44, 272, 410-3
    Funeral, 43 § *n*, 222, 225, 239, 295
      Ghost-excellence in, 239
    Imitative, 296
    of Witches and Wizards, 192
Dancing, Effect of, on Physique, 293
Dancing Skulls, story, 275-6
Dawn, Why the Bush Fowl always calls up the, story, 384-5
Dead, invocation of, 66, 139
    Lakes of, Ekoi, 23 § *n* * *et seq*.
    Names called in Juju, 53
Death, Ekoi ideas on, 17, 87, 200-1, 229, 230-2
    Return from, story on, 229
Death and Burial Customs, 44, 94, 139, 215, 226-7, 239, 287
    Ancient, 302, of Ekoi Clubs, 410
    Animal sacrifices, 19, 222, story on, 226
    Chiefs', 221 *et sqq*, 261, 295, 315
    Egbo Society, Dance, &c, 43 & *n*
    Funeral "Plays," in Folk-tales, 380-1, 384
    Shrines, 6-7
    Funerals of Women of importance, 224-5
    Human sacrifice in, 302, 328 *et sqq*.
    in story, 179, 180
    as to Widows, 116-7
Debts, Free-born pledged for, 326
    Recovery of, by Egbo Society, 45-6
Decorative art, Banana people, 290
Ekoi, *see* Wall-paintings
Deities, Ekoi, analogies of, 13 *et sqq*., 320
Dinosaur-like monster in Folk-tale, *see* Oporopóotop

Diseases, causes ascribed to, 407, story on, 280-3
    Divination concerning, 176, 278
    Infectious, *see* Small-pox
    Jujus of, 278
    to Prevent, 50, 225
    Most common, 279
Disguise of Nsibidi Club Executioners, 306
Dishes, Chiefs', &c., 210 *n*, 218
Divination, *see also* Charms, Magic, Ordeal, & Witchcraft
    Concerning Disease, 176, 278
    Concerning Snakes, 25
    Methods of, 174 *et sqq*, 324
    By Nimm women, 95
Diviners (*see also* Porcupine), Fee to, 177
    Functions, &c, of, 131, 174 *et sqq*
    in Folk-tales, 402, 403
Divorce, 113-4, story about, 114-7
Doctors, Native 278
    Fees of, How they were Regulated, story, 279-80
Dogs, in Folk tales, 252 *et seq*.
    Hunting, story on, 147-8
Dormouse, *Graphiurus crassicaudatus dorotheæ*, Dollm n,sp, Oban District, 468-9
    in Folk-tales, 46, 398 *et sqq*
    Huetr, in Folk-tales, 62, 349 *et sqq*., 398
Double Axe, in Crete, Egypt, and Egbo, 14, 15
Dowry, *see* Bride gifts
Drawing, &c, understood by Ekoi, 290-1
    Botanical, of Mrs P Amaury Talbot, 462
    on Egbo Pillar at Ndebbiji, 141
Dreams, two classes of, 231-2
Dress (*see also* Costume), Female native, 292, strictures on Europeanised, 292 § *n*.
Drill Apes (Nshum), specimens and skulls of, 78, 465
    Substituted for Human sacrifice, 78, story of their degradation, 78-9
    Tabu on, 408
Dropsy, Jujus of, 278
Drum-language, 298-302, 399, 413
Drum-names, 301-2
Drum-songs, 47, 48, 218, 300, 398
Drums, 285, 297, 302
    Club, 46, 217-8, 283
    Tone of, 297
    Town, 272, 297, 301
Dry season, How reckoned, 270

Duck and Frog as Messengers of Obassi Osaw, story on, 229
Duiker, various sorts, Oban District, 468
    Hunting Tabus on, 407
    Bay, flesh of, as offering, 95, in Folk-tale, 63, 398
    Small grey, or Blue Duikerbok (Ise), Oban District, 468, in Folk-tales, 233, 237, 362, 397–8; Horns of, in Divination, 175
    Yellow-backed, 468, in Folk-tale, 398
Dysentery, 279

EAGLE, Monkey-killing, Tabu on, 408
Ears, cutting off of, in Folk-tale, 344
Earth God, Ekoi, see Obassi Nsi
Ebangi Juju, 278
Ebony, male and female, 194 *n.*, plentiful near Ekuri Owai, 259
Ebu, Efa, or Idiong, see Divination
Ebu Nko, grade of Egbo, 41
Ebup Juju, 50
Eburuk Pabi, female Juju, 52, and Divorce, 113
Echann fish, Tabu on, 408
Edible Clay, 209 *n* †, 248
Effrigi, the, in Egbo ritual, 43
Efik, and Efik-named Clubs, 37, 412, 413
    Influence over Ekoi, 37–8, 42
    Language, *passim*, vocabulary of, 424–45
    Names, 131
    Ode to the Tatabonko fish, 2
    Song, in Folk-tale, 275
Efiks near Kwa Town, 318
    Physical characters of, 414
    Secret primitive Writing of, 305
    Secret Society of, 37
Efumi of Crocodiles and Elephants, see those heads
Efut, tribes near, Secret Society of, 37
Egakk leaves in ritual, 143, 194
Egbo Club, 2, 37, 39, 45–6
    Dances, 39, 41
    Drum of, 46
    Entrance to, 283–4
    Grades in, 40–2
    Officers of, 43
    Images, 39, 44–5
        How the first came, story, 46 *et seq*

Egbo Club—*continued.*
    Parallel to, 206
    Revenue of, sources of, 45
    Ritual ("Plays," &c.), 39 *et sqq.*, 284
    Whipping in, 44, 45, 65
    Secrecy of, how secured, 40, 41, 44, 45
    Totemistic elements in, 38–9
    Women in relation to, 44
    Feather (see also Feathers), 14
Egbo Houses, 6, 10, 39, 216–7, 257 *et alibi*; contents and decorations, 24, 96, 172, 220, 290, as Hotels, 76, 120, 212
    Plan of, 265
    Sites for, first to be chosen, 39, 262
Egbo Pillar, Drawings on, Ndebbiji, 141
    Stone, see Etai Ngbe
Egerton, Sir Walter, native sobriquet for, 5 § *n*
    Plant named after, 214
Egg-plant, legend on, 122, 236–8
Eggs, in Divination, 175
    and Egg-shaped things, in relation to Fertility, 122
    in Juju rites, 55, 67, 109
    in Sacrifice, 19
Egpatim Juju, 50
Egyptian analogies in Ekoi ideas, &c., 25 *et sqq*, 67, 217, 317
Egyuk, see Drums, Town
Eja Fetish or Juju, bisexual symbolism of, 74, 76, 157
    Feast of, 50, 76–8
    Yams at, 77, 269
    Human offerings to, 74–8
    substitutes for, 77–9
    "Medicine," 77, 212
    Priest, on Lakes of the Dead, 23–4
Ejame dance, at Chiefs' Funerals, 295
Ejame Juju, 50
Ejimm, story of, 101 § *n*, 102–4
Ejium (used in Cooking), in Folk-tale, 234–7
Ekabe Nkanda, hoop, uses of, 42
Ekandem and the Skull-folk, story of, 273 *et sqq.*
Ekang Club, 412
Ekarra, see Ekabe
Ekkonnanakku, Cave at, 84–5
Ekkpa or Oóm, Women's Club, Juju of, 225, 413
Ekkpe Club, Efik, at Calabar, 37
Ekkpo Njawhaw Club, 412, initiatory beating of, 284

INDEX

Ekoi, an Efik word, 153
Ekoi people, Characteristics, 11, 12, 141, 159, 191, 256, 266 et seq., 283, 287, 314–6, 320, 321, 322, 335
    Clubs or Secret Societies of (see also under Names), 37 et seq., 410–3
    Death and Burial Customs, see that head
    Efik Customs and Law adopted by, and Influence on, 37–8, 42
    Folk-Lore (see also Ghosts, and Stories, passim), 335 et sqq
    Houses of, see Compounds
    Hunters, Customs, Skill, &c., of, and Stories on, 38, 142, 147, Musical sense of, 147
    Industry and Trade of, 266–7
    Infant mortality among, 12
    Language, Short Grammar of, Appendix E, 417 et sqq.
    Vocabulary, 424–45
    Location, 1, and distribution, 318
    Magic the keynote of lives of, 2
    Marriage customs, see that head
    Name for themselves, affinity of, 153
    Origin, Bantu Strain in, 305, 317, deductions on, 172–3, 232
    Physical characters of, 293, 318–9, 414
    Religious ideas, &c,
    Before White rule, story on, 267–9
    Creation belief, 70, stories on, 98–9, 149–50, 341–9, 366–9, 373–4, 387–9
    Cult of Crocodile, 24, possible origin, 25
    of Nimm, Snakes venerated in, 24–5
    Lakes of the Dead, 23 & n * et seq
    Prayers to Sun and Moon, 21–2
    Secret Societies of, see Clubs, &c
    Symbolism of, Bisexuality of, 14 et sqq, 44, 67, 76
    Traces of a purer form, 13
    Two minds in, 231
    Secret writing of, see Nsibidi
    Shields of, 271
    Struggle of, for independence, 158–9
    Welcome, Sign of, 211 & n

Ekoi Towns, Entrances of, Charms at, against Ghosts and Leopards, 7
Ekoi-Akam inter-marriages at Abijang, 216
Ekoneman, 154, 158
    Cat-dances of, 151
Ekong, Jujus at, and Juju rites, 49–50, 65–7
"Ekpa Ntan," the, 39, 262
Ekpangpang, the Bat, 193, 466
Ekpangpang, washing-pan, 193
Ekpiri Ngbe, grade of Egbo, 41
Ekpo Juju, 87–8
Ekum Oke, 76
Ekuri Eying, Fungus near, and Houses at, 260–1
Ekuri fern, funeral use of, 287
    Language, Vocabulary, 424–45
    People, 245, 256
    Chiefs of, burials of, 261
    Physical characters of, 414
Ekuri Ibokk Cult or Juju, amulets of votaries, 32
    Axe-medicine, features of, 45
    Rain-making by Members of, 71
    Smelling-out of Witchcraft by, 198
Ekuri Owai, 256, Chief of, 257, Egbo House at, 257, Elephant ravages at, 258
Ekwaw and the Hat, story, 117–9
Elephant and Python, bested by Ants, story, 400–1
Elephant-tracks, 162
Elephantiasis, 279, 409
Elephants, 6
    Attack by, Ekuri Owai, 258–9
    Efumi of, 80, 82–3, 148, 246–7, story on, 247 et sqq
    in Folk-tales (Njokk), 144–6, 197–8, 208–11, 380–2, 385, 386–7
    Herd met, 213
    Hunting customs concerning, 148, 272, 407
    Prized by Ekoi hunters, 2
    Ravages of, 83, 161–2, 222, 223, 246, 258–9, 267
    Tusks of, in Folk-tales, 208–11
    as Were-beasts, see Efumi
Enyara Akum, see Bull-roarer
Enyere and Cactus, Sex of, in Magic, 194 n.
Enyere Juju, 97
Erim, Juju priest, cruelty of, 328 et sqq
Erong-Isonn Club, Efik name, 411

Esere Bean, Ordeal by, 31, 123, 165, 166 et sqq., 170, 191–2, 195, reason for eating, 124–6
Esere Ise Club, 411
Etai Ngbe, Egbo, or Leopard Stone, 40, 141, 172, 219, 263, 265
Etara, House-burial at, 215
Etokk Juju, Pains given by, 278
Eturi grade, Egbo Society, 42
Evil and Good, Jujus of, 129
Ewaw Club, 410
Ewaw-Offong, Fire customs at, 220
Exorcisms, 194–5
Eyelashes, beauty of, 293
Eyes (see also Pineal gland), Pepper in, Ordeal by, 171
for Seeing in the Dark, story of, 352
Used in Magic and Second Sight, 230, 232

FACE, Ghost's blow on, causing Death, 230–1
Face-form, Nigeria, &c., 414
Facial markings, and Painting, 108, 319–20
Familiars, see under Witches
Families, Jujus of, 50
Organisation of, 97
Fan, ceremonial, see Effrigi
Farm work, see Agriculture et passim
Father of all Jujus, see Crab
Fatting-houses in fact and story, 60, 273, 283, 329, 338–91, 357
Boys in, 284
Life in, 106–8, feast at leaving, 108
Use of, 8, real object of, 293
Wives' visits to, 130
Feathers (see Egbo, Nimm, and Nkundak), ceremonial use of, 108
Feminine attribute of Juju, Pot-symbol of, 52
Feminine deities, Ekoi ideas on, 17, 18
Ferns, Epiphytic, dedicated to Obassi Osaw, 21
Fertility, 10, 96, Aids to, 122–3, 219
Fetish Images, emblems of Juju male attributes, 67
Fines as punishments, 45, 311
Fire, How the Lame Boy brought it from Heaven, story, 370
Lighting, in New House, 263
Raked out, in Divorce, 113
Rainfall-hindering, 72
Fires outside Compounds, rules on, 51, 220

First-fruits, offering of, Eja Juju, 77
First thing caught in Husband's New Trap, tabu to Wife, 114, 408
Fish, in Folk tales, 186–8, 386–7
of Kwa river, 2
of Lake Ijagham, 154
of Oban District, 470
Poisoning of, 270, 341
Tabus on, 408
Story on, 409
Fishing, Women's occupation, 270, Juju of, 50
Flame in Folk-tale, 383
Flora, Oban District, 89, 462–4
Flower Child, The, story, 133–4
Flycatcher and Snake, association of, in Pompeian fresco, 26
Foe, Slain, Spirit of, as House-guardian, 272
Folk-Lore, and Folk-tales, Ekoi, 335 et seq., et passim
Analogies, length, and tone of, 335, 337
Folly, The, of the Mbabong, stories of, 155–7
Food of Ghosts, tabu to Living, 232, 336, 240, and see Stories
of Witch, tabu to others, 248 et passim
Food Tabus, 407–9
Foot Juju, 108–9
Forbidden Fruit, eating of, in Folk-tale, 377
Foreheads, designs painted on, 290
Protruding, of Leopard Society members, 38 n
Forest Demon, see Ada
Faiths, 191
Reserve, the, 213, 214, 262
"Forty Thieves" story, parallel to, 391–3
Fosbery, W., Plant named after, 214
"Four eyes," in Magic, 192, 230
Francolin in Folk-lore, 147
Free-born folk, Clubs limited to, 412
and other "Members," difficulties concerning, 326
killed by Slaves, stories of, 27 et sqq., 333–4
Murder of, punishment of, 311
Pledged for Debt, 326
Frog and Duck as Messengers of Obassi Osaw, story, 229
and Snake, why they never Play together, story, 386
Tree-nesting, homes of, 23
Frogs, Oban District, 470

INDEX

Fruit Child, The, story of, 134–5
Fufu, 35 *f n*, *passim*
Funerals, *see* Death and Burial Customs
Fungi (*see also* Geasters), Oban District, 462–3
Fungus Daughter, The, 135–6

GAI IGO T ILBOTI, Doll'm n sp, 463–6
Gall, 333–4, of Leopard, Python, and Snake, Magical Properties of, 27, Tabus on, 408
Game Reserve, 262
Games, &c, Children's, at Aking, 90
Gardenia physophylla, Kwa river, 1
Geasters, near Ekuri Eying, 260
Gecko, Oban District, 470
Genet, Hunting tabu on, 407
  West African, Oban District, 466
Genii of Trees, stories about, 31 *et sqq*, 231
Genitals of Animals slain by Hunters, tabu to Women, 409
Geographical Survey, Appendix L, 478–80
Geological formation, Kwa river, 204
Geology, Oban District, 6, 11
Ghost Town, Why Living Men can no Longer See the Road to, story of, 233 *et sqq*
Ghosts, 230 *et sqq*
  of Dead Mother returning, 334
  Ekoi name for, 230
  in Folk-tales, 56–9, 62–4, 99–100, 179–80, 208–11, 234–8, 280–2
  Food of, tabu to Living, 232, 240, 336, *and see* stories
  Inability of, to count Seven, 9, 240, 337
  Invocation of, 139, 148
  in Juju cults, 53
  Offerings, &c, to, 7, 176–7, 225, 232–3, story on, 7 *et seq*
  Precautions to Exclude, 6, 7, 231, 240, 272, story on, 7 *et seq*
Girl, *see* Lame Girl
Girls, Adornment on leaving Fatting-houses, 108
  Dress of native, 203
  Fattening of, for Marriage (*see also* Fatting-house), 8
Gneiss, Sex ascribed to, by Ekoi, 6
Goats in Folk-tales, 63–4, 376–7
  Sacrificed at Funerals, 222, 225, 226, story on, 226

God and goddess, shrine and figures of, Ekuri Eying, 260–1
Goliath beetle, 90
Good and Evil, Jujus of, 129
Good Fortune, River of, Carriers' Ceremony and Song at, 91
Government, 310 *et sqq*, 325
Grammar, Short, of Ekoi Language, Appendix E, 417 *et sqq*
Graves in Houses, 215, 222, story on, 227
Greater Plantain-Eater, *see* Nkundak
Greek analogies to Ekoi Symbols, 218
Ground nut, Shell of, Witches' Boats, 195
Groups dedicated to the Ekoi highgods, 21
Gun, Owner of, Why he gets all of his Kill save one Leg, story, 144 *et sqq*
Gun-firing, ritual, 411
Gunpowder, ritual use of, 272
Guns, Flint-lock, 271, 272, in Folktales, 359, 383

HAGIA TRIADA, Double Axe emblem at, 15–16
Hair, Arranging of, tabu on, story of, 281 *f n*, 282
  Curl, first, cut off, 131
  Cut off, in Divorce, 113
  Juju, 327
Hair's Revenge on Stomach, story, 394–6
Hands and Feet, How Pythons Lost, story, 374–6
  Why Snake has neither, story, 376–7
Hanging, story about, 404
Harnessed Antelope, Hunting Tabus on, 142–3, 408
Harp, 302
Hats, Why Women do not Wear, story, 117–9
Hausas as Porters, 318
Hawks, in Folk-tales, 383
  Why they haunt Rubbish-heaps, story, 189
Head-form, Ekoi, 317, 414
  Nigerian tribes, &c, 414
Heads, designs clipped on, 290
  Human, in War Dances, 261, 272
  Load-carrying on, 319
  Wooden, covered with Human Skin, 261
  Worn by Akum of Clubs, 412

490   INDEX

Heads of Houses, Administration by, 325 et sqq
Health, Recovery of, Juju for, 53, 54-5
Hearts of Pythons and Leopards, magic value of, 27 et seq, 408
Heaven, How the Lame Boy brought Fire from, story, 370-1
Herb Daughters in Folk-tales, 136-8
Herons, Kwa river, 2
Hippopotami, How the first came, story, 386-7
History, How it came among Men, story, 337
Horn, Gates of, 231
Horns in Divination, 175
  " Medicine " in, 139
" House," definition of, 325
House-Guardian, Spirit of Slain Foe as, 272
Household Juju, Sacrifice to, of expectant mother, 130
Houses (see also Compounds, and Egbo Houses), Graves in, 215, 222, story on, 227
  Shapes of, deductions from, 317
  Wall-paintings on, 90
Human Beings (see also Men, and Women), How they got Knee-caps, story, 394
Human Sacrifices, 74-8, 245-6, 259, 260, 272, 302, 328 et sqq
  Substitutes for, 77-9
Hunter, Why he may not Eat Apes killed in the Bush, story, 143-4
Hunters, Customs of, Jujus, and Stories on, 45, 49, 50, 142 et sqq, 148, 149-50, 269
Hunting Dogs, Concerning, story, 147-8
  Tabus, 407-9
Huts as Funeral Shrines, 6-7

Ibianshi Peak, 214
Ibibio Club, branch of, 412
Ibibio tribe, Physical Characters of, 414
Ibo tribe, and origin of Nsibidi, 305
  Physical Characters of, 414
Ibonn tree in ritual, 263
Ibum, Agriculture at, 214; Forest reserve near, 213, Migrations from, 215
Iffianga, tribes near, Secret Society of, 37

Ifunkpa, Uyanga town, 255
Igumi, Juju, never before seen by White Man, 223
Ikadum Club, 411
Ikkpai (Whip) Club, 412
Iko Akperem, First White Man's visit to, 256
Iko tribe, manners of, 256
  Towns of, Uyanga people at, 255
Ikpai, Mfam Juju centre, 139
Ikum, Chief of, Ojo Nkonmba, and the hired boy, 243-4, Head-gear, Official status, &c, 245
Illness (see also Disease), Mfam boughs in, 139
Image (Okum), in Egbo ritual, 39, 42, 44-5, 52-3, 206
  How the First came, story, 46 et seq
Imprisonment, Magical, in Trees, 31
Incantation of Tree-wedged Stones, 161
Infant Mortality, Ekoi, at Oban, 12
Inheritance, 314
Inoculation, Native, 10-11, Scars left by, 203
Insects (see also Goliath Beetle), Oban District, collection of, 470 et seq
Insignia in Egbo ritual, 42, 43
Insofan, Chief of, treasures of, 218
Invocations (see also Prayers), 22, 39, 66, 139, 148
Iron, dreaded by Witches, 123
  in Etai Ngbe stones, 265
Irun tree in ritual, 263
Isawm, Magic two-edged Knife, 127, 123
Ishut flower, sign of a Death, 287
Isinn tree, ritual use of, 266
Isse Obassi Nsi Juju, 123, case of, 123-6
Isua, Master of Ceremonies, lower grades, Egbo Club, 43 § n
Ita 'Ne Echi, story of, 274 et sqq
Ita Sakese, Chief, Oban, Rain-maker, 71
Itagbun, Head priest Ikpai, 139, treasures of, 141
Itaokui, Chief, Oban, 10
Itiatt Obbonn, 413
Itorok, Head Chief, of Oban, Funeral ceremonies of, 221 et sqq.
Itott bird, Omens from, 324
Iyamba, title of Head priest, Egbo Society, 43

INDEX

491

Jaws, Human, token of Victory, 257
Johnston, Sir H H, List of words chosen by, for Vocabularies, 424–45
Joseph, a modified parallel to, 128
Juju, Chalk as, 209 & n †
    Dance, and its object, Niaji, 328–32
    Emblems, 67
    Hair, 327
    Hunting, 45, 50, 142, 148
    in Club ritual, 412, 413
    Knives of Nimm women, 94, 95
    Man, famous, at Ekuri Eying, 261
    of Ojuk river, 89
    Posts, Skulls attached to, 257, 260
    Rites, 53 et seq
      of Revocation, 51, 65–7, 139–41
    Stones, Genii of, Propitiation of, 256
    Trees, 6, 10
      Weaver birds associated with, 14
Jujus (see also under Names), 49 et sqq
    Ekoi, feared by Efiks, 38
    of Good and Evil, 129
    in Litigation, 65
    of Special Diseases, 10–11, 278
    Women in relation to, 21, 96, 181

Kabila, or Ojo tribe (q v), Physical Characters of, 414
Kalbreyeri, Kwa river, 1
Keaka tribe, Ekoi affinity of, 318
Keith, Prof, M D, help from, acknowledged, 414
Keloids on Women, 203
Kingfishers, Kwa river, 2, Omens from, 324, Tabu on, 410
Knee-caps, How Human Beings got, story of, 394
Knitted garments of Egbo "Image," 44
Knives, magic (Isawm), 127, 128
    of Nimm Women, 94, 95
Kola-tree in Folk-tale, 307
    Nuts of, Oath on, 269
Korawp tribe, see Ododop
Kpifonn, "Members'" Club, mysteries of, 413
Kwa Language, Vocabulary, 424–45
Kwa river, Bridge over, 204
    Crocodiles of, 1, 3
    Flora and fauna of, 1–3, 204–5
    Geological formations near, 3, 203–5
    Magical character of, 2
    Navigable limit of, 3
    Scenery along, 1–3
    Source, 214
Kwa town, Ekoi and Efiks of, 318

Lake Ijagham, sacred to Ekoi, discovered by Mansfeld, 151, 153
    Legends of, 153
    Salt springs near, 317
Lakes of the Dead, 23 & n * et sqq, 153
Lamb, unacceptable as Sacrifice, story of reason, 67–70
Lame Boy, the, in Ekoi Folk-tales, 34 & n. et seq, 47, 48, 58, 280–2, analogies of, 336
    Fire brought by, from Heaven, story, 370–1
    in Stilt-Play, 285
    in West African ritual, 336
    Girl in Folk-tale, 248–9
Land of Obassi Osaw, how the Poor Boy came to, story, 18 et seq.
Land tenure, 262
Landolphias, Kwa river, 204
Languages, Oban tribes, see Vocabularies
Leaves and Boughs in Ekoi Symbolism, 44
    "Lucky" in Fishing, 270
    Magic, 8, 53, 54, 66, 67, 71, 249
    Ritual uses of, 44, 91, 95, 97, 121, 123, 140, 143, 240, 242, 263, 285
Legends, Ekoi, tone of, &c, 335
Lemurs in Folk-tale, 349 et sqq
    Oban District, 465–6
Leopard, Secret Societies of (see also Egbo, and Ekkpe), 38 & n.
    in Folk-tales, 337–40, 386–7
    Gall of, Magical properties of, 27 et seq, 408
    in Hunting Juju, 142
    "Medicine" for catching, 359, 362
    Slain, hunters' aid, 272
Leopard-child and Lamb, story of, 67–70
Leopard Stone, see Etai Ngbe
Leopards, 6, 213–4
    Charms and Juju against, 7, 50–1, 220
    Daring of, 50, 205–6
    Ravages of, 223
    Tabu on, 408
    as Were-beasts, 82, 83
Leprosy, Origin of, story of, 279
Lex Talionis, story of Nsibidi Club, 306–9
Libations, of Human Blood, 260, 272
    of Water, Wine, &c, 22, 67, 131, 139, 140, 148, 176–7, 217, 225, 263, 271, 272, 315, 352

Lichens, Oban District, 463-4
Lightning beliefs on, 73-4
  Party struck by, 92-3
Lilies, Kwa river, 6
Line, pure, delight in, of Ekoi, 290-1
Lions, in Folk-tales, 317
  Why there are no more in the Bush, story, 382-4
Living, the, Ghost Food tabu to, 232, 240, 336
  Why they can no longer see the Road to Ghost Town, 233 et sqq
Lizard, Song of, in Folk-tale, 379
Lizard's Head, Why it is always moving Up and Down, story, 378-80
Load-carrying on Heads, and Physique, 293
Lock-jaw, from Ghost's blow, 230
Lord of the Bush, story of, 400-1
Lord of Life and Death, see Obassi Nsi
Love charms, 112
"Lucky" leaves in Fishing, 270
Lumbago, Juju causing, 278
Lunacy and the Moon, 278

MACGREGOR, Rev J. K, on Magic, &c, of the Uyanga, 255,
  on Nsibidi, 305
Machauns, equivalents of, 146-7
Magic (see also Charms, Divination, Juju, Leaves, Witchcraft), importance of, to Ekoi, 2
  Plants, in Folk tale, 249, 250
  Sympathetic, 8
  of the Uyanga, 255
Magical properties of Gall of Pythons and Leopards, 27 et sqq, 408
  value of Manatees, 2
Maia, priestess of Nimm, Statue, 94
Malaria, common, 279
Male attributes of Jujus, emblems of, 67
Males, tabued from Women's Juju, Oban, 10
Mammals, Oban District, 465 et sqq
Man and Woman, Creation of, story, 373-4
Man, the, Who understood Animals' Speech, story, 99-101
Manatee, Kwa river, magic value of, 2
Mancala, the, 286
Mangroves, Kwa river, 1

Manners, Ekoi and Non-Ekoi, 256.
Mansfeld, Dr, 97, and Lake Ijagham, 151, on Ekoi struggle for independence, 159, on Nsibidi, 306
Mariba, or Etem-I-Ngbe ceremony of Egbo, importance of, 43-4
Markets, non-existent, 267
Marriage Customs, Ekoi (see also Fatting-house), 105 et sqq, 279
  Chiefs', 300
  Polygamy, 97, 109, 110
  Restrictions practically nil, 87, 110
Masks, Burial, Egyptian, Ekoi parallel to, 217
  of Ekuri Ibokk, 45
  in War Dances, 261
Mat and bag work, Men's and Women's share in, 270
Matchets, 272
Magic, 211
Matriarchy, traces of, 97, 234-6, 237, 238
Maxwell, T D, Efik Secret Writing discovered by, 305
Mbabong people, Migration of, to Oban District, 157
  Stupidity attributed to, 154
  Stories of, 155 et sqq
Mbaghe tree, and Witches, 195
Mbarakpa, Rest-house near, Native-made road to, 205
Mbeban, Egbo House at, symbolic Painting in, 14
Mbian Juju, 332 § n
Mbinda, Eja fetish from, 76, 157
Mboandem Frauen, Ekoi analogies of, 97
Mbonne fish in Folk-tale, 186-8
Meat and Fertility, 123
Medical beliefs, Customs, and Stories, Ekoi, 278 et sqq
Medicinal Knowledge of the Uyanga, 255
Medicine, Animal matter used in, 408
"Medicine," in Juju, 49, in Waist-cutting, 131
Melancholy of the Ekoi, 191
"Members," defined, Treatment of, 325 et sqq
  Clubs of, 413
  Duties of, 326
  Roman parallel to, 325
Members of Body, borrowed by Skull-man, story, 274-6
  Why they must serve Belly, story, 393-4

INDEX

Men, Black and White, How they Came on Earth, story, 98–9
Ekoi (*see also* Ekoi, *and* Hunters), Chief occupations of, 269
Fine form of, 293
Juju of, *see* Nchibbi
Tabus of, at Birth, 130
on Food, 407, 408, story on, 409
on Nimm mysteries, 96
Why they must Serve Women, story, 98
Mendi people, as porters, 318
Terrorised by Leopard Society, 38 *n*
Mentality and Memory, Ekoi, 320
Mercy to Mankind, why barred, story, 129
Metamorphosis (*see also* Efumi, Shapeshifting, & Werebeasts), Common belief in, 80 *et sqq*
Meteorology, Oban Station, Appendix K, 476–7
Meteors, Divination by, 324
Mfam Akabansi, *see* Ghost Town
Mfam Ane Achi (Land of Men of Heads), 274
Mfam Juju, age of, 51
Aru bird tabu to Members of, 408
at Ikpai, 139
Revocation rites, 139–41
Dropsy given by, 278
Tabu to Women, 21
Tree of, *see Croton amabilis*
Mfamosing, 163, 164
Ordeals at, 163 *et seq*
Mfepp Juju, Winds sent by, 73
Mfuor Club, 413
Juju, 50, 51
Amulets of votaries, 52
Rites of, Yams tabu before, 269
Mfut (Red fly), in Folk-tales, 28 & *n.*, 209–10
Mimosas, Kwa river, 1
Minds, Two, in Ekoi belief, 231
Mineralogy, Appendix J, 474–5
Minoan analogies with Ekoi religion, 13 *et sqq*
Mkpott, ruined town, Egbo House, &c, at, 219
Juju Skull from, 223–4
Treasure chamber in house at, 220
Mollusca, Oban District, 473
Money, conventionally drawn, 14
Monitors, Hunting tabu on, 407
Kwa river, 2
Monkeys (*see also* Apes, Baboons &c.), in Folk-tales, 345, 384
Originators of Nsibidi, 255, 305

Monni Njomm, 55
Moon, *see also* Sun and Moon,
Full, Dances at, 294
How it first came into the Sky, story, 344–9
Influence of, on Disease, 278
New, Women's Juju at, at Oban, object of, 10
Prayers to, Ekoi, 21–2
Ring round, Omen of, 324
Morel, E D, *cited* adversely to Europeanised clothing, 291 *n*
Mothers-in-law, 109
Mouse and her Story-children, story of, 337, 340
Mud couches, 263
Murder, punishment of, 311, stories on, 312–3, 401–4
Ritual, former, 222
by Witchcraft, 192
Murderer, Why he should Die in the same way as his Victim, story, 312–3
Murderers, Why they must die, story, 401–4
Murua, Rattle-bearer, at Egbo Plays, 43
Muscular ripple in Dances, 294
Music, Ekoi, 297
Within Witch's body, story of, 249, 251, 254
Musical Instruments, *see* Drums, Harp, Okankan, Pipes, Rattle, Wooden, &c,

NAMING of Children, 131–2
Napoleonas, Kwa river, 205
Alexandri, *Egertoni*, and *Fosberyi*, where found, 214
Nataba, Chief, cocoa-culture of, and fear of Witchcraft, 201–2
Native Court, 310
Willingness in Road-making, 5
Nature Forces, Ekoi Cult of, 13, 40
Juju of Lake of the Dead, Nsan, 23 *et sqq*.
Nchibbi Club, 412
Men's Juju, at Full Moon, Oban, 10
Ndebbiji, Egbo Stone at, 141
Ododop Secret Society adopted at, 37
Ndibu grade, Egbo Society, 41
Nenkui, Chief, Mfamosing, and Ordeals, 165 *et sqq*, fate of, 170
Netim, purely Ekoi town, 212–3, 242, 247
Nfam Juju, Head priest of, on Juju revocation, 65

INDEX

Nfunum, Treasure chamber at, 151
Ngapong Juju, 50
"Ngaw" creeper, used by Were-crocodiles, 95
Ngbe, *see* Leopard
Ngbe Abum Obbaw Juju, Oban, 50
   Fire forbidden outside towns possessing, 220
Niaji, site of, 92
Nigeria, Southern, Administration of, 325 *et sqq*
   Boundary of, 151
   Oil palms in, value of, 315
   Railway projects, and commerce, 267
Night Sounds, African, 190
Nilotic origin of Ekoi, 317
Nimm, nature goddess, 53, attributes of, 25
   Crocodile form of, 3
   Cult of, 2, 3, 94 *et seq*
      Analogies to, 97
      Feathers in, 94, 95
      Leaves in, 95, 97
      Mysteries of, tabu to Men, 96
      Snakes venerated in, 24-5
   Figure of, in Egbo house, 217
   Statue of, 94
   Stones, 218, 219, 242, 263, 395
   Women, "Done" by Sheep, story, 339-40
   Shrines, &c, of, 94-5
Nimm Asam Juju, 49-50, Poison of, 50, Rainbow-making by, 72
Njomm, meaning of term, 49
Njomm Ekatt (Foot Juju), 108-9
Njomm Aiyung (Blood Juju), 109, 201
Nkajokk Juju, 50
Nkami, last British town, 151
Nkanda, highest grade, Egbo Society, insignia, &c, 42-3
Nkokolle, *see* Ekuri
Nkundak Bird, Feathers of, used in Dances, 272 *et seq*, 412, Why they may only be worn by Warrior who has Slain a Foe, story, 273
   in Folk-tale, 196
   as Omen-giver, 324
   Tabu on, 408
Non-Ekoi peoples, Manners of, 256, Rural dwellings of, 256
Nose-form, Nigeria, &c, 414
Nsan, Juju tree of, 30
   Lake of the Dead near, 23 *et sqq*.
   Mfam Juju at, 51
Nsann Juju, Poisoners, 74; Storm-making, 73

Nsann, Thundertown, in Folk-tales, 207, 356, 361
Nshum, the Lazy Man made Ape, story of, 78-9
Nsibidi Club, 305, Functions of, story on, 306-9
Nsibidi Secret writing, 39, 217, 305, 306, 309, as Body decoration, 320, Egyptian analogies to, 317, Messages in, 309, origin of, and Author's collection, &c, 255
   Signs used, 267, 309, Appendix G, 447 *et sqq*
Nsippe Club, 413
Nsun meat in ritual, 263, 272
Nta Obassi and Ma Obassi invoked in Ekoi sacrifices, 17
Ntabe, Why he Warred no More, story, 268-9
Ntuanto Juju, 54, rites of, 55, meaning of word, 230
Ntui (Chief) of each Egbo grade, functions of, 43
Ntui Itabon, Rainbow maker, 72
Numerals, 422-3, signs for, 304
Nyampke grade, Efik Society, 41

OATH, on Kola Nuts, 269
Oban, position of, seat of government, 11, founding of, 262
   Circles of unhewn stone, at rites performed at, at full and new Moon, 10
   Clubs, typical, divisions of, 410 *et sqq*
   Egbo House at, 10
   Jujus at, 50, 51, Chief War Juju, 271
   Were-beasts at, 81
Oban District, Birds found in, previously unknown to exist in Nigeria, 469-70
   Botany, Appendix H., 462-4
   Butterflies of, 471
   Character of the region, 3
   Crabs of, 473
   Ekoi in, 318
   Fish and Reptiles, &c, of, 470
   Flora, 89, 462-4
   Fungi and Lichens of, 462-4
   Geographical Survey, Appendix L, 478-80
   Geology of, 3
   Insects of (*see also* Goliath Beetle), 470 *et sqq*
   Mammals of, 465-9
   Meteorology, 476

INDEX

Oban District—*continued*
  Mineralogy, Appendix J., 474-5
  Mollusca of, 473
  Natives of, Anthropometry of, Appendix C, 414
  Vocabularies of the Six Tribes in, 424-45
Oban Hill, healthiness of, 11
Oban Station, Meteorology at, Appendix K, 476-7
Obang tribe, Ekoi affinity of, 318
Obassi Abong, 52
Obassi Nsi, Earth god, Lord of Life and Death, 13, 44, 71, 139, Cult of, 16-7, 21, 271, in Creation myth, 188; feast of, 71, 139
  and Lamb, 68-70
  and the Chameleon, 91
  Children of, in Folk-tales, 29, 273 *et sqq*, 340-4, 351, 359
  Dwellings of, 70, 71
  Good Jujus sent by, 191
  Invocation of, 53, 66, 139
  Sacrifices to, 272
  in Stilt-play, 285
  in Stories about Women's position, 98-9, 103
  Yams associated with, 21
Obassi Nsi Juju, Funeral offerings to, 222
Obassi Osaw, Sky god of the Ekoi, 13, 44, characteristics of, 177, Lord of Witchcraft, &c, 191, Wind-sender, 72
  Cult of, 16, 17, 217, feast of, 149-50
  Dwelling places of, 70, 71, 177
  Eyes of, as Stars, 357
    Omnivision of, 118
  Ferns, epiphytic, dedicated to, 21
  How the Poor Boy came to the Land of, 18
  Invocation of, 39, 139
  Messengers of, as to Living again, story of, 229
  and the Osing Tree, 177 *et sqq*
  Sacrifices to, 263, 272
  in Stilt-play, 285
  in Stories about Women's position, 98-9, 103
  and Tortoises in Folk-tales, 9, 59-61, 397
  Wives and Sons in Folk-tales, 117-9, 128-9, 183, 207-11, 273 *et sqq*, 340-4, 351, 359
Obbonn, Efik and Ekoi Club, 412
Obepp, 151
Oberekkai, Witchcraft terror at, 201-2
Obung, Eja "medicine" at, 77, 212

Oburekkpe, Egbo House at, 259-60
  "War" tokens of, 257
Obutong, Rest House, Snakes at, 4, 5, surroundings, 3, 6, 203 *et sqq*
Ochitt (Nchitt) fruits, see Egg Plant
Ododop or Korawp tribe, Animal affinities in, 86-7
  Courtesy of, 163, 164
  Farms undevastated by Bush beasts, 87
  New town of, 84
  Physical type of, 163, 414
  Secret Society of, 37
  Vocabulary, 424-45
Offerings and Oblations (see also Libations), 39, 53-5, 148, 176-7, 200, 263
Officers of Egbo Society, 43
Offiong, E E, Chief, at Calabar, on Witch revels, 192
Ofiri, Juju, 49, 51, revocation of, 65-7
Oil palms, see Palms
Oji, the warder, and his Tree affinity, 31-2
Ojje, or Witchcraft (*q v*), 171, 178, 190 *et seq*.
Ojjen, never before seen by White Man, 223-4
Ojo Akangba, 244, 246
Ojo Nkonmba (see also Ojo people), Human sacrifice attempted at, 243 *et seq*
  Native name for, 244-5
Ojo or Kabila tribes, Efumi of Elephants, 246-7, trans-Calabar river, locale of, 242, 244; origin of, 245
Ojokk, 151
Ojuk people, sale by, of site of Oban, 262
Ojuk river, Juju of, 89
Okankan, 283, 302, tone of, 54
Okarara, devastations at, by Wild beasts, 161 *et sqq*
Oke Ewara, War Juju, Oban, 271
Okpata Juju and dance, 50, 295-6
Opke Club, 411
Oku Akama grade, Egbo Society, 41
Okum, see Clubs, *and* Image
Okun Ohin, hunter, dread of Elephant Efumi, &c., 243, 246-7
Okuri, Jujus of, 52, 157-8
Okuri Peak, pass near, 76, 157
Okuri people, and Esere Bean Ordeal, 126
Omens, 323-4
One-armed and one-legged Man, and the Cotton Tree, story of, 32 *et seq*

Onnuri Juju, Dropsy given by, 278
Oóm, play, 225
Oporopóotop, story of, 335, 371–3
Orchids, near Ojo Nkonmba, 244
Ordeals —
   Boiling palm oil, 165, 166
   Esere Bean, 31, 123, 165, 166 *et sqq.*, 170, 191–2
   Pepper in Eyes, 171
   Rope-walking, 402, 403
Ordinals, 423
Ornaments, Female, 49, 203, Votive, 218
Orthography, Appendix D., 415
Orui Achibbi Club, 411
Osa, High god of the Bini, 13 *n*
Osairri, *see* Kingfisher
Osaw Ifogi peak, Flora of, and Storm at, 92–3
Oshum njum ka etemm Club, 410
Osing Shells, 174–5
   Bisexual element in, 174
   Divination by, 175–8
Osing Tree, Why it can no longer Speak, save by the Charm, 177 *et sqq*
Owai Ifunkpa, Uyanga town, 255
Owl, Tabu on, 408, as Witches' Familiar, 195, story on, 196

PAINT HOUSE, analogy to, 108
Palm kernels in anti-Leopard Juju, 51
Palm leaf Juju, 278, 296
Palm leaves, &c, as Leopard charms, 7
   for Mats, rule on, story of, 306–9
   in Nimm cult, 95, 97
   Ritual uses of, 9, 257
   Oil, in Birth customs, &c, 130, 188
   Boiling, Ordeal by, 165, 166
   Rib, " violin," 302–3
   Stems, split, Nsibidi written on, 309
   Strips, Shields of, 271, 272
   Trees, Kwa river, 1
   and Water, How they came on Earth, story, 373–4
   Tops of, why Nki lives in, story, 397 *et seq*
   Wine, two kinds, 315, ritual uses, 9, 139, 140, 263, 272, 315, 352, 357
Pan, terror of, Nigeria, 13
Pangohn, Oban District, 466
   Hunting Tabu on, 407
Parents, Ekoi as, 159
   Expectant, Tabus on, 130
   Ghosts of, Sacrifices to, 232–3
Parrots in Folk-tales, 196, 253, 383
Pepper in the Eyes, Ordeal by, 171
Phœnician type of things found, 173

Physical Characters, Ekoi, Efik, &c, 293, 414
Pig, in Folk-tale, 146
   Wild, 6
Pineal gland, in Juju rites, 67, 242
Piper plant, leaves of, ritual use of, 285
Pipes (musical) of Crabs' Claws in Juju rites, 55
Pits for Trapping Game, 147
Plague, Rats, and Tutelary gods, 25 *et sqq.*
Plantain-Eater, Greater, *see* Nkundak
Plantains in Folk-tales, 9 *et alibi*
   Sacrificed to Ghosts, 232–3
Plants, Magic, in Folk-tale, 249, 250
   Souls of, 287
Plates, Funeral uses of, 215, 221
   Tabu to (some) Chiefs, 210 *n*
" Plays," of Children, 206, 217
   of Egbo Society, 43, 45, at Funerals 222, 223, a Ghost at, 238; Totemistic details in, 38–9
Pleurisy, Juju of, 278
Pneumonia, 279
Poison, Juju against, 50
Poisoners, Juju of, *see* Nsann
Poisoning, and Antidotes, 310–11, 332
   of Fish, 270
Poll-tax, German Cameroons, 157
Polygamy, Ekoi, 97, 109, 110
Pools for Ghost libations, 217, 218
Poor Boy (*see also* Rich Boy and), How he came to the Land of Obassi Osaw, story, 18 *et sqq.*
Population, Ekoi, Decrease in, Causes of, 201–3, Southward trend of, 245
Porcupine, as Diviner, 30, 181 *et sqq*, 234, 235, 237, 240, 241, 355–6, 365–6, Dog's enmity for, story, 147, Hunting Tabus on, 407, Oban District, 468
Porcupine Witch, story of, 181–2
Pot-hook, *see* Ejimm
Potions to enable Bush Souls to enter Animals, 80
Pottery (*see* Bowls, Dishes, Plates), Ekoi, 217, 219, 287–90, Funeral uses of, 223
Pots, emblem of Juju Female attribute, 52, 67, in Enyere Juju, 97
Powder in Egbo ritual, 41
Prayers (*see also* Invocations), 21-2, 242, 369

INDEX

Presidents of Age-classes, 283
Priest, Head, of Egbo Society, 43
Priestesses of Nimm, power of, 2
Prisoners of War, fate of, 271
Property, Inheritance of, 314
    Personal, in Funeral customs, 6–7, 17
    Most valued by Ekoi, 141
Proverbs, 156, and Omens, 323–4
Puff-adders in Rest House, 5
Python and Elephant bested by Ants, story of, 400–1
    of Lake of the Dead, 24
    Tabu on, 408
Pythons, Gall of, Magic properties of, 27 *et seq*, 408
    in Folk-tales, 346, 383, 400–1, How they Lost Hands and Feet, 374–6

QUARRELLING, when forbidden, 120
Quartz, Sex ascribed to by Ekoi, 6
Queisz, Leutnant, fate of, 158

RAILWAY projects, and Commerce, 267
Rain, How the First came, 340–4
Rainbow-making, 72
Rainfall, Oban, 476–7
Rain-making and staying, Ekoi, 71–2
Rainstorm at Netim, 213
Ram and Tortoise, story of, 371–3
Rats, in Folk tale, 395
    and Mice, Oban District, 468
    Plague-carrying, Chief enemies of deified, 25 *et sqq*
Rattle in Egbo Plays, &c, 43, 295, 302, 410
Records, Ekoi, 304
Religion of the Ekoi, see *under* Ekoi
Re-marriage of Divorced Women, and Widows, 116–7
Reptiles (*see also* Pythons, Snakes, &c), Oban District, 470
Rest-houses, 163, 205 *et alibi*
Rheumatism, &c, Juju of, 278
Rich Boy and Poor Boy and Osing, story, 178–81
Ridicule, Ekoi dread of, 283
Ring-decoration in Egbo ritual, 42
Rivers, see Calabar, Cross, Kwa, &c, heaps of leaves beside, 9–17, 242, How they all first came upon Earth, story, 366–9
    Pannings from, Mineralogical composition of, 474–5

Roads and Road-making, native attitude to, 5
Roman analogies in Nigerian House-building, 263–4
Rope Juju, 112
Rope-walking Ordeal in Folk-tale, 402, 403
Rubber, in Folk-tale, 398, 399
    Plants, see *Landolphias*
Rubbish-heaps, Why haunted by Hawks, story, 189

SACRIFICE (*see* Animal, *and* Human), to Cotton trees, 34, 36, to Ghosts, 232–3, at Town-founding, 263
Salt Springs, 317–8
Salutations on entering Towns, 297
Sambon, Dr W., on Rat-eating Snakes in ancient Rome, 25–7
Sanctuaries for Animals, 24, 213–4, 262
Sanitation, and Decrease in Population, 202
Sapele, Roads of, 5
Scars on Arms, Ekoi ideas on, 203
Scavenger Birds, Tabus on, 408
Sciatica, Juju causing, 278
Screw pines, Kwa river, 1
Second Sight of Animals and Men, 230, 232
Secret Chambers in Ekoi Houses, 265
Secret Societies (*see also* Egbo), 13, 410–3, origin, 37
Seven (the number), in Folk-tales, 9, 336–7
Seven Witchcrafts, The, 199–200
Sex-shifting in Folk-tale, 378–80
Shadows of the Absent, calling up of, by Egbo, 40, Ekoi belief on, 231
Shape-shifting (*see also* Efumi, *and* Metamorphosis); of Animals, 67–70, of Efumi, 243, Ekoi belief in, 191; of Witches and Wizards, 195, 199
Sheep, as Cunning beast, 337; Juju, in Folk-tale, 344 *et sqq*
Sheep and Leopard, in Folk-tale, 337–40
Shields, Ekoi, 271
Shinto beliefs and Ekoi parallels, 232
Shrew, Oban District, 466
Shrines of Nimm Women, 94–5
Sierra Leone, Leopard Society of, 38 *n.*

S.B.   K K

498

INDEX

Sight, Hearing, &c., Ekoi keenness of, 320
Signs, Flowers and Leaves as, 287
Singing, at Funerals, 239
Size, increase of, in Witch revels, 192
Skull People, and Town, story of, 274-7
Skulls, Dancing, in Folk-tale, 275
  Juju uses of, 217, 223-4, 257, 260, 261, 411
Sky father and Earth mother (see Obassi Osaw & Nsi), Wedding of, Ekoi parallel symbolism, 14 et sqq.
Slave-giving, to Husband, and Divorce, 114
"Slave towns," 325
Slave trade, Ekoi share in, 325
  Old centres of, 151
Slavery, 314, and the Egbo Society, 42, 46
Slaves, Cruelty to, case of, 328 et sqq
  Dead, disposal of, 326
  Escapes of, Juju against, 327
  How they killed the Free-born with Gall, story, 27 et sqq, 333-4
  Made by Efiks, of Ekoi, 38
  Prices of, 327, 328
  Slain at Funerals, 328 et sqq.
  in War time, fate of, 271-2
Small-pox medicine, 10
"Smelling-out" powers of Ekuri Ibokk, 45
Snails, Screaming and Springing, 473
Snake-form of Nimm, 2
Snakes (see also Cobras and Pythons), alarms from, 4, 206-7; Ekoi cult of, 24, 25, Fat of, in Medicine, 278, Kwa river region, 2, 4-5; of Lakes Ijagham and Nsan, 153, of Oban District, 470, Poisonous, as Juju, 91, as Were-animals, Egbo trial, 83-4
  in Folk-tales, 377, 383
    Snake and Frog, Why they never play together, 386
    Why Snake has neither Hands nor Feet, 376-7, & see 325
Societies (see Secret), various kinds, 48 & n
Songs (see also Drum Songs); of Boy without Hands or Feet, 375
  about Calabar river, 242
  of Carriers, at river, 91

Songs—continued
  at Eja festivals, 76-7
  of Ekandem, 275
  Funeral, Ghost-excellence in, 239
  of the Herb daughter, 138
  of Igwe, 102
  of Killing-thing, 235
  Mansfeld's Collection of, 153
  of Obegud, 101
  of Welcome to the New born, 120, 121, 122
  to Town Drums, 297
Souls or Spirits, Animal, see Bush Soul, and Efumi,
  Human, in Ekoi beliefs, 80 et sqq, 230 et sqq, 272
  Plant, 287
  Things, 232
Spears, 271, 272, Juju, 55, 130, 221, 222
Spiders, New Species, Bird-Eating, 471-2
Spitting, Ceremonial, 91, 141, 171
Spotted Antelope, tabus on, 142-3
Squirrels, Flying, 467, in Folk-tale, 362, Oban District, 467-8
Stars, Ekoi names for, 190
  How they all came, story, 349-55
  How the Two Biggest came into the Sky, story, 355 et sqq
Statue of Nimm at Niagi, 94
Stilt-walking, origin of, 284-5
Stomach, Hair's Revenge on, story, 394-6
Stones (see also Etai Ngbe, and Nimm Stones); Carved, 171-2, Unhewn, circles of, at Oban, rites connected with, 10, Wedged into Tree-forks, 160-1
Stories, How all came among Men, story, 337 et sqq
Storm-making Juju, 73
Strangers, Burial places of, 227
Streams, Oban District, 6
Sucking out Heart of Men and Things, 192-3, 208 & n., 232
Sun, How it came into the Sky, story, 357-9
  and Moon, How they went up to the Sky, story, 359-64
  Prayers to, 21-2
Sunset, Why sometimes Red and Stormy, story, 364-6
Supplication, sign of, 331
Surgery, Ekoi, 278-9
Surnames, 132
Sword dance, 413
Swords, Children's "Play," 217

INDEX

Symbolism, Ekoi, *see* Leaves and Green Bough, *and* Pots

TA AMAT Medicinal Juju, Oban, 10
Tabus, Hunting, 114, 407-9
   Juju, 181 *et alibi*
   Pre-natal, 130, 167
   Totemistic, 143
Tailor sewing Body together, story, 392
Talbot, Mrs P Amaury, accident to, 164, Adventures of, with Snakes, 4, 206-7, Botanical drawings by, 462, Dormouse named after, 468-9
Talbot, P Amaury, native drawings of, 90
Tallies, 304
Tatabonko fish, Kwa river, 2
Tegott river, Uyanga, of, 255
Temperance, Ekoi, and British, 314-6
Temperature, Oban Station, 476
Theft, Juju against, 50, 296, punishment of, 311
Thomas, N, on Lame Man in procession at Benin, 336, on Negroes as Porters, 318
Thunder, beliefs, and stories on, 23, 73, 207, 211
Thunder Town (*see* Nsann), in Ekoi Folk-Lore, story of, 207
Toads, Oban District, 470
Tobacco, Ekoi delight in, 290
Tomatoes, legend on, 122, 238-41, 336
Tom-toms, 297
Tooth-filing, 319
Tops, 286
Tornadoes, 366
Torque or anklet, in Ofiri Juju, 49
Tortoise in Folk-tale, 7 *et seq*, 371-3, 378-80, Cunning of, 337, How he got the Cracks and Bumps on his Back, 380-2, How Obassi Osaw proved the wisdom of, 396-7, & *see* 218; Why Sacrificed in Juju rites, 55 *et sqq*
Totem Animals, origin of, 81
Totem Peoples, inter-marriage of, 87
Totemistic details in Egbo Plays, 38-9
   Tabus, 143
Totems not eaten, 137, 138
Towns, Egbo Houses in, 39
   Entrances of, Leopard charms at, 7
   Hours for Ghosts to visit, 232
   Jujus of, 49-50

Towns—*continued*
   Moving of, to fresh sites, Typical cases, 201-2, 262 *et sqq*
   Sacrifices at Founding, 263
   Why Ape People no longer live in, story, 78-9
Trade and Trade Routes, Ekoi, 205, 266-7
Trance, Ekoi beliefs on, 231
Treasure Chambers in Egbo houses, 151, 220
   House, The, in the Bush, story, 390-4
   of Itagbun, 141
Tree and Bird worship, Cretan and Ekoi, 14
Trees (*see also* Juju trees, & *under* Names) in Folk-tales and sayings, 323 *et passim*, in House-building ritual, 263, Magic properties ascribed to, 30, 195, Souls of, 287
   Vocal, 31-2, story on, 32 *et sqq*
Twins, Ekoi attitude to, 120-3
Twitching of various parts of Body, Divination by, 324
Two-faced "Image," Egbo analogies of, 44

UKAI Club, 411
Ukpe Ewaw, Ball game, 285-6
Ukpon River, Cataracts and Crocodile of, 215
Ukwa Club (Calabar), 411
Unborn, homes of, 122
Uncle and Niece marriages, 110-11
Unloved Son in Folk-tales, 207-11, 355, 359, 363, 393-4
Utap-Anam Club, 412
Uyanga people, Language of, Vocabulary of, 424-45, locale of, 242, 255, Nsibidi of, 305, Physical characters of, 414, Renown of, 255

VEGETATION, Kwa river shores, 1, 6
Vengeance, Tree-sacrifices and 30 *et seq*.
Villages, Amusements in, 283-6
   Egbo houses in, 39
   Medicine in, 278-83
   Plan of, 266
Virginia creeper-like tree, properties of, 223
Vocabularies of the Six Tribes in the Oban District, List of Words chosen by Sir H. H Johnston, Appendix F, 424-45

INDEX

Vocal Trees, 31-2, story on, 32 *et sqq*
Vulture, tabu on, 408

WAKES, 222, 225
Wall-paintings, 90, 107, 263-4, 290
Wands, *see* Whip
War, Ritual preliminaries and Juju, 271-2
War-dances, 261, 272, 411
Warfare, 271 *et seq*
Washing, Personal, Ekoi, 12; Ritual of, 21-2
Water and Disease, story, 280-3
  and Palm trees, How they came on Earth, story, 373
  Ritual use of, *see* Libations
Water Chevrotain, 160; in Folk-tales, 352, 365. Hunting tabu on, 407, Oban District, 468
Waterways, 206
Weapons, *see* Guns, Shields, and Swords,
  within Witch's body, 250, 251 *et sqq*
Weaver-birds, Sacred, 14
Welcome, Ekoi sign of, 211 & *n*
Were-beasts, *see* Efumi
West Africa, Ritual of, Lame Boy in, 336; Population of, southward trend of, 245
Whipping, Ceremonial, 44, 45, 65, 284
White (*see also* Chalk), Ceremonial use of, 113, 186, 256
  Animals in Vengeance Sacrifice, 31
  Men, and Black, How they came on Earth, story, 387-9
Widows, re-marriage of, 116-7
Wild Boar in Folk-tale, 362
Wild Cat, in Folk-tale, 366, Ravages of, 223, Tabu on, 408
Winds, causes of, 72-3
Witchcraft, 132, Charms and Jujus against, 49 *et sqq*, 96-7, 148, 198, 200, Diseases due to, 278; Murder by, 192, Seven different kinds of, story on, 199-200, Terror of, 3, 201-2
Witch doctors, Exorcism by, 194-5
Witch, Outfit of, Crab-claws in, story on, 196-8

Witches and Wizards, Animal shapes assumed by, 195, 199
  Bat messenger of, 193, Cry, and Boat of, 195, Dances of, 192, Dead, beliefs on, 198-9; Familiars of, 193-4, 408, story on, 196, in Folk-tales, 223-4, 225, 237, 279, 402-4, Offerings to, 200, How kept at bay, 123, 195
Wives, attitude of, to Polygamy, 109-10, Faithfulness of, how secured and tested, 105, 108-9, 166, 224, Position of, 97, 109-10, 117, Property of, 314; Running away of, 327, story on, 114-6
Woman covered with Sores, in Folk-tales, 208, 234-5, 336
"Woman's day," 94
Women, Avocations of, 223, 263, 265, 266, 269, 270, 290 & *n*, Clubs of (*see* Ekkpa, and Nimm), 41, 412-3, Important, Funerals of, 224-5, in relation to Jujus, 10, 21, 44, 224-5, Keloids on, 203, Position of, stories on, 98-104; Subject to Trances, 231; Tabus for, on Food, 410, story on, 411
Why Men must Serve, story, 98
Why they do not wear Hats, 117-9
Wooden instruments used in Utap Anam Club, 412
Wraiths, visions of, 232
Wrestlers and Wrestling, 200, 285, 287
Wrestling Ghosts, 7-9
Wrist-cutting, 131
Writing, Secret, *see* Nsibidi

YAMS (*see also* Coco-yams), 18 *et passim*; harvest, &c , of, 269; sacrificed to Ghosts, 232-3, tabus on eating, 77, 269
  New, Festival of, dangers of, 242 *et seq*
Yaws, 279
Yellow, ritual use of, 41, 42, 221, 222

ZOOLOGY, Appendix L., 465-73

CPSIA information can be obtained
at www.ICGtesting.com
Printed in the USA
LVOW13s0830280917
550387LV00009B/112/P

9 781376 123500